NOT
YOUR
CHINA
DOLL

Anna May Wong sits poolside, circa 1931.

NOT YOUR YOUR CHINA DOLL

The Wild and Shimmering Life of
Anna May Wong

KATIE GEE SALISBURY

DUTTON

DUTTON

An imprint of Penguin Random House LLC
penguinrandomhouse.com

LIBRARY OF CONGRESS CATALOGING-IN-PUBLICATION DATA
has been applied for.

ISBN 9780593183984 (hardcover)
ISBN 9780593183991 (ebook)

Printed in the United States of America
1st Printing

BOOK DESIGN BY KRISTIN DEL ROSARIO

For Wong Liu Tsong

and for my parents,
Lee and Emilie Salisbury

When the bleak door of the ramshackle laundry opened, there emerged as quaint a bit of cream and jet girlhood as ever I saw. . . . A Yuan Chen poem, stepping from the embossed covers of a book of old lyrics. And then Anna May opened her mouth and spoiled it all.

—MYRTLE GEBHART, "JAZZ NOTES ON OLD CHINA,"
PICTURE-PLAY, MAY 1923

She seemed like a finely polished flint in the midst of a stack of moldy cornhusks. . . . The impression remained strongly that here was a person of force and character, of great inner unity and strength.

—BERNARDINE SZOLD FRITZ

CONTENTS

Anna May Wong, accompanied by Los Angeles mayor Fletcher Bowron and Chinese consul T. K. Chang, at the 1941 Moon Festival parade.

PREFACE

I t started with a black-and-white photograph. To most it was merely an artifact from a bygone era, snapped by a dispassionate photo-journalist on assignment. To me, however, it was remarkable. In the photo, a glamorous Chinese woman sat in the back seat of a convertible, the confidence of youth in her eyes as she smiled at spectators at a parade. She looked at once modern and chic, Chinese *and* American.

The woman, I soon learned, was Anna May Wong, Hollywood's first Asian American movie star. I was an impressionable nineteen-year-old beginning her first college internship at the Chinese American Museum in Los Angeles. I hardly could have imagined that a split-second gaze at this photo, while the curator gave me a tour of the galleries, would change the course of my life.

More than a decade later, when the idea for this book was merely an idle daydream, I contacted the museum and asked to see the photo again. The museum archives held exactly one photograph of Anna May Wong sitting in a convertible in a parade. It was from the 1941 Moon Festival celebrations held in Chinatown, and the dignitaries who accompanied her were Los Angeles mayor Fletcher Bowron and Chinese consul T. K. Chang.

The photo was not how I remembered it. I could have sworn the shot was closer up, her face more radiant in the glare from the flash-bulbs. But in this version of the image, Anna May wasn't even looking at the camera. For weeks, I continued to believe the photograph that had once dazzled me and converted me into a devotee was still out there somewhere, waiting to be rediscovered. Then I realized: just seeing her for the first time had been enough. Her aura shone through the black-and-white print and my imagination filled in the rest.

Before there was Constance Wu, Awkwafina, Lucy Liu, or what now seems like a plethora of Asian American female leads, there was Anna May Wong. Born in Los Angeles in 1905, when Hollywood was little more than a country town scattered with farmhouses and dirt roads, she was the original Asian American movie star. Beautiful, incredibly expressive on-screen, and shrewd at the art of self-promotion long before the advent of social media, Anna May Wong was a trailblazer. Silent films made her a star, and when the talkies caught on, she made the transition to sound seamlessly, surprising some, no doubt, with her flawless British-tinged English. Her natural magnetism, transmitted through the magic of film, made it hard to look away.

The importance of Anna May Wong's life and career as a figure in early Hollywood cannot be overstated. She introduced the American public to a compelling vision of Chinese American and Asian American identity at a time when our visibility was either limited or vilified. She was also, significantly, the first woman of color to become a movie star in the Hollywood system.

For me, the idea that there were any Asian Americans at all working in the movies back then was mind-blowing. Anna May's existence was a revelation that spoke to me in ways I'm still trying to comprehend.

Perhaps she understood this innately. Anna May once reflected that she was always looking for her father in her films, which is a sentiment I can relate to. It is human nature, I believe, to search for ourselves and the people who have shaped us, colored our everyday, intimate lives, in movies, television, books, art, and music. Growing up in the 1990s as a mixed child of Chinese and Anglo-Irish descent in an increasingly Asian suburb of Southern California, I could count on one hand the Asian American role models I looked up to: Michelle Kwan, world champion figure skater and Olympic medalist; BD Wong, the actor then best known for his recurring role as the forensic psychiatrist on *Law & Order*; and Margaret Cho, comedian and creator of *All-American Girl*, the first prime-time sitcom to center on an Asian American family.

So when I laid eyes on that photo of Anna May Wong, I instantly felt a pang of recognition. I had been searching for someone like her. That she'd lived nearly a hundred years before me was both a surprise and a reminder that Asian Americans have been here all along.

I thought I'd never seen anyone like her before, but in actuality I had. My Chinese American mother had been a black-haired beauty in the late 1960s, styling herself in A-line dresses and miniskirts that she sewed at home, not unlike a teenage Anna May, who wore the latest flapper fashions. Mom had told me stories about her childhood in Los Angeles's Chinatown: how her grandfather, a prominent Chinese immigrant who owned the eponymous Sam Ward Co. on Hill Street, stuffed her pockets with buffalo nickels and spoiled her rotten. Her father, Peter Moon Gee, could often be seen behind the counter at Sam Ward Co., ringing up customers for soy sauce, rice wine, cans of bamboo shoots, and other imported goods at the general store.

One year Sam Ward, who served as president of the Chinese Consolidated Benevolent Association of Los Angeles, a kind of unofficial mayor of Chinatown, presided over the ceremony honoring the Miss Chinatown pageant winners. He chose my mother, his prized granddaughter, to bring along with him. She's there in the publicity photos, a five-year-old girl posed next to the Miss Chinatowns in their elegant cheongsams. I remember examining those photographs with intense interest as a kid whenever I stepped into my mom's office, where they were displayed. The memory of this moment from my mother's childhood—a piece of Americana in its own right—came flooding back when Anna May Wong walked into my life.

Though separated by many decades, my mother's life and Anna May's share many similarities. And yet neither are the kind of stories we typically conjure up when we think of what America was like in the early to mid-twentieth century. By delving into Anna May's story, I realized, I could help restore her legacy as well as shed light on an often overlooked part of American history.

Anna May's career as an actress was filled with ups and downs, vacillating between periods when the gates of opportunity were opened wide and then, without warning, slammed shut in her face. Much has been written about the incredible challenges she had to surmount and the unspoken racism that plagued her constantly as the sole Asian American actress of popular recognition. Some have called her death in 1961 at age fifty-six, only weeks before she was to begin rehearsals for *Flower Drum Song*, a tragedy. Yet, in my opinion, it's impossible to truly understand her life within the Western concept of tragedy or through contemporary society's prevailing logic of success and failure, winners and losers. According to that model, Anna May is doomed to be a tragic figure, a victim of circumstance.

The Anna May Wong I know would never stand for such nonsense. Rather, I've found it helpful to examine her life through an Eastern lens and to see the highs and lows she experienced as the natural course of things in the undulating flow that is existence. Human lives do not necessarily follow the neat story arc of exposition, climax, and denouement the way we like to think they do. They are messy, composed of hundreds of narrative arcs big and small, and frequently difficult to make sense of. Take, for instance, the Taoist parable of the farmer.

The farmer is just living his life. Meanwhile, his neighbors take it upon themselves to comment on each and every turn of events that happens to him. They work themselves into a frenzy, alternately declaring the farmer's good fortune—"How fantastic!"—or lamenting his bad luck—"What a disaster!" The farmer responds to his neighbors' judgments with indifference. "Maybe," he says. Maybe whatever has happened is good; maybe it is bad. But the farmer knows there is no way to tell. The only thing he controls is how he responds to these events.

Anna May rolled with the punches as gracefully as she could. She survived and even thrived, outlasting many of her Hollywood peers and working in film, television, and theater for more than four decades. *Not Your China Doll* endeavors to capture the grit and the passion, the heartbreak and the outrage, and most of all the pure radiance of Anna May Wong's one wild and shimmering life. Somewhere between traditional biography and narrative-driven nonfiction, this book offers an immersive perspective into her world, based on years of extensive research. That said, it is by no means an exhaustive record of her life from cradle to grave, nor is it a catalog of her complete works, which other authors have ably tackled before me.

As I combed through thousands of newspaper clippings, interviews, photographs, pages of personal correspondence, 35mm prints, and studio files from archives across the country and around the world, a clear picture of the woman who has fascinated generations of moviegoers emerged. But if you ask ten biographers to write about the same person, they will inevitably produce ten different biographies, ten different refractions of who that person was. I don't believe there is such a thing as objective truth, at least not where people are concerned. And yet we still try our darndest to get as close to it as we can.

With *Not Your China Doll*, I did my best to chip away at the rumors and unfounded assumptions to reveal the true contours of Anna May's life. I prioritized primary sources in my research and have provided direct quotes wherever possible. For words in Chinese, I have employed Cantonese American spellings and Wade-Giles transliterations that Anna May would have used in her time, rather than the pinyin romanization system that is in popular use today.

Additionally, I consulted with Anna Wong, daughter of Richard Wong and niece to Anna May Wong. In fact, when we first met to talk about the book and I mentioned who my great-grandfather was, Anna exclaimed, "Well, Anna May Wong and Sam Ward must have been the two most famous people in Chinatown." Anna has since become a good friend and confidante in all things Anna May Wong. I also drew upon my own personal and familial knowledge of what it's like being Asian American in this country: how one never quite possesses the feeling of belonging to any single group, a phenomenon I have felt acutely as a multiracial person.

Like Anna May searching for her father, I, too, was searching for something in her. What I found was a woman who was adventurous, funny, imaginative, and kind. A woman who fought against convention and the ever-present criticism that she wasn't enough. A woman who refused to take no for an answer. And in her, unexpectedly, I began to see a little of myself. All my life, unbeknownst to me, I'd been quietly following in her footsteps.

I was born a native of the desert oasis they call Greater Los Angeles, just as Anna May was. Though I grew up in a leafy suburb outside the city, the familiar beats of L.A.'s Chinatown—Chung King Court, where my great-grandfather's shop once stood; the intricate wishing well I lost many pennies to; the sugar butterflies, deep-fried wontons dipped in syrup, sold at Phoenix Bakery; and Empress Pavilion, the site of many Gee family dim sums—were never far from my mind.

In my twenties, when I fancied myself a jetsetter, I traveled to London, Paris, Shanghai, and Beijing—all cities Anna May frequented—before finally settling in New York. I was studying, just as she did, the art of being a cosmopolitan woman and learning how to dress fashionably, hold court at cocktail hour, and leave a few errant lovers in my wake.

Then in my thirties I journeyed to southern China to trace my family's roots back to the rural countryside of Toisan. I visited the ancestral village where my grandmother, Ann Yin Gee, spent her childhood. Later I watched *Native Land*, the documentary Anna May made of her 1936 trip to the motherland. When I saw her walk arm in arm with her father, Wong Sam Sing, through a bamboo grove to look upon the lush rice paddies of Toisan, gleaming in the afternoon sun, it was like watching my own life played back to me.

Anna May knew instinctively how important it was for other Americans, especially Asian Americans and people of color, to see someone like her on the silver screen. She lived and died for her art, because for her it wasn't just about fame; it was about imparting a legacy of change. For a few bucks and a brief hour in a darkened theater, someone might finally see themselves reflected in the movies and feel their existence validated, not othered. The amazing part is that more than six decades after her passing, she still has that effect on people.

It's moments of recognition like these that have made me grateful for the opportunity to publish this biography and to introduce Anna May Wong to a new generation of readers and moviegoers. I felt an intense connection to her while I was writing this book, as if her spirit were sometimes floating outside my office window, giving me the fortitude to keep going. Her tenacity infected me in a way. It's because of her that I believed I could tackle a project like this and, in doing so, begin my career as an author. My hope is that, after reading this, you, too, will come to know and admire Anna May Wong's brilliance, her joie de vivre, and above all, her stubborn resilience. May it inspire you to change the world just as she did.

—KATIE GEE SALISBURY

NOT
YOUR
CHINA
DOLL

A movie set in progress, Los Angeles, circa 1920.

PROLOGUE

Still basking in the glow of the new year 1910, a ragtag crew, dispatched on behalf of the Biograph Company and helmed by a little-known movie director named D. W. Griffith, boarded a train in New York headed west. It was the first time many of the company had traveled beyond the tristate corridor. For five days they oohed and aahed at the landscapes that made up America, sights they'd only read about in schoolbooks and magazines: the snowcapped Rockies, the Great Plains, the red rock of Arizona, and the desert blooms of Joshua Tree. When they finally arrived at their destination by way of the California Limited in what should have been the dead of winter, a new era had already begun. They weren't the first movie people to arrive in Los Angeles, and they certainly wouldn't be the last.

Like all movie people, that dubious class of misfits, they came to California for the sunshine. The movies were a business, after all, and cameras required light—the more reliable the source, the better. The incandescent light bulb, perfected by Thomas Edison in 1879, wasn't powerful enough to illuminate an entire set, and the klieg light, with its intense, sometimes blinding rays, wouldn't be engineered for another year. Natural daylight was a movie company's best bet, but then there was the Northeast's mercurial weather to deal with. What good was it if you could only make pictures for half the year?

During the industry's youth back east, the studios had done their best to work around the forecast. Not to mention the relentless construction of high-rise buildings that obstructed more and more light.

To keep pace with New York's skyscrapers and their billowing shadows, the Vitagraph Company built its studio fourteen stories up on the rooftop of the Morse Building. Meanwhile, in West Orange, New Jersey, Edison concocted the Black Maria, a film studio covered in tar paper with a retractable roof. The entire structure could be rotated as the light changed, but it meant he was forever chasing the sun.

California had both sunshine and an incredibly diverse terrain. You could shoot scenes at a snow-logged cabin, a beachside resort, and a Spanish mission all on the same day. Plus, Los Angeles's rapidly growing downtown was a passable stand-in for other metropolises. Virtually any location you could think of or dream up could be re-created with a little spit shine and that dazzling, dependable sunlight.

There were other lures too. The myth of California preceded itself. Every wave of new arrivals launched a fresh marketing campaign when they wrote home to their mothers and sweethearts who'd stayed behind in places like Kansas, Montana, Iowa, and Illinois. The messages were scribbled on postcards of orange groves and crowded beach piers, palm-lined drives and fanciful carloads of giant peaches. Their authors swore the scenery looked exactly as pictured and always pledged to write again soon.

Word spread that California was a kind of paradise, a land of milk and honey. When the next wave of "hardy pioneers" disembarked from the train in Pasadena, their senses were not disappointed. The air was thick with the scent of citrus and eucalyptus, a heady perfume for those accustomed only to the dank drip of urban life. Even the train tracks were lined with ribbons of yellow wildflowers. As actress Leatrice Joy observed, "It was like heaven saying welcome to California."

More than anything, California represented the promise of the West and Manifest Destiny writ large. It was a place where anyone down on their luck and looking for opportunity could make a fresh start on virgin land free from the strictures of the old world. ("Virgin" only if you conveniently overlooked the Indigenous people who had lived there for generations.) A place where they could cast aside lesser versions of themselves and step into the shimmering possibilities of their summer skin.

Anyone could come to California, yes, but it didn't mean they broke out the welcome committee for you. Those most readily accepted into the fold of Los Angeles society circles were characteristically white Midwesterners of decidedly good stock.

Harvey and Daeida Wilcox, fervent supporters of the Christian Temperance movement, were one such couple. Mr. Wilcox made his money in Kansas real estate. Recognizing that the next boom was bound for the West, he took his young bride, thirty years his junior, to Los Angeles in 1883. On long drives through the countryside, the couple discovered the tranquil beauty of the Cahuenga Valley, which was little more than a quiet farming community known for its bounteous orchards. Smitten, Harvey bought 120 acres in the valley and Daeida, quite decisively, dubbed it Hollywood. The origins of the name have been disputed ever since.

Whether Daeida borrowed the name from a friend's estate in Illinois because she liked the sound of it, as one version of the story goes, or invented the word to pay homage to the bright red berries of the native toyon bushes that were easily mistaken for holly, the name stuck around long enough to take on a life of its own. In the end, it didn't matter where Norma Jean came from, only that she became Marilyn Monroe.

Long after her husband passed, Daeida carried on their shared mission of bringing "the right kind of folks" to the little Bethlehem they'd carved out for themselves in California. So when D. W. Griffith showed up in the village of Hollywood with the Biograph Company's band of nearly thirty people to make that nonsense garbage they called the "flickers"—the future marquee names Mary Pickford and Mack Sennett among them—the locals responded with all the warmth of a cold shower.

Notices advertising vacancies minced no words in making clear just who was fit to occupy them. NO JEWS, ACTORS, OR DOGS ALLOWED, the signs read. A brigade of do-gooder residents got so up in arms over the interlopers in their midst that they formed a league called the Conscientious Citizens and collected more than 10,000 signatures to force them out. They couldn't sit idly by while these troublemakers commandeered vacant lots and barns all over town to do God knows what.

"Those locusts are swarming into Los Angeles, building ramshackle studios from the beach to the mountains," theater impresario Oliver Morosco complained. "Literally, thousands are trekking west and this is resented by large groups of people, mostly churchgoers, who are forming committees to keep these ragtags and bobtails off the streets and out of our parks. These damn flicker outfits have even built more nickelodeons!"

The tides of change were on the side of the underdogs, however. When Griffith's Civil War epic and racist spectacle *The Birth of a Nation* was released five years later in 1915, audiences and critics almost universally embraced it as a work of genius, elevating motion pictures to an art form—and announcing that the "flickers" were here to stay.

On North Figueroa Street in Downtown Los Angeles, six miles from Hollywood but seemingly a world away, a little girl named Anna began to notice something happening. Something exciting. Normally, she spent her days at the Chinese Mission School or helping out in her dad's laundry, but recently, on her way home from school and in between deliveries to customers, she'd been glimpsing people in strange clothing playacting for some kind of crank-operated machine in the streets of Chinatown.

Her attention to her classwork and responsibilities at the laundry soon gave way to a growing obsession. Anna started playing hooky from her after-school Chinese lessons, knowing full well she'd earn herself a whipping from her teacher and later one from her dad. Like the boys who scaled telephone poles and clambered over fences to watch the movie people at work, she, too, became a regular onlooker.

"I would worm my way through the crowd and get as close to the cameras as I dared," she recalled years later. "I'd stare and stare at these glamorous individuals, directors, cameramen, assistants, and actors in grease-paint, who had come down to our section of town to make movies."

The first picture star she ever saw was forever burned into her brain: Mae Murray. In rags. That's right, the same Mae Murray of Ziegfeld Follies fame who starred in films alongside heartthrobs like Rudolph Valentino and John Gilbert.

"I was surprised and greatly disappointed to see such a famous person as Mae Murray, ragged and dirty," Anna later admitted. This being her introductory brush with a movie actress in the flesh, Anna hadn't yet realized the tattered getup was just an act for the cameras. But it led to a formative conclusion. "So this was the way a movie star really looked! I was quite disgusted. We children talked about it for days. Yet my first ambition to become a film actress myself was born at this time. Perhaps I thought I'd show Miss Murray how a movie star should dress."

In no time at all, she became known around sets in Chinatown as the Curious Chinese Child, for she was either observing the crew's every move in stoic silence or alternatively prodding them with countless questions about how it all worked. Now every spare nickel or dime, whether it was lunch money or the tips she earned delivering laundry, went toward the run-down nickelodeon in the Plaza or the theaters on Main Street. She cocooned herself inside the dark theater and stayed long enough to watch the reels play from beginning to end several times. The black-and-white frames beamed across the room, all Anna's synapses firing as she studied her idols Ruth Roland and Pearl White.

Determined to prove her chops as an actress, Anna often raced home from the movies to reenact the dramas she'd just watched. She started out with a set of tiny dolls she received for Christmas one year and, using her bed as a stage, orchestrated their every word and movement. Once her brother was old enough, she pressed him into service for her homegrown repertory theater. They got through two of Anna's invented dramas before he refused to submit to any more playacting.

Anna wasn't fazed in the least; she simply graduated to acting out her movie scenarios in front of the vanity mirror. "I would register contempt, shame, reproach, joy, and anger. I would be the pure girl repulsing the evil suitor, the young mother pleading for her baby, the vampire luring her victim." She was building up her reserve of stock expressions and histrionic outbursts, a repertoire of emotions she could call forth at the drop of a hat. This skill set would serve her well in the years to come.

Little Anna, ambitious though she was, had yet to envision the various forms she would later inhabit: a lovelorn Chinese maiden spurned by her American lover; a duplicitous Mongol slave held at knifepoint by an Arabian thief; a cunning and sinuous nightclub dancer in London's Piccadilly Circus; the loyal and murderous daughter of the supervillain Dr. Fu Manchu; a hard-edged courtesan who saves the day on the Shanghai Express; and finally, a Chinatown girl who makes good with her community. As an actress, she could live a thousand different lives. Just the thought of the possibilities was thrilling.

One afternoon, while playacting for the mirror, she worked up to doing a crying scene. Can you imagine it? A twelve-year-old girl, in the family living quarters above her father's laundry, sobbing her heart out over her dead lover or some such tragedy? That's when her mother walked in. "She must have been amazed to see me," Anna recounted, "with tears streaming down my face, clutching a bit of lingerie to my bosom."

Peculiar as this spectacle must have seemed, Anna's mother knew instinctively not to intrude on the world that had been constructed inside the looking glass. Instead, she quit the room without uttering a single word, leaving her daughter's performance intact. She did not know it then, though perhaps it was her earliest gleaning, but someday her daughter was going to be a movie star.

ACT ONE

Anna May Wong as a Mongol slave with Douglas Fairbanks
in *The Thief of Bagdad*, 1924.

1

IT ALL STARTED WITH A DREAM

Douglas Fairbanks couldn't make up his mind. What to do about his next picture?

Pirates. It had to be pirates. Besides, he'd already begun growing out his hair in anticipation of such a role. And a pirate film, he was convinced, had to be in color. He'd attended a screening of the latest two-color Technicolor film and was itching to make use of the cutting-edge technology.

But what about Monsieur Beaucaire? He'd been sitting on the rights to Booth Tarkington's novella of the same name for years now—about a French prince who flees to England to escape an arranged marriage and disguises himself as a lowly barber so that he may find a wife who will love him for who he truly is. Think of the costumes. The romance. The countless opportunities to wrest hearty guffaws from moviegoers with a comedy of mistaken identities. Think of the money he'd already spent on it. At $30,000, the rights to the book had not come cheap.

Robin Hood, his most recent flick, had been a roaring success, one of the best and biggest films of 1922. Box office receipts raked in $2.2 million in revenues for the Douglas Fairbanks Pictures Corporation, well beyond the $961,129.12 he had spent to finance the film, resulting in a net profit of almost $1.24 million (more than $19 million in today's money). This payday surpassed even Fairbanks's wildest ambitions, and his ambitions were famously prodigious.

There was no question. His next film had to be bigger and better, a tall order, since not only had *Robin Hood* been a box office smash, but it had even charmed the critics. They called Douglas Fairbanks the King of Hollywood for a reason.

His queen, Mary Pickford, the baby-faced beauty next door, the indisputable doyenne of the silent film era, was the only woman in Hollywood who could be considered his equal, creatively and financially. From the time she made her debut in silent pictures for the Biograph Company in 1909, where she appeared in forty films, many directed by D. W. Griffith, audiences interchangeably hailed her as "the Biograph Girl," "the Girl with the Golden Curls," "Blondilocks," and the moniker that finally stuck: "America's Sweetheart." More than a decade later, Mary Pickford by any other name—except maybe Gladys Smith, her *real* name—was still the wholesome, cherubic ingénue whom women aspired to be and men longed to love and protect.

Both had been married to other people when they first met in 1915, and yet they were inexorably drawn to each other. For years, whispers about their illicit love affair circulated, which they adamantly denied. Finally, Doug filed for divorce from his socialite wife in the fall of 1918. Mary, not wanting to prove the gossipmongers right, bided her time until March 1920, when she quietly secured an expedited divorce in Nevada. A few weeks later the love-smitten couple stepped out into the sunlight and were wed in a private ceremony in Los Angeles.

Despite their fears of the stigma that terrible d-word still carried, the public readily embraced the pair, who would be crowned king and queen, now and forever known as "Doug and Mary." They broke the mold and redefined Hollywood love for the Richard Burtons and Elizabeth Taylors of the world and the many other couples who would follow in their footsteps—Bogart and Bacall, Tracy and Hepburn, Brad and Angelina.

Mary loved to indulge Doug's numerous flights of fancy, and his growing obsession with swashbuckling buccaneers was no different. For Christmas 1922, she surprised him with an antique replica of a pirate ship's galley. But the man who never stood still was already onto the next idea: a Roman saga complete with togas, gladiators, and storied coliseums. His crackerjack team of researchers and scenario writers, headed by husband and wife Dr. Arthur Woods and Lotta Woods, and aided significantly by the talents of playwright Edward Knoblock, was presently at work on the script for this next project, if only he would pin down the concept.

"Last night I thought up a *great* story that happens during Caesar's time," Doug enthused one day to his foreign publicity director Robert Florey. "Can't you see the chariot races? The battles? That great old Roman architecture?"

The pirate paraphernalia and pictures of galleons that had multiplied on the walls of the director's office were taken down and replaced with images of Pompeii and the Roman Forum. Doug's team was used to this rigamarole and expected nothing less. Convinced they hadn't yet landed on the winning idea, one writer avowed to Florey: "You'll see. This devil will change his mind three times—if not more—before we start shooting."

It just so happened that Doug had recently been gifted a handsomely illustrated book of *The Arabian Nights* recalling the much-admired Art Nouveau–style renderings of artist Edmund Dulac. Doug rarely had the patience for books, but something in this particular tome gripped him and wouldn't let go. He'd picked it up one evening, hoping for some light reading before bed, not anticipating what happened next. Bewitched by the thrilling stories and quixotic illustrations brought to life on its pages, he stayed up the whole night and continued reading into the next day. Soon after, the ever-chipper Fairbanks stepped into a staff meeting to interrupt: "Let's do an *Arabian Nights* story instead!"

The other shoe had finally dropped. "We looked at each other with a dazed expression," one of the writers recalled, "and retired to our respective shells to meditate on the form the story ought to take." Without protest, the books and pictures of Rome went the way of the pirates. Reference pictures were unpinned and boxes' worth of research materials were shuffled away to make room for the volumes that would soon replace them: translations of *The Arabian Nights* by Galland, Scott, Burton, Lane, and Forster; papers on Middle Eastern architecture and decor; new illustrations and "delightful old woodcuts and engravings."

The exotic intrigue was hard to ignore. *The Arabian Nights* had everything Doug looked for in a story: romance, adventure, reversal of fortunes, and plenty of opportunities for physical hijinks and camera tricks. It was decided then. These classic tales merited the feature-length film treatment. And they would get just that.

"Our hero," Doug explained to his writers, "must be Every Young Man—of this age or any age—who believes that happiness is a quantity that can be stolen; who is selfish—at odds with the world—rebellious toward conventions on which comfortable human relations are based."

The moral of the story was boiled down to one snappy phrase—"Happiness must be earned"—and inscribed in twinkling stars across a midnight sky in the opening scenes of *The Thief of Bagdad*, as the film would be titled.

When an eighteen-year-old Anna May Wong arrived at the Pickford-Fairbanks Studios one July day in 1923, setting foot on the silent era's most extravagant set yet, she must have instantly felt the production's galvanizing sense of purpose. A deeply tan, bare-chested Douglas Fairbanks sat up, alert in his director's chair. With a megaphone in hand and wearing diaphanous pantaloons, he presided over the eighteen-acre lot bristling with activity like an ant colony humming with extras, carpenters, and camera assistants. A sign that read BAGDAD in all caps was installed atop the highest scaffolding lest a bypasser on Santa Monica Boulevard confuse the Moorish arches and silver minarets towering above the studio walls with some lesser production.

Anna May could feel it in her bones: this was going to be her big break. She had come to Doug's attention back when he was still attached to the idea of doing a pirate flick. He'd attended the premiere of *The Toll of the Sea*, the 1922 film in which she played her first leading role, to see whether Technicolor's newly reengineered two-color process used in it might work for his concept. Though his plans to make the pirate tale were ultimately shelved until a later date, the image of the anguished Chinese maiden lingered.

The Toll of the Sea was a somewhat unusual production. The men behind it were not filmmakers but scientists who had wanted to exhibit the possibilities of their color film. Their objective was to sell the technology, not box office tickets, which freed them in a way to cast an unknown actress like Anna May.

In her role as Lotus Flower, she rescues a man named Allen Carver, played by matinee idol Kenneth Harlan. Carver is an American cad who washes up on the rocky shores of Hong Kong. The script, written by Frances Marion, the highest-paid screenwriter, and loosely based on *Madama Butterfly*, follows Lotus as she nurses Carver back to health. She predictably falls in love with the handsome foreigner and he in turn becomes enchanted with her "exotic" beauty. Lotus strikes a pact with the ocean that has brought her this gift, vowing: "Ask of me anything in return, O Sea!" Their courtship ensues among the cherry blossoms until Carver is called back home to the United States. In his absence, Lotus Flower, who believes Carver to be her rightful husband, gives birth to a son. Several years pass before she spots him again from the shore, but she soon discovers he has returned with an American wife. Grasping the truth of her situation, Lotus Flower selflessly gives her son over to the care of Carver and his new bride so that the boy might live a better life. Having made the supreme sacrifice of a mother, Lotus throws herself into the sea.

The delicate, pink-hued face of Anna May Wong, only seventeen and virtually unknown at the time, framed in dramatic chiaroscuro, her eyes glistening pools of feeling, proved unforgettable. Doug's interest was piqued. *The Thief of Bagdad* was a different kind of film and a departure from the Westerns and romantic comedies Doug had become famous for. He understood that this film's "differentness" called for a unique cast. He wasn't looking for star power. He was looking for players with exotic flair, that whiff of otherness that would infuse the picture with ethereal charm and transport moviegoers to a place they'd never been before. And thus, Anna May Wong was plucked from her relative obscurity, an actress with only three credited roles to her name.

Amidst this fairy-tale world, Doug would play the mischievous thief, Ahmed, who, after fleecing his victims of their precious jewels and bags of gold coins, smiles broadly and laughs at his successful capers as if to say, "What fools!" Ahmed's carefree outlook changes in an instant, however, when he sets eyes on something he cannot steal: the heart of the caliph's daughter. In order to wed the princess, played by a willowy Julanne Johnston, Ahmed must outsmart her three princely suitors from the far-off lands of India, Persia, and Mongolia, and win the caliph's favor by presenting the most priceless gift.

No hero's journey is complete, though, without an outsized villain to defeat. The Mongol prince, played masterfully by Japanese actor Kamiyama Sôjin, is the calculating, diabolical foil to Ahmed, the earnest, lovestruck thief. Not only does Cham Shang the Great plan to marry the princess, by force if necessary, but he has secretly arranged for his Mongol army to surround the palace immediately after their alliance is consummated. If all goes to plan, the city of Bagdad will be his for the taking. But to achieve all this, the Mongol prince must rely on a strategically placed mole on the inside.

Enter Anna May Wong as the Mongol slave, the treacherous double agent who outwardly serves as lady-in-waiting to the princess of Bagdad while surreptitiously reporting to her true master. Anna May did not relish being cast as a villain. "I like roles that win sympathy," she told one reporter, "So-called 'sinister' roles—and I get plenty of them—I don't like so much."

So far in Anna May's fledgling career, she'd snatched at every conceivable opportunity, connection, and advantage that came her way. She'd modeled furs for a local furrier and leaned on relationships with Rob Wagner (a screenwriter and former customer of her father's laundry) and James Wang (a former pastor who regularly recruited Chinatown extras for Hollywood productions) for introductions to moviemakers. She had propelled her way onto sets during holiday breaks from school, where she took on her first uncredited roles.

She knew what a Douglas Fairbanks picture could do for her career and was willing to play her part, even a nefarious Mongol slave, in exchange for the international exposure it would surely bring her. The question, really, was who *wouldn't* be lining up to watch *The Thief of Bagdad* when it finally premiered.

Of course, Anna May was ethnically Chinese, not Mongolian, but in an era when Chinese and Mongol were racial types used interchangeably to describe anyone of the East Asian persuasion, not many people knew the difference. Anyhow, fudging ethnic lines was a minor deception, considering white actors were usually given a free pass to mimic the other races.

When Anna May looked around Hollywood, she rarely saw anyone who looked like her doing much more than extra work. Sure, Etta Lee, a fellow Asian American actress, would play a supporting part alongside her as one of the "slave girls" in the princess's escort, but her name would be left off the credits. At eighteen, Anna May had already made it further than other nonwhite actresses in Hollywood. In fact, she was hard-pressed to name any woman of color at all who possessed the title of movie star—the status she herself aspired to. Mexican actress Dolores del Rio was still two years away from making her motion picture debut; Lupe Velez and Merle Oberon would not emerge for another several years, though the latter hid her South Asian ancestry and passed for white.

As for Black people in the movies, their presence was felt only by proxy—through the white actors who painted their faces tar black using the ashes of burnt cork. Blackface minstrelsy predated the advent of cinema, so naturally the practice carried over into the flickers. In 1903, Edwin S. Porter's film adaptation of *Uncle Tom's Cabin* introduced the first Black character played by a white actor. Eleven years and four adaptations later, a Black actor was finally cast as Tom, but even that breakthrough proved to be an aberration. Thirteen more years would pass before a Black actor appeared in the role again.

Hollywood scripted Black characters for comic relief, to validate the white supremacist racial hierarchy, and "to entertain by stressing Negro inferiority." Just as Asian actors like Anna May and Sôjin were frequently asked to play exotic sirens and Oriental villains, Black characters were relegated to the stereotypes of coon, mammy, tragic mulatto, and brutal buck. Even so, the idea that a Black actor, male or female, might assume one of these dehumanized roles on the silver screen was virtually unheard-of at the time. Aside from a handful of Black child actors in a smattering of features like Hal Roach's *Our Gang* series, white actors in blackface dominated Black roles well into the 1920s.

From that perspective, Anna May Wong was lucky to act in a mainstream film, especially one of this magnitude. Doug had given her a running start, but if she wanted to make it in Hollywood, the rest would be up to her. Anna May quickly proved her mettle as production commenced, and Doug came to admire her diligence. He praised her as "a modest little person." Perhaps he even saw a bit of his younger self in her. Anna May found an unlikely role model in Douglas Fairbanks. The actor-producer embraced the exuberant American ethos of pulling oneself up by one's bootstraps, of making something of oneself despite obstacles.

Dozens of future actors, directors, and screenwriters (mostly male) would later cite Fairbanks as their childhood hero; they loved him for his effortless bravado, his graceful athleticism, and his good-natured rabble-rousing. But Anna May looked up to him for another reason: unlike other producers and studio heads, he had his finger on the pulse of American culture, especially at this moment of his career. In her opinion, Fairbanks was "the cleverest person in pictures." He somehow knew what moviegoers wanted and also when to put audiences onto the next big thing—the thing they didn't yet know they wanted.

In contrast to Adolph Zukor, Joseph M. Schenck, or Samuel Goldwyn, the businessmen turned producers who ran other studios, Fairbanks was an artist and a producer, in that order. He did not spend his days balancing the books or figuring out ways to trim studio expenditures, nor did he want to, which is why he sensibly hired his brothers to manage his money and business affairs. He was an entrepreneurial-minded creator who was up to the task, a filmmaker unafraid to take big risks, and luckily for him they nearly always yielded big rewards. There would be no corner cutting on account of the bottom line. Indeed, quite the opposite. *Thief*'s production costs, it was rumored, had already surpassed a million dollars by the time filming began.

Doug's Bagdad—no *h*—was an American boy's fantasy of the Orient, where every winding alleyway leads to another adventure, a treasure to unearth, an innocent maiden to rescue. It remained distinct from the historical Baghdad, known during the Middle Ages as the world's most advanced city, in that peculiar and exceptional way that only Hollywood films seem to achieve. The Bagdad at the Pickford-Fairbanks Studios on North Formosa Avenue and Santa Monica Boulevard was not so much a faithful reconstruction of a real place as it was a fabrication of a strange and whimsical world.

"A day on his set is like being taken by the nape of the neck and dropped into the *Arabian Nights*. . . . Baghdad is dazzling and amazing," *Los Angeles Times* reporter Harry Carr declared after visiting the studio two weeks into filming. Without seeing one frame of footage, Carr was sold. "No such motion-picture set has ever been dreamed of before. In every direction that you look your eye is met with the most quaint and charming composition. It is the last word—the final touch—in line and color and composition."

Thief's fabulous look and feel was principally thanks to William Cameron Menzies, a twenty-seven-year-old illustrator with an artist's soul and an architect's skills who had not yet made a name for himself in the nascent field of Hollywood production design. For months Doug struggled to pin down the artistic vision and had gone through a rash of illustrators and artists. He'd even hired celebrated painter Maxfield Parrish, but in the end the artist's renderings were dismissed as too complicated and impractical. Then Menzies strode into the office one Monday morning with a stack of 20-by-30-inch illustrated boards balanced on his head and presented his intricate ink drawings washed in vibrant watercolors. Doug's jaw dropped.

"Look at these," Doug exclaimed while brandishing the illustrations to a reporter. Arranged along the walls of his office were "large scenic drawings of startling beauty and originality. One showed the gateway to Bagdad, another a street scene. There was a drawing for a set at the bottom of the sea, another of the bedroom of the Caliph's daughter, showing the thief crossing a long bridge which leads into the moon-flooded chamber."

It was the handsome illustrated edition of the *Arabian Nights* sitting on his bedside table that had originally spurred Doug to embrace the concept that became *Thief*. And now, seeing Bagdad expressed on a grand scale in such beautiful detail, he finally saw that his vision was on its way to being realized. Over the following months, Menzies and his crew toiled night and day to transform Robin Hood's Nottingham Castle on the Pickford-Fairbanks lot into a stunning Art Nouveau rendering of ninth-century Baghdad.

At some point in preproduction, Doug realized there was one thing missing from his Bagdad. "A dream city should not look too well anchored on its foundations," he mused, "but sets built on the ground will look as if they were." To attain the sensation of a floating city, the concrete floors were painted black and buffed until they gleamed, creating an almost molten, sable-colored foundation that reflected the silvery structures above.

Tourists, locals, and Hollywood insiders alike flocked to the studio grounds, like incurable gamblers drawn to the electric lights of Las Vegas casinos. Tickets to tour the studio as filming progressed were sold daily. Harry Carr told his readers that upon arrival he was greeted by a cheeky sign that asked: ARE YOUR FEET CLEAN? Carr soon realized the reason for this imposition when he caught sight of the glistening floors and was handed a pair of felt slippers to wear over his shoes. Despite this effort to curb the attrition caused by constant visitors, the obsidian-like floor had to be re-enameled several times a week.

For all the agonizing hours of planning, assembly, and coordination that went into building the sets for *Thief*, the end effect of awe-struck wonderment was well worth the trouble. The reporter who once gazed upon Menzies's illustrations in the studio offices now pronounced the expectations that rested upon Douglas Fairbanks's thirty-seventh feature film: "If the plans of the artist and of the star are carried out with fidelity, the remarkable settings of *Robin Hood* will be entirely eclipsed and a new standard for beauty of lighting effects will be set."

One morning at the Pickford-Fairbanks Studios, reporter Helen Carlisle from *Movie Weekly* happened to be sitting with Julanne Johnston in her dressing room. She was there to interview the unknown actress who had been selected to play Doug's leading lady for her lithe dancer's body. Then in walked Anna May Wong wearing a smart new coat, the kind many chic young women could be seen strutting around Los Angeles in. She acknowledged the reporter with a nod and turned to her costar, seeking advice on the day's most pressing matter.

"Say, Julanne," Anna May began in her characteristic slang, "I got this coat at a bargain sale downtown and, gee, I don't know now whether I like it or not. You know how it is with anything you get at a sale. Afterward, you're apt to think it looks like something the cat dragged in."

Julanne admired the coat and told Anna May she quite liked it, which had the desired effect of dispelling any lingering buyer's remorse. The reporter, enchanted by the Chinese flapper who had suddenly materialized like a desert mirage and then just as swiftly "departed in the general direction of Bagdad," turned back to her intended subject in a daze.

"She surprised you, didn't she?" Julanne said with a smile. "But here's a peculiar fact about Anna May Wong. By the time you've talked with her for five minutes you forget that she is Chinese."

Anna May had learned through trial and error how to hold her own with her fellow Americans, even though many of them did not necessarily recognize her as one of them. The "worm turned," as she put it, while she was walking one day and "a truck came booming down the street." The driver yelled at her to get out of the way and called her a "chink." Well, the seventeen-year-old Anna May had had it. "To my own surprise I blazed back a remark equally insulting at him and he wilted. That was the turning of a corner for me."

Meanwhile on the lot, Doug could be seen good-naturedly schooling a crowd of extras on how to carry themselves as citizens of Bagdad. "This is the way we Americans walk," he asserted, and, by way of demonstration, propelled himself across the set at a brisk pace, his chin jutting out hyperbolically ahead of him as if it were pulling him forward "like the prow of a torpedo destroyer."

Then he began again: "But this is the way the orientals walk." And now his chin returned to its natural resting position and elevated slightly, Doug glided leisurely over the polished enamel floor for several yards, almost levitating. What made him an authority on variations of Eastern and Western manners of walking is anyone's guess. (He had yet to travel to the Middle East himself.) But Doug never promised reality; it was fantasy he was after. "The drab of historical accuracy will be utterly ignored," one reviewer touted of the coming attraction.

Recruiting enough people to fill a six-and-a-half-acre city was no easy feat and required hundreds, sometimes thousands of extras. Director Raoul Walsh proffered a creative solution: "A dark-faced Mexican with a head-rag hiding everything except his eyes and nose and mouth will pass for an Arab any time."

The casting director and three assistants drove buses down to South Central Los Angeles and enticed locals with the promise: "Free Ride! See Douglas Fairbanks in person making *The Thief of Bagdad!*" The buses filled up and "casting had a field day selecting desert-type faces." Costume designer Mitchell Leisen designed unique ensembles for 3,000 extras and made test shots of each and every one of them at Doug's request. Soon Bagdad's newest citizens could be seen shuffling about in a vibrant array of harem pants, faux jewels, and feathered turbans.

During her time on the production, however, a small uproar occurred when Anna May refused to go back to work. Doug later explained to the *New York Times* that he'd had a difficult time wrangling his "cosmopolitan" cast, with specific reference to several of the Asian actors he hired. An unreliable narrator predisposed toward charming reporters with tall tales, Doug claimed the trouble began when Anna May happened to mention that her Chinese name, Wong Liu Tsong, meant "Two Yellow Willows."

"A publicity man who had only half heard what she said sent out a yarn saying that Anna May Wong meant 'Two Yellow Widows,'" Doug explained. "It took some time to tell her that it was an error, and I finally, even then, had to write a letter to her honored parent before she would agree to put on the Mongol slave costume."

Yet, as Anna May tells it, after she mentioned her Chinese name, people on set "began kidding the other actors—[who] dubbed Snitz Edwards 'Two Lots in Glendale'; Julanne Johnston they called 'Couple of Peach Melbas,' and things like that." She may have swallowed her pride at first and tried to ignore the crew ribbing her for what was otherwise a beautiful name, but perhaps the studio's press memo spinning her name as "Two Yellow Widows" was a bridge too far. But was Anna May really willing to walk away from the professional opportunity of a lifetime because somebody got her name wrong? Or was there something else at play here?

Maybe it was the costume itself, a revealing bandeau-and-shorts combo. Its only concession to modesty was a flimsy silk panel draped to cover her midriff. Even Doug admitted with a wink that "Mongol slaves are merely attired for comfort." Anna May was acutely aware of her family's disapproval of her dabbling in the pictures. If she did balk at the getup she'd been asked to wear, it seems sensible that she demanded Fairbanks write a letter to her father assuring him that she would be participating in a reputable Hollywood production of the highest quality, not some tawdry one-reeler shown in brothels.

But the story about PR flubbing her name? More likely, Doug's humorous anecdote was meant to gloss over whatever had actually happened on set. Maybe the wisecracks didn't stop at "Two Yellow Widows." The majority white crew was not exactly sensitive to the daily indignities that many of the film's diverse cast regularly encountered. Raoul Walsh called Kamiyama Sôjin by the nickname "Sloe Gin" for the entirety of filming; he said it was "easier to remember." Whatever transpired, Anna May felt disrespected, and the incident was consequential enough that she had to put her foot down. There was no going back to that timid girl from before the worm turned.

Racism was rampant in early Hollywood but remained invisible primarily because it wasn't acknowledged as racism. Newspapers of the day saw it fit to print words like "Chinkville" and "the heathen Chinese" without apology or admonition. Racial epithets and insinuations were made openly and just as easily dismissed as a harmless joke—at someone else's expense.

To Doug's credit, he publicly eschewed bigotry of any kind (though this did not cause him to reconsider playing an Arab in brownface). During his early days in the film industry when he often worked with writer Anita Loos, whose sardonic wit is best remembered for *Gentle-*

men Prefer Blondes, he often sanitized her scripts of words like "n———" and "coon." Doug saw himself as a man of the people. He traveled the world and socialized with all types. He danced with the Hopi, played pranks on Mexican generals, and held court with H. G. Wells and the Duke and Duchess of Windsor, but his happiest moments might have been spent with the cowpunchers and stuntmen he regularly invited to hang around the studio.

For instance, Doug was fond of Black actor Sam Baker, whom he'd enlisted to play the sworder who guards the staircase entrance to the princess's boudoir. Sam, with his boxer's physique and seven-foot-plus height, cut an imposing figure both on screen and off. Doug and Sam could often be seen challenging each other's athletic prowess on the gymnastics equipment installed on the lot, and for a time, Doug backed Sam's professional boxing career. Julanne recalled what fun it was to do scenes with Sam, whom she described without a shred of self-consciousness as "a huge darkey with the funniest little piping voice and the biggest appetite for pies you ever saw."

His democratic worldview notwithstanding, Fairbanks was ultimately a product of his era. There were limits to how far he was willing to reflect on his white privilege or how race was portrayed in his films. Years later, when he traveled to China, locals threatened to boycott a local revival of *Thief* because of the way its most villainous characters were depicted. Principally, the scene where defeated Prince Cham Shang and his counsel are hung in the palace by their pigtails. Doug's rejoinder was to wholeheartedly agree with his detractors—"some American screenwriters were misrepresenting the Chinese"—but he insisted that the villains in his film were Mongolian, not Chinese.

In the end, Anna May donned the skimpy outfit, and in countless interviews following this period, she recast her Chinese name to the more accurately translated "Frosted Yellow Willows" rather than "Two Yellow Willows." (Being an American-born girl, she, too, got her own name wrong.) Bangles adorned her wrists and a giant bow of sorts with translucent panels was fastened to the back of her head. The resulting ensemble was unusual and eye-catching. The 1920s had seen women bob their hair and hike up their skirts to the ankles, which was a shock to the system for those who still clung to Victorian mores. But this was way beyond that. Of all the women players in *Thief*, Anna May's costume revealed the most skin. At least the playing field was leveled when Doug went shirtless for the first half of the film. For one scene he even stripped down to his waist-high skivvies, flaunting his flawless physique at age forty.

Even though production continued at a breakneck pace, with only Sundays and Christmas Day off, Doug still made time in between takes to cavort with extras, flash his million-dollar smile at tourists passing through, and entertain VIP guests who happened to stop by. One day it was Babe Ruth; the next day it was the Russian prima ballerina Anna Pavlova.

"Working in a Fairbanks picture was quite an experience," actor Adolphe Menjou recalled. "In some ways it was like going to a Hollywood masquerade party instead of to work. The set was always crowded with visiting celebrities and Doug's friends."

After the crew wrapped each day, he'd head home to his mansion in Beverly Hills. Pickfair, a portmanteau of Doug and Mary's surnames, was no ordinary house. The estate was anchored by a sizable mock-Tudor-style mansion where the King and Queen of Hollywood kept court. A company of live-in servants waited on them and managed the grounds, and though it may have been the first of many extravagant Hollywood mansions to come, none since have rivaled its reputation or lore.

Dinner was served at 8:00 every evening at a grand table set for fifteen. Mary's reasoning to the staff was that it was impossible to predict who might turn up. Perhaps Charlie Chaplin, Doug's meilleur ami and frequent partner in crime (the two indulged in constant pranks on and off the set), would join them at Pickfair, where he also had a dedicated bedroom. Other guests included friends visiting from afar or anyone who happened to be in their social rotation at the time. Assembled around the dining room table every night was a who's who of, well, the world: Albert Einstein, Gloria Swanson, Jack Dempsey, Greta Garbo, the king and queen of Siam, Amelia Earhart, F. Scott Fitzgerald, Henry Ford, Lord and Lady Mountbatten, among numerous others.

Meanwhile, at the end of another long day on set, Anna May Wong returned her costume to the dressing room and changed back into her street clothes. The work was exhausting, and yet it was thrilling just knowing that every day she was in the company of giants. Doug and Mary's success and fame surpassed that of any celebrity who had come before them. The pair was mobbed by fans wherever they went.

Anna May was seeing with her very eyes how the work ethic of the industry's biggest names had paid off. The stars in the Hollywood firmament had started from the bottom and made it to the luminous top. Now they were commanding thousands of cast and crew on million-dollar sets bankrolled by their own production companies, making movies watched and beloved the world over.

Was it crazy to think that one day she could be doing the same— that if she hadn't quite arrived yet, she was unequivocally on her way? "Just making a living was not enough for me," she explained in an interview. "I've always dreamed of becoming a movie star."

Visions of the future danced in her head as Anna May walked out the studio gates and scanned the curb for her ride. Most days her friend Philip Ahn, the Korean American boy whose family lived down the street from the Wongs, would pick her up. He'd be driving the convertible Studebaker Oldster she'd bought with her movie earnings but didn't yet have a license to drive. (Fairbanks had spotted Philip dropping Anna May off one day and immediately wanted to cast him into his company of exotic types, but Mrs. Ahn wouldn't hear of it.)

Other days, when Philip was tied up at school, Anna May made her way to Pacific Electric's Sherman Line stop on Santa Monica Boulevard, right outside the Pickford-Fairbanks Studios. She hopped on a Red Car trolley and, like any other girl Friday, commuted home with the nine-to-fivers until she reached her father's laundry on North Figueroa Street, a few blocks from Chinatown.

"She lives in a movie fairyland until the clock strikes 5:30," a reporter from the *San Francisco Chronicle* waxed poetic, likening Anna May to Cinderella. "Then her handsome suitors wash off the grease paint and go home, her jewels are placed in the studio safe, and her beautiful clothes are returned to the property room. It is then that Anna May steps from fairyland to reality."

Back at the laundry, she was met by a frenzy of activity as her family and half a dozen employees worked at the different tasks required to transform the piles of dispatched clothing, dirty and reeking of their owners, into packets of clean shirts and freshly starched collars. These would then be bundled in brown paper and string and stacked neatly into wooden cubbyholes flanking the wall. Hot coals used to heat the eight-pound sadirons and vats filled with boiling water kept the entire establishment at a sweltering temperature.

Douglas Fairbanks had astutely observed that Anna May Wong "was a very hard worker." That industrious spirit was learned from a young age, for she grew up in the laundry, where an idle hand was never wasted. There were always "books to be kept and many shirts to be pinned." And so it was that she arrived home from the studio every evening, ready to begin her second shift of the day at Sam Kee Laundry. Instead of standing by for her next scene as the mischievous Mongol slave in a Douglas Fairbanks picture, she returned to the stock character of Chinese girl in laundry, awaiting her next customer.

The Wong family, circa 1925. From left to right: Lulu, Roger, Mary, Lee Gon Toy, Richard, James, Wong Sam Sing, Anna May, and Frank.

2

FROSTED YELLOW WILLOWS

Anna May Wong was born on a winter's day in Los Angeles, a place where winter is often mistaken for summer. The weather on January 3, 1905, swelled to 79 degrees, though only a few days before a snowstorm had blanketed parts of the San Bernardino and San Gabriel mountains with a crisp, clean layer of white.

Whether or not it was an auspicious day, the wind blowing in from the northeast did not say. Still, inside the laundry at 351 Flower Street, Wong Sam Sing thought he must be cursed. His second wife, Lee Gon Toy, had disappointed him yet again by delivering another girl, another mouth to feed, and depriving him of the pride a father naturally feels at the birth of a son who will carry on his name.

His first child and only son was far away in the Toisanese countryside of southern China with his mother, Wong's first wife, who had declined to make the arduous journey to Gold Mountain. The money that arrived regularly from America made life quite comfortable for her and little Tou Nan. They were happy where they were. If he didn't like it, she said, egging him on, he could find a new wife in America. He wasted no time in doing so.

Slowly, against his better judgment, Wong Sam Sing warmed up to the baby girl he and Lee Gon Toy christened Wong Liu Tsong. The family doctor furnished her American name, Anna. Perhaps owing to the Chinese boy's cap her mother sometimes fitted on little Anna's head—to fool the senses into believing she was indeed a son—the child grew to be headstrong like a boy. She was born in the year of the dragon, and though dragons are typically associated with water in Chinese mythology, there was a fire in her belly nonetheless. Anna cultivated a taste for independence and a desire to cut her own path in life—not unlike a younger Wong Sam Sing, who was born in a mining town in Northern California, lost his mother at the tender age of five, and was sent back to China to grow up in the care of relatives. When he returned to America as a teenager, he survived solely on the strength of his wits and his willingness to work hard.

Anna had no interest in learning domestic handicrafts like other Chinese girls; she refused to return to the Chinese Mission School sewing circle after her first visit ended with a huff of disgust. Instead, she found her calling on the playground with the boys: "I could swing a bat and make a home run with the best of them. . . . I proved to 'the gang' that I could play ball and they accepted me."

But when Wong Sam Sing happened to catch sight of this "tomboyish creature," all bets were off. "Occasionally my father would unexpectedly come upon me," Anna wrote, "towsled [sic], grimy, with hair flying, having a glorious time with 'the gang,' and my actions troubled him. What was America doing to me, that at so early an age I showed a marked tendency to forget all my parents' teachings?"

This was not the way a good Chinese daughter behaved. At least not a daughter who would bring honor to her family by maturing into a decorous, well-bred lady, marrying a respectable Chinese man, and raising a family of her own one day. To correct this streak of American-bred insolence, Anna and her older sister Lulu were enrolled in additional hours of Chinese studies after their daily classes at the mission school concluded. From morning till night, the girls were subjected to lessons in arithmetic and grammar, and, the most dreaded thing of all, memorizing Chinese characters. When it came to their afternoon Chinese tutor, unlike the matronly Christian women who taught them during the day, he had no qualms about putting his bamboo switch to good use at the first sign of disobedience.

School remained a sore point for Anna, but in one particular aspect she was as dutiful and respectful as any Chinese child. She always pulled her weight in the family business. She was born in the laundry, played in the laundry, and, once she was old enough, learned the many tasks that went into operating the laundry.

"Running a Chinese laundry is no elemental art, as anyone knows that has lost his ticket or a collar," one reporter wrote in the *Los Angeles Times* after touring Sam Kee Laundry. "The laundry is a machine of human parts, as complicated as one of springs and wheels. The wash goes in one end and vanishes, the shirts one way, the collars another, the socks here, the underclothing there, and then they all come out together in neat piles. Everything is tied with a bit of string, and attached to it is a tag with the Chinese numeral on it. . . . Anna May Wong knows this routine thoroughly."

The laundry, in all its humid, stinking glory, was home. The familiar routine that unfolded within its walls day in and day out grounded Anna's life, lent it shape, and was comforting even in its regimented regularity. In this way—talking to customers, delivering packages, balancing the ledgers—Anna was imbued with the Wong family's industrious spirit and their working-class strivings.

As the family grew to eight children (Lee Gon Toy finally granted Wong Sam Sing's wish with the birth of four sons, not to mention two more daughters, though one unfortunately died as an infant), the parental stranglehold on Anna's doings eased up. Occasionally she pocketed the tip money she got from regulars and ditched Chinese class for an afternoon at the pictures. Whenever her father caught her playing hooky, he bemoaned the fact that she was squandering the money he put toward her private Chinese lessons. If she was going to play hooky, why couldn't she ditch her public school classes, which cost him nothing?

The nickelodeons at the Plaza were lousy with stiff chairs and only an electric piano to accompany the reels. The intertitles often ran in Spanish, catering to the largely Mexican American audiences that filled the theaters. Anna didn't mind. She lost herself in the latest picture with Ruth Roland or Olive Thomas, studying their every gesture and expression.

It wasn't long before she was taking advantage of vacations off from school or occasionally forging excuse notes from her parents, whom she kept in the dark about her new hobby so that she could thrust her foot in the door at the studios popping up all over town.

Like the invasive species that took root in Southern California before their arrival—the date palms that lured Back Easters to the newly coined "semi-tropical" climate—movie studios were suddenly and irrevocably entrenched in the local topography.

The self-styled Colonel William Selig, who built Chicago's first movie studio in 1897, was the first movie person to move to Los Angeles, where he found the climate much more amenable to filmmaking. In 1909, the Selig Polyscope Company commandeered a house next door to a Chinese laundry named Sing Kee (not Sam Kee, but close) and its drying yard on Olive Street; the film produced there, *In the Sultan's Power*, was one of the first to be shot completely in Los Angeles. Selig's permanent studio was built in Edendale, in what is now Silver Lake, that same year.

Not long after, in fall 1909, 101 Bison, a unit of the New York Motion Picture Company, set itself up in Edendale. Pathé, Kalem, Vitagraph, Lubin, Essanay, and Nestor swiftly followed. Then Biograph, helmed by D. W. Griffith, opened its permanent West Coast outpost on the corner of Pico Boulevard and Georgia Street in 1911.

The actors who arrived to work at the studios soon overran sleepy Los Angeles, which in the 1910s was little more than a rough-and-tumble Western town on the cusp of burgeoning into a legitimate city. The population was just north of 300,000, growing exponentially but still behind the city's big sister to the north, San Francisco (population 416,912) and a drop in the bucket compared to New York City (population 4,766,883). One could spot the theatrically inclined from a mile away, walking the streets in peculiar costumes or riding the trolley cars in strange makeup, like ghouls on All Hallows' Eve.

Anna was one of them, only she hadn't needed to travel very far to join this band of outsiders. Though she made half-hearted attempts to get conventional jobs as a typist and at the Ville de Paris department store, her strategy of turning up at Hollywood studios and leaving her name with the casting department eventually worked. She got a call-back that led to doing crowd work in several productions over the course of a year. Her first extra part earned her $5. The actual work of making movies, she found, was not quite as glamorous as the silver screen made it seem. "It was grueling and long before the day ended I was tired out. But my passion for film work wasn't killed. I loved it enough to carry on in spite of the hardships."

She knew exactly who could help her get noticed, but she'd have to work up the nerve to approach him. James Wang was a former Protestant pastor who quit his ministry in Evanston, Illinois, and, heeding the call of Hollywood, moved to Los Angeles. In addition to the supporting parts he played in movies like D. W. Griffith's *Broken Blossoms*, he became well-known in Chinatown and Hollywood for acting as an intermediary between the two communities. These were the years before Will Hays, president of the Motion Picture Producers and Distributors of America, established the Central Casting Corporation in 1925, which functioned as a registry for extras and often supplied studios with the "ethnic types" called upon to fill in as background. Wang was a valuable liaison and regularly recruited people from Chinatown to do extra work. Despite the questionable reputation of early movie studios, the exceptional pay of up to $7.50 a day (equal to about $136 today) was enough to lure many naysayers out of the shops and back alleys of Chinatown. Who wouldn't mind trading the back room of a laundry or a hot kitchen for twelve hours spent putzing around in "coolie" pants?

Then the Spanish flu epidemic hit Los Angeles in mid-September 1918. Suddenly, Wang's once plentiful roster of extras dwindled to a few dozen as more and more people caught the virus or decided they'd rather not tempt fate and stayed put at home. School was dismissed and those hated daily Chinese lessons came to a grinding halt. Anna saw an opening and she took it.

"Consumed by my ambition to become a film actress, I decided, unbeknownst to my parents, to find the all-powerful James Wang," Anna later recalled. "Trembling, I told him of my admiration for Pearl White, Mary Pickford, Olive Thomas, and my desire to make room for myself on screen."

Anna was in luck. Wang happened to be assembling several hundred Chinese extras that day for a Metro picture starring the famed Russian actress Alla Nazimova, but so far he'd been able to gather only about fifty. He offered to take her along to the studio. Clutching his arm, Anna squealed with gratitude: "Oh! Thank you, thank you! Do you think I will become a great actress?"

Wang looked her up and down. "Wong Liu Tsong," he responded in earnest, "you will be lost in the midst of three hundred extras, but I am sure you will be noticed, for your face is like a tangerine, you have big ears, a big nose, and especially big eyes."

Unfazed by Wang's dour prognosis, Anna was happy for the introduction. After one day on set for the Nazimova vehicle, she was singled out by the director to appear as a lantern bearer in an upcoming scene. *The Red Lantern*, as the film was titled, was set in China amidst the Boxer Rebellion of 1900 when Chinese citizens, tired of the preferential treatment given to the foreign powers that routinely pillaged their wealth and resources, took up arms against the "foreign devils," including many Christian missionaries. All of the principal Chinese characters were performed by white actors in yellowface.

A common trope of the 1910s was to center the drama on two characters pitted diametrically against one another—one good, one bad, one rich, one poor, one white, one mongrel—and cast the lead actor in both roles. In *The Red Lantern*, Nazimova played two half sisters: Blanche, the legitimate daughter of an Englishman, and Mahlee, the Englishman's daughter by his Chinese lover. Mahlee pledges to live among Europeans and espouse their Western values, but in the end finds she must defend her Chinese brethren when the uprising breaks out. The film was a cinematic allegory of sorts, as many were then and now, implying that "Orientals" could not be trusted by Westerners. Many years later, Anna May herself would question this trope with exasperation: "Why is it that the screen Chinese is nearly always the villain of the piece? And so crude a villain—murderous, treacherous, a snake in the grass!"

It's doubtful any of this crossed Anna's thirteen-year-old mind. In the family's living quarters above the laundry, she prepared herself for what she hoped would be the role of a lifetime. "I felt the responsibility for the whole movie industry on my shoulders," she reminisced. "I borrowed my mother's rice powder rag and fairly kalsomined my face. With the most painstaking effort, I managed to curl my straight Chinese hair. As a finished touch, I took one of our Chinese red papers, wet it and rubbed off the color onto my lips and cheeks."

The director was distraught when little Anna showed up on set that day looking like a clownish Blondielocks. She was sent immediately to makeup and wardrobe, where two women wiped her face clean and washed out the curls. Returned to her natural state and once again looking the part of a young Chinese girl, she played her role as lantern bearer along with two other extras in the procession behind Nazimova.

This being her big debut, Anna eagerly awaited the film's release in the spring of 1919. She abstained from lunch for an entire week to save up enough money to bring several girlfriends with her to the California Theater on Main Street, where they viewed the film from balcony seats. Anna's breath caught in her throat as the scene flickered onto the screen, her eyes trained on the three girls carrying lanterns.

"Which one is you?" one of her friends asked.

"I . . . I don't know," Anna stammered. "I think I must be the outside one."

To tell the truth, she didn't know which of the girls was her. How do you like that? She had made her first visible appearance in a film and she couldn't even recognize herself.

Disappointment and rejection, she was learning, were part and parcel of this acting business. But she'd grown a thick skin, quite literally, since the days when her white classmates at the California Street elementary school stuck burrs in her pigtails or, as the boy sitting behind her did, jabbed pins into her through her coat to see "if the Chinese have the same feelings we do." Anna's solution had been simply to put on another coat. As far as she was concerned, the uncredited role in *The Red Lantern* was just the beginning of her journey, the first hurdle to becoming a bona fide film star.

She continued to do background work as a glorified extra for another year. One day while tagging along with James Wang to the Universal lot, where he was making a Western picture, Anna caught the eye of "a handsome man with an ingratiating smile." Whenever there was a break on set, he casually ambled over to where she sat and struck up a conversation. His name was Marshall Neilan, Mary Pickford's favorite director, but everyone who knew him called him Mickey.

Enchanted with this young, spunky Chinese girl, Mickey cast Anna in his 1920 film *Dinty* as Half Moon, mistress to the Chinese drug lord played by Noah Beery. The role was uncredited but set her in the company of established movie actors like Beery, Colleen Moore, and child star Wesley Barry.

Anna subsequently fell ill with Sydenham's chorea, a mysterious childhood disorder that causes jerking movements and involuntary tics. During her long bout with this affliction, she was convinced she would never work in movies again. So when she miraculously recovered, she decided not to return to classes despite completing only two years of high school and instead pushed full steam ahead with her career. A steady progression of small parts over the next year continued to get Anna noticed. Among them were a tragic part in a Norma Talmadge film for which Anna turned on the waterworks ("Somebody throw Anna May Wong a raft," the assistant director cried); the Chinese girl in the background behind Lon Chaney in director Tod Browning's *Outside the Law*; another uncredited role in director Fred Niblo's *Mother o' Mine*; scenes in Japanese heartthrob Sessue Hayakawa's *The First Born*; and the part of Lotus Blossom in *Shame*, starring leading man John Gilbert.

It was around this time that she shed "the girl named Anna" and refashioned herself as Anna May Wong. She didn't like the way "Anna Wong" sounded. It didn't roll off the tongue. "Anna" was a common name, and so was "Wong," at least where she was from. But "Anna May Wong"? There was something about those four syllables that rang out pleasantly, and it also made for a prettier signature. She chose "May" because it was her favorite month and suggested a kind of eternal spring.

Anna May Wong's profile was growing. Slowly but surely, her dream of making it as a movie star was becoming ever more real. Her parents could no longer turn a blind eye to their daughter's unusual extracurricular activities, budding career or not.

When Anna first announced her plans in the motion picture business, her parents, in her words, "hit the ceiling. The Chinese had old-fashioned notions about play-acting." Those notions regarded actors as vagabonds and prostitutes, people who were among the lowest ranks of Chinese society. Even the culturally legitimate arena of Chinese opera did not allow women on the stage; instead, female roles were impersonated by male actors who spent a lifetime perfecting their performances in drag.

Wong Sam Sing, like any concerned father, worried about his daughter's propriety and safety. He knew what men were capable of. Movie people weren't exactly respectable from a Chinese point of view—or an American one, for that matter. "Hooligans" was more like it.

Anna May fired back. "I defended myself, saying that I didn't see anything wrong with a business in which so many of their old friends were engaging." Wong Sam Sing and Lee Gon Toy couldn't believe the words coming out of their daughter's mouth. Then they saw several studio buses pull up outside the laundry on Figueroa Street. Inside were no less than "a hundred fifty Chinese on the way to the studios to play extra parts and my father and mother knew most of them. They stayed so long gossiping in front of the house that the picture was kept waiting; but meanwhile I had slipped without further objection into the bus."

Wong Sam Sing made a habit of scanning the passengers aboard studio shuttles to suss out whether other Chinese women were present. He indulged Anna's obsession up to a point. It didn't hurt that she was bringing home a paycheck to "buy pretty dresses," as he jokingly told one reporter, and earning $150 a week (more than $2,500 today). But he wasn't a fool who was about to let his daughter ruin her reputation and risk becoming unmarriageable.

One day a boy in a car showed up, explaining he was there to drive Anna May to a studio in Culver City. Wong Sam Sing stood resolute.

"No other girl going?" he asked, stone-faced. The boy answered in the negative. Anna was forbidden to leave the house. And that was that.

Lee Gon Toy had another reason for objecting to her daughter's work in the movies. She pleaded with Anna not to have her photograph taken so often because she feared the cameras would steal her soul—in the most literal sense. This apparent superstition was not as unfounded as it might seem. Motion pictures were a startling innovation that burnished the image of the world onto celluloid film and then projected its exact likeness onto a screen, reviving moments long since passed. How could one explain such a mysterious technology except to believe it must be some form of sorcery?

When the Lumière brothers first screened their short film *The Arrival of a Train* in 1896, audiences jumped out of their seats for fear the locomotive shown rolling into a station was about to leap from the screen and into their laps. The film was only fifty seconds long.

Such was the power of the medium. Film didn't merely document the world; it transformed it, sharpened it, re-created our mundane reality into something that was familiar yet astonishing at the same time. Somehow the movies began to feel more real than our own lived experiences, giving rise to the expression "It was just like the movies"—a new way to describe the feeling of witnessing an extraordinary event.

Movies could even reanimate the dead. Douglas Fairbanks and Mary Pickford learned this firsthand. On their honeymoon, the newlyweds stopped in the Arizona desert to visit the Hopi tribe featured in Doug's recent film *The Mollycoddle*. Doug was keen on showing the film to his Hopi friends and arranged for it to be screened in the reservation schoolhouse.

The Hopi watched the film with interest, not unlike a Broadway audience, applauding Doug's various stunts. However, when they saw the playback of themselves performing a sacred dance, the schoolhouse erupted into commotion. There, on-screen, was Chief Loloma, who had died since filming, now seemingly resurrected.

"To us, of course, it was nothing but a harmless screen image," a reporter at the screening observed, "but to the Hopis it was the spirit, if not the flesh and blood of Loloma who had come back from the underworld to greet them."

The Hopis were right, though. They intuitively understood what a decade of moviegoers took for granted. Doug's film *had* brought Chief Loloma, his likeness and spirit, back into the world, just as subsequent films have done for a hundred years hence, restoring countless people and places, the infamous and anonymous alike. If movies elicited such wild, visceral responses from audiences, it was because moving pictures were truly miraculous.

Lee Gon Toy and Wong Sam Sing, both born in California to Chinese immigrant parents, came into the world amidst one of history's greatest transformations, and certainly during a pivotal moment in American nationhood. In 1860, the year Wong Sam Sing was born, the West was still wild.

Wong's parents, like nearly every other Chinese who ended up in America in the nineteenth century, hailed from Toisan in southern China, a rural countryside tended by farmers ninety miles southwest of the bustling port city Canton, or modern-day Guangzhou.

Though far from the imperial capital in Beijing, Toisan was but a stone's throw away from British Hong Kong and the proverbial barbarians at China's gate. In some ways it was a forgotten place at the mercy of domestic instability—poverty, famine, civil war—in a nation bowed by colonial forces. Yet, Toisan also sat at the crossroads of change and its inhabitants were some of the first to receive news of opportunities in faraway lands. Young men from Toisan's several dozen market towns increasingly looked to the West for a chance to make their mark, immigrating to the United States as laborers as early as the 1830s.

When gold was discovered at Sutter's Mill in 1848, the news of the gold rush traveled across the globe. President James Polk substantiated the claims in his 1848 State of the Union address to Congress. With that, the floodgates were flung open and California, wrested from Mexico at the close of the Mexican-American War, was hastily inducted into the Union. Within two years 100,000 men from all over the world had flocked to California, including thousands of men from Toisan. The call to adventure and a shot at a piece of treasure across the Pacific proved hard to resist.

Little is known about Wong Sam Sing's early life. We are left only with the stories he chose to tell his family, which were later filtered through Anna May's own recounting. "My father proved his originality by being born in Michigan Bluffs [sic]," she later wrote, which situated Wong smack dab in Placer County, the heart of gold country.

Wong grew up in the transient, somewhat manic atmosphere of a Western mining town. His parents had been lured to California by the promise of gold, but, rather than toil as a hapless miner, his father owned two stores that catered to Michigan Bluff's growing population. It was Wong's loss of his mother at age five that prompted his first trip to the family's ancestral village in Toisan, China. He then stayed behind in the village with relatives while his father sailed back to the United States to tend to his business. According to Wong's own recollections, he returned to California thirteen years later as a young man eager to try his chance in the mines.

Wong Sam Sing interacted daily with white miners and other settlers on the frontier. "He must have been very popular with the children of the town," Anna May recalled in one of her memoirs, because he had shown her "a lot of pictures taken with them gathered around him." Even so, he was not white, and though many fellow Chinese had roamed the hills of Placer County for about as long as any other claim-jumpers, he would always be seen apart from the white men who declared Manifest Destiny as their God-given birthright. Wong's years in Mother Lode country likely strengthened his connection to the Old World and hardened his identity as a Chinese man in a strange, lawless land.

In short order, the "Big Four"—an infamous partnership among Leland Stanford, Mark Hopkins, Collis Potter Huntington, and Charles Crocker—joined the race to pave the iron road of the future: the transcontinental railroad. The railroad would be built with the era's most cutting-edge technology: a man with a pickaxe. As such, the Central Pacific needed manpower, and lots of it. The company was desperate to hire strong, reliable laborers, but the supply of white men, mostly Irish immigrants, was limited, and many refused to do the backbreaking work of laying track twelve hours a day.

Though Stanford had previously disparaged the Chinese as "a degraded and distinct people" exercising "a deleterious influence upon the superior race," his partner Crocker's decision to hire a group of fifty Chinese workers on a trial basis reversed his opinion. Stanford was skeptical that the diminutive Chinese would be able to muster the muscle power required, but, watching them work, he was impressed by their discipline and endurance. Not only could they do the work, but they did so efficiently and for a fraction of the wages he paid white men.

With the help of some 20,000 Chinese laborers, the Central Pacific route of the transcontinental railroad plowed, tunneled, and blasted its way through the solid granite rock of the mighty Sierras. The line was finished in 1869 in half the time originally slated for its completion.

The introduction of the transcontinental railroad was world shattering. It transformed what had once been a dangerous and uncertain journey across land and sea for many months into a straightforward matter of buying a ticket and sitting aboard a steam-powered car that traveled coast to coast in a week. Like clicking to buy a product on Amazon and having it show up on your doorstep twenty-four hours later, it was that kind of magic—but it came at a cost.

The railroad was a symbol of American ingenuity and progress, but it was the entrepreneurial figureheads who got all the glory, not the laborers who had sweat and bled to make it a reality. Stanford, along with his colleagues Huntington, Crocker, and Hopkins, became absurdly rich. At the same time, the competition for jobs and market share rose to new heights, and, rather than unlocking opportunity, the opening of the railroad created a bottleneck that propelled the country into a financial crisis and the Panic of 1873.

Wong Sam Sing would feel the ripple effects of the railroad on his own life when he returned to Michigan Bluff in 1878 as a young man. Thousands of laborers suddenly found themselves out of work. Unemployed white men did not take kindly to the idea of having to compete yet again with Chinese workers for jobs they felt were rightfully theirs. The trauma of the Civil War, which had concluded in 1865, was still fresh in the hearts and minds of the men and women brought west by the railroad. Now that Reconstruction was underway, the dregs of racial animus consolidated around a new enemy: the "Heathen

Chinee." The white man in the guise of the Workingmen's Party of California wanted the Chinese gone. Angry mobs often took these matters into their own hands, burning down Chinese businesses across the West, running their owners and employees out of town, and sometimes outright lynching them.

Just as hostilities against the Chinese reached their peak, a nineteen-year-old Wong decided to set out for China to find himself a bride. When he returned, the U.S. Congress had passed the first racially based immigration law in American history. The Chinese Exclusion Act of 1882 effectively ended the immigration of Chinese into the United States, aside from a small quota of diplomats, merchants, and students. What's more, the act put into place measures to track the entry and exit of any Chinese who had rightful claims to residency within the country's borders.

The Chinese who remained in America had to strategize novel ways of making a living without treading on the perceived rights of the white man. What the West sorely lacked were women to do the work women were supposedly best suited for: cooking, cleaning, and washing and mending soiled garments. By some accounts, laundry service was so dearly needed that miners began sending bags of dirty clothes on four-month journeys to Hong Kong and back for the exorbitant cost of $12 for a dozen shirts. The absence of women in the West, in addition to their subordinate position in society, paved the way for the rise of the Chinese hand laundry.

That Anna May Wong's father went into the laundry business in the last quarter of the nineteenth century would surprise almost no one. More than three fourths of California's laundries were operated by Chinese in 1880. The motivations behind the rapid expansion of Chinese laundries were clear. Setting up a laundry required very little capital. In most cases, all that was needed was a storefront (which often doubled as living quarters), a few irons, coal to heat the irons, soap, water, and a drying yard. The laundryman, unlike the railroad laborer, was his own boss, and if he decided to marry and raise a family, as Wong Sam Sing did, the laundry naturally became a family business with extra hands to help lighten the load.

As a laundryman, Wong's interactions with the white world were bounded and diminished, though racism against the Chinese persisted where it could. People sometimes showed up at the laundry demanding parcels of clean clothing without providing their claim tickets, or a customer might scour their clothes looking for stains and tears so that they could insist on a refund. Delinquent children threw rocks at the laundry windows and, in winter, dirty snowballs at clean washing hung out to dry.

Campaigns to root the Chinese laundrymen out of Los Angeles were waged in the law courts as well. In 1913, when Wong was arrested because of a bunk ordinance that arbitrarily prohibited laundries in certain districts, he hired a lawyer and fought the case all the way to the California Supreme Court. He was not one to put up and shut up when he knew his rights were being violated—a brand of stubbornness he unwittingly passed on to his daughter.

———

Even as a teenager, Anna May Wong understood the power of an origin story. She'd watched one materialize right before her very eyes to account for the meteoric rise of her native city. Los Angeles, once a frontier outpost, grew into a major metropolitan center that surpassed San Francisco in population by 1920. The city sprung up, like a mirage of an oasis, in the middle of a desert where a city was never meant to be.

Like the movie stars she looked up to as a girl, Anna May crafted and recited her origin story for the press again and again. She was the daughter of a Chinese laundryman. Perhaps what made it so irresistible, so worthy of reprinting, was that it appeared to be the unvarnished truth, wholesome in its plainness. Certainly, it was unusual to see such a girl become a movie actress. The Chinese laundry was a place many Americans frequented, picking up and dropping off their shirtsleeves and collars, yet it existed on the periphery of American life.

It wasn't that other actors came from particularly well-off households or theatrically talented families. On the contrary, Anna May's humble beginnings weren't that dissimilar from those of the flickers' biggest stars. Most movie people, especially in the industry's early speculative days, came from working-class backgrounds where money was always tight and the task of putting food on the table a daily existential quest.

Mary Pickford's father was an alcoholic who abandoned the family; the eldest of three children, she began acting in the theater at age five and quickly became the family's breadwinner. Douglas Fairbanks, whose real name was Ullman, was the son of a bigamous Jewish lawyer who later deserted the family; he was ashamed of his Jewish ancestry and took that secret with him to the grave. Charlie Chaplin, the bastard child of a sometime prostitute who called the madhouse home, scraped by in the streets of London as a juvenile.

Screenwriter Anita Loos observed these humble origin stories in her recollections of Hollywood, clarifying that money and sex appeal were often the only things separating movie stars from their servants. "To place in the limelight a great number of people who ordinarily would be chambermaids and chauffeurs, give them unlimited power and instant wealth, is bound to produce a lively and diverting result."

Through the rose-hued lens of studio PR, Fairbanks's father became a silver speculator in Colorado and a well-known scholar of Shakespeare. The Pickford patriarch was remembered as a loving family man taken too early by a tragic accident aboard a steamship. Chaplin was the son of boisterous music hall performers and nothing more.

Hollywood's heavyweights deftly tidied up the unsavory aspects of their narratives, the modest truths of their previous circumstances they'd rather no one knew about. Anna May told it straight, mostly.

She had learned as a child to hold her head high. Her devotees and detractors should know the truth about the challenges she'd overcome.

In a two-part memoir written for *Pictures* magazine in 1926, Anna May recalled that as a child she had known no difference between herself and the white children she went to school with. That was until the day a group of boys from school accosted her and her sister Lulu on their way home and "the world came crashing down." "Chink, Chink, Chinaman," her classmates chanted, inducing the girls to flee. Once in the safety of their father's arms, they asked him between sobs what it all meant. "Why had the little boys pulled our hair, slapped us, driven us from the sidewalk? We had done nothing wrong. We had tried always to behave in a proper manner."

Wong Sam Sing, who had faced the specter of racial violence since he was a young man in Michigan Bluff, took his daughters, one on each knee. "Perhaps our father was sad at heart, to find that social ostracism had come to us so early," Anna May reflected. "Perhaps he was resentful. But he showed nothing of this. . . . He explained to us, gently, that it was no disgrace to be Chinese, that indeed we must be proud always of our people and our race. But, he told us, our position in an American community must at times be a difficult one."

The next day the girls put on a brave face and returned to school. The taunts continued at recess, and this time their girl classmates joined the chorus of boys. Though Lulu and Anna May never cried in front of their tormentors, as their father insisted they must be "too proud to cry," eventually the girls were switched to the Chinese Mission School, where they could study in peace, as their classmates were Chinese like them.

Anna May would never again forget the distinction of her race in American society. But as she was coming to understand, the thing about celebrity is that singularity sells. Difference sets one apart, indelibly imprinting one's persona onto the hearts and minds of fans. What had once been a liability in the schoolhouse became a noteworthy advantage on the silver screen.

So when the reporters came calling with requests to interview the seventeen-year-old actress, Anna May welcomed them into Sam Kee Laundry and gave them the grand tour. She told them with pride, "I was named Wong Lew Song, which means Frosted Yellow Willows. A rather unusual name, isn't it?" And they lapped it up.

"Imagine that name in electric lights," one columnist exalted. Anna May Wong, he confided to his readers, was one of the most remarkable interview subjects of his career.

A glamour shot of Anna May from *The Honorable Mr. Buggs*, 1927.

3

HAPPINESS MUST BE EARNED

An expectant hush fell over Los Angeles at the beginning of July 1924 as Sid Grauman's Egyptian Theatre on Hollywood Boulevard went dark for three days. The city's denizens waited with baited breath for "the greatest event of the cinema season" to come to town. While the doors to the theater remained closed to the public, inside the Egyptian's plaster-cast walls made to look like the limestone bricks of the pyramids, "extensive and elaborate" preparations were vigorously underway for its next feature presentation, *The Thief of Bagdad*.

Principal photography on *Thief* had commenced one year prior almost to the day. All told, with the initial months of frenzied research and planning, as well as postproduction edits and the composition of the original musical score, the film had taken more than sixty-five weeks to complete and cost the Douglas Fairbanks Pictures Corporation a whopping $2 million.

The Egyptian Theatre, which had opened fortuitously in 1922 mere weeks before the discovery (and later plunder) of the tomb of Tutankhamun, was the obvious choice to host *Thief*'s long-anticipated West Coast debut. Grauman's resplendent movie theater was not only on-brand—the hieroglyphs and sphinxes decorating the venue spoke to the same exotic yearnings as those of the cinematic Bagdad—but it was also the site of the first-ever Hollywood movie premiere, securing its place in show business history for the rest of time. The initial film screened there two years prior had been none other than Douglas Fairbanks's *Robin Hood*.

By the early 1920s, Los Angeles was earning its stripes as the booming new capital of the film industry, but the shadow cast by New York City's cultural eminence still loomed large. As custom dictated, *Thief* made its world premiere on Broadway in New York on March 18, 1924. Promoter Morris Gest flooded the papers with ads and puff pieces in the weeks leading up to the event. His "de luxe press-agent tactics brought them from the highways and byways," as one *New York Daily News* reporter commented. On opening night the pavement outside the Liberty Theatre and the entire block of Forty-Second Street between Broadway and Eighth Avenue were thronged with 5,000 fans. Doug and Mary were nearly bum-rushed by admirers when they arrived fashionably late, ten minutes after curtain time. It took a five-man police escort, one man hooked around each of the stars' arms plus an extra man for good measure, to get them safely to their seats.

In the end, the excessive hype and hoopla, "the beating of drums, the droning of voices in dirge-like songs and the odor of incense that emanated from the theatre," paid off. *Thief* was an absolute triumph with the New York critics. "A film which will exhaust fans' superlatives for some time to come," hailed the *New York Daily News*. "The wealth of magic that is applicable to pictures has finally been adapted by Fairbanks," declared *Variety*. The last word in film criticism, the *New York Times* exalted: "An entrancing picture, wholesome and beautiful, deliberate but compelling, a feat of motion picture art which has never been equaled."

The film's rollout continued across the Northeast, opening in Boston and Philadelphia in the spring of 1924. After attending the New York premiere, Doug and Mary boarded a ship for Europe and commenced on one of their post-film gallivants, which in its own way served as a de facto press junket, drawing thousands wherever they traveled. Meanwhile, the folks back at home—the same Angelenos who had watched the minarets go up on Santa Monica Boulevard, mingled with the scores of extras commuting to the studio daily on Pacific Electric's Red Cars, and seen the officious Bagdad sign glittering in the sunlight from afar—waited patiently for their turn to revel in the movie that had occupied the local imagination for the past year.

Some 20,000 persons had visited the Pickford-Fairbanks studio during the filming of *Thief*, and soon they would get a souvenir reminder of the exploits they'd witnessed on set. A month ahead of the Hollywood premiere, studio secretaries began mailing visitor passes back to their owners in a well-timed advertising stunt. The *Hollywood Daily Citizen* dedicated an entire four-page spread to pre-coverage of the film's Southern California premiere along with pages of ads and special promotions from local businesses eager to ride the Bagdad wave.

Not to be outdone by Morris Gest's New York showing, Sid Grauman set about orchestrating a premiere extravaganza "that would go down in the history of motion-picture presentations as its greatest prelude." On the evening of July 10, 1924, cast members, VIP guests, and a few lucky ticket holders were greeted by a massive swarm of onlookers lining the Egyptian's regal courtyard and the boulevard beyond.

Among the guest list was Anna May Wong, and what a thrill it was for her, this sudden thrust into the limelight. For years she had stood on the other side of things, just another face in the crowd, jammed in with the riffraff, maneuvering for a spot with a clear view of Hollywood's finest. But tonight she found herself mingling with important names like Norma Talmadge, Jackie Coogan, Jeanie MacPherson, King Vidor, Samuel Goldwyn, Elinor Glyn, Cecil B. DeMille, and even her old idol Mae Murray. Brushing shoulders with the stars in their "beautiful gowns and handsome jewels," Anna May was no longer a star gazer but one of the gazed upon.

Flashbulbs discharged as she strolled demurely past the life-size elephant statues with elaborate howdahs that Grauman had installed. The musky parfum of Fleurs de Bagdad, the self-proclaimed "aroma of Arabia," hit Anna May's nose as soon as she crossed the threshold into the theater lobby. Inside, usherettes draped in "the long veils of the harems" handed out leather-bound souvenir programs and directed guests to their seats. Colorful balloons, rich tapestries, a profusion of burning incense, and a smattering of Oriental deities positioned throughout the lobby only intensified the carnivalesque atmosphere.

Grauman's Egyptian was a far cry from the nickelodeons of Anna May's youth, where the lights were best left off. Looking at the intricate columns painted in vibrant golds, greens, and reds, the winged scarab filigree, and the giant gilded sunburst rising overhead against the deep cobalt blue of the auditorium ceiling, Anna May understood why these theaters were called movie palaces. Tutankhamun would be turning in his grave.

Guests made their way through the bazaar of attractions to their seats as Grauman's opening act, "The City of Dreams," began. The lavish presentation had been in rehearsals for weeks while the local papers endlessly touted the expenditure invested in the show: a full orchestra, one hundred "native" performers, and $100,000 spent on costumes alone. Grauman had helped to pioneer the movie prologue, as these live performances were called, to lure in audiences and persuade them to pay higher ticket prices. For *Thief*, he pulled out all the stops.

The show before the show was filled with "camels, flying rings, Arabs, and pretty girls" as the stage was transformed into a scene "of bazaars and hanging rugs and curved archways and minarets and everything symbolical of the Orient." There was no doubt in Grauman's mind that his production was "a spectacle more brilliant, I am sure, than anything so far staged in connection with a picture."

When at last the preliminary entertainments were concluded, actor Milton Sills took the stage to introduce the film and pay tribute to Douglas Fairbanks, the Thief of Bagdad himself, who was still very much vacationing in France thousands of miles away. Then, one by one, Sills called up the actors in attendance. Anna May Wong took her place in the spotlight as the fifth-billed player, a rather high position in such a large ensemble cast, and graciously acknowledged the round of applause that reverberated throughout the auditorium.

Then the lights were dimmed and "the velvety blackness gradually [changed] the mood," making way for the main act to begin. The members of the orchestra, who had not escaped Grauman's attention, were dressed in turbans and sheiks' robes as they launched into the overture and the opening title card flashed on-screen.

Since the earliest days of the cinema, most silent films were accompanied by a live pianist or an electric piano that played a repertoire of short compositions strung together into one long improvised soundtrack. The accompanist struck a suspenseful, wicked-sounding note to foreshadow a dramatic development and played a blissed-out, triumphant melody when the good guy got the girl. There would be no such stock music in *Thief*. Instead, Doug hired classical composer Mortimer Wilson to draft an "original" score for his opus, though the finished soundtrack borrowed liberally from Rimsky-Korsakov's *Scheherazade*.

From the very first note, the audience was spellbound. The tentative sounding of woodwinds gave way to melancholy violin and the mystical undertones of a harp being strummed languidly. Wilson's "symphonic masterpiece," which was said to be "the first time a musical accompaniment for a photoplay has been written as the story was filmed," was the final ingredient in the magic formula needed to recast the everyday into fantasy. As the music soared, so, too, did moviegoers. Though Anna May had been on the set day after day and seen how the sausage was made, there was almost no comparison between the experience she'd had shooting the film and the one she was now having watching it.

The world presented on-screen was as foreign to her as it was to every other audience member that night. And in the final scenes when the thief becomes a prince and alights with his bride on a magical carpet ride, their capes fluttering in the wind, it didn't matter one jot that Anna May knew full well the simple method behind the camera trick: a giant eighty-foot crane hoisted the royal couple over the tops of Bagdad's minarets using a steel-reinforced rug and invisible cables painted white. The witchcraft wasn't in the mechanics but in the sheer miracle that a piece of flickering celluloid could actually make you feel something.

———————

The Thief of Bagdad played to standing room only through every evening performance the first two weeks of its run at Grauman's Egyptian, eclipsing ticket sales for the theater's two previous feature presentations. The Los Angeles critics were just as bowled over as the New York ones, if not more so.

"*Thief of Bagdad* Beggars Description," read the headline in the *Los Angeles Daily News*. "It may be said without any exaggeration," the reviewer elaborated, "that *The Thief of Bagdad* is the greatest cinema of its kind ever to be projected on the silver screen." *Visual Education* applauded it as "a great artistic achievement." Meanwhile, the *Los Angeles Evening Express* heaped praise upon the film's visionary producer: "No one but Douglas Fairbanks could have turned the trick of corralling the highly sophisticated and making such an allegory, a gossamer thing of pure fantasy, seem real and full of meaning and beauty."

Edwin Schallert, drama critic for the *Los Angeles Times*, wrote simply, "I have no words to evoke its magic. . . . One of the most splendid films, if not in certain ways the most transcendent, ever made. . . . There is in all this glamour something that sweeps and carries you away with it."

Anna May performed the role of Mongol slave with aplomb. Her dexterity as an actress was on full display. In one scene she might evince genuine fear and panic—say, when she discovers Ahmed, the thief, has stolen into the princess's bedroom. He holds her at knifepoint with a dagger to the back and pushes her toward an alcove off the cavernous chamber, where he wedges the dagger in place using a pillow propped up against the wall. As she writhes in fear against the blade poised behind her, little does she know that Ahmed has left her and the knife behind to inspect the princess's dainty shoes. This moment of slapstick was a crowd-pleaser that stuck in the minds of many moviegoers.

In another scene, the ladies-in-waiting divine the princess's future from the sands of Mecca and foretell that she will marry the first suitor who touches the rose tree in the palace garden. You can see the wheels turning in a close-up of Anna May's face as her expression changes from one of revelation to malevolent scheming. With a subtle shift of her gaze and narrowing of her brow, her countenance reveals all the audience needs to know: the devious Mongol slave will use this newly received information to aid her master in winning the princess's hand in marriage and becoming the next caliph.

For all the fuss made about Julanne Johnston's graceful dancer's body, her performance as the princess was unremarkable despite the ample amount of screen time given to her. And in comparison to Doug's pantomime-like rendition of Ahmed the thief, Anna May's understated yet forceful artistry was a welcome tonic. *Photoplay* had predicted as much in the caption that ran with a portrait of the young actress in its March 1924 issue: "Advance reports say that she walks away with quite a bit of the applause." Schallert later concurred: "Anna May Wong, to my mind, does one of the best bits of acting as the intriguing Chinese girl."

A number of reviewers, male and female, couldn't help but notice the Mongol slave's costume, or lack thereof. "If Miss Johnston is to be considered the season's 'find,'" Carolyn Carter trilled in *Movie Weekly*, "little Anna May Wong, the Chinese girl, is surely the season's 'exposé'—she wears nothing and very little of that, and is very, very easy to look at."

Though Wong Sam Sing had acquiesced to Anna May's continued interest in doing film work, perhaps somewhat uneasily, he had little to say about his daughter's performance in *The Thief of Bagdad*. In fact, it took some coaxing from one of his sons to finally get him into the movie theater for a screening—supposedly the first and only film of his daughter's he ever watched.

When the fantasy ended and the harsh lights were flipped back on, his son asked, "Well, father, what do you think of Liu Tsong?" The sixty-four-year-old laundryman simply smiled. He hugged his sides and, pretending to shiver, said, "It's cold." Clearly, the Mongol slave's meager uniform had not escaped his notice either. This thing called "acting" sure was strange work but good money if you could get it.

Those in the know, however, were plenty vocal about what they saw in the young actress. It was fast becoming clear that out of all the newcomers and "curious, exotic, and sinister types" in *Thief*'s ensemble cast, Anna May Wong was the breakout star that movie columnists and fans were clamoring for. Full-page portraits of Anna May dressed in her Mongol garb and various exotic costumes ran in *Photoplay*, *Picturegoer*, and *Motion Picture Classic* in a span of a few months. Indeed, her name and face had been popping up in newspapers and magazines across the country ever since news of her role in Doug's film had been made public. Now that the film was finally out, moviegoers could come to their own conclusions as to whether she was more than just easy on the eyes. "Anna May Wong as the little slave girl who is a spy for the Mongol prince, proved herself a fine actress," *Variety* pronounced.

Interest in the bewitching "Oriental beauty" intensified. Anna May could be seen modeling luxurious ermine wraps and posing next to a top-of-the-line 1925 Studebaker Special Six sedan on the regular. Profiles in *Movie Weekly* and *Photoplay* soon followed. Oddly enough, reporters described her without fail as "little" and "diminutive," despite her natural height of five foot six. They couldn't get over the fact that her Chinese appearance belied her exuberant American girl patois and style. To illustrate the two jarring personas combined in one woman, *Photoplay* juxtaposed an image of Anna May wearing an old-fashioned cheongsam and with a somber expression next to another image of her dressed in a smart cream suit and tie, complete with a cloche hat, heels, cane—and a good-natured American grin.

"Improbable as this sounds . . . Anna May Wong, among Americans, is so thoroughly one of us that her Oriental background drops completely away," Helen Carlisle attested in the pages of *Movie Weekly*. "Does she, chameleon like, become as thoroughly Chinese when among her own people? Are her Americanisms merely part of a clever pose?" Carlisle wondered. "Which is the real Anna May Wong? The Chinese maiden or the American one?"

By the end of September 1924, *Thief* was nearing its 150th performance at Grauman's Egyptian Theatre. A special showing was arranged to mark the milestone and the *Los Angeles Times* announced that Anna May Wong, the "diminutive almond-eyed star," would serve as the guest of honor. As part of this publicity stunt, Anna May personally presented souvenirs—"a surprise package engraved with a design representing Doug's winged horse flying above the Egyptian Theater"—to attendees in the theater's courtyard.

The public recognition of her performance as the Mongol slave, of all things, was validating. Her parents might never understand or wholly approve of her vocation, but who needs filial piety when you can get your kicks from thousands of adoring fans? Outside of the fame and money that came with success, Anna May was having a grand ol' time. She was nineteen, beautiful, and whip-smart despite never having completed high school. She had a quip or a comeback for everything, and that made her amusing fare at cocktail hour. She was a creature in demand in adolescent Hollywood, where there was a party going on somewhere every night of the week. One night it could be drinks at the Montmartre Café, the next night dancing at the Cocoanut Grove, and the next a late supper at Henry's—or all three in the same evening.

The Jazz Age was in full swing by 1924. Prohibition may have wrung out legitimate channels for manufacturing and selling alcohol, but in Hollywood, young people—as they did everywhere in America—found a way to keep the booze flowing. This new generation, the sons and daughters of prim Victorians, was decidedly different.

F. Scott Fitzgerald, the veritable voice of his generation, set the tone for the Roaring Twenties with his best-selling novel *This Side of Paradise* (which everyone who was anyone had read). His protagonist, Amory Blaine, registers the same shock and awe that many of his peers must have felt at the changing times: "Amory saw girls doing things that even in his memory would have been impossible. . . . [He] found it rather fascinating to feel that any popular girl he met before eight he might quite possibly kiss before twelve."

It was the era of fast cars and fast women. As the Chinese flapper, Anna May knew a little something about both of those things. "I never seem to have any money saved up," she admitted to one reporter. "Gee, it disappears as soon as I get it." She'd bought herself a car with her movie earnings, but it wasn't long before she totaled it while "trying to beat a motor cop to a bridge." The moral of the story? "I beat him all right, but I missed the bridge." Reports of her traffic exploits were simply more fodder for the newshounds.

As far as any potential love interests, Anna May didn't kiss and tell.

"Who's your favorite movie star?" one reporter asked.

"Say, you don't get me with that one," she responded with a laugh. "I told an interviewer once I admired Richard Dix, and I've been kidded about it ever since. Well, it's a great life, isn't it?"

Hollywood's rumor mill entrapped the appealing young actress all the same. The very celestial qualities—"celestial" being a synonym for Chinese, as in "not from the planet Earth"—that had induced her male classmates to yank her pigtails and stick her with pins were presently something of a draw. Or maybe her unusual face had always been a turn-on and those boys had merely become men who were now responding accordingly.

Whether she wanted it or not, Anna May got plenty of attention from the opposite sex. The white male directors she inevitably worked with couldn't keep their hands off her. Tod Browning, who directed Anna May in *Outside the Law* (1921) and *Drifting* (1923), made advances toward his underage actress, to which she seemingly responded.

Rumors of their dalliance circulated on studio backlots and in back-stage dressing rooms. "He was in love with her," MGM production manager J. J. Cohn said. Others suggested she was merely the flavor of the week, a foreign-seeming girl to satiate his chronic desire for the unusual. When Browning's wife found out, she left him.

The man Anna May fell hardest for, a first love of sorts, was the unforgettable, larger-than-life Marshall "Mickey" Neilan, the biggest boozehound of them all. Gloria Swanson once described him as the "omnipresent playboy" who "always knew where the good gin was hidden, where the best party was going on, where the best band was playing." Romance novelist and Hollywood gossip Elinor Glyn dubbed him "a hero out of F. Scott Fitzgerald."

Mickey was an Irish kid from San Bernardino, a jokester and a playboy with a restless soul that always seemed to get him into trouble. Fittingly, his break into showbiz came via one of his many odd jobs: chauffeuring theatre impresario Oliver Morosco, who was then direct-ing the stock company at the Burbank Theatre. This led naturally to another job chauffeuring D. W. Griffith, who encouraged Mickey to break into the movies. In the early 1910s, Mickey started getting parts in silent films and within a few years had charmed his way into the director's chair. It turned out he had a knack for directing. He worked gigs at all the early studios, like Kalem, Selig, Bison, Famous Players-Lasky, and Biograph. When he directed fellow Irish pal Mary Pick-ford in the 1917 hit film *Rebecca of Sunnybrook Farm*, his reputation as a hotshot director was sealed.

By 1921, Mickey was raking in $125,000 for every picture he di-rected. His pockets were so overstuffed with cash, the money did more than burn a hole in his pants; it set them on fire. But Mickey was a generous high-roller. His wallet was like a sieve, and he was content to throw the money away on a good time for one and all. He started his own production company, as was the trend of successful directors at the time, but often made capricious decisions that upended production schedules. Other times, he showed up late to set after an all-night bender, or sometimes not at all if he got carried away at a party in San Francisco or Catalina.

"I always said that one reason I wanted my own company was so that I could hire an efficiency man and then can him," Mickey joked. He hated the egos and moneymen who ran Hollywood; his feuds with Louis B. Mayer and Cecil B. DeMille were legendary.

Never one to forget his humble beginnings, Mickey made a habit of casting unknowns in his films. His most famous discovery was the freckle-faced Wesley Barry, who became a child star. Mickey did the same for Anna May when he scouted her for his film *Dinty* in 1920, her first credited role, but only after persuading "her father to allow her to forsake her shirt-pinning activities."

Wong Sam Sing was right to be wary of the wily picture people who kept turning up at Sam Kee Laundry. But there were only so many times he could lock Anna May in her room when a casting director came calling. The thing about Mickey Neilan was that he fell in love with every beautiful woman he set his eyes on. Rumors soon swirled about the true nature of Mickey and Anna May's director-actor relationship. Was selecting her for his films how he rewarded her for submitting to the casting couch? Even more scandalous was the fact that Anna May was merely a child. Mickey was thirty to her sixteen. A sexual relationship with an underage girl, whether consensual or not, was statutory rape as laid out by California law.

According to director and friend Allan Dwan, the couple's affair was an open secret in Hollywood. Mickey, newly divorced from his first wife, Gertrude Bambrick, said he wanted to marry Anna May, only they'd have to run down to Mexico for the marriage license in order to skirt anti-miscegenation laws in the United States. The scandal such a union would stir in the papers, especially at a time when Hollywood was under siege for its loose morals, could ruin his career, friends close to him argued. Mickey thought better of it and the marriage was off before it was ever really on.

Complicating matters was the fact that Mickey had been linked to actress Blanche Sweet in the press. The two had known each other since their early days at Biograph. Anna May's feelings may have cooled precipitously when the gossip rags divulged that Blanche was expecting an imminent proposal from Mickey. Meanwhile, behind the scenes, Mickey was making moves on Gloria Swanson, who had succeeded Mary Pickford as Hollywood's biggest star. The pair had been circling each other since 1919 when Mickey swept Gloria onto the dance floor, away from her soon-to-be-husband Herbert Somborn, and told her he was going to marry her one day. He admitted that he wasn't yet at liberty to walk down the aisle, seeing as he was then still married himself, but added, "You and I are both probably going to be married a number of times. I just want to get my name on your list."

Funny thing is, he'd said the same thing to Mary Miles Minter, only she never took his proposal seriously. Mickey's standard seduction strategy, apparently, was the marriage proposal, but as it turns out, he was much better suited to being a lover than a husband. Gloria realized this over a weeklong tryst with Mickey in Paris. His fun-loving jaunts swiftly turned into drunkenness. Following a crack-up fight in the Hôtel de Crillon, Gloria convinced Mickey to phone Blanche long-distance and promise to marry her as soon as he got back stateside.

In the midst of this romantic turmoil, Mickey was working on his next movie of 1921, *Bits of Life*, a film composed of four vignettes, including one about a family living in San Francisco's Chinatown. Anna May was given a substantial role as the wife of a brutal half-Chinese man, impersonated by character actor Lon Chaney, the Man of a Thousand Faces. In the vignette titled "Hop," the husband flies into a rage when he learns that his wife has delivered a daughter instead of a son. Anna May played the scene in which her husband nearly chokes her to death with convincing terror. It wasn't exactly light fare, but it got her noticed by critics and earned her praise.

"Anna May Wong, an attractive little Chinawoman who has often been seen in bits, is provided here with an opportunity to really act and let it be announced that she puts it over in a manner that would be highly commendable," the reviewer for *CAMERA!* wrote. "We have a great desire to see Anna May again." Ads for *Bits of Life* billed her name just underneath the three other principals: Wesley Barry, Lon Chaney, and Noah Beery.

Their affair notwithstanding, she had nothing but good things to say about her director-muse. "Mickey Neilan is the prince of directors," she gushed to a *Picture-Play* reporter. "None of your plush-lined ballyhooers can equal him. He lets you be yourself and, while I don't know a darn thing about art or acting, I do know that that is the truest expression of any talent."

Whether there were tears shed over Mickey or lingering feelings of resentment, she never showed it. Anna May was learning the ways of the world and her career was taking off, which meant she was going places that she'd never been to before. The borders of her universe were, little by little, stretching past the Los Angeles of her girlhood.

———

Not long after Anna May's work on *Thief* wrapped, she moved out of the family laundry and into a bungalow in Hollywood. Famous Players-Lasky, Adolph Zukor's motion picture company, hired Anna May for three films, and, in addition to the films she made at other studios, she worked steadily throughout 1924.

At the end of May, she was off to Banff, Canada, with the cast and crew of *The Alaskan*. She would play an Eskimo girl named Keok, a slight departure from her normal schtick as the Oriental girl. Rugged he-man Thomas Meighan would assume the male lead along with love interest Estelle Taylor. Herbert Brenon would direct and James Wong Howe would serve as director of photography.

The town of Banff looked like something out of a picture book of the Swiss Alps. Nestled amidst the majestic snow-covered peaks and the stunning glacial lakes of Banff National Park, it had those chalet vibes and the brisk mountain air to go with it. For Anna May, though the work was demanding as always, being on location on her first trip outside the country felt like a holiday. In between scenes, she sometimes watched from her perch next to the camera atop the roof of the Banff Springs hotel while her costars staged scenes a thousand feet below. When she wasn't in front of the camera, she was busy taking in the scenery, adopting the Britishisms of western Canadian culture, and attending a local Indian stampede and roundup.

"Cheerio, old top," Anna May began in a "breezy letter" to the *Los Angeles Times*. "It seems as though there isn't an ugly spot anywhere in the landscape up here. Though I must admit I should like a peep of real California sunshine, for it manages to rain sometime during the twenty-four hours on the sunniest days here. We have one saving thing, though—the long daylight hours. It seems so funny to have dinner at 10:30!"

The rain proved to be a boon in its own way. Every day the shoot was rained out, Estelle Taylor and Anna May went swimming in the hotel's heated pool. "Anna May cannot swim," Estelle disclosed to Grace Kingsley at the *Los Angeles Times*, "but she has all the nerve in the world—would dive from a height where I wouldn't think of going."

However, the trip north wasn't all fun and games.

"We got into Vancouver in the middle of the night," Estelle recounted. "There was a little difficulty over Anna May Wong and Jimmie How [*sic*], cameraman, because both are Chinese. The trouble was, it had been feared that the two might not be able to get back into California again, once they had left."

The Chinese Exclusion Act of 1882 was still the law of the land and its ban on Chinese immigration to the United States ruled not merely the lives of Chinese nationals who hoped to immigrate across the Pacific, but also thousands of American-born citizens living in the United States who happened to be ethnically Chinese. In contrast to their fellow Americans, Chinese Americans were not given the benefit of the doubt. They had to prove that they were indeed who they said they were every time they exited and entered the country.

Anna May kept up a brave face as the situation was hashed out at the border, but privately this confrontation with U.S. immigration officers was alarming and put her into a frightful state. Sure, she'd encountered the long arm of the law before—exhibit one: speeding away from that motor cop. And she'd seen some things in her day, such as the unpleasantness of certain customers at the laundry who resented patronizing a Chinese business, and the time her father was hauled off to jail on account of an ordinance that criminalized Chinese laundries. But the thought of not being let back into her own country and birthplace, the only home she'd ever known, was likely something she'd never considered before. How could the government— her government—do such a thing?

"But having been born in California, somehow the matter was finally arranged," Estelle concluded. "Somehow" is right. Unlike Anna May, James Wong Howe had not been born in the United States. Somehow this technicality was overlooked or flubbed for the sake of the film's production schedule.

James Wong Howe was no stranger to anti-Chinese sentiment, otherwise known as racism in America. Born in Canton, China, he immigrated to Pasco, Washington, at age five to reunite with his father, who ran a general store there. As a child, he didn't understand why the other little boys were always poking fun at the way he looked and calling him "chinkie." Thinking he could remedy this situation and maybe make a few friends, he skimmed candy from his father's store and offered it up to the white children. "I wanted to be like them. I wanted to get away from the Chinese thing," Howe later explained. Instead, he mostly played with Native American kids, who noticed his braided queue and assumed it meant he was one of them.

By adolescence, this genial approach to racial adversity had changed course to one of striking back. Jimmie decided he wasn't gonna take any more lip from ignorant white kids, so when the racial epithets were flung his way, he responded with his fists. It was on the streets of Pasco that he first learned to fight. Though he was small at five feet two inches, his skillful jabs and muscular physique landed him on the local Northwest boxing circuit. Oddly enough, it was boxing that led him to a career in cinema.

When his father died suddenly and he got sick of his stepmother's demands, Jimmie dropped out of high school. He quickly realized that boxing was not a good long-term career option, so he skipped town and traveled down the West Coast, picking up odd jobs along the way. Eventually he arrived in Los Angeles, where he found work as a bellboy at the Beverly Hills Hotel. On his days off he wandered around Chinatown, which felt like a familiar place, a home away from home. Then one Sunday when a Mack Sennett production was filming in the neighborhood, he ran into an old boxing partner who was working as a cameraman. His friend bragged about the $10-a-week pay and told him he should hurry up and join him in the movie business.

Jimmie turned up at the gates to Famous Players-Lasky Studios, pronto. His only relevant experiences were his childhood experiments with a Brownie camera, bought from a local drugstore by collecting glass bottles, and a short stint assisting photographer Raymond Stagg, who'd fired him when he caught him using his equipment after hours to shoot passport photos for friends. Somehow Jimmie talked Alvin Wyckoff, head of the Lasky camera department, into giving him a janitorial job sweeping up the camera room, and slowly but surely he climbed the ranks from fourth assistant to principal cameraman.

Cecil B. DeMille was notably amused when he watched a batch of dailies and saw the stout, round-faced Jimmie in a flowery shirt, holding the slate and grinning for the camera, a giant cigar hanging out of his mouth. "Where'd you get him?" DeMille reputedly said. "I like his face. Keep him with me."

For all the Wyckoffs and DeMilles who encouraged and valued Jimmie's growing prowess as a cinematographer, there were plenty of detractors too. Jimmie was regularly referred to as "the Chinaman" on sets and some crew members held their nose at the idea of working for someone who wasn't white. They complained that he was too small to lug the camera equipment himself. Others, like Jimmie's first public school teacher, who refused to instruct a Chinese pupil, simply up and quit.

But Jimmie had an eye for composition, a flair for lighting, and a mind for ingenious problem-solving even in the most constrained circumstances. For example, he rigged a setup for photographing Mary Miles Minter, the actress who'd wisely ignored Mickey Neilan's marriage proposal, that captured her beautiful blue eyes on film. Because of the blue-sensitive orthochromatic film used at the time, most exposures washed out her eyes. Not so, Jimmie discovered by accident, when a piece of light-absorbing black velvet was hung in front of the camera with a hole cut out for the lens. From that day forward, Minter insisted that James Wong Howe be the one to photograph her. Blue-eyed starlets throughout Hollywood were suddenly requesting the Chinese cameraman.

His talent and artistry as a cameraman—today we'd call him a director of photography—was undeniable. Those who recognized it kept him employed for fifty-seven years and later bestowed him with sixteen Academy Award nominations and two wins for Best Cinematography. But despite Jimmie's virtuoso photographer's eye, the studio counseled him to go by the de-ethnicized, vaguely white-sounding name "James Howe." Fearing a potential backlash, they preferred the public didn't know he was Chinese, and so "Wong" was kept out of his name in screen credits until 1933.

While Jimmie could hone his craft and focus on his work behind the camera somewhat anonymously, Anna May never had that luxury, for her career as an actress demanded that she be seen and scrutinized in titillating detail. The threat of exile and the assumption that Anna

May Wong and James Wong Howe were not legitimate American citizens because of their Chinese ancestry, however, would continue to dog the two friends for decades. Being Chinese and American was a novelty in the eyes of most white Americans at a time when the phrase "hyphenated American" was thrown around as a derogatory term, not as a symbol of a thriving multicultural melting pot.

And yet, the Chinese had been in America for more than half a century by the time Anna May was born. Their presence was documented in U.S. Census records as early as 1830. According to some estimates, the population grew to 150,000 at its height following the Gold Rush and efforts to recruit Chinese labor for the construction of the transcontinental railroad. Their numbers decreased drastically, however, in the wake of the 1882 Chinese Exclusion Act. By 1920 the Chinese population had declined to 61,639 or 0.1 percent of the United States' total population of 105.7 million people.

A Chinese woman like Anna May was even rarer, as the 1875 Page Law prohibited the immigration of Chinese, Japanese, and "Mongolian" women, who were suspected of being sex workers. Indeed, Chinese women made up only 12.6 percent of the U.S. Chinese population in 1920. In California, Anna May was one of only 4,582 Chinese women, less than one fifth the number of 24,230 Chinese men residing in the state.

In everyday life, the Chinese were functionally invisible. But the perception of their presence in the United States and the threat that many felt they entailed were outsized. The hatred and animosity they experienced was completely out of proportion to their actual population. Fear of the so-called Yellow Peril was certainly reflected in the cinema of the time in films like *The Red Lantern*, *The Forbidden City*, and *Broken Blossoms*. The Asian characters who did appear in movies were frequently portrayed as gamblers, opium addicts, conniving cheats, grinning halfwits who spoke only in pidgin, or the worst of the lot, white slavers—unsavory characters who traffic white women into prostitution against their will.

Chinese Americans picked up on this inflated, unflattering trend. They bemoaned the negative stereotypes broadcast to the world through Hollywood films and in some instances even fought back. Several months before Thomas Meighan arrived in Banff to shoot *The Alaskan*, he found himself caught in the cultural crosshairs in New York's Chinatown. Dressed in a blue sailor suit, Meighan was walking down a cobblestone lane while the cameras filmed exteriors for Famous Players-Lasky's *Pied Piper Malone* when suddenly "an old parlor lamp, bearing the mystic symbols of a language older than our white civilization, left a Doyers Street window, hurled by the sinuous strength of a hidden yellow arm."

The lamp narrowly missed Meighan's head and was promptly followed by a "barrage of stones" that forced cast and crew to scatter and seek shelter. A six-man search into the houses on Doyers failed to reveal the culprits as "a veil of sinister secrecy, as impenetrable as the cunning duplicity which lurks in the slant-eyes of Orientals, hangs over the most daring interference that the motion picture industry" had yet witnessed, at least according to one *Movie Weekly* reporter.

A local Chinese merchant offered a more pragmatic explanation: "Murder and shooting matches are plentiful in most every scene depicting Chinatown in the movies. This gives Chinatown a bad name and hurts all the decent and orderly people who live here. I supposed that the attack against Mr. Meighan and his company was made because the residents thought additional propaganda was being created against them."

On this occasion, the locals prevailed and the desired scenes were never made, but, on the whole, Hollywood seldom bowed to complaints from ethnic communities about their on-screen representation. They weren't the moviegoers Hollywood had in mind anyway.

The demand for Asian roles continued and was filled primarily by white actresses. Yellowface was so common, donning ochre powder and pulling one's eyes into a slant were practically a rite of passage for rising starlets. From Mary Pickford to Norma Talmadge, Alla Nazimova to Pola Negri, Colleen Moore to Bessie Love, it seemed like all of Hollywood's leading ladies appeared in yellowface sooner or later.

The flip side to this anxiety, the transgressive appeal of the forbidden, also expressed itself in these same films. As in D. W. Griffith's *Broken Blossoms*, where a saintly Buddhist missionary takes in a young woman who has been beaten and abused by her father, the prospect of interracial love was presented as both a hazard and a temptation. Of course, miscegenation was never consummated or allowed to end happily in these early movies. The nonwhite lover's fate was, more often than not, death, whether by murder, accident, or suicide. Hollywood was willing to satisfy America's thirst for the exotic up to a degree, but the lesson was clear: racial mixing was a line not to be crossed.

Twenty-two-year-old journalist Myrtle Gebhart, a Texas native who'd traded her dreams of becoming a screenwriter to report on Hollywood's stars, pulled up in her jalopy to the Sam Kee Laundry one perfectly sunny Los Angeles day and waited for her interview subject to come out.

She could already see the copy: "When the bleak door of the ramshackle laundry opened—"

Out popped Anna May Wong into the late morning sunshine. She walked up to Myrtle's car, her appearance as lovely as ever: flawless, dewy skin, eyes twinkling with youthful confidence, glossy black hair pulled back into a pseudo-bob. In Myrtle's eyes, Anna May was a vision of "a Yuan Chen poem, stepping from the embossed covers of a book of old lyrics."

Looking smart in a tan sport suit, Anna May opened her mouth and spoke: "My, what a nifty car! It's the kitty's eyebrows, what?"

In an instant, the reporter's romantic longing for talk of "moon blossoms, lacquered vases, Oriental mysticism" was thoroughly dashed. She took a beat to compose herself. "Anna May made it plain to me," Myrtle admitted to her readers, "that she's an American girl and didn't want any of that Oriental bunk said about her; we got along famously." The two young women grinned at each other like "two understanding souls, two typical flappers out to worry the traffic cops."

As Myrtle drove them up and down the hills of Downtown Los Angeles, Anna May talked candidly of her six siblings—"No, we aren't a family—we're a dynasty"—her plans to invest in real estate, how she'd taught Constance Talmadge to eat with chopsticks for *East Is West*, of her dreams to play alongside Mary Pickford and to one day build a Chinese-style home with a garden in the Hollywood foothills.

They stopped for a banquet-sized feast at her sister Lulu's chop suey café, and Myrtle gorged herself on delicious Chinese stir-fry "in anticipation of a checkless week." After lunch, the conversation turned to Anna May's love life.

"All I hear is 'Get married, get married!' That's my father's daily—what d'y' call it?—litany. He still believes in the old Chinese customs and thinks girls should marry early. We have some merry battles," Anna May explained with a huff.

Wong Sam Sing had not looked kindly upon a recent picture of Anna May in the local paper that showed her smoking a cigarette and wearing rolled-down hose that revealed her bare knees. The last thing he needed was one of his daughters outed as "the modern Chinese flapper."

"Why should I marry?" Anna May continued. "I won't marry a Chinese boy because they think all women are for is to cook and work for them and have many children. And Americans—" Here she sighed, leaving the air pregnant with the unspoken.

"But," she began again with spirited optimism, "I should lift a weary eyebrow! I'm independent. I won't marry until I get good and ready. So there!" This final act of cheerful defiance was clinched with a snap of her "highly polished nails" in true flapper style.

When Anna May's tête-à-tête with Myrtle Gebhart ran in *Picture-Play* under the heading "Jazz Notes on Old China," Wong Sam Sing must have been greatly displeased to learn that his improvisational, "flapper at heart" daughter had declared to the world she would not be marrying a Chinese boy. The clash at home between traditional Chinese values and the modern flapper aesthetic intensified. Six months later, Anna May reversed course and told reporters with feigned certainty, "I shall marry a man of my own race."

The question of love and marriage for a girl like her who was thoroughly American yet respectful of her Chinese heritage may not have been fully resolved in her heart and mind, but Anna May carried on as if it were. In any case, she was busy riding the wave of fandom *The Thief of Bagdad* had generated and eager to get back to the thing she did best, acting.

That fall and winter the series of films she appeared in capitalized on her newfound fame to draw in moviegoers yet cast her in supporting roles without much substance. Regrettably, the hype around *The Alaskan* fell short and the melodrama was mostly panned by critics who said the breathtaking scenery trumped the confusing storyline. Anna May's characterization of Keok did not go unnoticed, though. "Anna May Wong as an Indian girl scored nicely," *Variety* observed.

Anna May next assumed the role of Tiger Lily in Famous Players-Lasky's adaptation of J. M. Barrie's *Peter Pan*. She teamed up with Herbert Brenon and James Wong Howe for a second time, and this go-around their efforts fared much better at the box office. The fantasy film came out just in time for the Christmas holiday and delighted adults and children alike with its fairy-tale landscape brought to life, pulling in more than 6 million moviegoers. Anna May was appealing as always as the strong-willed Tiger Lily, but her screen time was so slight, it hardly registered with the public. Viewers were preoccupied with the cherubic Betty Bronson and her lighthearted incarnation of Peter Pan.

With the money she earned from her stint in Never Never Land,

Anna May bought herself a new car to replace the last one she'd totaled. She sped toward 1925 with open arms and into a vast new world of possibilities. At the beginning of the year, she signed on to join a troupe of Hollywood up-and-comers like herself, backed by a little-known venture called the Cosmic Production Company. Billed as the "Transcontinental Tour of Movie Stars," these bright-eyed young'uns were set to depart in mid-February on a nearly fifty-city tour across the United States and Canada. At each stop they planned to put on a show of entertaining vaudeville acts and host little dances where locals could Charleston with a real-life motion-picture star.

The tour was a DIY affair from the get-go, with the stars trading their coats, furs, and handbags for mops and brooms in order to clean up the train car for their departure. Lulu, who had begun to help manage her sister's business affairs, went along on the tour as chaperone, and it's a good thing too. When the troupe turned up in Kansas City, they showed up to a theater with 18,000 empty seats and were nearly laughed out of town. The Cosmic Production Company had failed to do much in the way of advance promotion. A few bad checks later, with nothing to show in ticket receipts, Anna May and several of her fellow Cosmics were obliged to make an overnight stay in the Omaha town jail. Their crime? Skipping out on hotel bills. In truth it was the production company that had failed to pay up. By the end of March, the ill-fated Cosmic enterprise came to a rocky end, but Anna May, always looking up, took the opportunity to continue east and make her first trip to New York. While there, the handsome Mexican stage actor Romney Brent sloughed off his duties organizing a revue for the Theatre Guild to take the "beautiful, beautiful Oriental actress" out on a date.

Anna May returned to Los Angeles sometime in the spring but did not go back to making pictures. Around the time her name recognition exploded in connection with *Thief*'s knockout success, a man named Forrest B. Creighton, a self-styled producer, had approached her about backing a production company in her name. Anna May aspired to produce and star in movies based on classic Chinese tales, so the deal presented by Creighton was immediately appealing. She had said yes.

Hypothetically, this was a smart move on her part. Plenty of big-name actresses, like Mary Pickford and Norma Talmadge, had launched their own production companies to conceive and create new and compelling pictures for themselves. This gave actresses more control over their public images and the kinds of projects they decided to take on; it also significantly furthered their careers by ensuring they were the stars of their own films. Usually, such ventures were funded by businessmen with deep pockets and a knack for marketing. In Norma Talmadge's case, it was her husband, Joseph M. Schenck.

Unfortunately, Anna May's business partner was no Schenck. In actuality, the deal was rubbish—just another grifter's attempt at making a quick buck off an unsuspecting starlet. Creighton had promised to secure $400,000 in funding for Anna May Wong Productions; however, in the time since she had signed the contract, all Creighton had produced were debts in her name. Anna May had quietly sued Creighton the previous summer, claimed malfeasance on his part, and requested that the courts void the contract and absolve her for Creighton's debts. While she waited for the suit's resolution, the production company that bore her own name refused to release her from their contract. Aside from parts in *Forty Winks* and *His Supreme Moment*, which were filmed in late 1924, she remained off the screen for the entirety of 1925.

It seemed like only yesterday that she'd walked into the Egyptian Theatre a relatively unknown actress and then walked out the season's "It" girl sensation. The dream that she had worked so hard for was finally taking flight. Anna May knew that success was never assured and public opinion was fickle, but she hadn't expected everything to come to a screeching halt so soon. As much as these missteps with Creighton and the Cosmic Production Company stung, they taught her an important lesson. Now that she was a known entity, the trouble wasn't getting noticed but rather doing due diligence on all the offers that came her way. Anna May had to be selective about who she got into bed with, figuratively speaking. She couldn't afford any more one-night stands with dubious production outfits.

That's when a call from Sid Grauman, the inimitable showman, came in. He was as official Hollywood as you could get, and the memories of his impressive grand opening for *Thief* had not faded one bit. He asked if she would christen the launch of his next big project: Grauman's Chinese Theatre. Now, this was a cause Anna May could get behind.

On a November day in 1925, surrounded by workmen in overalls, suited dignitaries, and the Hollywood press corps, Anna May Wong posed for the cameras in a boiler suit and an oversized pair of leather workman's gloves. Then, with the bluster only a laundryman's daughter could muster, she drove the first rivet into the huge steel trusses that would undergird the new theater. Cheers rang out through the McClintic-Marshall steel plant. A Chinese movie star to consecrate a Chinese movie palace was auspicious as all get-out. It sure made for good copy too.

ACT TWO

Anna May models her "East Meets West" style
in one of her silk sports frocks for MGM publicity, 1928.

4

YEAR OF THE FLAPPER

For 364 days out of the year, the shopkeepers, butchers, laundrymen, and cooks of Chinatown worked tirelessly at their trades, serving their community as well as the thrill-seeking gweilo who passed through on a "slumming" tour or turned up for a bowl of chop suey and a few souvenir trinkets. But come Lunar New Year, the faithful worker finally abandoned his post. The shopkeeper shuttered his storefront, the butcher hung up his bloodied apron, the laundryman turned a blind eye to the soiled shirts piling up, and the cook snuck off on his break, the first of many, to join his fellow Chinese Americans in celebrating the start of a new year.

Lunar New Year 1927 saw the streets of Los Angeles Chinatown filled with revelers: aunties and uncles dressed in their Chinese best, young married couples in smart-looking suits and dresses, some with babies in tow, and even the tired old bachelors who could hardly believe the Western frontier town they helped found had sprouted into a modern metropolis all these years later. Strings of flags and paper lanterns decorated the streets from above, while boxes of fresh lychee nuts and candied fruits beckoned from store windows. There was no want of entertainment, what with the rat-a-tat-tat of firecrackers flashing in alleyways and confetti bombs coating everyone and everything like a sheet of colorful snow.

The only things that could part the great sea of people were the competing lion dance troupes, whose chants and pounding drums heralded the arrival of the lion. Decked out in brightly hued red, gold, and orange fringe, the mystical lion and his bushy mane zigzagged through the crowd. Two men manipulated the lion's every move from underneath, cloaked in the beast's festive hide. In the middle of its boisterous dance meant to chase the evil spirits away, the lion pulled up to an unsuspecting spectator or a shopkeeper watching from a doorway and, with eyes blinking and mouth ajar, waited for an offering. According to tradition, one must feed the beast in exchange for good fortune by tossing coins wrapped in red paper or a fresh piece of produce into the creature's gaping mouth. The latter oblation is then unceremoniously gobbled up and shreds of cabbage leaves regurgitated into the air. The rush of excitement one got from this ritual never waned, whether it was your first Lunar New Year or your fiftieth.

As the festival carried on, upstairs, tucked away in one of Chinatown's cafés, another kind of celebration was underway. Anna May Wong and friends Moon Kwan and Jimmie Wong Howe had banded together to usher in the Year of the Rabbit with a lavish fete for all their Hollywood friends. "I shall never forget Chinese New Year's of 1927," Hollywood reporter Harry Carr, one of the trio's guests, declared in his column for the *Los Angeles Times*.

Chopsticks were passed around the table and the uninitiated given a quick lesson in how to use them. Anna May then instructed her guests how to say "Gong hei fat choy!" with feeling. Waiters in loose-fitting black jackets and trousers stacked the table with dishes of rice cakes and dumplings, steamed fish and candied ginger, and the most unusual delicacy of them all: bird's nest soup. The fifteen-course banquet transitioned seamlessly from one course to the next, likely through many rounds of jasmine tea and bathtub gin, coming at last to a final, filling dish, such as longevity noodles to encourage a long and fruitful life.

"Jimmy raises English bulldogs and shoots craps; Anna May Wong is a flapper of the flappers, and a great belle; Moon Qwan is an up-to-date young journalist," Carr explained, tendering his hosts' American credentials. "But down in that dim old cafe—digging into strange and exotic foods with our chop sticks, they all slipped out of the jazz age as one takes off a coat. And were Chinese again."

This idea that being Chinese and American was a contradiction in terms had been weighing on Anna May ever since she was thrust into the limelight. It was as if the rest of America's populace had conveniently forgotten their families had once called foreign shores home too. Indeed, her race had become the central refrain of every press piece and interview she did. Rudyard Kipling's famous line of poetry—"Oh, East is East, and West is West, and never the twain shall meet"—was quoted so often in articles about her, perhaps she was beginning to wonder whether she also deserved a cut of the royalties that were certainly due to him.

People formed preconceived notions about her based on looks alone. She'd learned to steel herself against the suspicious and condescending stares that seemed to follow her everywhere. Secretly, she hated the way people judged her. They saw a Chinese girl and intuited she must be foreign, primitive, and unfeeling—when she felt that she was something else entirely. What did they know about her true nature, anyway? Winning the attention of reporters and gossip columnists was her chance to set the record straight, or so she thought.

Anna May took great pleasure in subverting her interviewers' expectations, and she worked hard at it too. The indelible icon of the Roaring Twenties was the flapper, a persona Anna May embraced wholeheartedly. But she wasn't just any flapper. She was queen of them all. Dressed to the nines in "a tiptilted hat, pure Parisian heels, sheer silk stockings, and a Persian lamb wrap," she talked circles around journalists in her jazz girl jargon, and waxed poetic about her sky-high career ambitions as a new woman. She made damned well certain they saw she was no shrinking lotus, but everything one had come to expect of an American "It" girl. "She's never been to China," they would invariably spout. Somehow, they didn't think to mention Anna May had never been to Paris either.

The strategy had worked so well, her reputation as the "Chinese flapper" now preceded her. Her independent streak had also led to not a few arguments at home with Wong Sam Sing and looming threats that he would marry her off to the next eligible suitor. Some in Hollywood questioned why she continued living at home when, with her movie star salary, she could easily afford to get a place of her own. Caught between the expectations of her Hollywood friends and her traditional Chinese father, she wavered with indecision. The last couple of years had seen her move in and out of the laundry on Figueroa Street several times, alternately despising the hectic workplace and its cramped quarters, and then, once alone in her lifeless flat, desperately missing her brothers and sisters and the family meals they regularly shared together.

"Anna May Wong cannot make up her mind as to her residence," *Photoplay* complained. "She moves from Hollywood to Chinatown and back again at regular intervals. . . . Anna is our leading Chinese star. Likewise, she is one of the brightest of our flappers."

By the fall of 1926, though she had not completely made peace with it, Anna May had come to an understanding of her identity and of her position in America's racial politics. For years the media had editorialized their encounters with her, selectively quoted certain comments over others, and emphasized aspects of herself that somehow read sensationally to fans when they seemed perfectly ordinary to her. All this talk about her flapper image had made her realize that it wasn't truly her: it was an act. Like any other part she'd played in the movies, she'd donned the persona when it suited her, which meant she could also drop it.

It was time for the public to hear her story unfiltered, in her own words. In a two-part commentary in the pages of *Pictures*, she set to work right away on dispelling the most pernicious misconceptions about her.

"A lot of people, when they first meet me, are surprised that I speak and write English without difficulty. But why shouldn't I?" Anna May began. "I was born right here in Los Angeles and went to the public schools here. I speak English without any accent at all. But my parents complain the same cannot be said of my Chinese. . . .

"I'll explain as best I can," she continued, "how it *feels* to be an American-born Chinese girl—proud of her parents and of her race, yet so thoroughly Americanized as to demand independence, a career, a life of her own."

She told readers the story of how her grandparents came to the United States seeking gold; how her father was born in California and worked hard to earn enough money to marry and buy land in China; how her maternal grandparents submitted a picture of her mother to a Chinese matchmaker in San Francisco and subsequently married their daughter to her father as his second wife at the age of fourteen. "Chinese men have it all over the rest of us," she added, explaining their right to wed as many wives as they desire. For Chinese women, marriage was not necessarily a cause for celebration but a matter of course. Thus, the bride wept on her wedding day.

"You can see that the Chinese woman's life is not a particularly enviable one. She is considered far beneath the male members of her household, and is a servant to them. I just [don't] see myself being let in for anything like that!"

Anna May spoke candidly of the moment she first realized the way others saw her—when the boys and girls at school taunted her for being Chinese—and of her education in the differing expectations of American and Chinese cultures. She recalled wryly not having any compunction about skipping class to make her way onto movie sets; she endured the whippings that followed rather stoically.

She complained of the familial hierarchy created by her father's two marriages. His first wife, who bore him a son, remained "first" in every sense of the word. Wong Sam Sing faithfully forwarded money to her despite not having been back to China in nearly thirty years. Meanwhile, his son, Wong Tou Nan, was not only the first child but, as the eldest son, was considered next in line to be the family patriarch. Wong Tou Nan and his mother regularly sent missives from China to the Wong clan in Los Angeles directing them on how to order their lives. And yet, when Wong Sam Sing sent his son and first wife a clipping of Anna May modeling a mink coat in the paper, Tou Nan wrote back self-servingly, "Tsong is indeed very beautiful but please send me the dollar watch on the back of the picture." Anna May firmly put her foot down when her father suggested she send some of her own earnings to her half brother in China, who at thirty-six years old already had a family of his own that was in large part supported by theirs.

"But, though I love father dearly, and am proud of my people, I can see their faults. It is the cause of much conflict in me, sometimes. I don't suppose an American girl can begin to realize that conflict. . . ."

In previous interviews, Anna May had sometimes turned philosophical. Occasionally, she might probe her interviewers for answers to some opaque problem she was working out in her head. "Say, do you ever wonder what life's all about, anyway?" she once asked Helen Carlisle. Here, most tellingly, she put into words the thing that had caused her so much consternation and soul-searching.

"Do not think it is easy for me to throw over the traditions and customs of my people. I have behind me countless centuries of Chinese ancestors who have unquestioningly obeyed the rules laid down for them by *their* ancestors. No people revere their parents as do the Chinese. The father's word is law in the household, never to be disputed. The Chinese child is born with ages of superstitious belief traditions in his blood. It is no light thing to cast them all aside, in one generation, believe me. Sometimes when I have defied my father, who is the kindest, gentlest man alive, I have gone off by myself and wondered if, after all, I was in the right. I have wondered where my course will lead me."

The conflict was not the fact of her being both Chinese and American. The two sides of her identity were not at war with one another. No, the contradiction was in others' insistence that she be one thing or another, that she live up to their expectations in lieu of the ones she had clearly set for herself.

"I just tried to explain to [my mother] that my life must be lived along different lines than hers had been. It might not be a happier life, but that was for time to tell."

She said it plainly and unequivocally to the world: "It is my life."

At the same time, Anna May had tried so hard to fit in and be like the other girls, she nearly lost herself in the process. But now she had finally registered what it meant to be Chinese American; the script for that role didn't yet exist, so she was free to write it herself.

The Lunar New Year of 1927 brought with it an opportunity to turn over a new leaf. The flapper joke had grown stale and the hedonistic euphoria that had fueled the decade-long party they called the Jazz Age was wearing thin. Anna May was ready to hang up her cloche hat and slip dress. Sensing this and wanting to resolve the discord that had come between them, Wong Sam Sing extended an olive branch to his daughter: "Anna May, if you will come home, I will build you a house which shall be all your own."

Anna May returned home with equanimity, knowing that it was exactly where she was meant to be. "I had my fling in Hollywood," she told her old friend Rob Wagner. "After my first big success as the Mongolian slave girl in *The Thief of Bagdad* I thought living there the thing to do. The publicity men were doing their best to Americanize me and I appreciated it, for I am an American: also I appreciated the confidence placed in me by my father when he allowed me to leave home, a very hard thing for a Chinese father to do. I employed a sort of governess who tried to make an American 'lady' of me but all the time she was instructing me I could hardly keep from saying: 'Be yourself, madam: be yourself!'

"In fact I grew to think there was no use in learning to act, for in Hollywood everybody was acting," Anna May reflected. "Even the houses seemed artificial and finally I began to feel that I was dwelling within a world of 'sets.' Then I decided to go back to the laundry and to my family, where I would hear the truth!"

Wong Sam Sing built her a little bungalow behind the laundry that was hers alone, yet close enough to her parents and beloved brothers and sisters that she could seek out their company and counsel at almost any hour of the day.

Life had changed and improved for the Wongs at 241 North Figueroa Street. Lulu was running a café in Chinatown and pitching in part-time as Anna May's business manager. James was studying business administration at the University of Southern California, an education that Anna May was more than happy to fund. Mary and Frank were in high school. Roger was twelve going on thirteen and old enough to help with various tasks at the laundry. And Richard, the baby of the family, at four years old, was still a little boy and the main object of his mother's attention. The laundry, meanwhile, was staffed by several "cousins" brought over from the Wong clan in China.

Happily ensconced in her new lodgings, Anna May fully expressed her hybridized identity by styling the space into a kind of Oriental boudoir with a carefully curated selection of antiques and treasures, such as ivory elephants for good luck. A gold-and-purple tapestry hung on the wall and fans made of ivory and sandalwood were scattered about. An upright piano, which she had to give up on account of her long fingernails, and an autographed portrait from Doug and Mary were the only objects in the room that hinted at her occupation.

It was here that she established herself as a social force to be reckoned with, extending and receiving invitations to socialize with various cliques in Hollywood. Incense burned in the background as she served her guests tea in thimble-sized teacups atop a lacquer table. "Men and women from the world of art and letters seek her out," Helen Carlisle wrote in *Motion Picture Magazine*. "Many a celebrity has visited the little house where she serves tea in a truly ceremonious manner."

Anna May maintained a vibrant coterie of friends that included writers, directors, artists, intellectuals, and of course other actors. One night she might take writer friend Grace Wilcox out to dinner in Chinatown; another night she could be found at New York artist Harrison Fisher's Ambassador bungalow for a small party. She became a favorite guest of German actor Emil Jannings and his wife, Gussy Holl, who entertained the smart young actress on a number of occasions. When the German ambassador to the United States, Baron Ago von Maltzahn, visited Los Angeles, the Janningses threw a party in his honor. Who else but Anna May Wong was invited to glamour up the evening's post-dinner dance and garden affair?

Moving among these exalted circles, Anna May began brushing shoulders with sophisticates from around the world, and Europe in particular. Through Jannings she met many of his German comrades, including actor Conrad Veidt, famous for his role as the nefarious somnambulist in *The Cabinet of Dr. Caligari*; director Josef von Sternberg; and the millionaire dilettante turned playwright Karl Vollmöller. These Europeans were quite taken with Anna May, for Chinese women, a rare presence in America, were almost mythical in Europe, so sparse was their population there. Unlike most Hollywood starlets, she was well-read and full of droll repartee, a delight for the eyes and the ears.

It may have been at one of these parties that Anna May came across a familiar face. Forty-one-year-old Charles Rosher had just returned from a yearlong stint in Berlin working at UFA, Germany's renowned film company. Charles had been the cameraman on *Dinty*, the Mickey Neilan film in which Anna May made her debut. Like Neilan, Rosher first garnered attention as a cinematographer because of his association with Mary Pickford, becoming known as her exclusive cameraman. He'd shot every one of Mary's films since 1918, including *Dorothy Vernon of Haddon Hall*, which filmed on the Pickford-Fairbanks Studio lot at the same time that production on *The Thief of Bagdad* was underway. Near the end of 1925, Mary had kindly released Rosher from his contract so that he could study the artistic approach and camera techniques of the German expressionists, whose work had earned international praise.

Now, one year later, Charles was back in Hollywood and directing photography for F. W. Murnau, one of UFA's acclaimed directors, who was making his first American film. Charlie was a "camera operator" in more ways than one. He remembered Anna May the girl, and here she was a woman of twenty-two, finally of age. This time when he set eyes on her, the gears began spinning, working out how he was going to woo this new potential conquest and get her into his bed.

Lucky for him, he was just Anna May's type: older, Anglo-Saxon, worldly, and an artist in his own right. Charles had been born in London and retained his charming British accent. After starting out as a photographer of royals and European dignitaries under Richard Speaight, the court photographer of London, his curiosity got the better of him and he left for Los Angeles in 1911. Fifteen years in the business had not only nurtured his craft as a cinematographer but also fed his thirst for adventure. He enchanted Anna May with tales of his filmmaking capers and travels around the world.

In Mexico, he rode with General Pancho Villa and kept his camera rolling as the former bandit commanded his rebel forces in combat against Federal troops in the Mexican Revolution. He told her, with a twinkle in his eye, what it was like to get caught in the crosshairs of war: the film crew's bulky cameras were easy targets for Federal marksmen. "I had to film everything: men digging their own graves, executions, battles. I was right in there, in the trenches, listening to the ping-ping-ping of the bullets hitting the air above me." And how at the Battle of Ojinaga he was captured by Federal troops but narrowly escaped the firing squad when an officer noticed the Masonic pin on his lapel.

The bright-eyed Anna May was enthralled. Here was a man who had truly lived, and not the kind of living spent guzzling champagne until the wee hours of the morning and showing up hours late to the studio the next day (although no one said he was opposed to a good time, especially where alcohol was involved). Charles was dedicated to his art, so much so that he had put himself in the line of fire to get the shot. He'd tasted death and lived to tell about it. What could possibly be sexier than that?

A romantic affair between Anna May and Charlie commenced, and the fact that he was married was conveniently overlooked by both. The two lovers often rendezvoused at his cottage nestled in the lush, overgrown woods of Rustic Canyon, an undeveloped area in the eastern Pacific Palisades at the foot of the Santa Monica Mountains. Where once the Tongva people had made their homes among the sycamores and eucalyptus trees and fished along the coastline, a rowdy gang of movie people, businessmen, and cowboy types called the Uplifters Club had newly taken up residence. Charles was a dues-paying member of the Uplifters, and his house was one of a number of cabins and ranch-style houses built on a parcel of land they called the Uplifters Ranch.

Despite the social club's reputation for debauched, booze-laden parties, the group was composed of a wealthy and prominent roster of men. Plumbing magnate Harry F. Haldeman, banker Marco Hellman, newspaper executive Sim Crabill, and film producer Hal Roach were all members. L. Frank Baum, author of *The Wonderful Wizard of Oz*, came up with the club's name, calling it "The Lofty and Exalted Order of Uplifters."

Rustic Canyon was a real-life Never Never Land where powerful men could carry on their illicit affairs with starlets and mistresses away from prying eyes. Will Rogers was an honorary member and other Uplifters from the movie colony included Harold Lloyd, Busby Berkeley, and Darryl F. Zanuck. Anna May Wong became such a local favorite at the club that the ranch's fourteen hired groundskeepers were asked to develop a garden of exotic plants and interconnected spring water pools in her honor. They called it the Anna May Wong Garden.

Enamored of his paramour's porcelainlike beauty and impeccable style, Charles built a shrine to her in his home. Down a few steps on a lower split-level of the fairy tale–like cottage was a separate chamber decked out in full chinoiserie. Every last detail down to the doorknob and light fixtures was selected to evoke the Far East. Anna May likely helped him pick out the Chinese objets d'art that filled the room, including a stunning black lacquer bed. Coffered beams in red and jade green, some with intricate patterns painted on them in black, cut across the ceiling. A metal box lantern hung in the corner by the window, its ornate filigree casting unusual shadows upon the walls. It was in this room that the couple carried on their moonlight trysts.

If Anna May had waffled over the years about whether she intended to marry a Chinese man or a man of another race, with her newfound Chinese American identity came a reassurance and trust in her own desires and needs as a woman. She finally had an answer to the question all the movie rags wanted to know, and it wasn't the one they expected.

"I don't suppose I'll ever marry," Anna May said to a reporter unprompted. "Whom could I marry? Not a man of your race, for he would lose caste among his people and I among mine. And so far, I have never found a Chinese man whom I could love."

She spoke of her situation pragmatically, without a whiff of sentimentality. The truth was, the men she was attracted to could not marry her legally and the men she was expected to marry were not attracted to her. Many Chinese American men expected a wife who would cook and clean and raise a family.

"I couldn't live as my mother always has, under the domination of my father. I don't believe that woman is an inferior creature. How can I?"

Anna May was too Americanized for their tastes, too independent and stubborn. Like the men she became romantically involved with, she was married first and foremost to her career. But it was deep in the annals of Chinese philosophy, ironically, that she discovered wisdom for her unusual situation. She had been reading up on her illustrious ancestors and found much in their ancient credos that was worthy of adoption.

"My philosophy of life is contained in that beautiful expression of Lao-Tze: 'To meet the good with goodness: to meet the bad also with goodness,'" she explained to fellow Chinese American Mamie Louise Leung. "I believe life should be met as it comes, without trying to shirk the responsibilities and sufferings that are inevitable. No, I'm not entirely a fatalist. The passive attitude of leaving all to fate is wrong, for one must deserve his happiness and work for it."

And as if she couldn't resist hinting at something more, a sly smile found its way onto her lips: "I suppose that I'm just in love—in love with life."

———

Professionally speaking, 1927 was Anna May Wong's busiest year yet. Ever since her success in *The Thief of Bagdad*, studios had been keen to capitalize on her name recognition and her seductive appeal with the movie-going public, yet they had stopped short of giving her roles with substantial screen time that would justify top billing.

That year Anna May played bit parts in the dramas *Driven from Home* and *Streets of Shanghai*. She also got a chance to try her chops at comedy in two Hal Roach shorts called *The Honorable Mr. Buggs* and *Why Girls Love Sailors*. The second film starred the comedy duo Stan Laurel and Oliver Hardy of Laurel and Hardy fame, but Anna May's scenes were ultimately cut from the final print.

She was pleased to win another role alongside Lon Chaney, the master of disguise, in *Mr. Wu*, but she had to endure being relegated to the sidelines while French-born Renée Adorée played the lead female role of Nang Ping, Mr. Wu's cherished daughter, in yellowface. Anna May good-naturedly taught her costar how to use chopsticks, but the habit did not seem to take with Renée once the cameras stopped rolling.

One M. H. Shryock from Arlington, Texas, wrote in to *Photoplay* in dismay: "WHY, oh WHY did Metro, etc., use Renee Adoree for Mr. Wu's daughter? With a perfectly charming little Chinese girl like

Anna May Wong, not only in pictures, but right there on the set, and playing her part nobly, WHY should they give a pretty little plum like that to Miss Adoree."

Then she was cast as an Indian nautch dancer, not once, but twice—in Gilda Gray's *The Devil Dancer* and in *The Chinese Parrot*, the first of the Charlie Chan films. Despite being billed third in the former, after Gray and leading man Clive Brook, Anna May's character meets an untimely death when she is caught in an illicit love affair with a monk and sentenced to be buried alive. In the latter film, she assumed the role of dancing girl, with an exposed midriff and a silvery hula skirt revealing her bare legs. Caught wearing a strand of pearls "strung with death," her character dies in the opening scene.

The complaints from critics and moviegoers, who plainly saw that Anna May's brilliance was being sidelined, were one and the same: "The reviewers deplore the scant opportunities given Anna May Wong, whose brief appearances in pretentious pictures keep interest in her at high pitch and inevitably cause comparisons with those who play leads in the same pictures. The comparison is always to the credit of the Chinese actress, whose talents are thought to be wasted in the brief roles given her." Even the director, Fred Niblo, admitted as much. He thought Anna May "a great little trouper" but sighed and said, "I only wish I could direct her in something worthy of her talents."

Anna May certainly wasn't the only Asian actor being pigeonholed because of her race. On several of these productions, she was reunited with friend and colleague Kamiyama Sôjin. The two Asian actors had become friends. Sôjin invited Anna May to parties at his home, where she first sampled Japanese dishes like zaru soba and sashimi. He later recalled in his memoir that she often carried an English edition of *The Analects* of Confucius with her and would ask his opinion about it. Aside from Sôjin's onetime role as the benevolent detective Charlie Chan in *The Chinese Parrot* (Warner Oland in yellowface would soon replace him in succeeding films), he was back to his regular schtick as Oriental villain extraordinaire. Meanwhile, Etta

Lee, who also appeared in the film, was merely attributed as "Girl in Gambling Den."

The work Anna May was garnering with her newfound fame was disappointing. But there were other aspects to the job of movie actress that she found enjoyable and rewarding, like being introduced into elite social circles and getting to travel across the country in the comfort of first class.

Although she only played a small part in *Old San Francisco*, which starred Dolores Costello, Warner Bros. sent her along with the rest of the principal cast to make a personal appearance at the New York City premiere in June that summer. On this second visit to New York, Anna May got more of a chance to take in the big city, which didn't seem all that different from Downtown Los Angeles, except that its buildings were taller and its avenues stretched far beyond the vanishing point. Angelenos might walk fast when they were in a hurry, but New York City was an entire metropolis full of harried pedestrians. There was a manic, creative energy pulsing through the Manhattan grid. The people were different, too—direct and to the point, which was refreshing compared to the fake Midwestern civility one usually received in California.

The week preceding *Old San Francisco*'s premiere, she attended a luncheon held in Dolores Costello's honor, hosted by Warner Bros. at the swanky Park Lane. Anna May was her usual witty self and gamely chitchatted with the press as they doted on the "smilingly beautiful" blonde, Dolores Costello. Privately, one began to wonder why a similar party had never been thrown for Anna May. The most attention she got for the film was a single line at the end of the *New York Daily News* review: "And Anna May Wong, as usual, is a cute, clever Chinese maiden." As usual. What if she was tired of the usual?

The always enterprising Anna May used part of her time in New York to meet with theater producer Gilbert Miller about the possibility of arranging a future stage debut. Since this was her first press trip to the Big Apple, she also took the opportunity to do a tour of the city.

She visited the Woolworth Building, then the tallest building in the world, walked the streets of Greenwich Village, and rode through Chinatown in a taxicab. She knew immediately when they had arrived, for she detected that familiar musk, something she loved about Chinatown. Her evenings were spent in the theater and, on one night in particular, in a Harlem nightclub.

In recent years, Harlem had surpassed Chinatown as the gritty ethnic enclave where white flappers and boozehounds went slumming late nights and weekends. Curious visitors found their way uptown one way or another. Anna May went to see for herself the vibrant quarter, with its jazz clubs, dinner cabarets, and dance halls, from which nearly all the era's hippest dance moves—the Charleston, the Black Bottom, the Lindy Hop—had originated or at least been perfected.

But Harlem was more than just a New York neighborhood; it was also a movement and a beacon for educated and upwardly mobile Black Americans, many of whom had lately migrated north. They called it a renaissance. Black writers, artists, and thinkers were molding a new vision of what was possible. The "New Negro" was free finally to reclaim their own narrative, put their best foot forward, and recast their image as a step toward political power and self-actualization.

Some of the twenties' most astonishing art was inspired by Harlem and its residents. *Shuffle Along*, an all-Black musical revue written by Eubie Blake and Noble Sissle, set the whole thing off with its Broadway debut in 1921. The show became a record-breaking hit and helped kick-start the careers of future stars Josephine Baker, Paul Robeson, and Fredi Washington. Within a few years the names of writers and poets like Langston Hughes, Zora Neale Hurston, and Claude McKay were beginning to mean something to people outside of Harlem. These artists weren't bound by Manhattan's geography either. They traveled the world. Anna May had undoubtedly heard about Robeson's and Baker's arrivals in London and Paris respectively a couple of years before. Word on the street was that Europe was more enlightened than its American offspring. To the Old World— that was the place to go if one wanted to experience true freedom.

For Anna May, Harlem must have been a glimpse of something familiar. Like Chinatown, it was a community where people could kick back and be themselves without being scrutinized by white folks. It was a place of belonging. Probably she smiled with a knowing she could not express as she listened to the jazz band play hot and loose in that Harlem nightclub.

Anna May had been in New York for just over a week when she received a telegram that she'd been selected to play the Native American girl in *Rose-Marie*. She had a press interview scheduled that day, but the sudden change in plans meant she'd have to catch a train that same afternoon. As a compromise, magazine writer Virginia Morris agreed to interview Anna May over lunch in her suite at the Ambassador Hotel. She briskly responded to Morris's questions, charming as ever, while she hurriedly stowed things away in her wardrobe trunks.

Morris surveyed the room while the actress continued packing and couldn't help but notice "an exquisite cluster of delicate orchids" from an unknown admirer basking on one of the tables. She spied a well-worn copy of cartoonist Milt Gross's comic strips as well as a bottle of Parisian perfume that had been delivered to the room with a gentleman's card. Anna May had not shared the contents of the card; rather, she read it discreetly before tucking it away. Many beautiful garments were strewn about the room: tulle evening dresses, sport frocks, and elegant afternoon gowns all with "a touch of the East . . . a bit of Asia on them somewhere."

"I love American clothes," Anna May confessed, "but I realize that I look better if my gowns have a suggestion of China about them. And it's good business, too!"

Their conversation was interrupted momentarily when a small bellboy came to the room to collect the autographed headshot Anna May had promised him.

"What would you like for me to write?" Anna May asked.

"Wudja mind puttin' 'To my pal, Al?'" the boy stuttered shyly.

"Sure thing! Why not?" She dashed off the requested greeting and signed her name in both English and Chinese before handing the picture over to her trembling fan. "So long, Al—don't forget your umbrella!"

Everywhere she went, it was clear to Anna May that people loved and adored her. Everywhere except Hollywood. She received fan mail weekly by the hundreds and poems, too, inspired by her beauty:

TO ANNA

> *Dear little Anna May Wong,*
> *She's a dream—a picture—a song.*
> *If I had my way I would watch her all day,*
> *My beautiful Anna May Wong.*

> *M. S. (Southampton)*

Rob Wagner noted, "When a girl who has been given only the smallest parts calls forth a fan mail of five hundred letters a week—more than many of the stars receive—it would seem that there are plenty of people who could fall deeply in love with a Chinese star."

Even the critics were in her corner: "In picture after picture this lovely and graceful little Chinese girl has demonstrated remarkable ability as a cinema portrayer, and yet never is she seen in anything but minor roles. In *Mr. Wu* she played just a bit, and yet in her few scenes she showed how absurd it was to cast even the excellent Renee Adoree for the leading role when she was available for the part. Now in *Old San Francisco* she appears in perhaps five scenes, as chief assistant to the villain, and in a role of no importance she is just about the most interesting and alluring feature present."

Though she held out hope that "some day some one will write a story *demanding* a real Chinese girl—then perhaps I'll have my chance," as she told Wagner, Anna May kept getting the cold shoulder from casting directors. That and feigned enthusiasm about parts they promised would be much bigger than they were. A couple weeks into filming for *Rose-Marie* with Renée Adorée and director William Nigh, Metro-Goldwyn-Mayer decided to recall the company. The studio brass didn't like the dailies and demanded rewrites. When the new script arrived, the director and cast were swiftly replaced. Just Anna May's luck. Maybe it was time to reevaluate her relationship with Tinsel Town, especially if she was wanted elsewhere.

She was making back-to-back films at a frenetic pace, saying yes to nearly every project that came her way, no matter how flimsy the role. And yet she felt as though her career was headed nowhere in a hurry. It was like trying to break free from quicksand. Every time she thought she'd found a script that might throw her a lifeline and pull her to safety, the movie's release would see her sink deeper into the sludge of cinematic obscurity. Active, yes, notable to many, but never taken seriously enough to land a title role.

"The directors seemed to believe that a pathetic death was the only thing I could do with art: *The Alaskan, Peter Pan, The Chinese Parrot*. In *The Devil Dancer*, I only had two scenes before I was dramatically killed," Anna May protested.

The trend continued into 1928. *Across to Singapore* saw her cast in yet another third-rate role that even the screenwriter dismissed as "a lovely slut." To add insult to injury, her lusty scenes with Ramon Novarro and Ernest Torrence were cut by the censors and her name was conveniently left out of the credits. Costar Joan Crawford's character got the guy in the end, since the whole film had been about men fighting over her, not Anna May. At least she'd had fun acting opposite Ramon, who became a friend. The Mexican actor rose to fame in 1925's toga saga *Ben-Hur* and became Hollywood's de facto "Latin lover" after Valentino's untimely death in 1926. Though his matinee idol good looks attracted a rabid female fan base, Ramon preferred men and discreetly carried on affairs with Hollywood reporter Herbert Howe and others for most of his career.

In *The Crimson City*, Anna May again played a minor supporting part, while Myrna Loy—the Montana-born actress of British and Swedish extraction—performed Onoto, the lead female role, in yellowface. Four years prior, no one even knew the name Myrna Loy. She was merely one of the many anonymous nautch dancers hired by Sid Grauman for his prologue to *The Thief of Bagdad*. Myrna had risen dramatically through the ranks since then. Perhaps Anna May should have requested an additional consultation fee since she was asked yet again to coach her white costar on how to hold her chopsticks properly. Myrna herself later admitted how absurd she'd felt in the role. "They cast me as a Chinese in *The Crimson City*, with Anna May Wong," she recalled in her memoir. "Up against her, of course, I looked about as Chinese as Raggedy Ann."

Anna May Wong was fed up. Hollywood couldn't get past her race and what it dictated for her gender on-screen. Naturally, the studios always found rather vague and insincere ways of explaining it to her. But she knew it and they knew it. "There have been several attempts to show me in leading roles, but it's very difficult in Hollywood because of the race issue," she explained to a member of the foreign press. "In American terms, a colored woman is not allowed to marry a white man, and since films in America almost always end with a happy ending, I have not been given a leading role there." In not so many words, happy endings could not be permitted to someone like Anna May Wong, a woman of color.

Luckily, where American directors saw a liability, others saw opportunity. Karl Vollmöller, the German playwright and screenwriter she'd met at one of Emil Jannings's parties, had become a somewhat influential go-between for the German and American film industries. He first garnered attention in 1911 with his play *The Miracle*, which was staged by Max Reinhardt and later adapted into a film. As early as 1920, Vollmöller began splitting his time between Hollywood and

Berlin. He was a millionaire, after all, and liked to socialize with interesting and attractive personalities. His ability to broker deals on both sides of the Atlantic only added to his drawing power. Apparently, he'd been so smitten with Anna May that when he returned home to Berlin, he cranked out a novel written with her in mind for the lead in the adaptation.

Schmutziges Geld, or *Dirty Money* in English, is the tragic story of star-crossed lovers. In a fit of jealous rage, Jack Houben attacks a man for flirting with his lover, a renowned dancer, and pushes him overboard from a ship's deck. He jumps into the sea after his victim to avoid being taken in by the law and flees to an "Eastern harbor." Song is a destitute Malaysian girl living by her own wits in the same foreign port city. When two sailors threaten to assault her, who should step in and save the damsel in distress but the down-on-his-luck Jack. The two scrape together a living by working the city's nightclub circuit, Jack as a knife thrower and Song as his assistant and dancer. Though Song has fallen in love with her protector, he still pines for his ex, who comes into town right on cue. Who will Jack choose?

The story was full of sorrow and misfortune, the kind of melodramatic script that Anna May could really sink her teeth into. Song, in fact, was named after her—for Tsong in Wong Liu Tsong. The film was soon retitled after its leading lady and referred to simply as *Song*.

"The role is perfect," Anna May effused, "it is *my* role like none before."

Vollmöller took the screenplay to director friend Richard Eichberg, one of the continent's "starmakers" who had launched the career of Lilian Harvey. Some considered Eichberg the "most American" of European directors, as he was known for making action films and melodramas. Without hesitation, Eichberg agreed to direct. An offer from UFA, Germany's illustrious film company, quickly followed. The six-month contract stipulated that Anna May was to make films in both Germany and England, as part of Film Europe, an effort to coproduce and distribute pan-European films internationally to compete with the likes of Hollywood. Thus, she was contracted to star in films such as *Song* at UFA and later productions managed by British International Pictures (BIP).

Signing with UFA could completely change the trajectory of her career. It could also end it. Would Hollywood forget her while she was away working in Europe? God knew how quickly people seemed to forget you in Hollywoodland if your photograph or name stopped appearing in print for a season. What if *Song* was a failure? Or, worse yet, an utterly forgettable mediocrity? What if she went to Berlin and never came back?

For all her gumption, Anna May had never before been faced with such an important and difficult decision. The possibilities were tantalizing, and though she was daring, she couldn't afford to be reckless or impulsive. Still, she could already taste the sweet satisfaction of walking out on Hollywood.

"I sought the advice of many relatives and friends. I considered all they said. Many of them advised against such a difficult and uncertain venture," Anna May Wong later recalled of the opportunity to work abroad and the unknown future that lay ahead. "Then I made up my mind—I would go."

Anna May Wong as Shosho, dazzling her coworkers in the scullery, in a scene from *Piccadilly*, 1929.

5

THE GIRL WHO CAN'T HELP
BEING CHINESE

t seems to us the greatest pity in the world that the Hollywood producers are going to let that uniquely talented young oriental actress,
Anna May Wong, slip through their fingers," the *Los Angeles Times*
lamented upon learning the news of Anna May's imminent departure.

In truth, Anna May had been contemplating a European sojourn
for quite some time. She began making plans to depart for Europe as
early as June 1927, when she submitted a request to leave the country
to her local U.S. Immigration Service office in Los Angeles. Form 430,
as it was known to all Chinese Americans, was just a flimsy piece of
paper, but it symbolized much more than that. It was the bane of
many, a bureaucratic indignation, a reminder that the Chinese,
American-born or not, were second-class citizens in the United States
of America. When the Chinese Exclusion Act was made permanent
in 1902, all Chinese living the United States were required to register
and obtain a certificate of residency. In addition, Form 430 had to be
filled out each and every time an American citizen of Chinese ancestry wished to leave the country and return without any major
complications—like, say, being deported from one's own birthplace.

"As nothing was developed tending to show that [Anna May
Wong's] status is other than that claimed, to-wit, a native of this country, it is respectfully recommended that her application be approved,"
wrote J. C. Nardini, the immigration inspector assigned to the Wong

family. He had known Anna May and her parents for a number of years and had helped her siblings register their status and apply for identification papers on a trip to Mexico in 1925.

With her UFA contract in hand and her state passport issued, Anna May made preparations for her first transatlantic voyage. Sailing alone to a foreign land at twenty-three would be no small feat. She had not forgotten those lonesome days of living alone, away from her family, in a Hollywood flat. Besides, her parents had already objected to the entire endeavor, as she knew they would. Lulu didn't give it a second thought and volunteered to travel with her sister as chaperone, which seemed to calm their worst fears. Lulu was more than just an older sister and confidante; she was also a valuable asset to Anna May's business of being a movie star. She'd traveled with Anna May on the hapless Cosmics tour a few years back and persevered through all the troubled hiccups of that kooky venture.

J. C. Nardini recommended Lulu Wong's Form 430 for approval on March 16, 1928, stating, "This applicant is a native of Los Angeles, California. . . . She is to accompany her sister, Anna May Wong. . . . It is believed that she intends to visit all the important countries of Europe." Several days later, Lulu's application was approved.

The Wong family and Anna May's good friend Grace Wilcox made up the small group of well-wishers who saw the two sisters off at the train station as they embarked on the first leg of their journey to Germany. As Grace recalled, Anna May was "dripping with flowers and baskets of fruit, trying to smile stoically, as Chinese people are supposed to do." In the end, Grace was the only one who managed to keep it together, while Wong Sam Sing, Lee Gon Toy, and the rest of the Wong children cried openly "with tears streaming down their faces."

In New York City, Anna May's hotel suite filled up with flowers sent by friends, admirers, and colleagues. When the two sisters boarded their midnight ship to Germany at the end of March, the scene was much the same. Their stateroom overflowed with more flowers, steamer baskets, and books. A journalist who caught up with her in New York before her departure remarked, "Anna May Wong is in a class all by herself in the movie world: and some of her Occidental sisters must envy her popularity. One reason for her success must be her humbleness. She has neglected to acquire the airs and trappings of stardom. She remains a wise, quiet, mysterious little Oriental. . . . We wish her good luck!"

Two weeks at sea brought them to the docks of Hamburg, Germany's largest port. The cold, wind-whipped city built on the Elbe River, whose frigid waters feed into the North Sea, tendered a bleak welcome. Hamburg was like a fortress. Massive red brick warehouses situated along man-made waterways stretched in either direction as far as the eye could see.

Anna May and Lulu made their way through Hamburg's maze-like network of canals to the main train station. Once there, they stood in the station, surrounded by their luggage, uncertain of how to proceed, looking very much like two strangers stranded in a foreign land. Neither of them spoke a lick of German, but they had their wits about them and turned their ears to the announcements being made over the loudspeaker. "Berlin" was the magic word they listened for, so that they might pluck it from the blaring, incomprehensible sentences made of harsh guttural tones and follow it to their desired destination. When the sisters heard "Berlin" uttered by a nearby group of travelers, they scurried in their direction to the train.

Fortunately, Berlin gave Anna May a much warmer, spirited welcome than Hamburg. The American movie star, who had traveled all the way from Hollywood to make a film for the German cinema, disembarked from her first-class train car wearing a fabulous fur-lined coat. She smiled and waved for the cameras while clutching a bouquet of roses.

Berlin had risen from the ashes of World War I and refashioned itself into something completely unexpected. This unlikely European capital had earned its place in the cosmos by the end of the 1920s as the world's most decadent city. Although Germany arrived late to the Jazz Age, it swiftly made up for lost time. With the Great War lost, rampant inflation, and millions of dollars in war reparations haunting the country like a hungry ghost, most Germans, Berliners especially, longed to forget, shake off their shame, and experience the pleasures of the living once more. The streets were alive with music, dance, theater, and a nascent sexual energy.

After many years of penury, Berlin was suddenly the wellspring of the ultramodern, a place where traffic lights and pavement were held up as miracles of progress. Anna May Wong, with her lacquered bangs, sunny American disposition, and Chinese looks—vestiges of her flapper persona still clinging subtly to her manner of speaking and dress—must have been an otherworldly vision even to those smart, cross-dressing residents of Charlottenburg catwalking down the Kurfürstendamm. Anna May, however, didn't have time to watch them pick their jaws up from off the floor.

She went to work on *Song* with Richard Eichberg and her costar Heinrich George, who played Grot in Fritz Lang's *Metropolis*, at the UFA studios almost immediately. The language barrier was decidedly more difficult than she'd anticipated. Her and Lulu's first days in Germany were a comedy of errors, but they usually had a good laugh about such incidents.

"The first day on the set I was puzzled by the small leather books that everyone on the set except my sister and myself was carrying," Anna May observed. "Then I discovered that they were English-German dictionaries which the people there hoped would enable them to converse with me more easily. However, I decided that it would be easier for one person to learn German than for an entire company to master English."

If Anna May planned to work in this language, or at least attempt to, she'd have to find a way to bridge the gap. She hired a tutor and threw herself into intensive German lessons, studying six hours a day. "Within a week I could take direction in German—if plenty of gestures were thrown in for good measure." She learned the language with a zeal she had never committed to her Chinese studies all those years before. The difference was that Anna May had come to Germany of her own volition and chosen to leave that provincial American colony behind. Now she was here reaping the rewards—a starring role in an Eichberg film written specifically for her, along with heaps of adulation from a public uninhibited by her race. Instead of being seen as a problem and a hurdle to overcome, her Asian-ness was received quite favorably. It drew them to her like a magnet.

There were less than a thousand Chinese people living in Germany in 1928, only a handful of whom were women. Unlike in America, where Chinese immigration had been blocked by the Exclusion Act, the Germans bore no animus toward the Chinese since there were so few. German citizens were not knowledgeable of Chinese culture or the distinction of Anna May's Chinese American identity. To them, she was simply an unusual specimen, a kind of endangered species rarely seen in the wild. In reviews and news articles, the press often referred to her as "the Asian artist," "the Mongolian from Hollywood," or simply "the Chinese woman."

The *New York Times*, playing the role of spurned lover in the wake of Anna May's departure for Europe, grumbled that the German press was a little too fixated on her embodiment of the "Chinese waif," underlining the fact that they "neglect to mention that Anna May is of American birth. They stress only her Chinese origin."

Another draw was Anna May's singular ability to cry on cue without the aid of glycerin tears, a skill she had become well-known for back in Hollywood. Her tragic turn as Song called for plenty of waterworks. When German fans caught wind of this special talent, many drove all the way to the UFA's Neubabelsberg studios in Potsdam, nearly an hour's commute from Berlin, to see her famous tears. Despite the sorrowful airs she put on while working a scene, Anna May was having the time of her life.

"I am very happy in Berlin—so happy, as I have rarely been

before," she told the readers of *Mein Film* in early May 1928. "I really enjoy my work in Berlin, and I also work very well with director Eichberg. . . . I hope that this film will be quite a success so that people in Europe will appreciate me as an actress."

Anna May Wong was already proving to be an enthusiastic success socially among Germany's elite. Invitations to various social functions and private soirées abounded. On one such occasion two months into their stay in Germany, she and Lulu attended an intimate gathering at a society host's Berlin home. As Anna May gracefully made her way into the party, the idle chatter went silent and everyone's attentions whirled to the sleek, five-foot-six swan presently in the room.

Dressed in a tailored navy suit and a light blue blouse, a yellow handkerchief tied at her neck with a flourish, Anna May sat down with the small party around a low wooden table, flanked on all sides by curious gazes. The other guests, each a distinguished personality, peppered her with questions and ingratiating witticisms, hoping to crack open her doll-like exterior and excavate the depths of her beauty and poise. The novelist asked whether she rehearsed her roles in front of a mirror. The illustrator on her left and the American journalist on her right took turns vying for her recognition, perhaps hoping to possess a small piece of this Oriental goddess's good favor.

Of course, they were no competition for twentieth-century Germany's most eclectic thinker, Walter Benjamin. As the two heavyweights in the room, Walter and Anna May said little at first, each surveying the other in silence, allowing a truer image of their famous personalities to form while the others prattled on. Then, finally, Walter Benjamin spoke, and the night's interview began. Little by little, he drew Anna May out, asking her opinion on her part in Eichberg's latest film, her thoughts on the Chinese cinema, her life's story from laundryman's daughter to international movie star.

He probed her on her craft and playfully challenged her dedication to it. "What means of expression would you use if the film wasn't available to you?" Unable to imagine a life outside of her art, Anna

May responded cheekily with two words: "Touch wood." The entire party hollered merrily at this rejoinder and pounded on the table in moral support.

Contrary to the image of the tragic Chinese maiden, the picture that developed of Anna May Wong in the flesh, according to Benjamin, was a vision of her that fans rarely saw.

"I can already guess that her unclouded, cheerful self-expression is not deceptive," he mused, "and that the deeper her love for sadness is, the more balanced and cheerful her everyday life is. Her sister can confirm it. In this good, healthy girl, who, despite all her charm, looks so earnest and genial as if life had already revealed its true nature to her, you don't see anything of the film star."

The meeting of these two minds made the room feel as if there were no one else in it—at least, no one else who had the courage to utter a word or the authority to interrupt. The party continued without them as Benjamin and Anna May moved to another room, where they persisted in their private exchange.

Benjamin went straight to the heart of it and inquired about her work as a screen actress. Anna May, thousands of miles and an entire ocean away from home, spoke freely and frankly. "The truth, if it is bitter, is only heard from friends," she opined. "I want to hear even the bitter truth from friends."

"Do you have role models, teachers?" Benjamin asked.

"No. There are actresses I admire, Pauline Frederick for example. But the only time I copied someone else's gesture was from the dumbest, most inexperienced actress, according to the general belief in Hollywood, that we had there."

Her words cut to the quick. But the intended targets—those hacks in Hollywood—were far away and blissfully unaware. Anna May was nothing if not serious about her profession, and she held herself and her peers to accordingly high standards. This may have further endeared her to the infatuated German philosopher. For in Walter Benjamin's eyes, she remained as bewitching as ever.

Reclining in a comfortable chair, perfectly at ease with herself and the world, Anna May unspooled her long hair, which she usually wore neatly in a chignon at the nape of her neck. Despite the rumors of her flapperdom par excellence, Anna May had cut her hair short only once and, having learned her lesson, let it grow long again. Thereafter, she merely fabricated the illusion of having bobbed her hair. Victorian women were famous for their extensive, uncut tresses. A woman's hair, naturally, was her most valuable asset and a symbol of her virtue. The flapper revolted by chopping the whole damn thing off. But letting one's hair down was something else entirely—the ultimate transgression. As Anna May loosened her hair with her immaculately manicured fingers, stroking and restyling the fringe across her forehead, Benjamin no doubt caught a thrill.

"Everything that is courageous and dear seems to be reflected in her eyes. I know I'll see her again," Benjamin predicted, "in a film that may resemble the fabric of our dialogue of which I say in the words of the author of the Iu-Kiao-Liu: *The fabric was divinely draped, / but the face was even finer.*"

During her nearly three months in Germany, Anna May was consumed by her work on *Song*. She saw very little outside of Berlin, to say nothing of the Continent, aside from a few trips to German spas and "healing baths." Though she already had offers to do more films in Germany, Eichberg encouraged her to visit England and France first. With production on the film completed by mid-June, Anna May decided to use her time off to take a little vacation. She and Lulu hopped a train to France.

Paris, like Berlin, opened up new worlds for Anna May and fed her wanderlust. The City of Light was loud and boisterous like every city she had been to, yet even its roar evinced a sense of timeless elegance and refinement. Maybe it was the graceful sloping mansard roofs on the apartment buildings, which cut a uniform horizon across an endless blue sky. Or the tidy rows of trees, trimmed to precision, that lined the Jardin du Luxembourg. Or the way Sacré-Coeur glowed, jewellike, from the crest of Montmartre each evening, serenading all of Paris with its splendor at sunset.

Anna May had never seen women quite like Parisiennes—except maybe in movies. Their clothes were sophisticated and well-tailored. They wore red lipstick as if it was second nature to them. Their bodies moved freely in dangerously high heels. Daring little hats propped on the tops of their heads were the final punctuation to the entire look. She saw lovers embrace in the streets, on bridges, and along the banks of the Seine. Kissing in public was not off-limits as it was in the United States but à la mode.

On one of her first nights in Paris, Anna May went to see Serge Diaghilev's world famous Ballets Russes at the Théâtre Sarah Bernhardt. The ballet, choreographed by a twenty-four-year-old George Balanchine and set to music composed and conducted by Igor Stravinsky himself, was sublime. Here, dancing before the footlights, was the truest form of the dramatic arts, the story of Apollo told solely through melody and the fluid movements of the human form.

The cunning of Hollywood's artifice fell away in the presence of its superlative source material. One could see where Douglas Fairbanks had taken his inspiration for *The Thief of Bagdad*, yet it left one wondering how the film industry could possibly compete with European high art. Somehow Hollywood movies managed it. Box office revenues didn't lie. The regular workingman and -woman couldn't sail to Paris to see the rapturous Ballets Russes for themselves, but for a buck and some change they could watch a knockoff version of it. Cinema had turned the world upside down and the masses were now the arbiters of art.

After the ballet ended, Anna May found her way backstage, probably flashing her movie star smile to get past security. She stole a few moments with several of the ballet dancers, including Serge Lifar, who had danced as Apollo. Serge and the other performers happily indulged Anna May's effusive admiration and autographed her program.

Then, who else should she run into backstage but her friend Ramon Novarro. Their hot and heavy embrace in *Across to Singapore* hadn't made it past the censors, but tonight they were in Paris—at liberty to cross the lines policing race and gender back home. Nothing could stop them from enjoying this heartfelt reunion. Ramon insisted on marking the felicitous occasion with an inscription of his own. "A mi simpática amiguita Annita May Wong," he wrote in a corner of her program, "como un recuerdo de esta noche en Paris!" Did these two pals celebrate the fine summer night by supping under the stars at the charming Château de Madrid at the edge of the Bois de Boulogne? Did they take a nightcap at Chez Joséphine in Pigalle and dance until the wee hours of the morning with the Black Venus herself? Movie stars don't kiss and tell. Suffice it to say, they did what rich, famous twentysomethings anywhere would have done. They tore up the town.

Paris, ultimately, was a whirlwind affair, but one Anna May hoped to rekindle at a later date. After only a fortnight, she and Lulu moved on to London. The sisters settled into an apartment on Park Lane across from Hyde Park, the leafy neighborhood that was home to London's most fashionable society. Anna May didn't care much for the flat's stuffy, antique aesthetic, but she made the best of it by adding a few touches of her own: a Chinese vase here and there, brightly colored cushions, and an embroidered Chinese shawl draped across a settee in the sitting room.

And just as it had done in Germany and France, Anna May's cultlike status ripped through the British papers, tabloids, and magazines. Publications raced to tout the arrival of the Chinese movie star from America. Pictures taken years before of her horsing around in boxing gloves at Hal Roach Studios were released to the British press. Local artists and photographers like Paul Tanqueray, Dorothy Wilding, Nicholas Michailow, and Frank Arthur Swaine clamored for a sitting with her. While the whole of London was abuzz, Anna May and Lulu went about seeing the sights of London. They visited the infamous Tower of London, the site of so many terrible executions, as well as the London Scottish Drill Hall, where twenty lusty bagpipers played pibrochs for the sisters. Paparazzi captured Anna May reading the Chinese news bulletin in Limehouse, London's Chinatown.

During this period of downtime in between flicks, she also acquainted herself with the local theater scene and went to see Noël Coward's hit musical revue *This Year of Grace* at the London Pavilion. Her next film, in fact, was set in a dinner theater club in that same section of the city: Piccadilly Circus, London's entertainment and nightlife hub.

The source material for *Piccadilly*, as the project was titled, had been written by famous British novelist Arnold Bennett. Anna May was well-acquainted with Bennett's novels, potboilers that had been circulating in the United States since the 1910s with great success. Bennett was "the most conspicuous figure in English light literature," according to the *New York Times*. Emphasis on "light." So the best-selling novelist wanted to try his hand at the movies? *Piccadilly* was vigorously hyped as Bennett's first "original play for the screen."

The story, Anna May surmised as she flipped through the treatment's pages, began with successful nightclub owner, Valentine Wilmot. The bulk of the action would take place at his Piccadilly establishment, where star dancer, Mabel Greenfield, headlines the main act and also moonlights as Valentine's lover.

In this stock setup for "happy couple confronts unexpected obstacle to their enduring love," the first signs of trouble erupt when a guest, played by a young Charles Laughton, lodges a complaint in the midst of one of Mabel's performances.

"Dirty plate!" the lone diner shouts at the head waiter as he repeatedly pounds his fist on the table, attracting fellow patrons' snickers and stealing their attention away from the dance number. Valentine, a shrewd entrepreneur, knows the club cannot afford any dips in attendance due to a disgruntled customer. He follows the trail of the dirty plate to its logical culprit: the scullery, the part of the kitchen where the lowliest staff wash the dishes.

None of the dishwashers notice Valentine's presence, however, because they're all enraptured, lost in "passionate attention" to the young woman dancing for her workmates on a makeshift platform. "This youthful creature had slanting Chinese eyes. She was the slatternliest of slatterns, and she was dancing," the screenplay indicated. "The scene was a sinister replica on a small scale of the scene in the large dance-hall, except that where Mab in the large hall had not held her audience, this girl was unquestionably holding her audience. She was indeed holding it so tight that not a soul save herself had noticed the arrival of the supreme master of the establishment."

Within the first few pages of the script, the Chinese scullery maid emerges as a powerful rival to Mab, the "slatternly" girl's well-established white counterpart. Anna May was intrigued. Holding an audience captive—that was certainly something she knew a thing or two about. She'd done it for as long as she'd been around the movie business, in spite of the limitations imposed on her. In every frame in which she appeared, slight though the scene might be, she pulled viewers in like a lodestar. Her on-screen charisma was undeniable.

"The young girl, as she danced, happened to catch sight of Valentine," Anna May read on. "She was passionately absorbed in the dream of her dance. Her facial expression was the expression of a fanatic. . . . For perhaps a full thirty seconds the girl continued to dance—the strangest dancing that Valentine had seen in his life. He neither liked nor disliked it; he knew only that it puzzled and somehow fascinated him."

That the script tapped into the exotic lure of a young and vital Chinese girl was hardly surprising. The scullery maid named Shosho no Kimi, her name a mash-up of Chinese and Japanese consonants, merely personified a new variation on an old Orientalist fantasy. What separated Shosho from the Lotuses and Madame Butterflys whom Anna May had played before was a subtle but key difference: Shosho had agency. She goes from back-of-house scullery maid to the Picca-dilly Club's main attraction, becoming the talk of all London and converting the club into a solvent business again. Shosho triumphs over the washed-up Mab and wins Valentine's all-consuming infatuation.

The movie industry has always been flush with stories of rags to riches and instant fame, a favored Hollywood trope, but none could have been more fitting for Anna May Wong than *Piccadilly*. The film neatly resembled her own life's trajectory, only instead of folding clothes at the laundry, she would be scrubbing dishes in the scullery. Art imitates life, as the saying goes. Taking on this part was, in a way, a chance for Anna May to tell her own story—to remind people of her humble beginnings before she became a film star.

Even so, Anna May wouldn't receive top billing as Shosho, though it was plain to see hers was the starring role. Marquee placement would go to Gilda Gray, the "Queen of the Shimmy Shakers," who had risen to fame for her outrageous dancing style. The shimmy—the twerk of the Jazz Age—was the most naked expression of sexuality yet to be displayed in pictures, much less in public. Using her out-stretched arms to send convulsions through her core, Gray's ebullient quivering sent tremors into audiences. The shimmy was one of the first dance crazes, of many to follow, that spread like wildfire through the dance halls. "[Gilda] knows just what her admirers want," one movie reviewer commented, "dancing primarily—and she gives them plenty of it."

Although Gilda had played in half a dozen films and amassed a small fortune for her celebrity, *Piccadilly* was the first movie to offer her a role that entailed more than just shaking her wares. She was cast as Mabel Greenfield, yesterday's dance sensation whose worn-out cho-reography and frown lines are beginning to show at the ripe old age of twenty-eight—which just happened to be Gilda's actual age at the time. To play a role so precariously similar to her current circum-stances, especially a role that forecast a career in decline, took guts.

Anna May had first become acquainted with Gilda on the set of

The Devil Dancer, one of the many movies she'd played a bit part in during the hectic year of 1927. The film was set in Lhasa, Tibet's Forbidden City, and produced by Samuel Goldwyn. It was a far-fetched tale by any stretch of the imagination: the daughter of white missionaries is raised by lamas in a Buddhist monastery where she must remain as their sacred dancer. That is until the heroic white man, played by Clive Brook, shows up to whisk her back to civilization. "The story of this production may not be widely different from the familiar tropical narratives of a white man who rescues a white woman," the *Times* critic conceded, "but few pictures have been filmed with equally faithful modes and moods."

Anna May's performance as the unnamed Indian nautch dancer who is buried alive went without mention in the review. For her part, Gilda delivered her signature routine as "girl of swaying hips, rippling arms, and writhing muscles" and was paid $250,000—$3.6 million in today's currency—helping to make her one of the highest-paid actresses of the era.

Gilda and Anna May were kindred spirits, of a sort. Both had broken free from the traditional strictures of womanhood, in Gilda's case literally running away from home to escape the husband and child who had defined her existence as a teenage wife. She and Anna May were women who understood the capriciousness of fame and the concessions one sometimes had to make as an entertainer, baring your soul and body for all to see.

Except Gilda didn't have the recurring problem of being limited to characters who meet ghastly ends because of their forbidden sex. *Piccadilly,* despite its more progressive impulses to portray Shosho as a savvy, independent woman, surrendered its heroine to the same hackneyed fate of Anna May's many previous characters. In the end, Shosho dies for her racial transgression, but not at the hands of a righteous white zealot. It is her jealous friend and sometimes lover, Jim, a fellow Chinese, who shoots her after he realizes he's lost her love to Valentine.

Shosho's death is predictable and disappointing, precisely the kind of thing Anna May wanted to get away from when she left Holly-wood. But, unlike the other roles she'd played where the characters were often lowly slaves, unnamed prostitutes, or minor villains, Sho-sho was set apart as an exceptional talent, a flame who dared to burn too brightly and was extinguished because of her brilliance.

What's more, the script called for an on-screen kiss between her and Jameson Thomas, the British actor who would play Valentine. This was something Hollywood filmmakers had never even dared to put in writing. Whether progressive or prurient, Europeans appeared to embrace a more relaxed morality code. An interracial kiss would certainly ruffle some feathers back home in puritanical America. This time, dying for her art—at least for the cameras anyway—just might be worth it.

———

Filming for *Piccadilly* began in earnest in August 1928 with the arrival of its ostensible star, Gilda Gray. Meanwhile, sitting in her dressing room at Elstree Studios, wearing a striking blue-and-silver kimono, and casually reclining in a chair while reading a paperback novel to kill time, was Anna May Wong, looking every bit the show stealer. She had the singular power of transforming an ordinary room, cluttered with bric-a-brac, dirty makeup brushes, and perfume bottles, into the most extraordinary scene.

Miss Wong, they're ready for you on set.

With that, the actress sprang to life and into action. Anna May sat up as an assistant hurriedly lowered a gilded headdress atop her head. When she stood up and disrobed, it was as if she were Arthur drawing Excalibur from its sheath, revealing a virile, sharpened blade. Her costume—a throwback to her Mongolian slave days—was a scant, shimmering two-piece, more armor than apparel. Each shoulder ended with a curved, twisted point, while the headdress framed her face with jewels and a crown of spikes.

The costume was provided by Nathan's, the famous firm of

costumiers known to house 50,000 garments in its archives. A representative of the company affirmed that "every actor and actress of note since 1790, in England and many on the Continent and in the Colonies, has passed through our hands," and now they had added Anna May Wong to their rolls. Though her costume was nothing like the long robes and flowing sleeves of the Chinese and more aptly resembled those of Siamese Khon dancers, there was no denying the look was a showstopper.

Anna May stepped onto the set, glinting in the studio lights. She was about to perform the most important scene in *Piccadilly*, the one on which the entire film's credibility hinged: when Shosho takes center stage as an anonymous ingenue and leaves it transformed into a star. Sure, she knew how to Charleston like any good flapper, but although she was frequently asked to twirl and gyrate in roles like Song and Shosho, Anna May was no dancer. To ensure the performance had the spellbinding effect indicated in the script, she recruited Noranna Rose, principal dancer at Drury Lane Theatre. Noranna taught her the fundamentals of classic dance and helped her choreograph the final number so that it would enrapture all who watched it unfold.

British International Pictures and director Ewald André Dupont, a German emigré well-known in German expressionist cinema, reportedly spent in excess of £8,000 constructing the set for the Piccadilly Club, the largest and most elaborate yet built in a British studio. BIP had only recently changed its name from British National Pictures to British International Pictures, signaling its bid to break into the international film market and compete with the American studios. Hence, *Piccadilly* became its most expensive and prestigious production at Elstree Studios, a series of production facilities in the sleepy hamlets of Elstree and Borehamwood, fifteen miles northwest of London. Part of England's ambition to assemble a world-class film industry, the area was branded the British Hollywood. It eventually succeeded as a hub for British and international film productions, but

Elstree never supplanted Hollywood in the glitz and glamour department.

E. A. Dupont, like Anna May, was happy to be working far away from the censure and constraints of Hollywood. His last film there—*Love Me and the World Is Mine*, a romance set in Vienna—had been a total flop, mostly due to studio meddling. Ironically, Dupont had signed with Universal Pictures because he thought he would be afforded more artistic license in America.

The producers at Universal, however, were less concerned with Dupont's distinctive eye than they were with playing up the film's setting of Old Vienna, to which they believed Dupont could lend an air of cultural authority. The effect of Universal's demands was a film overrun by nostalgic kitsch. The movie did so poorly, Carl Laemmle sent Dupont packing and terminated his three-year contract.

So here they were, Wong, Dupont, and Gray, three immensely talented artists who had all seen some measure of success before being marginalized, misjudged, and cast out by Hollywood's ruthless machine. They had come to England looking for an outlet to express their genius. What was left unsaid was the underlying desire they all harbored of returning to America triumphant—and wanted.

The lights on set dimmed and the more than three hundred extras dressed as club patrons in velvet gowns and tuxedos quieted themselves in anticipation of the performance about to unfold on the dance floor.

Film rolling!

Anna May walked out to take her place at center stage. She pulled her arms across her golden breastplate and assumed her opening pose, remaining "calm and cold as a statue." Giant flickering candles installed on rotating pillars surrounded her petite figure on every side, reflecting tiny shards of light onto the faces in the gallery.

Then, summoning Shosho's life force from some invisible reservoir of feeling, Anna May inhaled and lifted her eyes to meet that evening's audience, revelers who had come to drink her in, for they were no longer extras milling about idly but curious Londoners thirsty for their next fix. All eyes were on her—Anna May, now Shosho—as she began to twist and sway her body. Sometimes briskly with her fingers trilling to the music and her arms unfolding into right angles, echoing the spikes of her crown; at other times languorously slinking across the stage, her hips swinging back and forth. Every movement was cast into stark relief by a kinetic shadow projected onto the stage floor by an overhead spotlight.

Shosho's performance was peculiar. Uncomfortable. Hypnotic. "The strangest dancing" you'd ever seen, if you could even call it dancing. And yet . . . it was absolutely, undeniably, viscerally mesmerizing. Some watching may have felt the blood rise to their heads, a dampness begin to collect involuntarily in the soft crevices of their bodies, a sudden and urgent thumping in their chests.

Her conquest complete, Shosho lowered her outspread hands in front of her face and kneeled on the floor, signaling the end of her dance. The crowd seated around the perimeter of the stage leapt to their feet for a standing ovation. There was a feeling of wonder and astonishment wafting through the soundstage, as if they had all witnessed history in the making.

Shosho stood and composed herself back into the statue she had entered as—true to the script's direction—and silently exited stage left, returning to whatever world she had been conjured from by her vessel Anna May. Whether the applause was for the actor or her character was of no importance. The former knew she had given the performance of a lifetime. Gilda Gray and E. A. Dupont knew it. So did the entire soundstage. And it had been imprinted on film for the ages.

———————

In the midst of filming *Piccadilly*, Anna May took a brief leave from Elstree in order to attend the premiere for *Song* in Berlin. The Alhambra theater on Kurfürstendamm was as grand as any movie palace in

Hollywood, perhaps grander. Its stone facade made up of Ionic columns and oval-shaped windows felt more appropriate for an opera house than a cinema. Indeed, the film was accompanied by a live orchestra. She had never been to a premiere quite like this before, where her name was on the lips of every onlooker, shouted out in a foreign tongue. "Maia Wong," as they called her, was finally the star of the show.

Her director had shot two endings for the film: one where Jack realizes his missteps, swears off his ex, and reunites blissfully with the steadfast Song; and another where the pair remain star-crossed lovers to the last. Eichberg, ultimately, chose Greek tragedy over happily ever after. What's more, scenes from the script that called for intimate touching and kissing were never filmed. Because UFA intended to distribute *Song* internationally and to the United States, it was still beholden to America's racially restrictive mores. Eichberg's scriptwriter, Adolf Lantz, regretted that he had to give Anna May's character such a joyless resolution but reasoned, "It's better to choose the lesser evil. Better not to insist on the 'happy ending' than deprive a hundred million people of experiencing this unique actress."

In the version screened that evening, and at all subsequent showings, a remorseful Jack arrives at Song's new cabaret in time to watch her final performance, a dance among razor-sharp swords on a rotating stage. When the two lovers meet eyes from across the room, Song loses her footing and collapses on one of the blades to her death.

Despite her character's rather melodramatic finale, Anna May rendered it so exquisitely, like an ethereal angel finally ascending to heaven, that the film concluded on a luminous note. Sitting in the audience that night, she could hardly believe the audience's response. Their standing ovation to her artistry lasted a full twenty minutes. By the time she made it out to the packed lobby, she was surrounded by fans, which induced an out-of-body experience: "I seemed suddenly to be standing at one side watching myself with complete detachment. It was my Chinese soul coming back to claim me."

One of the German critics praised Eichberg for making a thing of beauty out of Karl Vollmöller's tired script, adding: "He discovers Anna May Wong not only for Europe, but perhaps for the cinema, because for the first time he puts this highly talented woman on the big screen, turns her into an Asian Mary Pickford, who has an exceptional partner in Heinrich George."

The film debuted in London a month later as *Show Life* and the English reviewers said much the same. Auberon, the critic for the *Bystander*, put Anna May in the same class of actresses as Greta Garbo. "With Anna May Wong in the leading rôle success is ensured," he continued, "but how she shows up the lesser talent of the other players! . . . She stands out as being one of the most talented screen actresses of to-day."

Around this time, as her accolades abroad cropped up in U.S. papers, Anna May received an offer from Hollywood screenwriter and talent agent Ben Hirschfield. Her reply made its way into the pages of the *Los Angeles Times*:

> Your offer sounds very interesting, but I doubt very much my getting back to Hollywood before Christmas. Many thanks for your kindness and courtesy.
>
> I starred in a wonderful film in Berlin, the story of which was specially written for me. It is now titled *Song* and will probably be released in America shortly. It had its Berlin premiere a couple of weeks ago and was a tremendous hit and am happier to report it was a great personal success. They take film openings in Berlin, especially big ones, as seriously as they do in Hollywood.
>
> *Piccadilly* is the most lavish production ever attempted here in England. I have a wonderful part, one of the three featured roles.

One can hardly blame Anna May for boasting of this long-overdue triumph and throwing a touch of shade at good old Hollywood. Her faithless lover had finally come running back to her, jealousy in his eyes, but it was too late. The woman he'd discarded—and on a whim wanted back—had unmistakably moved on.

———

Production at Elstree picked up again with the scene following Shosho's magnificent first show. On the set that day was a French reporter who'd come to interview Anna May for *Pour Vous*. They chatted underneath the blistering heat of the klieg lights in between takes. Resting in her actor's chair with WONG LIU TSONG written on it in "charming Chinese hieroglyphs," Anna May told him why she loved Europe: because the people there had less contempt for the colored races. She also shared stories from her childhood and talked of her family back home. For this, she pulled out a photo of her youngest brother, Richard, with his cute "buttonhole eyes."

Just then Dupont reappeared with his sleeves rolled up, cigar in hand, and a look that said he meant business. Anna May quickly dispensed with the interview and returned to her mark in front of the camera. The reporter gazed on as he watched the artist become her subject. "Anna May sits in the corner of a filthy room, knees tight, face quivering," he described the scene. "Goodbye memories, here she is living her role. Shaped by the mastery of Dupont, the man who is best at handling actors, she curls up against the worm-eaten wood carefully fabricated by the set decorator, and becomes a tiny Chinese shadow in a Whitechapel slum."

In the film, Shosho awakens the day after her winning performance to a knock at her door. It's Jim, who has come, newspaper in hand, to share the first review of her performance: "SHOSHO, THE CHINESE DANCING WONDER—Sensational Triumph of a young Chinese Dancer—Stroke of Luck for the Piccadilly Club."

Shosho turns from the newspaper back to Jim, giddy from the spoils of victory, and lowers the outspread paper before finally leaning in to give him a kiss. A jump cut from this scene to a second shot of the newspaper headline zooms out to reveal another pair of eyes perusing the review—Mab's, whose reaction is not quite as sanguine. Shosho's rise signals her own demise as the Piccadilly Club's former headliner and Valentine's ex-paramour.

It's hard to say if fiction took its cues from reality in this case or if the drama on-screen divined real events still to come.

Piccadilly premiered in London at the end of January 1929 at the Carlton Theatre, marking the first time a West End theater was booked for the presentation of a British film. Although reviews were mixed on the film overall, the verdict on Anna May was clear. "Acting honours undoubtedly go to the Chinese," the *Stage* wrote. "Anna May Wong gives a brilliantly clever performance."

An American movie star worth her mettle was now among the Brits, and they went crazy for her. "It was England who made Anna May Wong a star," one critic in *Picture Show* quipped, "[and] gave her the reward that America had withheld." Indeed, illustrated posters for the film advertised Anna May as a larger-than-life figure posed topless above Piccadilly Circus, as if the film belonged to her alone.

It's hard not to replay the scene where Shosho reads her review in the paper and imagine the nearly identical scene that must have played out when Anna May read the reviews for *Piccadilly*. The hard-won validation she must have felt. The cultural gatekeepers, of Great Britain no less, were at last acknowledging the talents she'd always known she possessed.

Gilda presciently sailed back to America as soon as production on the film was completed, leaving Anna May to bask in the glory of her newfound English admirers. Her swift fame made traversing the city on foot suddenly difficult, for nearly everywhere she went she was mobbed by fans. Her style, too, began to seep into popular culture. All over London, girls began turning up with blunt-cut bangs, their faces powdered a pale ivory, dressed in beautifully embroidered Chinese coats with knotted buttons.

Unsurprisingly, Gilda did not fare as favorably with the critics and was unable to outshine the fierce glow of her costar. "Gilda Gray, the originator of the 'Shimmy,' is starred," one reviewer noted, "but her performance sinks into insignificance when compared with Anna May Wong's artistry."

BIP succeeded in exporting the film abroad, and six months later *Piccadilly* opened to American moviegoers at the Little Carnegie Playhouse in midtown Manhattan, next door to Carnegie Hall and the Russian Tea Room. By the end of its one-week run, showings were limited to standing room only. Reviewers on the other side of the Atlantic made much the same observations as their British counterparts: "Just a whisper, the little Chinese Anna May Wong, steals the picture from the lighter skinned heroine, Miss Gilda Gray."

Of all the critics, Freddie Schader at *Motion Picture News* was the one to finally say what everyone else was thinking:

> Whoever permitted Gilda Gray to take the role that she plays at *Piccadilly* showed very poor judgment, for Anna May Wong's role entirely overshadows that of the Golden Girl of the box office. The little Chinese player troupes like a house afire and makes the most of the opportunity given her, and what is more she looks decidedly good.

A house afire, indeed.

Many years after Anna May Wong's celebrity died down to a murmur—a name brought up at cocktail parties that eluded most people's memories, despite the familiar rounded vowels—the image of her body enshrined in Shosho's golden armor remained like a glowing ember, a last remnant of what was once a raging inferno. That showstopping dance number outlived her, cropping up in documentaries of her life, on YouTube, in the endless scroll of Instagram, and in the private flirtations and jokes of DMs the world over, her undulating hips forever memorialized as a GIF.

But if art truly imitates life, then we are obliged to look beyond the dazzling dance number and consider a scene that must have haunted Anna May long after the applause for her dance subsided.

Once Shosho secures her status as London's latest "It" girl, she moves out of her shared rooms and into her own flat in Limehouse, which she promptly decks out in chinoiserie. She is, after all, earning £100 a week for her sold-out show. One evening after her nightly performance, Valentine offers to accompany Shosho home and has his chauffeur drive them to Limehouse.

Gone are her ordinary street clothes and stockings with runs down the front. In their place she sports a chic velveteen dress trimmed with fur around the collar and hem, paired with a matching fur muff. Her eyes peek out from underneath a tight-fitting cloche hat with tapered ends, and she wears gloves, of course, to keep her hands soft now that they have escaped the drudgery of the scullery. Valentine and his starlet walk arm in arm down the deserted streets of Limehouse before stopping into a local saloon.

They try to blend in with the rough-and-tumble crowd and install themselves toward the back of the bar, where they down their drinks. Valentine places his hand tentatively on Shosho's. His gentle caresses go unnoticed because the dance floor is hopping with couples and singles and fine young things showing off their Charleston moves. "You see, this is *our* Piccadilly," Shosho says, grinning slyly at Valentine.

But even in a Limehouse saloon that serves all color and kind of folk, there are limits to the lax propriety afforded to the down-and-out. A Chaplinesque Black man wearing a creased top hat dances cheerfully on his own until a tall white woman enters the saloon and makes his acquaintance. The pair continue dancing together.

Seeing an unspoken rule broken, the saloon's proprietor steps in and breaks the two apart. "Yer know that's not allowed in my place— dancing with a white girl. Get out!" he screams in the man's face. The Black man doesn't need to be told twice and backs away, leaving the woman standing alone amidst a crowd of people who have stopped dancing.

Embarrassed, the woman says nothing at first, eyes lowered, as the owner and another woman give her a public dressing down. Something wells up inside her, though, as the owner's harangues continue and the crowd throws insults and nasty glances her way. The camera returns to Shosho and Valentine, who have awoken from their private infatuation. They move closer to get a better view of the spectacle.

The woman's expression has changed. She raises her head high, casting a righteous stare at the saloon owner, and delivers what might be the most rousing, vitriolic comeback of the silent era. There are no intertitles to tell us what she's saying, but you can feel the heat just looking at her mouth move.

It is this moment of confrontation—a white woman standing up to the mob for their rebuke against racial mixing—that hits a nerve. Shosho cannot bear to watch the scene any longer, so she jerks herself away, turning her back to the camera. When the episode is finally over and the white woman has been shooed out of the establishment by a chorus of raised fists, Valentine whisks Shosho out to the street and into the night.

Shosho appears stricken, no longer in the mood for frivolity, because she has been reminded of her essential lot in life. She can't help being Chinese, yet she's hanging on the arm of a white man—a man she may entrance and seduce but never win, because she will never be white like him. Society frowns on their commingling, perhaps less so since Valentine is a white man, in contrast to the white woman in the saloon whose entire worth depends upon her pristine race.

Still, the mob has spoken. No amount of success, money, or fame can ever transmute the reality of what Shosho is. In truth, she knows her reception as an exotic import—THE CHINESE DANCING WONDER—is in part the reason for her success.

Shosho no Kimi and Anna May Wong both found stardom

through sheer force of will and a little luck. They faced the same challenges of poverty and racism. They were Cinderella stories sans Prince Charming. Anna May played Shosho as if she were simply playing herself.

The saloon scene was not in the original story by Arnold Bennett but rather was an invention of E. A. Dupont's that appeared only in the German shooting script. As a German émigré in Britain, Dupont would have been keenly aware of what it felt like to be "other." That such a scene made it into the finished film is both miraculous and startling. And yet most of the critics failed to give it much notice, save the *National Board of Review Magazine*, which commented, "Shosho and Valentine may not see the analogy but the incident invites the spectator to do so. It is a good example of the camera doing its own talking."

Piccadilly was hailed in the United States as "the first serious contender of our American product to reach these shores from English studios"—though the *New York Times*, strangely, said nothing of Anna May's performance. Wong, Gray, and Dupont—the foreign help—had done their part to put BIP's Elstree Studios on the map of international cinema for one fleeting moment. The British media enthusiastically praised the picture as "our greatest effort yet" and "one of the finest films that has ever come from a British studio." Anna May renewed her contract with BIP until May 1930 and signed on to do another four "super" productions with Richard Eichberg.

And she got her kiss in front of the cameras. While shooting one of her final scenes, Anna May and Jameson Thomas consummated Shosho and Valentine's affair with a lip-to-lip kiss. A still from the film was included in Arnold Bennett's accompanying book. The image captures Valentine and Shosho entwined in the moments before their kiss with the caption:

"Kiss me," she said, very softly. "I like you."

Against Dupont's directorial wishes, those precious few frames ultimately landed on the cutting room floor. Even then, censors in the United States, Canada, and Australia cut scenes showing "Wilmot fondling the arms of Chinese girl," "Shosho wiggling her hips and stomach when doing the hula dance," and "Shosho reclining on a couch tempting Valentine." The world, it turned out, was not ready for interracial love. Not in 1929. Not ever, quite possibly.

Anna May with Marlene Dietrich and Leni Riefenstahl
at the Reimann Art School ball, Berlin, winter 1930.

6

CURIOUS BEASTS

K iss or no kiss, Anna May Wong had work to do. In no time, she was back in Berlin for her next film with Richard Eichberg. By all accounts, *Pavement Butterfly* did not have the most original screenplay. It was merely another thinly veiled variation of *Madama Butterfly*. This go-round she would be playing Mah, better known by her stage name Princess Butterfly, an exotic dancer down on her luck in an unjust world, spurned by her artist lover on account of a duplicitous man from her past. The exciting aspect of the movie was that it was set primarily in France, and the exterior shots would be filmed on location in Paris, Nice, Menton, and Monte Carlo.

Anna May would miss the 1929 Lunar New Year celebrations back home in Los Angeles's Chinatown, but the bizarre and rowdy merrymaking of Nice Carnival was a fitting substitute. The fete was in full swing by the time cast and crew arrived on the French Riviera. The boisterous parade through the Place Masséna was a sight to be seen. Grotesque effigies and floats—a bathing beauty riding a giant lobster, a brigade of "gaily dressed" Frenchmen holding puppets on their heads, and even King Carnival himself draped in a toga like Bacchus of the Côte d'Azur—rolled past the Casino Municipal as the crowds cheered them on. Eichberg seized the opportunity to capture footage of the festivities, which would later be spliced into the film.

What *Pavement Butterfly* lacked in story it made up for with striking cinematography. These were some of the strongest images Anna May had ever seen of herself on the screen. Her nighttime scenes on the steps to the casino in Monte Carlo, for example, had come off marvelously with the soft glow from the overhead lanterns and the nighttime mists rising from the nearby Mediterranean Sea. And who could forget the dramatic contrast of her lone figure, standing in a dimly lit corner of a deserted Paris street? The scene would soon make its way onto posters for the film.

This was her first time to the Riviera, land of languorous holidays and pleasure cruises, where Coco Chanel and the haute set put new meaning into the French maxim "profiter de la vie." Luckily, Anna May had arrived in style. Her costumes were richly designed, especially the sparkling evening dress and silver cape she wore at the casino, which gave her the air of an Erté design brought to life.

Every scene felt like something out of a dream—or, more specifically, one of the many make-believe visions she'd entertained while playacting in front of her mother's vanity as a little girl. Here she was, feeling as though she really were some kind of Princess Butterfly, a creature who had flown far away from home in order to transform herself into a thing of splendor and nobility. Though she would never forget her humble roots, Anna May Wong was a laundryman's daughter no more. The mountains of fan mail she'd been receiving since the knockout successes of *Song* and *Piccadilly* were proof enough.

Throughout the two months Anna May worked on *Pavement Butterfly*, another enterprise was steadily taking shape. The idea of making her debut on the legitimate stage, as the old-timers and critics were wont to refer to live theater, had been kicking around in her head for almost as long as she'd been on the screen. On a previous trip to New York, she had met with theater producer Gilbert Miller to discuss her prospects for making her stage debut under his management, but their conference failed to result in anything definitive. In Germany, she was courted by the famed Austrian theater director Max Reinhardt to play a part in the play *Artisten* but declined out of a desire to stick to film for the time being.

With all the hullabaloo around *Piccadilly*, even those predisposed to sneer at the cinema began to take notice of the Chinese movie star causing everyone in London to lose their minds. She had produced solid work on British soil and had the box office receipts to attest to the fact that she was more than just an overhyped Hollywood face.

Producer and director Basil Dean, whose name was both feared and respected in the London theater world, soon came calling. For his next show, he intended to put on the first English production of *The Circle of Chalk*, a Chinese play dating back to the Yuan dynasty. The poet Klabund had translated it into German several years prior. While he was at it, he took it upon himself to refashion the Chinese morality play—a King Solomon–esque allegory about two rival women fighting over a baby each claims is theirs—into a tale of star-crossed lovers. This generated a tried-and-true romantic theme more appealing to Western audiences, and the eminent Max Reinhardt staged the play in Berlin in 1925 to great acclaim. Now that James Laver had translated the German version into English, the play was ready for its debut across the channel.

Dean wanted Anna May to play the lead. Chang-hi-tang is a young woman of noble birth sold into prostitution (why, of course, another prostitute!) after her family's fortunes take a turn for the worst. She meets a young man whom she falls in love with at first sight, but before her would-be suitor can buy her out of bondage, the wealthy Ma Chun-shing purchases Hi-tang to be his second wife. Thus proceeds a woe-filled drama of murder, entrapment, and hidden identities.

The plot was complicated, yes, but with all those twists and turns, no one could say it was boring. Besides, the chance for Anna May to make her legitimate theater debut while starring in a Basil Dean production on London's West End was almost too good to be true. Through a series of long-distance telephone calls, Anna May hammered out the terms of her engagement and negotiated a generous salary the likes of which the West End had never seen before. As soon as her work on *Pavement Butterfly* wrapped, she was on her merry way to London to begin rehearsals for *The Circle of Chalk*.

A cast of West End regulars had been assembled, including a young, up-and-coming thespian named Laurence Olivier. All of the actors, aside from Anna May and Rose Quong, a Chinese Australian actress selected to play the treacherous first wife, would assume their roles in yellowface. As in America, the practice went unquestioned as it was de rigueur for the day. Where would they find enough qualified Chinese actors to speak in the Queen's English, anyway?

Anna May had only a couple weeks to learn her lines for what would effectively be her first speaking role. The advent of sound films—or "talkies," as everyone was calling them—had been gaining traction ever since Al Jolson's song-and-dance numbers in 1927's *The Jazz Singer* shocked and thrilled moviegoers on both sides of the Atlantic. However, sound technology was still cumbersome and difficult to adapt to the current mode of filmmaking. Up until now, all of Anna May's films had been silent, and—unlike on a studio soundstage—in the theater there were no cuts or retakes in front of a live audience. She had done her best to learn her lines in time, retyping them wholesale on her typewriter until she memorized them, a technique she had often employed with movie scripts.

The Circle of Chalk opened at the New Theatre on March 14, 1929. That night Anna May's dressing room was filled with so many bouquets, it looked like a florist shop. Following the performance, Lord and Lady de Walden threw her a party at their ritzy home in Belgrave Square. Twelve hundred guests attended and the party didn't break up until 5 a.m. Princess Beatrice, King George V's aunt, came to the theater on another evening to personally congratulate Anna May on her performance.

London's theater critics, however, proved they were not as easily charmed. They complained the play, like Basil Dean's previous efforts, was "ever so much too long," which by the end had the effect of reducing the audience to "a state of collapse." The opulent sets and costumes were stunning, done up in colors "as rich and bright as a set of old prints," but Dean's penchant for the extravagant got the better of him. "There is a lack of austerity in his vision," one critic commented. Unfortunately for Anna May, their remarks did not end there.

For a play with significant stretches of dialogue presented in verse, not enough attention had been paid to the delivery of speeches, several ventured. Of course, it was universally agreed that Anna May Wong was a pleasure to behold. She was "a dainty personality, one of those sweet things that one adores in porcelain or on vellum" whose movements onstage were "exquisitely graceful."

"To watch her," the *Tatler*'s critic wrote, "is a fascinating experience and something of an enigma." But she failed to modulate and emote through her voice, the critics pointed out, and played the "long-suffering heroine" "somewhat monotonously."

The most offensive aspect of her performance, according to these London observers, was the vexing realization that Anna May Wong, an American, spoke not in the mild, muted tones they ascribed to a Chinese courtesan but with an abrasive American nasality more befitting of Broadway than the West End.

"It comes as a shock to one—a shock from which one never recovers—to listen to a harsh nasal twang emitted from a figure of ancient China—which Columbus surely never could have heard, or he would have declined to discover America," wrote the *Bystander*. "No wonder—if this is the average film star's voice—that the talkie pictures from U.S.A. are an offence to the ear!"

The *Graphic* was no kinder: "Speaking with an American accent that is fluent without being agreeable, she betrays no sign of understanding what a lovely thing a single word can be. Her Chinese cast of countenance is insufficient compensation for this."

"Her speech is tinged with Hollywood accents," complained the *Sketch*. "An English actress—say, Miss Valerie Taylor—would have made much more of the part, and the Chinese racial characteristics were far more evident in Miss Rose Quong's impersonation of the wicked wife than in Miss Wong's portrayal of the younger one who had all sympathy with her."

And, as if the *Graphic* hadn't gotten its point across the first time, the next issue's theater guide contained this zinger: "With Anna May Wong talking so American that Anna May Twang might be an apter name."

Of all the things to find fault with! Anna May was used to encountering people who assumed she didn't speak English at all. It had sometimes been funny to watch their faces fall when she opened her mouth and flawless English came out. But this was something else entirely. The West End critics had gone to town on her . . . for what? Speaking like an American? And yet their same publications had lavished her with blurbs and profiles and full-page photo spreads in the weeks and months leading up to her stage debut. Days after the show opened, she graced the cover of the *Tatler.* They knew her popularity would help sell their papers like hotcakes.

Would they have dared to air the same grievances about Louise Brooks or Colleen Moore if one of them, with their dark bobs and Dutch boy bangs, had assumed the role of Hi-tang instead? Those Hollywood "It" girls were as fluent in "flapperese" as she was. Maybe the English simply had a bad case of China Doll syndrome. They delighted in gazing upon Anna May Wong's "enigmatic" veneer, but once the woman inside spoke, her voice rang out like a gong, shattering the illusion that she might really be made of porcelain. The thing is, dolls are never wanted for their voices, much less their souls.

The Circle of Chalk ran for only five weeks. The bad reviews were gutting. Somehow this stung more than previous flops in her career. The way English critics attacked Anna May's Americanness, a designation that felt precarious at best when she was home in the States, was disorienting but also hurtful. They called into question the legitimacy of her Chinese heritage. According to them, her Chinese looks were a mirage of sorts, because she sure didn't sound Chinese. Perplexing, really. For what is a Chinese person supposed to sound like?

Not long after the show closed, Basil Dean and beloved English actor Sir Gerald du Maurier hosted a luncheon at the Savoy Hotel, where Anna May was called upon to say a few words. She expressed her frustrations with the critics finally, "quite gently and charmingly" so, and all that they had said about her "terr-bul Amurrican accent."

As with most disappointments in her life, Anna May had learned to swallow back her tears and keep moving. Wong Sam Sing had taught her that. So had Douglas Fairbanks and his meticulous collection of negative reviews.

She was determined to take her detractors' comments in stride. Their preference for the soft, lilting tones of British English was duly noted. She intended to make the transition to talkies, she explained over lunch. In fact, she had already invested a hundred guineas in elocution lessons. If she could learn to speak German in a matter of weeks, surely she could put in a few hours to acquire an English accent. Even so, she couldn't resist making light of the whole affair.

"Now I will speak in a language you cannot criticize," Anna May said before bursting forth in several lines of Cantonese. The dining room resounded with applause as she returned to her seat.

However, one of the reporters present couldn't help but retort in the following week's edition of the *Bystander* that Anna May Wong had "achieved a curious distinction in the annals of the British stage." He continued, "She is the only leading lady who started to take lessons in acting a week after her play was produced."

Four months later, when the news of her sour treatment reached Los Angeles, Anna May's hometown paper proudly stuck up for one of its own. Apparently, the report surmised, "Londoners liked the Chinese plot, the Chinese music and the Chinese setting, but declared that the Broadway accent to the star's Chinese did not fit into the production."

With Anna May's disappointing theatrical interlude in the rearview mirror, things had shifted back into perspective. The demand for all things Anna May Wong had reached a fever pitch in England. Any of her films that UK movie theaters could get their hands on, including many of the B movies that had spurred her to leave Hollywood in the first place, were hastily released. Newspaper ads enticed English moviegoers to catch a glimpse of the "well-known delineator of Oriental roles" in showings of *The Crimson City, The Devil Dancer, Mr. Wu,* and *Across to Singapore* up and down the British Isles.

Meanwhile, Anna May had been enjoying the success her leading roles had finally earned her. What it came down to was respect. She'd always known that she could rise to the occasion if given half a chance. Hollywood painstakingly groomed, pampered, and coached plenty of other actresses of lesser talents in order to mount their leading-lady moment in the movies. So why not her? Well, they were white (Dolores Costello, Loretta Young, Estelle Taylor) or close enough (Dolores del Rio, Lupe Velez, Merle Oberon). She, on the other hand, despite her flapper persona—would not—could not ever be white. Nor did she want to be.

In Europe, nobody cared about one's "race"—or at least they pretended not to. This obsession with the color of one's skin was a uniquely American dilemma. Europeans who asked Anna May and her compatriots abroad to explain it to them often left such conversations feeling more puzzled than when they started.

"I like the English people; they are kind and courteous," Anna May told a reporter who called on her at her Park Lane apartment. She relished her time in England, for it was "the only country I have visited to which I have felt a desire to return." Her life there was no longer constrained by the racial codes of American society, which silently but forcefully dictated what station one could assume in life, how one was spoken to and must speak to others, where one could dine and with whom, and so on.

In London, Anna May did what she wanted and went wherever she pleased. She lunched at the Ivy, the West End café patronized by actors, politicians, and the who's who of London. On occasion she caught up with old friend Edward Knoblock, the English playwright who had worked on *The Thief of Bagdad*, and asked for his sage advice. Her visit to the Law Courts with a barrister friend apparently caused a minor commotion. Gazing upon a group of bewigged High Court judges, she declared, "Aren't they cute?"

English men were not shy about expressing a romantic interest in her. Although social ostracism often impeded interracial relationships, there were no laws prohibiting such unions in Britain. "For many months," Anna May later admitted, "I did not buy myself a single meal." In addition to eating well, she attended as many plays and musical revues as her schedule would allow.

On one particular outing, the brilliant composer and bachelor Constant Lambert accompanied her to the opening night of Puccini's *Turandot* at the Royal Opera in Covent Garden. Anna May turned quite a few heads in her stunning brocade mandarin coat in vermilion and gold, paired with a matching pink brocade dress and "pretty pink trousers" underneath. Close observers silently noted her male companion. Constant had been not so secretly obsessed with Anna May since he saw her in *The Thief of Bagdad* years before, inspiring him to pen a series of compositions that set Tang dynasty poet Li Po's poems to music. Her exotic luster seemed to magnify his romantic vision of the Orient, and friends recalled how he often drank Chinese wine that tasted rather like "embalming fluid" in her honor. Constant dedicated *Eight Poems of Li-Po* to Anna May before he had ever met her, so when she arrived in London and made her theatrical debut, he found his way backstage posthaste to meet his muse. It was whispered he had fallen head over heels for her, that he had even proposed marriage. So when he was seen escorting Anna May around town, the rumor mill had all the proof it needed.

Constant Lambert certainly wasn't the only victim of Anna May's charms. "When I was in Europe," Herb Howe wrote in the pages of *New Movie*, "the name of Anna May Wong was a society feature. . . . And, of course, there were the attendant stories of princes and even kings being madly in love with her."

She was also becoming something of a local fashion icon. Her habit of dress always exhibited some element of the Orient, whether subtle or dramatic. The hunger for Chinese fashions surged correspondingly. Anna May was only too happy to oblige the craze she had inspired. She modeled Chinese shawls "embroidered with exotic flowers in brilliant tango shades" and smoking suits in "duck's-egg blue" crêpe de chine for Debenham and Freebody in the pages of the *Graphic*.

The city's gardens were another frequent attraction for the film star. She could oft be spotted riding a horse through Hyde Park in black pantaloons and one of her many silk cheongsams. The photographers loved her for these extravagances because they made for such fine pictures.

When the incessant whir of fame became too much, Anna May decamped to the English countryside. "What I like about English country life," she told a reporter, "is its restful sanity." She was all too happy to accept an invitation from friend Eddy Sackville-West, a well-to-do writer associated with the Bright Young Things. Knole, his family's fifteenth-century estate with its idyllic grounds in Sevenoaks—the same sprawling estate Virginia Woolf would later make famous in her book *Orlando*—was just the place to quiet her nerves. She returned the favor by hiring a private chef and hosting a Chinese feast in one of the estate's many vaunted chambers.

Anna May loved the quaint charm of England and its centuries-long traditions, but that same quality disposed the country to falling behind the times in other aspects. English women ages twenty-one to twenty-nine had only recently won the franchise and were about to cast their first votes in what was being called the "flapper election" on May 30, 1929. As a twenty-four-year-old reformed flapper, Anna May intended to celebrate the momentous occasion like Londoners: out in the streets by the thousands, dancing at hotel parties and dinner shows, crowding around makeshift screens in Trafalgar Square, waiting anxiously for the polling results to come in.

Her first stop was a party thrown by friends from the theater world, where the guests of honor were a curious-looking American man with a shock of white hair that shone like the regal plumage of a whooping crane, and his petite wife, an arresting Russian woman with eyes the size of saucers. Together, they were Carl Van Vechten and Fania Marinoff of New York City. Anna May had met them only a few days before at Kitty Williams's tea. The Van Vechtens had arrived in London in mid-May and were on a holiday tour of never-ending cocktail parties, financed primarily by Carl's spate of best-selling novels.

It was no secret that Carlo, as all his intimate friends called him, was an absolute lush, but he was the sharp-witted, humorous kind. Anna May got on with him and Fania right away. His reputation as patron saint of the Harlem Renaissance preceded him. He was the man who had written to Alfred A. Knopf and told the esteemed publisher that he simply had to publish Langston Hughes, Zora Neale Hurston, and a long list of African American writers and poets. Their manuscripts might never have seen the light of day if it weren't for his vision, but there were some in Harlem who felt Van Vechten hogged all the credit for the artists he claimed as his "discoveries."

Van Vechten was a polarizing figure, to say the least. His 1926 novel *N——Heaven* put a spotlight on Harlem and introduced white Americans to the hopes and struggles of the "New Negro." Whether one welcomed his effusive love of Black folks or despised it, his influence on Black artists and their reception among the greater American public was undeniable. More important, unlike most white

Americans, he had no qualms about entertaining mixed company; he was a pioneer in that sense. His and Marinoff's New York parties were legendary, and not merely because they allowed Blacks and whites to mingle freely.

Tonight's event was no exception. Interesting personalities of all stripes and colors gabbed their way around the room. In one corner, English pianist Harriet Cohen played a tune while West Indian cabaret star Leslie Hutchinson sang. Among the many jubilant faces was another well-known figure in London. The man was hard to miss with his ebony skin and six-foot-three athlete's build. He had a generous smile that instantly put people at ease and a deep, resonant voice that cut through the chatter like the prow of a sailboat gliding through choppy waters.

Paul Robeson was striking in his beauty. The Van Vechtens, who were two of Robeson's earliest champions, no doubt made the introduction to Anna May, their newest friend in their eclectic set. The all-American athlete scholar from Princeton, New Jersey, who had abandoned a career in law for one on the stage, was coming off a triumphant ten-month run in the British production of *Show Boat*. Although his role as Joe, a dockworker on the banks of the Mississippi, was minimal, his reprisal of the tune "Ol' Man River" throughout the show won audiences over. English theatergoers were astounded by Robeson. He was the son of a formerly enslaved man, a human link to America's barbaric past. So when he sang "Ol' Man River" or any of the Black spirituals he grew up performing in his father's church, there was a sorrow and solemnity in his voice that brought people to tears.

Paul, like Anna May, knew what it was like to be typecast and to nonetheless say yes to such stereotypical roles for the small push forward they might engender. They were both actors of color, which bonded them in a certain respect, as they would soon discover.

If Anna May Wong was the China doll and by turns the dragon lady, then Paul Robeson was the magical Negro of legend, exceptional in every way. This trope may not have always expressed itself through his theatrical roles, but for the first half of his life as Paul Robeson the man, he was looked upon by an adoring public as a marvel. He possessed a preternatural poise and charm: when people first met Robeson, his cool self-assuredness put them instantly at ease. He was doing things and going places that no Black man had ever gone before. And his success—not only as an actor on the stage and soon to be in films, but also as an athlete, a scholar, a lawyer, and a concert artist—belied the herculean efforts and resolve that got him there.

As his biographer, Martin Duberman, would later write: "To the white world in general, Robeson seemed a magnetic, civilized, and gifted man who had relied on talent rather than belligerence to 'rise above his circumstances.'" Here was an example that could be held up as validation and allow whites to "persist in the comfortable illusion that his career proved the way was indeed open to those with sufficient pluck and aptitude, regardless of race—that the 'system' worked."

With sufficient pluck and aptitude, Robeson had overcome countless blows to his body and his dignity. For one thing, Jim Crow attitudes prevailed in his hometown of Princeton, New Jersey, even though it was squarely in the North. One day while walking home with a friend, a gang of white kids followed close behind him, chanting, "N——! N——! N——!" Swap the racial slur and the story recalls a nearly identical incident from Anna May's childhood.

At Rutgers College, where he was the third Black student to matriculate in the entire history of the institution, seventeen-year-old Paul was beaten within an inch of his life when he tried out for the all-white football team. He limped off the field that day with a broken nose, a sprained shoulder, and other assorted wounds that required ten days in bed to recover from.

With sufficient pluck and aptitude, Paul defied the odds, graduating valedictorian of his class and giving the commencement day speech to great applause, all while suffering the humiliations of segregation. For instance, most of the clubs and societies he belonged to barred him from traveling with them or excluded him from social events; at one college dance, he watched from a balcony as his classmates enjoyed themselves on the ballroom floor below.

With sufficient pluck and aptitude, he continued to law school at Columbia University and moved to Harlem, where he would meet his future wife, Eslanda Cardozo Goode. At Essie's urging, he nurtured his acting and singing career on the side, taking roles in landmark shows like *Shuffle Along* and *Taboo* and occasionally giving private concerts to supplement their income. After he earned his law degree, Robeson was hired by the law firm Stotesbury and Miner, but his time there was short. As the only Black lawyer at the firm, his presence was met initially with unpleasantries and silent microaggressions, then head-on. The day a stenographer refused to take dictation from him, stating, "I never take dictation from a n———," was the day he realized he would never be able to progress, let alone excel, in the legal field.

Paul turned to the stage out of exasperation. The life of a performer, ironically, offered a more practical, less restricted pathway forward. If you entertained white folks with a little song and dance, they tended not to mind the color of your skin so much, at least for as long as you kept them laughing.

His first notable role came in *All God's Chillun Got Wings*, a new play by Eugene O'Neill about an interracial relationship between a Black man named Jim and a white woman named Ella. The mere idea of a Black actor—rather than a white actor in blackface—playing opposite a white actress who would kiss her costar's hand in the course of the play, generated a massive controversy. The mob to protect white purity responded with intimidation of all kinds, including a bomb threat on the Provincetown Playhouse in Greenwich Village.

All God's Chillun opened in the spring of 1924, and despite all the hubbub, the experimental play was received favorably by the average New York theatergoer. With sufficient pluck and aptitude, Paul quietly endured the threats of violence, the patronizing reviews from white critics, and the ones from Black critics accusing him of pandering to white stereotypes of Blacks. In spite of everything, his back-to-back runs at the Provincetown Playhouse, first in *The Emperor Jones*, and then *All God's Chillun*, propelled him into a new stratum of celebrity.

Robeson was now a known entity in the theater world, but his existential woes remained. While he was performing in Greenwich Village every night, the only places in Manhattan where he could sit down for a meal on account of his color were at Penn Station or up in Harlem, a long train ride away. So, yes, sufficient pluck and aptitude and a whole lot more got Paul Robeson through to the other side of success. By the summer of 1925, he was off to open the English production of *The Emperor Jones* in London.

Like Anna May, Paul found English society quite welcoming. Everyone wanted to meet the young, talented, larger-than-life African American performer who'd shaken up New York's theater scene. The Robesons went from one dinner to the next, making new friends and alliances as they circulated about London. To Essie's annoyance her husband was never lacking in attention from the opposite sex; women swooned over Paul. Still, the Robesons got on swimmingly in their new surroundings. Paul continued to garner roles in West End productions and his salary rose correspondingly, allowing them to settle into a late-Victorian house up on Carlton Hill in St. John's Wood that came furnished with everything they needed: silver, linen, and servants. There were few reasons to travel back to the States, other than for a few months' concert tour, and their years in London ticked by.

It was a relief to work and live in a country where one's race was not seen as an impediment and where one could move about freely among different types of people. Maybe this is what other Americans meant when they waxed poetic about their holy freedoms. But to say that a person of color was not at all aware of their race in Europe was a stretch. The European public's positive reception of American entertainers like Paul Robeson, Josephine Baker, and Anna May Wong was merely the flip side of the coin. Where Americans saw uppity and inferior social climbers who refused to stay in their places, Europeans saw rare creatures of beauty, like a white tiger behind bars at the Berlin Zoo. They were novelties, too strange—too unfamiliar—to be scorned.

But there were perks to being a novelty. It usually meant you were in demand and sailed to the top of the guest list. By the end of election night 1929, Anna May had made her way from the party with Robeson and others to the most exclusive event in town: Mr. Selfridge's Election Party. "Everyone who is anyone in London society will attend," the *Sketch* trumpeted. Indeed, more than 2,000 hapless B-listers found themselves relegated to the waiting list.

For the occasion, Mr. Harry Gordon Selfridge, the self-made American businessman who brought the department store to Britain's high street, closed off an entire floor of his flagship Selfridges store on Oxford Street. Instead of the regular clientele, H. G. Wells, Princess Ingrid of Sweden, Elinor Glyn, and enough lords and ladies to fill a dozen manor houses lined the shop halls, guzzling bottomless champagne and stuffing themselves with hors d'oeuvres. The Van Vechtens also counted themselves among the privileged few.

Carl recorded the night in his daybooks: "On to the . . . election party on the top floor of Selfridge's store, the most marvelous party I have ever seen, with the crowd in the street below." While Anna May and the luminaries upstairs were busy partying, ordinary Londoners crammed into the street outside to watch the election results projected on Selfridges' facade. The woman of the hour may have been Miss 1929, but Anna May Wong was following hot on her heels.

In mid-May, friend and creative collaborator Grace Wilcox traveled to England to write a play for Anna May and assist with details related to the Chinese atmosphere of the potential theatrical work. But no sooner did Grace arrive in London than she received news of her husband's sudden death. It was decided that Lulu, who had accompanied Anna May on her sojourn for more than a year now, would make the long journey back to Los Angeles with the grieving Grace Wilcox so that she could attend to her husband's funeral rites.

As the full bloom of summer 1929 approached, Anna May became restless. Alone and with no immediate projects to occupy her time, her normal "work hard, play hard" routine felt off-kilter. She had her fun orchestrating mahjong matches at a party thrown by French impresario André Charlot. News of her "Gambling Den" was faithfully reprinted in the society pages. But when every night is a party, one night tends to bleed into the next until your week is just one long, frivolous soirée.

Believe it or not, Anna May much preferred curling up at home in Park Lane with a novel by Somerset Maugham or Donn Byrne. She had been away from home for more than a year now, and the touch of homesickness was beginning to wear on her. This wasn't the first time she had experienced the lows that sometimes come with fame. When Anna May had completed work on *Piccadilly* in the fall of 1928, she was in a terrible state about a romantic relationship gone wrong and checked herself into the Godden Green sanatorium in Kent to recover from a "nervous breakdown."

To break out of her funk during this idle period, Anna May flew to Paris. It was the first stop on her way back to Berlin to see whether she'd been assigned to her next film at UFA. A reporter from the French movie magazine *Pour Vous* happened upon the actress one morning as she strolled through the Tuileries Garden. He didn't recognize her at first. Her long, self-assured strides down the gravel path were like those of any American woman; there was nothing about her elegant figure that suggested the aura of a Chinese girl. "She was a film actress like a hundred others. That is all."

The crestfallen reporter reasoned that "her life with the Anglo-Saxons had completely de-ethnicized this tall girl with nearly white skin and that there was nothing left in her of that mystery we always imagine we glimpse among the yellow race." Then suddenly his eyes fell upon her ungloved hand and his disappointment vanished at the sight of her unusually long nails, lacquered and filed to a fine point. "I rediscovered the mystery, the smile of the distant East and that slight anguish that we always experience in the presence of beings we do not understand."

Anna May jauntily agreed to do an interview with him as long as he didn't mind accompanying her to the Louvre, where she was headed. She could tell him all about her origin story on the way.

Always generous with reporters, she repeated the tale of her unlikely rise from laundryman's daughter to international film star as they walked down the Grande Allée, past seventeenth-century fountains and perfectly manicured beds of flowers. The trees of the Grand Couvert section provided some temporary shade, cooling the pair as they walked, but when Anna May brought her life's story up to the present, she faltered.

She mentioned the thrilling work she'd done with E. A. Dupont on *Piccadilly*, which she hoped would be released in France soon, and then admitted, "I don't know what to do next. Maybe shoot a big movie in Germany." In a heartbeat, she returned to the charming, poised film star. "I can't tell you anything about it. Shhhh . . ."

In the mood to elaborate, she continued: "These are the external events of my life. I see that French journalists are not as intrusive as their American colleagues. You haven't asked me yet if I've had any love affairs, how they ended, if it was me or the partner who broke it off, the names of my lovers, their profession, their residence, their hair color and their favorite dessert!

"This is what pleases me so much in France and in England. The old ladies seem to claim that good manners have disappeared (they must have disappeared with the roses in their cheeks and their real teeth) but everywhere I go, here and on the other side of the Channel, I feel calm, and am well received; I'm not pushed around, I cease to feel like some curious beast. I am no more extraordinary than you or this passer-by, cher Monsieur. I have yellow skin and slanted eyes and if my soul is not like yours, what can I do? Is it my fault?"

Anna May smiled and added, "Maybe I'm not quite Chinese anymore and not yet fully European. It might be a drama, you know! The two halves of my soul fighting it out like cat and dog: 'For East is East and West is West. And never the twain shall meet.'"

By this time they had made it to the second floor of the Louvre and were standing in front of a painting by Camille Corot. Anna May fell silent as she looked upon *The Road to Sevres* and its portrait of rural French life: a man on a mule and a woman on foot traveling separately down a country road as wisps of clouds float above. This was her second viewing, as she'd visited only a few days before. The painting was miraculous, she remarked, and she wanted to commit every brushstroke to memory so that she could recall the image whenever she was unhappy.

She drank in the scene with a profound, unwavering gaze, and when she was sated, they made the rest of their way through the Louvre without speaking. Anna May punctured the silence as they exited: "It's Corot who helped me understand the French. He opened a big door for me."

Outside in the Tuileries again, Anna May bounded happily over to a small herd of goats harnessed to miniature carriages, one of the park's attractions for children. She lovingly petted the goats, then plucked the rose pinned to her dress collar and offered it to her new friends, who grazed it hungrily. And just like that, the brooding young woman of only a few moments before vanished.

———

Anna May arrived in Berlin the second week of July 1929 to begin work on what she believed would be her next film toward her joint contract with BIP and UFA. The papers reported her "hard at work filming in Germany," but in actuality the two-studio coproduction had not yet decided on a definite project for her. There were discussions about her next picture being a talkie, but UFA was still scrambling to assemble the appropriate studio space and equipment. Meanwhile, Warner Bros. in the United States had been refining their sound recording process since 1927. European studios had only just caught up to their American cousins in the art of producing silent films. But now it was back to the drawing board. If they wanted to keep up, they'd have to join the race to produce world-class talkies.

Anna May went to a few plays here and there and kept up with her Berlin network but she was beginning to grow impatient. She was not one to remain idle. Weeks of inaction had stretched into months. By the end of September, UFA and BIP had finally reached a decision. She would film her first talkie in England. Brightening as a result of this development, Anna May wrote to her new friend Carl Van Vechten, who had since returned to New York.

September 26th, 1929

Dear Carl Van Vechten:

What a shame it would be if the traffic got airy, one would never get nice notes from people as it is now. Thanks for yours.

I was most frightfully sorry you weren't able to get over this way and give the Berliners a treat. A great many friends have been here and hello and goodbye. Was a continuous performance by me, but it's been much fun and I was having a holiday on salary so I've just been having a glorious time.

After changing their minds a few times, British International Pictures finally decided we would make our new talkie film in England's Hollywood Elstree.

So all I've accomplished since I saw you, is speaking German like nobody's business as I have to speak both German and English in the new film. It's been most interesting to master what formerly seemed like an impossibility. But we sometimes even surprise ourselves at what we can do.

How's the new novel coming along? I am looking forward to it with much interest.

I hope the most important thing is as it should be, that you are well and happy.

Please give Mrs. Van Vechten my kindest regards and let's see you both all of a sudden if not sooner.

Ginger snaps to you.

Ever sincerely,
Anna May Wong

Anna May arrived in England in mid-October with a bounce in her step. Within a few weeks she was back on set at Elstree with director Richard Eichberg, who'd signed a deal to make four "supers" for BIP. The first would be *The Flame of Love* (sometimes called *The Road to Dishonour*), yet another variation on the "Chinese dancer caught in a tragic love triangle" trope that stalked Anna May. The character's name was Haitang, and this time, the action would be set in Russia and the love interest was a Russian military officer named Boris Borissoff, played by British actor John Longden.

Mayhem ensues when Boris's superior, the Grand Duke, takes a shine to the lovely artist. For no man who falls in love with a Chinese songstress and dancer, whether her name is Shosho or Haitang, ever arrives at the happy ending he envisions. Haitang's cards were dealt: After her brother Wang Hu defends her honor by shooting the handsy Grand Duke in the arm, Haitang gives herself to the Grand Duke in order to save her brother from execution. She then commits suicide by poison and breathes her last in the arms of her bereft-but-still-living lover Boris, who arrives a moment too late.

While production on *The Flame of Love* progressed at Elstree, a Scottish paper publicized a recent controversy between Paul Robeson and the Savoy Hotel in London. Only one month prior Robeson had announced that he would take on the role of Othello in the Shakespeare play to much fanfare. Then something happened that made Paul consider whether the English were truly color-blind.

On the floor of Parliament, MP James Marley read aloud from a letter Paul had written to a friend: "Do you remember that we were talking one day not so long ago about the lack of prejudice against negroes in London? At that time I thought that there was little or none, but an experience my wife and I had recently has made me change my mind and to wonder unhappily whether or not things may become almost as bad for us here as they are in America."

During the incident in question, Paul and Essie arrived at the Savoy grill room to join a group of white English friends for "a drink and chat." The waiter, who recognized Robeson because he had served him on many previous occasions, told the couple that they were not allowed to enter the dining room. Confused, Paul assumed there must be some mistake. "I sent for the manager, who came and informed me that I could not enter the grill room or the dining-room because I was a negro, and the management did not permit negroes to enter the rooms any longer."

When his friends inside the restaurant found out what the commotion was all about, they came out and made their own appeals to various managers, to no avail. In outrage and solidarity with the Robesons, the entire party left. Savoy Hotel officials questioned by the press later denied that they enforced any such policy. "We have no recollection of the incident to which Mr. Robeson refers. He has dined at the hotel on many occasions, and the colour bar is certainly not applied here."

The following spring of 1930, Paul Robeson became the first Black actor to play Othello in a century. Though he had a fine Desdemona in the young English actress Peggy Ashcroft and a talented supporting cast, the production was troubled from the first by its own producers.

Paul was "wild with nerves" by the time the show opened at the Savoy Theatre on May 19—the theater connected to the same hotel that had denied him service months before.

Anna May, who had become a loyal friend during their time in London, sat prominently in the audience that evening. She went over to Essie Robeson's seat during breaks "to offer her moral support and to compliment her on her white satin gown." The performance was a resounding success, at least according to the audience, who summoned Paul back to the stage twenty times after the curtain fell. The critics were another matter.

That same evening after the play, Anna May attended a supper party on Buckingham Street with many of the British literati present, such as Evelyn Waugh and Nancy Mitford. Evelyn later wrote in his diary of that evening that Lord Redesdale commented, "A.M.W. like a brontosaurus." A legendary animal that also happened to be extinct, that's how peculiar the English baron found the Chinese American actress. When Waugh went to see the great *Othello* for himself, he noted the event in his diary with this entry: "Hopeless production but I like his great black booby face. It seemed to make all that silly stuff with the handkerchief quite convincing."

Conceivably, London's "colour bar" existed solely in the clandestine whispers between guests at exclusive social gatherings and in the private diaries of its denizens. Which is why its continuance was seldom confessed in public.

Only a couple weeks after the Robesons' incident at the Savoy Hotel in the fall of 1929, another news item would pierce a hole in England's supposed lack of colour bar. "When It's Wong to Kiss: Censor's Ban on New Film" ran the ill-advised headline. The British Board of Film Censors had made it their business to issue an edict on the occurrence of interracial romance in *The Flame of Love*. A kiss between Anna May and John Longden's characters had been written into the script. In the British censor's opinion, it was "unseemly for English eyes to watch a kiss between an English actor and an actress whose skin is not white." The Germans would keep the kiss in their version of the film, but the English had once again ruled it out.

"It's all absolute rot!" Longden complained to a reporter. He skewered the ban's illogical reasoning: "We are to have many love scenes. I have to sit at her feet, stroke her hand, and sing to her, but never am I permitted to kiss her, because she is Chinese and I am white. This seems absurd, in the circumstances, but those are my instructions."

In the end, Anna May wasn't much concerned with *The Flame of Love*'s kiss or lack thereof. This wasn't her first time at the rodeo. There was something else on her mind, so when a reporter asked her about the ban, she let it fly. "Once again, I have to die."

———

Back home in the United States, the stock market crashed on October 29, 1929. Black Tuesday came and went, the consequences of which still felt a world away to most Europeans. It was said that people were throwing themselves off buildings in New York. But in London and Paris and Berlin, for those of a certain insulated class, the party raged on.

Anna May returned to Berlin, the gender-bending capital of the world, sometime at the beginning of 1930. Here, nobody blinked at the sight of men draped in pearls dancing with one another in the hot, crowded ballrooms of Charlottenburg. In fact, the capital's bustling nightlife scene encouraged such encounters. Clubs like Clärchens Ballhaus furnished each table with a telephone so that guests could surreptitiously flirt with each other and arrange their rendezvous. Everywhere one looked, bodies were on display and love was for sale. Plenty of people came to spectate too. As Franz Hessel wrote in his flâneur's guidebook, all were welcome in this bohemian bastion, including those with more conservative tastes: "Visitors who like to dance with the opposite sex are also allowed into these mellow orgies."

The city was mad for costume balls, a trend that began in earnest in the mid-twenties and crested by the end of the decade. From mid-December to March, the calendars of the glamorous, the wealthy, and the wannabes were jammed with balls to celebrate the final thrust of carnival. For several months straight, thousands of Berliners attended these opulent, champagne-drenched bacchanals hosted by groups and institutions of all kinds: the Fashion Ball, Actors' Society Ball, Police Officers' Ball, Alpine Ball, etc. "While the German capital has no money to end housing misery, it will soon have the largest and most luxurious palace for festivities in the world," the *New York Times* reported.

As a member of this self-selecting crowd, Anna May attended the Reimann School of Art and Design's Gauklerfest, or Imposters' Ball—the party where high-society Berliners went to see and be seen. Along with her came Richard Eichberg and a coterie of UFA actors and directors. The grand Marble Hall of Berlin's Zoological Gardens was packed with revelers, many of them students who had designed their own carnivalesque costumes in checks and stripes. Unbeknownst to the evening's pleasure seekers, history was being made in a private room off the main dance floor. Two little-known German actresses were sidling up to Anna May Wong, the celebrity in the room, hoping to rub off some of her golden Hollywood sheen.

One was Leni Riefenstahl, an actress with a few films under her belt, mostly patriotic mountaineering adventures in the Swiss Alps meant to evoke a feeling of national pride in German audiences. Leni was the spitting image of Aryan beauty with her blue eyes and blond hair. She had previously attempted to bill herself as a dancer, but when that endeavor failed, she moved into film acting. Her wealthy lover and patron, Harry Sokal, had ponied up the money for this career change, likely with a bit of cajoling, and handily funded her first film role in Arnold Fanck's *The Holy Mountain*.

The other woman was Marlene Dietrich, whose reputation among Berliners was well established. She'd acted in nearly two dozen German silent films, including starring roles in *Café Elektric* and *I Kiss Your Hand, Madame*. What finally turned people's heads and got her the notoriety she always seemed to be craving was a little tune she sang with Margo Lion in the 1928 revue *It's in the Air,* written and produced by Marcellus Schiffer and Mischa Spoliansky.

Margo and Marlene, dressed in matching black dresses, danced together on stage as they sang the duet "My Best Girl Friend," a song about two female friends who know each other so well they seem to forget they have husbands.

Marlene had fastened bunches of violets to her and Margo's shoulders to give their outfits "a friendly touch of colour," as she put it in her memoir. In truth, the violet was the symbolic flower of "the girls." The revue was a smash hit and, thanks to that song, everyone in Berlin now knew Marlene Dietrich's name.

As Marlene, Leni, and Anna May circled each other at the Reimann ball, there was a feeling of electricity in the air, something more than the usual buzz of excitement that surrounds any big party. A young photographer named Alfred Eisenstaedt, who had recently quit his job selling buttons and belts to embark on a career as a photojournalist for the Associated Press, felt it too. This was a moment worthy of capturing on film. Why? He couldn't say as of yet, but he let his intuition guide the women in front of a gilded mirror.

Anna May stood in the center, tall and lean, wearing a sleeveless, sheer black dress, a single strand of pearls knotted below her neck, draping down to her waist, and a single flower affixed just so to the chignon at the back of her head. She had assumed the uniform of the prototypical flapper, her answer to the costume ball's assignment. Leni stood to her left in a long, shimmering dress that looked as though it were made of the most delicate chain mail. On her right, the intrepid Marlene was done up in a pirate outfit of her own making: a low-cut top with fluttering sleeves and black lace, double-breasted pants with a sash tied at the waist, a twisted rope necklace resting in her cleavage, bangles on either wrist, a feathered hat, and to complete the look, a dainty pipe hanging from her lips.

All three women looked directly into the camera as Eisenstaedt clicked the shutter close. Only one of them was truly famous—Anna

May Wong, the international sensation—while the other two "imposters" were merely playing at being somebodies, striking a pose for the infamy that awaited them. The photograph helped them in that regard; it quickly became the stuff of legend. People liked to talk. The picture invited all sorts of lurid conjecture. For three gorgeous women at a Berlin ball looked like trouble. Those knowing grins—their faces said it all. Had Marlene Dietrich, a known libertine who courted men and women, snared the Chinese American actress as her latest conquest? Was Leni also vying for Anna May's affections? The fantasy of all three enmeshed in a twisted ménage à trois was almost irresistible. Except that Marlene hated Leni (her judgment would later be proven right about the flailing actress), and Anna May had everything Marlene dreamed of one day usurping.

The party atmosphere seeped into the rest of the images Eisenstaedt made that night, as the girls soon reverted to cavorting with the other guests in the room. Richard Eichberg bounded into the frame at one point, hugging the two German actresses on either side of him. In another photo, Anna May laughingly placed Marlene's pipe back in her mouth. Eisenstaedt also caught Marlene, in a moment of repose, sitting next to her director, Josef von Sternberg. The diminutive genius stared absentmindedly into the distance with a cigarette perched between his fingers. Marlene and Jo were basking in the afterglow of having just completed their first film together, *The Blue Angel.*

Josef von Sternberg was Austrian by birth but American by pedigree, having grown up in the United States from the age of seven. Taking a page out of Erich von Stroheim's book, he'd added the "von" to his name when he began climbing the ladder in Hollywood, though he later denied it. Movie people liked to think they had aristocratic Europeans working in their ranks whose sophisticated tastes would elevate the commercial dross they regularly pumped out. After a number of fits and starts, von Sternberg found his footing in the business with a series of commercial successes, such as *The Docks of New York* and *The Last Command,* starring Emil Jannings.

In the summer of 1929, UFA production manager Erich Pommer and Karl Vollmöller negotiated a deal with von Sternberg to reunite with Jannings and return to Europe to direct Germany's first talkie. The story was based on the Heinrich Mann novel *Professor Unrat* and retitled *The Blue Angel*. An exhaustive search was held to cast Lola Lola, the female lead, but it wasn't until six weeks before principal photography was to begin that von Sternberg set eyes on her perfect embodiment: Marlene Dietrich. Or rather, Marlene Dietrich's legs. One look at them, so the story goes, and Jo was entranced.

At the same time that Anna May was in London filming *The Flame of Love* with Richard Eichberg, Marlene was spending long days with Jo on set at UFA's Neubabelsberg studios, shooting *The Blue Angel*. By day, Jo dictated Marlene's every move, word, and expression, often dismissing the entire cast and crew in order to coach her English pronunciation (the film was being shot simultaneously in English and German). At night, Marlene dominated "the little man" in the bedroom. Both Jo and Marlene were married, but this was Berlin at the close of the Golden Twenties. Sex with one's lover was as expected as sex with one's spouse. Even so, von Sternberg's American wife eventually got tired of her husband's extracurricular activities, which included making love to Marlene "on a tiger skin in a bedroom with a mirrored ceiling." Upon their return to the United States, she filed for divorce.

In late February, several weeks following the Reimann ball, Anna May attended the premiere for *Haitang*, the German title for *The Flame of Love*, at the Capitol am Zoo cinema. "It's amazing the skill with which Anna May Wong masters the German language," one observer commented in *Der Kinematograph*. It seems those shiftless summer months in Berlin "speaking German like nobody's business" had paid off.

A little more than a month later, Marlene attended a premiere of her own, the sold-out gala opening for *The Blue Angel* at UFA's Gloria-Palast. She wore a flouncy chiffon dress and full-length ermine coat, all in virginal white from head to toe. Lola Lola was a lewd and vulgar woman, but she, on the other hand, wanted the people to know that Marlene Dietrich was a class act—irrespective of any rumors they might have heard about her vast sexual appetite.

Jo was already back in Los Angeles, where he was still under contract to Paramount Pictures, formerly Famous Players-Lasky. As for Marlene, von Sternberg had urged Paramount to sign her and cultivate her as a rival to Greta Garbo, MGM's exotic Swedish import. Without yet knowing how *The Blue Angel* would fare with audiences, Paramount offered Marlene Dietrich a seven-year contract at $500 a week. She played hard to get and demurred several times, complaining that she did not want to leave her husband and young daughter behind— that if it turned out Hollywood was not for her, she would not want to be kept in bondage to fulfill a seven-year contract. Her husband, Rudolf Sieber, told her not to be stupid. In the end, she said yes.

As *The Blue Angel* played in the packed theater, Emil Jannings, who had made a career of playing once-great men reduced to positions of humiliation and disgrace, watched with eyes wide open as Marlene stole the spotlight away from *him*—the illustrious Emil Jannings, the greatest German actor of his generation!

Silence fell upon the entire theater after the final scene faded to black, followed by resounding applause. "Marlene! Marlene!" the people shouted. Her thirty-six pieces of luggage awaited on a truck parked outside the backstage door as she spoke to the audience; she was to leave for Hollywood that very night. Jannings joined Marlene on the stage but looked at her as if he could kill her. "I don't leave Berlin lightly," she said. "First, because Berlin is my home. Second, because Berlin is . . . Berlin. Though I shouldn't say it, I am a little afraid of Hollywood."

Marlene had nothing to fear in Hollywood. It was Germany where things were beginning to change. Berlin was the pinnacle of this zeitgeist, the place where welcoming the new and embracing a spirit of experimentation were paramount virtues. Yet Weimar culture was primarily a movement made up of artists and intellectuals, an elite and insulated class. While many were seduced by the ebullient glow of the Golden Twenties, many more looked upon what was going on in Berlin as a depraved freak show, a modern-day Sodom and Gomorrah that had brought about a diseased Germany. The common man was ailing, living on credit, never knowing where his next meal was coming from. In a few short years, a man named Adolf Hitler, chairman of the Nazi Party, would rise to power as chancellor of Germany (and Leni Riefenstahl, now his chosen film director, with him). For those who knew how to read the signs, the writing was on the wall. The Weimar Republic was on its last legs.

Such thoughts, however, must have been far from Anna May's mind. She bounced around Europe for the rest of spring 1930, making a personal appearance at *Haitang*'s opening in Budapest (though the film was later banned in Hungary for it's supposed "anti-monarchist" theme), then on to London for the British premiere. While there, she went to the theater, took up flying lessons, and made the rounds on the cocktail circuit.

In June, Anna May returned to Paris to film the French version of *The Flame of Love*, or *L'amour, maître des choses*. She hired a strict tutor who drilled her in the intricacies of the French language from morning till night. Ultimately, she performed the part of Haitang in three languages: French, English, and German. She'd yet to meet an American movie star who'd accomplished a similar feat with such sangfroid, thank you very much.

As the summer progressed, Anna May signed on to star in a Chinese operetta called *Tschun Tschi*, or *Springtime*, in Vienna. She received such a frenzied welcome there, the police were called to disperse the crowds that had gathered to see her. Friend and former costar Jameson Thomas remarked that "Anna May is the most popular stage star of years in that city." Still, she couldn't shake the unexplained feeling of foreboding that had come over her. After twenty-five performances, she ended her run in mid-September. She was preoccupied with a dream she'd had more than a year prior: "I dreamed that Grace

Wilcox, the writer, and I stood under a willow tree. . . . [And we] wept, but held no speech. . . . I interpreted the dream to mean my family was in danger."

But when she wired Grace, who was then in New York en route to London, everyone in the Wong clan was confirmed to be in good health. Then the news of Grace's husband's sudden death came, which seemed to account for the dream. For whatever reason, the image continued to haunt Anna May into the following year. She had been in Europe for two and half years. It was time, she realized, to return home—maybe not forever, but at least long enough to see if the winds in Hollywood had changed and, of course, to spend some quality time with the Wong clan, whom she missed dearly.

Anna May embarked on the RMS *Aquitania* at Southampton and sailed for New York at the beginning of October with only one trunk and a few bags; the rest of her belongings remained scattered across Europe in anticipation of her return. When she disembarked at the port in New York City, she had every intention of continuing on to Los Angeles via train, but as she made her way off the boat the theater producer Lee Ephraim flagged her over. He was carrying the manuscript for Edgar Wallace's play *On the Spot*, which had opened that spring in London with Charles Laughton and Gillian Lind. Anna May chanced to meet Wallace while she was still on that side of the Atlantic; she'd also gone to see the play and enjoyed it. Ephraim and Wallace wanted her to play Minn Lee, the Chinese mistress of a Chicago gangster and bootlegger, in the play's Broadway production. Tony Perrelli, the "bogus wop gang leader," would be performed by Crane Wilbur—the actor Anna May had grown up watching in the beloved Pearl White serial *The Perils of Pauline*. Dreams, she was reminded, sometimes do come true. Anna May signed the contract in the time it took the customs officers to finish going through her baggage.

She arrived in New York on a Saturday and began rehearsals for *On the Spot* on a Monday. The play opened on Broadway a mere two weeks later. In the audience that evening were her friends Carl Van

Vechten and Fania Marinoff, as well as the head of Paramount Pictures, Jesse L. Lasky. Reviews from the first night's performance were glowing. But Anna May would soon come to regret not having gone straight home from Europe.

A week and a half into the play's run, she received distressing news from Los Angeles. Her mother had been struck by a car while crossing the street in front of their home. She was in the hospital with serious, almost certainly fatal injuries. Two days later, major newspapers across the country carried the news: "Anna Wong's Mother Dies."

The mysterious omen in her bad dream with Grace Wilcox had portended two deaths, not one. Life had finally caught up to Anna May. It had caught up to them all—the flappers and boozers, the speculators and spendthrifts, the socialites and expatriates, the soldiers and revolutionaries, and, most of all, the hard-up working class.

"I've just been admitting it. . . . We're swine, filthy swine," David Westlake, the protagonist of Carl Van Vechten's recently published novel, *Parties*, declares in a rare moment of sobriety. The book caricatures a group of New York well-to-dos who drown their boredom with round after round of sidecars, highballs, and gin rickeys. Its publication neatly capped the booze-drenched twenties and was the last novel Van Vechten would ever write.

"We'll get drunker and drunker and drift about night clubs so drunk that we won't know where we are," Westlake says, reflecting on the aimless existence he and his ilk have surrendered to, "and then we'll go to Harlem and stay up all night and go to bed late to-morrow morning and wake up and begin it all over again."

The great Jazz Age party had passed its peak. The reckless good time had gone on too long, so long it was now the stuff of satire. Anna May Wong's European daydream ended the moment she set foot in Depression-era America. There, the Roaring Twenties had already been flushed down the drain—and the rest of the bathtub gin with it. The decadent decade was over. And Lee Gon Toy, her one earthly mother, was dead.

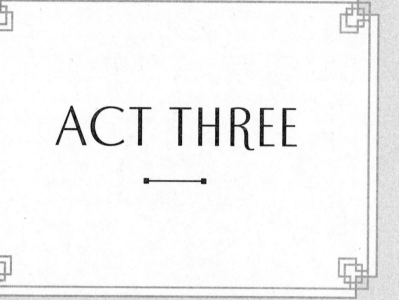

ACT THREE

A publicity shot from *Daughter of the Dragon*, 1931,
autographed by Anna May and signed "Orientally yours."

7

THE PRODIGAL DAUGHTER RETURNS

Los Angeles was plagued by a two-week-long heat wave in the run up to Halloween the fall of 1930. Ninety-degree highs lingered well into the first week of November. But the city's fever finally broke, with temperatures dipping back into the moderate seventies, just a day before Lee Gon Toy decided to do the most ordinary of things: cross the street in front of her home at 241 North Figueroa Street.

It happened there, on the sloping hill at the edge of Downtown Los Angeles where Sam Kee Laundry had stood for two decades. The same hallowed ground where the industrious Wong family had expanded in tandem with the city they inhabited, watching the mirage in the desert become a true, if sprawling, metropolis.

All the while, Lee Gon Toy toiled quietly in the background, helping out at the laundry, taking care of her husband and their seven children, dutifully performing the role of a devoted Chinese mother and wife. No matter that she'd been a child herself the first time she set eyes on Wong Sam Sing at age fifteen. Her own parents were a distant memory. After they returned to China, she never saw them again.

Anna May Wong was mindful of her mother's sacrifices. Indeed, it was observing her mother at her father's beck and call that partially led Anna May to steer clear of anything remotely resembling a life like her mother's. The feeling was mutual.

Lee Gon Toy struggled to make sense of her daughter's profession—and the money and fame that came with it. She didn't like that her daughter was constantly having her picture taken, her soul slowly drained out of her, and that her work took her to far-off places. She worried about her health and whether she was getting the right kind of sustenance to balance her qi. She worried about her safety, alone in the world among men. This concept of the independent woman was a bizarre and radical idea; surely it wouldn't last. When was her daughter going to quit this movie business and settle down?

At least, these are the thoughts one imagines must have run through Lee Gon Toy's mind in rare moments of solitude, if only someone had asked her.

We don't know what Lee Gon Toy was thinking, where she was headed, or whether she looked both ways before stepping out into the road she'd crossed thousands of times before without incident.

On the night of November 10, 1930, the dimly lit street was nearly pitch-black. Lee ventured midway into the street, but when a car suddenly appeared, barreling toward her, she jumped back. She successfully avoided one car only to step directly into the path of another. The second car struck Lee head-on with devastating force, leaving her broken and bloodied on the unforgiving asphalt with a basal skull fracture, shattered leg, and numerous internal injuries. The receiving doctor at the Georgia Street hospital held little hope for her survival.

The driver, Joseph Rodini, was not held by police. Within twenty-four hours a coroner's jury ruled the death accidental and exonerated Rodini. News reports did not disclose how fast his car was going at impact or what became of the first car. Instead, the coroner's jury determined the blame rested with the victim: "Mrs. Wong was negligent in crossing a poorly lighted street in the middle of the block."

The night of the incident Wong Sam Sing sent an urgent telegram to his daughter in New York City. Was the message waiting for Anna May Wong backstage in her dressing room at the Forrest Theatre, after she made her final bow at that evening's curtain call? Or did the news come in the middle of the night while she slept soundly in her hotel suite? However or wherever, the message was received. Her father told her to come home at once.

The irony of this moment in Anna May's life and career was not lost on the press, many of whom considered her a friend. She "had to go to Europe to find fame and fortune," and now that she'd returned triumphant, her acclaim had earned her a gig on Broadway, delaying her reunion with the Wong clan.

"Then the terrible news of her mother's death reached Anna May," Grace Kingsley wrote sorrowfully in her column for the *Los Angeles Times*. "Life certainly plays some hard, cynical tricks on us poor mortals."

Anna May faced an impossible dilemma. She must decide whether to return to Los Angeles for Lee Gon Toy's funeral rites—"It was unthinkable that a Chinese girl should be absent from the funeral of her mother"—or stay in New York and continue her nightly performances as Minn Lee in *On the Spot*. Traveling by train to and from L.A. would eat up two weeks' time. If she left now, less than two weeks into the show, the play might close, which would mean a great financial loss for its backers. However, if the producers wanted to recoup their money, they'd find a way to carry on. The same day her mother's accident made headlines, Jeanne Winters was announced as Anna May's understudy. The show would go on, with or without her.

There were no words to accurately convey the flood of grief and anguish that gripped Anna May as she considered what to do. Every ounce of her being told her to go and be with her family. Yet the mother who had borne her, raised her, and so cleverly placed the boy's cap on her head so that her father would finally smile upon her, was gone. Nothing she could do would bring her back.

The thought of having to abandon the thing she had worked so hard to get—recognition—was insult to the injury.

Lee Gon Toy did not pretend to understand her daughter's life, but had she still been there, selfless mother that she was, she would have recognized the path that Anna May must take.

Against the wishes of her family, Anna May Wong would remain on Broadway, performing night after night, her actor's mask skillfully concealing her broken heart. She found solace in the beliefs of Christian Science, "which looks upon death beautifully as but the passing through a door." The Wong family proceeded with the funeral for their dearly departed mother in Anna May's absence. Still, Wong Sam Sing could not resign himself to burying his late wife without the presence of his daughter Liu Tsong. The body would be placed in a vault and held there until she returned.

———————

Meanwhile, on Broadway, the great world kept spinning. Edgar Wallace, the prolific author behind *On the Spot*, was best known for his thrillers and detective novels. He'd turned to writing as a young man primarily as a means to support his flashy lifestyle, which was always just beyond his means, and the constant debts he racked up due to his enthusiasm for horse racing. Luckily for him, he had a knack for pulp. Once Wallace got going on a book, play, or short story, he stopped only for a smoke and a cup of tea. He wrote his books back-to-back, sometimes dictating a 60,000-word manuscript in the space of three days.

On the Spot was not his first foray into playwriting, but it was certainly his most successful. Based on a recent trip Wallace had made to Chicago, the play lampoons an Al Capone–esque gangster named Tony Perrelli, played by Crane Wilbur, and the seedy underworld he supposedly holds dominion over. For all the villainous treachery Perrelli is capable of—including betraying his own men to a rival gang— his downfall comes at the hands of a woman. When Perrelli's Chinese girlfriend, Minn Lee, turns up dead, the police pin him for her murder, even though in truth she died by suicide.

This rollicking picaresque of a play, scripted with the authentic flavor of "the gangster's grotesque jargon," was a sensation when it first opened in London in the spring of 1930. Trinculo in the *Tatler* called it "tremendously entertaining; one of those fact-is-stranger-than-fiction plays in which 'good theatre' is favourably matched with bad morals."

American audiences embraced the "comic unreality of the nouveau riche underworld" Wallace fashioned for the stage even more so. *On the Spot* titillated New York theatergoers, perhaps because they felt they were in on the joke: they'd experienced prohibition firsthand, along with the booze racketeers and all-night speakeasies that came with it. The subject hit a little too close to home for Chicago mayor Anton J. Cermak, however, when he learned the play was to open in his city. He threatened to take police action against the production if he found it was "injurious to Chicago's reputation" in any way. The manager wisely stripped all mentions of Chicago in advance of its run there.

The *New York Times* lauded Wallace's wicked sense of humor and regarded the play as "refreshingly amusing in the simple vein of footpad make-believe." The flush of success extended to Anna May as the play's leading lady, earning her praise in the *New York Times* and *Vogue*. *Harper's Bazaar* proffered her as one of the theater's exciting new talents, adding that her final scene in *On the Spot* may well have been "the best suicide known to minor tragedy."

Every night, as the play reached its climax, Anna May as Minn Lee would enact her own death with a literal knife to the heart. Gounod's "Ave Maria" was cued up to play on the gramophone as she lay lifeless on the stage. One night a stagehand accidentally put the wrong record on and "a selection of Negro melodies," likely something jazzy and up-tempo, played instead. Well, Anna May could hardly contain herself. As she recalled, "The audience saw my 'dead' body convulsed with most inopportune laughter."

On the Spot ran in New York for five months and a total of 167 performances. When it closed on March 1, 1931, Crane Wilbur, Anna May, and the rest of the cast and crew simply picked up and launched into a five-city road tour through Brooklyn, Boston, Pittsburgh, Chicago, and Philadelphia.

A continuous flow of praise and admiration was heaped upon Anna May as she traveled from city to city. Everybody loves a comeback kid, and she had proven to be just that. The media was quick to pounce on her underdog story and quicker still to lay blame at Hollywood's feet.

"[Anna May] went out every morning to glow and dazzle. . . . Now that she has become world famous, Hollywood tries to assure us that they knew her all the time," Harry Carr observed in his column for the *Los Angeles Times*. "But this is not true."

"Because Miss Wong could only be cast in a limited number of roles in this country, she went to Germany," Rosa Reilly of *Screenland* added to the chorus. "Once out of Hollywood, few come back. But Anna May *has* come back. She shows more outstanding dramatic talent than any one screen woman who has appeared on the New York stage. And it isn't luck. She prepared herself!"

There was talk of Anna May deserving a big fat contract if she consented to return to Hollywood. "The producers, after letting Anna May slip through their fingers . . . , are now wanting her screen services," Grace Kingsley snapped. "I hope they pay for them."

Various offers for Anna May to star on the screen were suddenly forthcoming. A famous English producer envisioned her featured in various Shakespearean roles, the first of which he suggested should be Ophelia in a film adaptation of *Hamlet*. Paramount wised up just in time to get an offer of their own in the ring while Anna May was considering her options. Negotiations ensued. At the end of March, she made her decision. She would sign a contract with Paramount and begin work on a new film as soon as her run in *On the Spot* finished.

Paramount announced the deal with nonchalance, simply stating that Anna May Wong had been added to the studio's roster along with Dolores del Rio and others. The "I told you so" crowd, on the other hand, was just revving up.

"Back in the old days Anna May Wong was frequently seen in the movies. Then came the fade out. Apparently the barons who control the pictures couldn't see Miss Wong any more," began a long tirade in the *Pasadena Post*.

"After becoming a sensation [in Europe] she became a small riot and had 'em all at her feet. Her triumph was complete. She returned to New York. The little motion picture actress they couldn't see scored an American success. Then the magnates, the bright boys who know a thing is good after the world has proclaimed it, broke their necks to get her name on a 'long-term contract.'"

All the hubbub, evidently, elicited Jesse L. Lasky, the cofounder of Paramount Studios, to say a few words about Anna May's recently inked deal. "In Miss Wong, we feel confident that we have obtained rare talent for the talking screen in which youthful beauty is combined with mature acting powers.

"Press and public have united in New York," he continued, "in proclaiming her exotic charm provided by a piquant face, fine figure, and fascinating personality."

The *Pasadena Post* wisecracked, "And all this, reader, Jesse has just discovered!"

By the time Anna May finally made it home to Los Angeles, it was June 1931. Her gamble had paid off, and now the winds of Hollywood were happily blowing in her favor. But she'd been gone for three long years. Within the Wong family, some bristled at the late return of the prodigal daughter.

Indeed, she went to work at Paramount on her next film right away. In lieu of returning to the old bungalow behind Sam Kee Laundry, she rented herself an apartment at the Castle Argyle, sometimes touted as "the finest address in Hollywood." She tried her best to make time to visit her father and siblings in between studio calls, but rehearsals regrettably kept her from attending her brother James's graduation ceremony at the University of Southern California. Now in his seventies, Wong Sam Sing had given up the laundry business, and

Anna May talked of buying a house where the whole family could live together. The Wong patriarch stubbornly declined to live under any roof but his own.

Unhappy with the jury's decision to absolve of fault the driver of the car that had hit Lee Gon Toy, the Wong family had sued Joseph Rodini earlier that year for $50,000 in damages. Seven months had passed since her mother's fatal accident. What could Anna May possibly say to assuage the grim decision she'd had to make between family and career. Her father would never understand, but she had her reasons. Lee Gon Toy had sacrificed for her husband and children. Anna May had sacrificed for her art.

There was no point in mincing words. Better to demonstrate her penitence through action, by paying her respects to the dead. At long last, Liu Tsong arrived at the little Los Angeles chapel where Lee Gon Toy's body had been waiting all these months. Inside, she kneeled quietly at her mother's side and wept.

For her first picture at Paramount, the studio settled on a feature called *Daughter of the Dragon*, based on a book by Sax Rohmer, the British pulp writer whose fertile imagination had invented the evil Dr. Fu Manchu. As a villain, Fu Manchu was the summation of the West's unspoken fears about the East: a Chinese man who was fluent in the modern conventions of Western civilization, knowledgeable "of science, past and present," and rich and powerful with "all the cruel cunning of an entire Eastern race." Rohmer dared to make such anxieties legible in one character and described him memorably in his first book as "tall, lean, and feline, high-shouldered, with a brow like Shakespeare and a face like Satan . . . the 'Yellow Peril' incarnate."

Anna May would play the starring role as Princess Ling Moy, a celebrated dancer who on the night of her last performance in London discovers that her father is none other than Fu Manchu. When "the 'Yellow Peril' incarnate" reappears from the dead after twenty years' absence, he enlists his long-lost daughter to spill blood for the House of Fu. He wants her to finish the job he began and kill off the remaining members of the Petrie family, who are supposedly responsible for the death of her mother and brother. Coincidentally, the Petries live right next door to her London home.

Daughter of the Dragon was certainly not a prestige film, but from Anna May's perspective, if Paramount was willing to back it in a big way, the picture stood the chance of becoming a commercial success. Which might also result in broader exposure and proof of her box-office potential. But even her triumphant return could not completely change the way Hollywood viewed her. In their eyes, she was an Oriental actress who was fit to play Oriental roles. Except, of course, when the producers wanted a white actress to depict an Oriental instead. *Daughter of the Dragon* was the first starring role she had been cast in since *The Toll of the Sea* in 1922, nearly a decade earlier.

Warner Oland, whom Anna May had previously worked with on *Old San Francisco*, was by now a staple character actor in Hollywood known for playing scoundrels, half-breeds, and most notably, the unfeeling Jewish father in Al Jolson's *The Jazz Singer*. The Swedish actor would reprise his role as Fu Manchu in *Daughter of the Dragon* for the third and final time.

Another long-absent name from Hollywood would also be making a splashy comeback in *Daughter of the Dragon*. Silent cinema heartthrob Sessue Hayakawa, who'd made American women swoon as the handsome but devilish ivory merchant in Cecil B. DeMille's 1915 film *The Cheat*, was slated to play the upstanding Chinese detective Ah Kee.

In the film, two things prevent Ling Moy from executing Fu Manchu's dastardly plan. Ah Kee, working for Scotland Yard, attends to the case with a righteous vigor, his only weakness being Ling Moy's beauty. The second is that Ling Moy has the soft heart of a daughter, not a son; she falls in love with the blond-haired Ronald Petrie and bungles her first attempt at killing him.

Ronald Petrie and his wife, Joan Marshall, are saved in the end by

Ah Kee's loyalty to his profession and a rather useless band of men from Scotland Yard. Despite his love for Ling Moy, Ah Kee is the one to shoot her dead only moments before he, too, collapses, having revived momentarily from a five-story fall. With his hand resting gently on the expired Ling Moy's head, he utters his final words: "A flower need not love, but only be loved . . . as Ah Kee loved you."

Whether good or bad, the Oriental characters, members of that "tragic race," all die. The white people, both victims and victors, live on. The Fu Manchu franchise at its core was a dubious morality tale of white might against yellow villainy, told over and over. The premise of every film in the series was always "absurdly fantastic and unreal," but Fu Manchu was a reliable box office earner, especially with the kids.

Despite the financial wreckage of the Depression, which had eventually hit home in Hollywood, it was clear that Paramount had spent a good chunk of change on staging the production "with dragons on the walls . . . and several persons arrayed in embroidered silken garments." The final budget clocked in at $270,000 ($5.2 million today). Travis Banton, the head costume designer at Paramount, along with his assistant, Edith Head, gave Anna May the full star treatment. In every scene she is dressed in fabulous creations: a silk kimono sparkling with sequins, an impeccably tailored dress with tasseled sleeves and a delicately pleated skirt and train, a velour robe magnificently draped over a short cheongsam, and, for Ling Moy's dancing act, a skintight bodysuit studded with crystals and topped with a showstopping bead-fringed headdress. Each superbly designed outfit accentuated Anna May's sinuous frame and graceful carriage. In total, they tailored seven individual looks for her at a cost of $1,400 (more than $27,000 today).

Divine wardrobe or not, *Daughter of the Dragon* was a B movie at best and received middling to bad reviews. "Weak entertainment owing to a preposterous and draggy story," *Film Daily* reported. "Too much effort concentrated in the wrong directions," *Variety* added. The most noteworthy aspect was not the film itself, but the fact that it served as a vehicle for reintroducing Sessue Hayakawa and Anna May Wong to American audiences. Seizing upon this angle, Paramount produced glamour shots of the two Asian stars and sent them out to do press together. *Motion Picture Magazine* accordingly ran the headline "Famous Oriental Stars Return to the Screen" with an interview of the two actors.

"Unimportant as a picture, save for those who relish their gelatin spiced with knives, gun play shrieks, secret panels, and torture chambers," Muriel Babcock began her review in the *Los Angeles Times*, "*The Daughter of the Dragon* is significant in bringing Miss Wong and Hayakawa to attention again."

Hayakawa had left Hollywood in 1922 around the time that his popularity began to wane and his controlling stake in his production company, Haworth Pictures Corporation, became increasingly meaningless. The United States was also experiencing a surge in nationalist sentiments, which culminated in the passage of the Immigration Act of 1924 that instituted a national origins quota system and effectively barred emigrants from Asia. Hayakawa sensed the growing agitation against Japanese Americans in California and, following an attack on his life while shooting one of his films, decided it was time to move on.

Like Anna May, he traveled to greener pastures first in New York, where he featured in the Broadway play *Tiger Lily*, and next Europe, making films in France and England. Then he returned to Japan, where professional actors must be born into their trade by family lineage, and broke with tradition by becoming the first man to appear on the Japanese stage without any such theatrical legacy. He had to be convinced to come back to Hollywood and only after an exchange of twenty or so cablegrams between Japan and the United States did he decide to accept the role of Ah Kee. Paramount's offer of a $10,000 flat fee likely did the trick.

"I am very happy to be filming alongside Sessue Hayakawa," Anna May told the press. "He is a great artist, whom I have always admired and who knows how to express feelings with a sobriety of expression and means that have never been equaled." This was the first time most American moviegoers would hear Anna May's rich and mellow low-toned voice, no doubt subverting expectations that she would sound ditsy and high-pitched. But as far as making the jump to talkies, her transition was seamless.

Reviewers were not as impressed with Hayakawa's performance in *Daughter of the Dragon*, which was also his first talking picture. The famous Japanese actor, whose crazed lady fans once threw their fur coats over a rain puddle in his path to save him from dirtying his feet, was mentioned almost as an afterthought in most reviews. "He does moderately well," Mordaunt Hall of the *New York Times* wrote, "even though his lines are not always spoken so that one can understand them."

At age forty-four, Hayakawa retained his good looks. His performance was most convincing when he let his anatomy do the talking with those searing gazes he'd been known for in the silent era. Whenever he opened his mouth to speak, his monotone delivery coupled with a heavy Japanese accent unfortunately marred the illusion his countenance had worked so hard to create.

"He does not manage to endow his performance with a quality of emotional interest," Muriel Babcock judged. "He is too staid and stiff even for the popular conception of the Oriental."

Who could have believed that Hollywood's first heartthrob, the man even Rudolph Valentino admittedly modeled himself after, would one day get passed over? Or that an actor once considered in the same league with Chaplin, Fairbanks, and Pickford would find himself all washed up? The talkies drew a stark line in the sand between actors who could work in sound and those who could not. Hayakawa's comeback was over before it began.

Any strong points the film possessed were instead attributed to Anna May and Warner Oland. Harry Carr, always a booster of Anna May's work, wrote favorably of the film. "As a general thing the studios must leave the direction of the 'Dr. Fu Manchu' pictures to the janitor, but *The Daughter of the Dragon* is a beautiful piece of work." Harry closed with a plea to Paramount: "But the next time they screen Anna May Wong I hope she doesn't have to be the villainess."

Warner Oland, Hollywood's favorite villain, was approaching the zenith of his career. Paramount paid him handsomely to appear in *Daughter of the Dragon*: $12,500 in all (about $243,000 today) for his twenty-four minutes on-screen. Paradoxically, both Asian stars earned less than the white man in yellow makeup. Anna May's salary was a mere $6,000, less than both her costars', and yet the film was her starring vehicle.

When filming began on *Daughter* at the Paramount studio in Los Angeles, Oland had just returned from shooting *The Black Camel* on location in Hawaii. The film was his second impersonating the affable Chinese detective Charlie Chan. This "lovable Chinaman," as Charlie Chan was sometimes called, was the diametric opposite of the nefarious Dr. Fu Manchu. Chan was a gentleman, cultured in the ways of the West, who used his powers of observation and acumen, never brute force, to solve murders and serve justice to the bad guys. He did this work cheerfully and with aplomb, all while spouting ancient Chinese aphorisms to elucidate his working theories.

And yet, like Fu Manchu, an evil brother from another father, Charlie Chan was dreamed up by a white man who knew almost nothing about the Chinese. Earl Derr Biggers from Pasadena, California, was reminiscing about a previous vacation in Hawaii when he happened upon an interesting item in a Hawaiian newspaper. Years after he read about a real-life detective on the Honolulu police force named Chang Apana, Derr Biggers penned the 1925 novel *The House Without a Key* in which the fictional Charlie Chan would make his first appearance. Derr Biggers hadn't set out to write a bestseller—he was simply a writer looking for his next meal ticket—but his character would soon take on a life of his own.

Hollywood quickly latched on to the idea of bringing Charlie Chan to the silver screen. *The House Without a Key* was adapted into a ten-episode Pathé serial in 1926, followed by a film version of Big-gers's next novel, *The Chinese Parrot*, produced by Universal in 1927. Anna May had a small role in the latter. A third film, *Behind That Curtain*, was made by Fox in 1929 with a local Chinatown business-man slotted into the detective role during the last ten minutes of the film. Although all three films featured Asian actors in the role of Charlie Chan—George Kuwa first, then Sôjin, and finally Edward Leon Park—for whatever reason, none of these pictures caught on with moviegoers and the original prints for the first two films were either lost or destroyed. It seemed that Charlie Chan, the movie star, was dead in the water.

During this time, Warner Oland was busy playing the heavy in various Hollywood productions. There was, however, a specific brand of villain that casting directors believed he excelled at most: the wicked Oriental.

Born Johan Verner Ölund in Nyby, Sweden, in 1879, "the Swede who became a Chinese," as one reporter described him, arrived in the United States with his parents, sister, and brothers at age thirteen. Oland built a prosperous career on the stage long before he made his debut in motion pictures. He was not an obvious candidate for the facile tastes of Hollywood. Oland had erudite interests. He married a painter and, together with his wife, Edith Gardener Shearn, was the first to translate August Strindberg's plays into English. But following a few bad investments, principally in theatrical shows he produced on his own dime, he was ready to consider a more serious foray into the movies.

Then, after fifteen years in motion pictures, Oland gained a repu-tation for being the on-screen Oriental of choice. "If you asked the average person to name the two most typically Chinese things in America," one journalist posed, "he would reply at once, 'chop suey and Warner Oland.'"

His transformation from Swede to Chinese required almost no makeup. Rather, Oland simply brushed his eyebrows up, combed the ends of his mustache down, and added a pointed goatee to his chin. The epicanthic folds in his eyelids, which he spuriously attributed to his mother's Russian blood, gave him the almond-shaped eyes so frequently associated with East Asians.

Oland's appearance fooled people on and off the set, whether they had never met an Asian person or were a Chinese national with an entire lifetime of experience. He made a point of wearing his mustache turned up at the corners when he wasn't working. "You have no idea how tired one gets of being a type actor. Of being branded 'that Chinaman of the movies' wherever you go," Warner explained. "A workman can take off his overalls, but I can't take off my face. I just can turn up the ends of my whiskers."

Whether he naturally looked the part of an Asian or not, Warner Oland was still a white European American putting on a minstrel act, assuming the role of Asian characters in yellowface. By casting him instead of Asian American actors, Hollywood perpetuated America's unspoken racial hierarchy. In film after film, Oland was deemed more appropriate to play an Asian character than Asian actors. One reviewer of *Daughter* concluded, "So far as the picture proves, the white actors impersonating Orientals seemed more the Chinese type than did the two principal Oriental players." This same irrational logic was used against Anna May Wong time and again when casting directors denied her roles that were clearly scripted as Asian.

The strange and troubling practice of yellowface did not go unremarked by those in the mainstream press. "Miss Wong is a flaming and brilliant personality, but it means seeing some American actors trying to act the part of Chinese. And they are always terrible," Harry Carr concluded.

Anna May's return to Los Angeles similarly prompted Grace Kingsley to muse: "It may yet come to pass that producers will realize that gluing an actor's eyes back and putting him in oriental clothes do not suddenly transform him into an Oriental. There are subtle qualities of mind and feeling that no Occidental can convey."

Up until 1931, Oland had mostly portrayed Asians as criminals and evildoers. He was tired of being pigeonholed, though. "It is my hope to be given a part some day that does these people justice," he told an interviewer in 1929. "It is extremely foolish to represent the Celestials as nothing but opium smugglers, tong men, and white slavers. China is a land with a great culture and you will find more Chinese with philosophy in their heads than with hatchets in their sleeves."

Fox purchased the rights to Earl Derr Biggers's *Charlie Chan Carries On* and *The Black Camel* in 1931 and made a renewed attempt at establishing a popular Charlie Chan series. The studio tested more than twenty actors before they landed on Oland to star as the Chinese detective. His slightly rotund, linen-suit-wearing rendition of Charlie Chan was an immediate hit and would define the series for years to come. Oland spent the better part of 1931 dashing between portrayals of Charlie Chan and, alternatively, Yellow Peril figures like Fu Manchu. Only in Hollywood could one person embody two such divergent yet inextricably linked characters.

The one thing that set Oland apart from other actors who dabbled in yellowface was that his impersonations were not a passing fad or a way station on the path to something bigger. Charlie Chan was *it*. The character became synonymous with Warner Oland, to the point that people dispensed with his given name and called him by Chan's instead.

"This Charlie Chan is rather a nice person, you know. I've had a long time to study him since we made the first picture, and I feel that I know him very well. . . . I've learned a great deal from him," Warner reflected. "Much as I love the part, I do wish sometimes that I might be known as an individual."

Charlie Chan was but the other side of the coin, a kindly foil to the dastardly Fu Manchu. Though Chan may have been cultured, considerate, and clever beyond reason, his emergence as a positive stereotype was only evidence of the same binary thinking Hollywood employed to characterize Asians and all other minorities. The racial other was either pure evil or virtuous to a fault, but never human. Being Charlie Chan day in and day out took its own toll on Oland. He began speaking to his wife in Charlie's elevated pidgin even in the privacy of their home. Keye Luke, the Chinese American artist who would play Charlie Chan's Number One Son, recalled how Warner drank before scenes to loosen his tongue. "He imbibed between shots and the more he imbibed, the fuzzier the dialogue became and the funnier and more hilarious the excuses that he made for muffing his lines." Occasionally he went missing from the set.

Needless to say, Charlie Chan also made Warner Oland a very rich man. He was initially paid $10,000 per film, but by 1935 his contract with Fox was revised to $20,000 a picture. On average, he made three Charlie Chan films a year, usually one right after another. In due time, he and his wife acquired four homes: a sprawling estate in the Carpinteria Valley near Santa Barbara; a Cape Cod–style farmhouse in Southborough, Massachusetts; a small bungalow in Los Angeles for when Oland was in town working; and, the most extravagant of all, a 7,000-acre island off the coast of Mazatlán, Mexico, called Palmetto de la Virgen.

Despite the enormous and discriminatory gap between their salaries, Warner and Anna May were chums. They played on the same team. Both were tasked with imbuing stereotyped characters with humanity, dignity, and charm. Being cast in Asian parts also meant they were frequent collaborators. In *Old San Francisco*, Warner and Anna May played lovers. They met again as parent and child in *Daughter of the Dragon*. This prompted Oland to remark: "Husband and wife? Father and daughter? This is getting pretty incestuous." The two actors would find themselves working together again in short order.

———————

Anna May Wong scarcely had a chance to consider whether *Daughter of the Dragon* turned out to be the moneymaker she hoped it would before she was on to her next engagement. And it's a good thing too.

Negotiations with Edward Belasco and Homer Curran to bring *On the Spot* to Los Angeles had led Anna May to sign on to a reprisal of the much-talked-about Edgar Wallace play. Crane Wilbur would join her onstage again as well. Contracts were inked in July, rehearsals began in August, and the play opened at the Belasco theater at the end of summer.

Anna May's effusive homecoming tour continued. Family and friends had heard so much about her "sensational rise to dramatic prominence in Europe and the East" and were eager to break out "the brass band and the welcoming committee for the home-town girl who has made good." One journalist saw the outpouring of love with their own eyes when they visited the actress backstage one evening: Anna May's dressing room was filled with flowers. She was enjoying her success "because, for once, she doesn't have to be the villainess."

There was a notable difference in the movie star who left Hollywood a "hoydenish and slightly crude young girl" and returned a woman of worldly distinction and poise. "I am very happy to now be back in Hollywood near mine and able to rest from the fatigue of London social life," she told reporters. "I still prefer a good book to all the brightest parties."

In a series of interviews, she reflected on her career thus far with a thoughtfulness and maturity the American press had never seen from her. "I always say it is better not to expect anything. Then you are not bitterly disappointed," Anna May explained. "And if you succeed, it is doubly wonderful. I never try to make things come out as I want them. I just let things alone, and let them take care of themselves."

Except that her triumph was in large part a result of her personal agency. As one writer pointed out to readers, "[Anna May] has shown great determination and sagacity in planning her career, and has helped Fate along by studying and perfecting herself in everything that might further it."

Hollywood had been forced to recognize her popularity abroad. Paramount kowtowed and finally gave her the starring role she had been agitating for all along. For a brief moment Anna May felt supremely happy and at peace, as if everything had fallen into place. She was enjoying this victory lap and all the honors that came with it.

"I feel I am a very fortunate person," she continued. "All people have their dreams, and it's wonderful just to have them. But when they actually come true, you are happy and lucky beyond what you have any right to expect."

More and more, she saw how important it was for the world, Americans especially, to see a Chinese American woman like her on the silver screen. "I couldn't give up my career, because I feel it is really drawing China nearer, and making it better understood and liked," she explained.

"People tell me I've changed so since my European experience, and that I don't look like a Chinese girl any more," she told another interviewer. "I believe the mind and spirit show through the features. My face has changed because my mind has changed."

One thing that hadn't changed was the media's obsession with her love life. Did she have plans to marry? At twenty-six, she wasn't getting any younger.

"Wasn't it Byron who said 'Happiness is a twin that cannot be shared'?" Anna May responded serenely. "My happiness now is in my work. I hope to find it there for many, many years to come. When that is finished there will be time to think of marriage.

"I still want to see life and some more of the world alone," she went on, invoking her independent streak. "I want to visit Alaska, India and, oh, so many other places. I want to feel for a while yet that freedom which makes every new place and every new thing a new adventure.

"I want a youth that is full and an old age that is free of everything save rest and peace—probably in that land I am saving until the last."

The land she was speaking of was China, a place she had yet to visit. With her mother gone, her father grew restless to return to the terra firma of their ancestors. The country to which Anna May supposedly belonged but had never been to—much like Lee Gon Toy, who was born and died in the United States without ever leaving its borders—seeped into her consciousness like incense languorously diffusing into the musty air of a temple shrine. The scent traced a line from her to China, where she, too, envisioned one day retiring in a state of perfect tranquility.

So when another reporter posed the marriage question to her, Anna May answered quixotically: "It is my dream to marry a splendid Chinese, preferably a scholar, and one who has lived in the Occident, so that I will not seem too alien to him. And I shall go to China—and never, never, never come back."

Anna May and Warner Oland in a scene from *Shanghai Express*, 1932.

8

NOBODY'S CHINA DOLL

Though China remained many thousands of miles away, Anna May Wong would soon receive an opportunity to walk onto its closest approximation: a Hollywood set dressed to look like a Peiping (modern-day Beijing) train station in Josef von Sternberg's *Shanghai Express*. For her next film, Paramount offered her the role of Hui Fei, a reformed courtesan on her way to meet her fiancé, who embarks on the train to Shanghai along with a motley cast of characters. Perhaps Anna May's dream of marrying a Chinese man would come true?

The fates collided to reunite her with Marlene Dietrich and Josef von Sternberg. Their two names, the German actress and her director, were almost universally spoken in the same breath now. The pair had made two films in the year and a half they had been working together in Hollywood: 1930's *Morocco*, a desert romance about a cabaret singer who follows the rogue soldier she loves into the sand dunes, and 1931's *Dishonored*, the doomed saga of Mata Hari, the spy who must pay for her love with her life. Marlene had become the face of the femme fatale, her latent sexuality smoldering from the depths of her penetrating gaze.

Anna May had scarcely seen or heard from *the* Marlene Dietrich, whose celebrity reverberated through the Hollywood Hills, since they had last seen each other in Berlin on that memorable night at the Reimann art school ball. She had watched from afar as Marlene's career soared under the faithful tutelage of Josef von Sternberg. It was breathtaking, really, how one meeting with the right director, one buzzworthy film that no one in America had even seen, could take an unknown entity and turn her into Tinseltown royalty overnight. Jesse Lasky admitted as much many years later in his autobiography.

"[Jo] kept raving in his letters about a girl in [*The Blue Angel*] and urging me to bring her to America," he recalled. "So I gave her a contract to star in Paramount pictures without seeing so much as her passport photo. I was never sorry I did."

No one could blame Anna May for wondering what her own career in the United States might have looked like if she'd had Richard Eichberg, E. A. Dupont, or any other important director in her corner, fighting for her interests inside a powerful studio like Paramount. But she tried not to go there. What use was it to dwell on things that hadn't come to pass? But Anna May did what she could to give herself a leg up. Around this time, she lopped off two years from her age, changing her birthdate from 1905 to 1907. No one was the wiser.

Ironically, Anna May had known Josef von Sternberg longer than Marlene, though never intimately. They became acquaintances when she first circulated among Hollywood's foreign contingent, primarily the Germans and the Brits. Jo had long harbored a fascination with the Orient. He found Anna May enchanting in her own way and saw her as an emissary to the East, someone he could probe when his autodidactic tendencies hit their limit. One can only speculate whether he might have let his interest slip into infatuation if his attention wasn't otherwise occupied. Being Marlene Dietrich's director was a full-time job.

When Marlene arrived in Hollywood in the spring of 1930, she had relied totally on Jo to help her navigate the foreign setting. It was he who had made sure only "Studio-controlled press" would be waiting for her when she disembarked at the Pasadena train station. He who had rented her "a pretty little house" in Beverly Hills, staffed with two maids. He who had insisted the studio send her a lavish welcome gift: a green Rolls-Royce that came equipped with a chauffeur. And it was he who had opened a bank account in her name with $10,000 from the studio and showed her how to write a check. All that for an actress who had then yet to screen a film on American soil.

Jo and Marlene were caught in an addictive, self-perpetuating codependency. He had made her a star and she was grateful. The public's growing obsession with her—the "Great Find of the Century"—in turn made his films into commercial box office hits. People murmured that Jo was the seducer, the scheming Svengali to Marlene's Trilby. However, the dynamic worked both ways, and, more often than not, Marlene herself held all the strings.

Shanghai Express was an ensemble piece, but its overriding purpose was to serve as another starring vehicle for Marlene Dietrich. The film was to follow a group of foreigners, each with something to hide, traveling by train from Peiping to Shanghai. When the train makes an unexpected stop in the middle of the night, the first-class passengers are thrust into an unforeseen drama and find themselves collectively at the mercy of a dangerous Chinese revolutionary.

Marlene was to embody Shanghai Lily, a "notorious coaster" and woman of easy virtue known for breaking hearts up and down the China coast. (Somehow her screen roles were always remarkably like the woman herself.) Lily runs into a man from her past on the train. Dr. Harvey, in fact, is the only man she has ever loved. Five years have passed since they last saw each other. She tells him, with not a little self-satisfaction, "It took more than one man to change my name to Shanghai Lily."

British actor Clive Brook was set to play Dr. Harvey, Shanghai Lily's jilted lover, who also doubles as the ensemble's upstanding member of society because of his duty to save lives—although it's questionable whether he ever does. Brook's roles had not changed much in the intervening years since his turn as Gilda Gray's savior in *The Devil Dancer*. His rather wooden acting and dashing looks made him the perfect "man who gets the girl." All he had to do was show up at the end and kiss the leading lady like he meant it.

On the other hand, Hui Fei, a Chinese woman of dubious

background, is classed in Lily's camp. As women of the night, presumably, they naturally gravitate toward one another and decide to share a compartment. Under the disapproving gaze of their fellow first-class passengers, they proceed to smoke and play the phonograph in their den of iniquity. High-class prostitute though she may be, Hui Fei was a dramatically different part than any Anna May had played in the past. She was neither the helpless and tragic Lotus Blossom nor an out-and-out Dragon Lady like the murderous Ling Moy in *Daughter of the Dragon*. No, Hui Fei was a clear-eyed, determined spirit, a woman unafraid to travel alone and heedless of the other passengers' disapproval.

Production on *Shanghai Express* was scheduled to begin in October 1931. Anna May, however, was still in the midst of her commitment to *On the Spot* at the Belasco. To secure her for the film, Paramount had to buy Anna May out of her contract with Belasco and Curran to the tune of $6,000. Further negotiations upped her salary from $1,500 to $1,800 a week, netting a total fee of $8,100 for her engagement in *Shanghai Express*. Small gains for Anna May were but a drop in the bucket for Paramount in comparison to the $78,666.67 lavished upon Marlene, whose compensation for this one production dwarfed the salaries of every other cast and crew member involved in the film, including the director. Jo took only his standard fee of $50,000.

The film called on Anna May to act opposite Warner Oland again, but this time as his adversary. Oland was cast in his usual Oriental role, the Eurasian merchant Henry Chang, who is in actuality the rebel leader of the forces that will overtake the train en route to Shanghai. Eugene Pallette, Louise Closser Hale, Lawrence Grant, Emile Chautard, and Gustav von Seyffertitz, all playing a colorful array of personalities, would bring up the rear.

As for the script, well, Josef von Sternberg made no efforts to hide that he regarded such documents contemptuously. The same was true of the actors he employed. As the director, he would tell the actors what to say, how to say it, and when. Marlene, for instance, never worked from a script. She simply looked to her creator to put the words right into her mouth.

Studios and the moneymen that ran them, however, usually insisted upon a final script. What's more, the Motion Picture Association of America (MPAA), operated under the auspices of chairman Will Hays, had a new mandate to review, modify, and approve scripts and final cuts in compliance with the Motion Picture Production Code established in 1930. More commonly referred to as the Hays Code, this official set of rules was intended to guide studios in self-regulating their productions so that no picture would "lower the moral standards of those who see it."

The script for *Shanghai Express* entered the world, according to von Sternberg, as "a single page" written by Harry Hervey—a screenwriter known for features set in far-flung locales based on his travels in Asia. Jo then took Hervey's seed of an idea and dictated a new outline to writer Jules Furthman to set down on paper. Of course, the MPAA would gladly interject to remind Jo of the story's moral failings. But whether he ever looked at that piece of paper again to ensure that he was faithful to it is anyone's guess.

Jo had bigger fish to fry. For *Shanghai Express*, he would need to create his own filmic version of China, a place he had never been. He'd already proven he was adept at fabricating such camera tricks with *Morocco*. "He was miraculous," Henry Hathaway, Jo's assistant, recalled. "He took an old Mexican street on the Universal back lot and said, 'Bring me some eucalyptus poles and palm leaves,' and then we had *Mogador*! His 'desert' was at Guadalupe, just a little tiny beach with sand dunes."

This illusory mirage had been so successful, it fooled even the pasha of Marrakesh, who asked Jo why he hadn't called on him while he was filming in his city. "He smiled when I told him that this was no more than an accidental resemblance," Jo reflected, "a flaw due to my lack of talent to avoid such similarity."

Realism was not the goal of a von Sternberg film. He was a painter of light and shadow. Every frame, every detail, was rendered in service to the image, to beauty, not verisimilitude. And yet, Jo's "papier-mâché" China, unlike Douglas Fairbanks's Bagdad, was not the stuff of comic book fantasies. Rather, his sets gave off the uncanny sensation of being more real than reality itself.

The exterior scenes in *Shanghai Express* were shot at the San Bernardino station on a stretch of the Atchison, Topeka & Santa Fe Railway in Southern California closed expressly for the purposes of filming. Von Sternberg ordered all manner of Chinese bric-a-brac, livestock, and decorative flourishes to dress the train station: "Chickens, goats, paper lanterns, straw-hatted coolies, ragged urchins, scrawny dogs, bags, trunks, crates, and boxes, roped parcels in all shapes and sizes." The attention to detail was almost maniacal. Wherever possible, signage with the unfamiliar swirls of Chinese characters was installed. Even a self-evident water tower had to be labeled with the character 水 for water. "A sea of banners, long, narrow white cloth panels painted with Chinese letters," was strung above the train tracks. In addition, B-roll footage from James Wong Howe's recent trip to China would be projected as the scenery outside passenger windows to simulate the train moving through space.

Hundreds of Chinese Americans were recruited to populate the station and the chaotic, bustling environment around it. Another fiction peculiar to Jo's China was the fact that the Chinese extras did not speak Mandarin, the dialect common in Peiping, but the southern dialect of Cantonese. The Chinese diaspora in America at that time, largely descendants of gold seekers and railroad workers who had come from southern China, much like Anna May's forebears, was largely Cantonese-speaking. Hence, most extras spoke in their native dialect when asked to put on a show for the cameras. This inconsistency was simply a facet of the wholly fictional place Jo invented within the frames of *Shanghai Express*.

Set against this backdrop, Anna May as Hui Fei is the first to make her entrance at the start of the film. The train whistle blows as a tracking shot glides past the side of the train. Harried pedestrians walk by in the foreground, revealing glimpses of the packed third-class car in the background. A pagoda-like sedan chair carried by Chinese manservants comes into the frame, then stops at the foot of the stairs to the first-class car. Hui Fei steps out from her lacquered box wearing a dark flowing cheongsam, her back to us as she waves away the porter's hand outstretched to assist her. She climbs into the train and only then, in mid-ascent, does she turn to look tentatively about the crowded station, her earrings dangling in the strip of sunlight that cuts across her comely face. Surely this is the arrival of a force to be reckoned with.

As production on *Shanghai Express* progressed, Marlene and Anna May settled into a chummy on-set friendship as if nothing had changed since they last saw each other—only their positions in the food chain. Marlene was now the attention-commanding star and Anna May the lesser personality made to play second fiddle. Their scenes together positioned them as two of a kind. Shanghai Lily and Hui Fei are independent, sophisticated, experienced women—perhaps too experienced. They are perceived as vulgar aberrations in the veneer of respectable society and its insistence that the ideal woman must be chaste, married, or a spinster. This clash in moral values is displayed superbly when Mrs. Haggerty, the boarding house mistress, stops by the ladies' compartment to introduce herself.

"It's a bit lonely on a train, isn't it? I'm used to having people around. They put my dog in the baggage car," Mrs. Haggerty prattles on. "I have a boarding house in Shanghai. . . . Yorkshire pudding is my specialty," she says as she hands out cards to Lily and Hui Fei. "And I only take the most respectable people."

"Don't you find respectable people terribly dull?" Lily responds with a sly smirk on her face.

Alarmed, Mrs. Haggerty answers breathlessly, "You're joking, aren't you? I've only known the most respectable people. You see, I keep a boarding house."

"What kind of a house did you say?" Lily asks with widened eyes in mock surprise.

"A boarding house," Mrs. Haggerty counters, tight-lipped. She turns to Hui Fei instead and says, "I'm sure you're very respectable, Madame."

When the elegant Chinese woman looks up from her game of solitaire, cigarette in hand, and finally speaks, her voice intones in a lofty, British-inflected elocution: "I must confess I don't quite know the standard of respectability that you demand in your boarding house, Mrs. Haggerty."

The joke is on respectable society and those who hew to its outmoded standards. In life, as on the screen, Anna May and Marlene were both mavericks in that respect. They were ambitious women who found a way to prioritize their careers above all else, whether that meant remaining single and unattached or conveniently fashioning one's husband and child into manager and personal assistant. They were cultured women, unlike the rest of Hollywood's women who Marlene skewered for having no brains. They read books, loved art and the opera, worshipped the intellectual mind, had an eye for fashion. They gave their love freely and turned a blind eye to the strictures of marriage. And, for different reasons, they both saw through Hollywood's bullshit. Except that Marlene didn't have to play nice the way Anna May did. She didn't live in fear of her big fat paycheck being cut off by the Paramount execs. Jo would be there to catch her when she fell.

Instead of rehearsing between takes, the two women lounged side by side in their actors' chairs with Marlene's six-year-old daughter, Maria, settled quietly nearby. Sometimes they listened to records by Richard Tauber, a mutual friend from Berlin, in Marlene's spacious dressing room. They sipped coffee through straws so as not to mess up their makeup and conversed in soft tones. "She liked Miss Wong much better than her leading man," Maria mused many years later. Clive Brook, it turned out, was little more than "a photogenic jaw," and a stiff one at that.

Marlene "fussed over Miss Wong's square bangs" as a kind, caring girlfriend would do. She even lobbied Travis Banton to redesign one of Anna May's cheongsams in a more flattering way. Anna May received this act of generosity with graciousness. Still, it was more gesture than deed. Travis and Marlene had left nothing to chance when it came to Shanghai Lily's intricate travel frocks and sumptuous smoking gowns. They'd spent several solid weeks holed up in the wardrobe department for twelve hours at a time, combing through endless bolts of silk and lace. More than $1,600 was spent on Lily's four looks, whereas Hui Fei's three outfits cost $300, a hundred dollars less than Dr. Harvey's officer's uniform.

On the first day of filming that fall, Marlene Dietrich emerged from her chauffeured limousine, little Maria in tow, and strutted into the "dramatic confusion" of a train station in a faraway land. She looked flawless, dressed all in black. She had refused to wear any other color for fear the cameras would reveal the fifteen pounds she'd gained while on holiday in Germany. Black, being the darkest of color values, was difficult to photograph distinctly. But when Jo was asked to comment on Shanghai Lily's costumes, he turned to Marlene and said matter-of-factly in German: "If *you* believe I am skilled enough to know how to photograph this, then all I can offer you is—to *do* the impossible."

There was no question. Marlene's look had all eyes on her. A flurry of inky black feathers, plucked from a Mexican fighting cock, "the rarest black bird imaginable," encircled her shoulders and neck, their green iridescent sheen glimmering in the sunshine. A black crepe dress extended past her ankles—there would be no bare legs in this Dietrich flick—and black-and-white kid leather gloves were impeccably fitted to her hands. A cock-feather hat and veil, which imprinted

Marlene's face with the most exquisite pattern—delicate stripes made as if by pinpricks—was the pièce de résistance.

Whatever sense of duty had been channeled by the extras, crew members, and livestock milling about the tracks suddenly ceased at the sight of the film's inspiration. Jo had been sitting next to the train and painting shadows onto its side when the uncharacteristic silence tipped him off. He looked up to see his leading lady, in all her crested glory, single-handedly bringing the set to a standstill. He smiled as if to say everything was as it should be, then shouted: "Let's get back to work, boys!"

Otherwise, the atmosphere on set was tense. Jo had gained a reputation for being officious and domineering, and his comportment throughout the filming of *Shanghai Express* only validated that observation. His view on actors was straightforward.

"An actor is turned on and off like a spigot," Jo would later explain. "How can a sculptor be honest with the piece of clay that considers itself more important than the hands that mold it? The intelligent actor knows this and submits without a question. He accepts that he is part of an entity over which he has little control, and he wastes no time demanding that he be handled with kid gloves."

This notion led to a number of preposterous demands. For instance, Jo opined, as he informed his cast, that people on a train always talk in accordance with the rhythm of the machinery that conveys them. Thus, he set out a metronome. "Now, that's the rhythm of the wheels. Talk in time with that," he commanded.

During exteriors, he barked commands through a megaphone until his voice was hoarse. Then the production manager hatched the bright idea of providing him with a microphone and loudspeaker. Once the crew returned to the studio in Hollywood, the same public-address system was hooked up inside the soundstage. A bewildered and amused Jesse Lasky remembered entering the stage one day and hearing "the booming voice of the director reverberating through the enormous structure like a train announcer's in Grand Central Station." As he recalled, "Joe was staging an intimate close-up of Marlene and Clive Brook, almost breathing in their faces as he gave them directions, but still using the microphone!"

Jo's obsessive need for control led him to act out all the parts before the entire production. "First, he was Clive Brook kissing Marlene, and then Marlene kissing Clive Brook!" cinematographer Lee Garmes reminisced. "You should have seen Clive Brook's face! His impersonation of Anna May Wong had us all in stitches. But we didn't dare show our amusement."

Jo and Clive constantly tussled over how the latter should impersonate his character. "Clive Brook wanted to be Clive Brook. Von Sternberg wanted him to be von Sternberg," Garmes explained. The two leading men in Marlene's life went around in circles like this for hours yet never raised their voices at each other. Instead, they muttered in soft half whispers, "Oh, you fucking son of a bitch!"

Warner Oland didn't fare much better with the tyrant von Sternberg. He haughtily boasted of his theatrical talents, saying, "They call me One-take Warner." Oland's rising profile and salary requirements, thanks to Charlie Chan, had made him complacent. That and the supplemental swigs of whiskey he'd been gulping down while filming Chan flicks to slur his speech to the delightful pace of the contemplative detective. A swig here or there had rapidly transgressed into full-on stupors and late-night benders.

Jo formed his own acrid opinion of Oland's claim to fame. Far from getting his lines down in one take, Jo claimed, "It took me hours in one of the scenes of *Shanghai Express* to get Mr. Oland to say no more than 'Good morning'—and this with the aid of a blackboard."

Grace was extended solely to Jo's cherished one. To this end, Marlene was allowed to position a full-length mirror on wheels next to the camera so that she could see her image in real time while film was rolling and instantly correct any unflattering angles. If she struggled with the pronunciation of a word in her accented English or looked visibly frustrated, Jo made the call. "Clear the set!" Those three magic words sent the entire production packing.

"The crew seemed quite used to this ominous exodus," Maria recalled many years later. "It meant getting out into the bright sunshine, having a smoke, leaning against the wall improving their California tans, while Dietrich was inside being taught how to act."

"She wasn't sure of herself, she had to be guided in everything," Lee Garmes noted. "Joe knew how to handle her; he was very considerate of her. . . . Von Sternberg never made her 'act' through a whole scene."

It was no secret that Marlene was more eye candy than substance, but she was willing to put in the work. She would do as many takes as Jo demanded, 140 or more, even if it killed her.

In contrast to some of her costars, Anna May found Jo's direction invigorating. It was inspiring to work with someone who took such ardent ownership over his art, despite driving some crew members batty with his perfectionism. Jo's interest in Chinese culture also opened the door for Anna May to exert a small crumb of influence over the final script and story. Before shooting commenced, she pulled an all-nighter with her brother James, flagging details and scenes, bits of dialogue that she felt "did not tell the tale very truly." The next day she waited many hours for the production manager to show up to their prearranged appointment so that she could present her constructive criticism, and finally "some change was effected."

The MPAA also submitted changes of its own. Lines like "I haven't lived in this country ten years not to know a strumpet when I see one" and "It took more than one man to change my name to Shanghai Lily" were a little too transparent in their references to Lily and Hui Fei's profession for the MPAA's tastes. It succeeded in modifying some of these utterances, but not all: the administration still lacked the teeth to enforce its rulings, and Jo was not one to easily give in to censorship. The MPAA also took issue with a proposed interlude in which Mrs. Haggerty takes her dog out to pee, as well as some scenery highlighting human skulls skewered on poles; both were cut from the final film.

But most of all, the MPAA worried about the character of Reverend Carmichael, a proselytizing minister traveling through China who expresses a rather rigid and judgmental worldview. In the original script, he is to be revealed as phony in the end, a con man posing in "the garb of a priest only to cover a crime." However, this was modified in the final film, based on the MPAA's guidance: "Our fear is that you may be charged with misrepresentation of the Protestant clergyman in foreign countries, revealing him as a picayune, irascible and narrow-minded man." Reverend Carmichael was duly transformed into the only true believer of Lily's holy reformation.

The question of whether any of the material might offend the Chinese was breezily waved away. "We are very hopeful that the Chinese will have a favorable view of the picture since, it seems to us, you have respected their point of view throughout," the MPAA reassured Paramount.

Though her lines are sparse, the role of Hui Fei presented Anna May with a rare occasion to exhibit a hardness absent from her previous parts. She was still playing the "exotic Asian," yes, but with a shrewd gaze and a sharp edge. Gone are the baby-fat cheeks and youthful grin that distinguished her in *Piccadilly* and *Song*, her finest silent films. In their place, Anna May's Hui Fei is sober and world-weary, slightly gaunt, with her bangs slicked down the middle of her forehead and her bare nipples peeking through the thin silk of her dress. She nevertheless carries herself in a dignified manner, regardless of what others assume about her character, and her somewhat understated cheongsams are a welcome contrast to Shanghai Lily's conspicuous femininity. Unlike her coaster friend, Hui Fei is not foolish enough to believe in love and chivalry. She has no illusions about the dangerous and violent world they find themselves in as single women, and this discernment is likely the reason Hui Fei travels with a dagger.

Warner Oland as Henry Chang, a man of mixed Chinese and European ancestry, is the unequivocal villain of the film. There is something off about him from the get-go. When the train's departure is delayed by a cow standing on the tracks and the cantankerous Reverend Carmichael expresses his exasperation, Chang is the voice that declares: "You're in China now, sir, where time and life have no value."

Further into the journey, the wagering, wisecracking Sam Salt looks at Chang and says what everyone else is thinking: "I can't make head or tail out of you, Mr. Chang. Are you Chinese or are you white or what are you?"

"My mother was Chinese; my father was white," Chang says rather dryly.

"You look more like a white man to me."

Now irritated, Chang replies, "I'm not proud of my white blood."

The MPAA was similarly concerned with Chang's remarks because, as it said, it "may be objected to on the grounds that it shows the white race unfavorably in contrast with the yellow." It is no surprise, then, when this self-hating half-caste who clings to a uniquely Chinese strain of nihilism is revealed to be the revolutionary insurgent the Chinese authorities have been searching for. After his right-hand man is discovered on the train at an impromptu passport check and arrested, Chang sends an encrypted telegram to his men in hiding to stop the Shanghai Express in the middle of the night. They will hold one of the foreign passengers hostage in return for the safe passage of his officer.

After a thorough interrogation, the other first-class passengers are released and allowed to return to the train. The only passenger of value, as it happens, is Captain Harvey, who is traveling to Shanghai in order to perform a lifesaving operation on the governor-general. Harvey remains in Chang's custody to wait for the release of Chang's officer.

There is a twist to this seemingly straightforward prisoner swap, however. Chang propositions Shanghai Lily, suggesting that she stay with him as his lover. Captain Harvey, listening at the door in his holding cell, breaks down the door just in time to stop Chang from laying a hand on Lily. Rebuffed by the white lady and her savior, Chang sends for Hui Fei. Rebel soldiers drag her from the train into Chang's lair as all the passengers watch in silence; they know what he means to do with her. Sometime later, she returns to the train with her hair undone, her clothing ruffled, and a lust for vengeance in her eyes.

Chang, meanwhile, has not forgotten Dr. Harvey's insult. This is Hollywood's China, mind you, where the most trivial of slights must be avenged with a cruel act of violence. Chang vows to blind Harvey before he releases him. But Lily, overwhelmed by her love for this old flame, makes the ultimate lover's sacrifice and offers herself up to Chang so that Harvey may escape unharmed.

Hui Fei, whom everyone is too ashamed to look in the eye, fetches her dagger from the train car and steals into a shadowy corner of the commandeered train station. She lies in wait for her opportunity, and when it comes, she reemerges from the darkness to stab Chang to death. Hui Fei notifies Harvey in passing that Chang is dead and that he should go retrieve Shanghai Lily. The long-lost lovers are swiftly reunited.

The Asian characters in *Shanghai Express* exist on a separate plane from their Western counterparts. Whatever happens to them seems incidental to the fates of the expats aboard the train, who look about helplessly, counting on their prayers to bring someone to save them. But no one is coming to save the Chinese from themselves. So Hui Fei does the dirty work and, in doing so, saves one and all. She is, in the truest meaning of the word, a femme fatale.

The rescued Lily returns to the train, where she finds Hui Fei calmly playing solitaire.

"I don't know if I ought to be grateful to you or not," Lily says, visibly shaken.

"It's of no consequence," Hui Fei states plainly. "I didn't do it for you. Death canceled his debt to me."

When the train finally arrives in Shanghai, Lily and Hui Fei go their separate ways without so much as a parting glance.

The logic of *Shanghai Express* is such that there is room for only one happy ending, that of Captain Harvey and Shanghai Lily. The heartless escort is redeemed by her true and pure love for a respectable white man, a British officer no less. They kiss and live happily ever after. The detail about Hui Fei traveling to Shanghai to marry her fiancé was dropped from the completed film. Love never enters the picture for her, and she is not recognized with any special feeling for her brave deed; she simply walks off with the Chinese government's $20,000 reward money for Chang's head. "I was glad for once not to die in the last fade-out," Anna May asserted. For once, she was nobody's China doll.

Jo's lighting magic cast a reverential spotlight on Marlene in so many of the film's scenes, it was easy not to notice Anna May's powerful performance. Many still did.

Peter Ballbusch, an assistant designer who worked on the film, observed Anna May from the sidelines while on set. He scribbled in the margins of his script somewhat breathlessly: "Anna May is picturesquely marvelously beautiful with her hair let down." But, he added with a tone of regret, she had never had a director wholly devoted to her, "who peeled her out of the shells of habituation and daily wear and tear as HE does with Marlene." Jo, presumably was the "HE" referred to.

Despite rumors that Anna May and Marlene had a special connection all their own—which were principally stoked by one publicity photo in particular, in which the two women stood arm in arm in their *Shanghai Express* costumes and stared knowingly into the camera—they did not keep up their on-set friendship once production ended. Even Maria, the keeper of her mother's secrets, who would later write a tell-all memoir of the great Dietrich's affairs, never believed for a second that her mother and Anna May had entertained a one-night tryst, much less a full-blown lesbian love affair. The actresses were well-behaved rivals, plain and simple.

In early 1932, Marlene invited actor friend Martin Kosleck, one of the latest arrivals fleeing Germany's sky-high inflation and crumbling film industry, to watch an early cut of *Shanghai Express* in one of Paramount's private screening rooms. Marlene "sat looking critically at herself on the screen, criticizing or praising her own face and hair," Kosleck remembered.

"Oh, God! My *acting*! Now I move my eyes this way, now that way," she laughed at herself. In every scene her eyes bounced around in their sockets like pinballs, searching for a focal point. Marlene's self-deprecation put Kosleck at ease, so he chipped in his two cents: "That Chinese girl is wonderful." Marlene's snickering ceased and the room went silent.

"I must have been crazy to have said such a thing," Kosleck later recalled. "The atmosphere grew distinctly chilly after that."

China did not look kindly upon Josef von Sternberg's latest creation. Less than a month after principal photography wrapped, editors at the Chinese publication *Pictorial Weekly* caught wind of the less-than-flattering portrayal of China's political situation in *Shanghai Express*. Except they didn't fault the director. They laid the blame squarely on the only recognizable Chinese actress in the film.

"Paramount Utilizes Anna May Wong to Produce Picture to Disgrace China," the headline read. The article didn't stop there, but continued to harangue its target:

> The Oriental Star in Hollywood, Anna May Wong, is working as a featured player in America. Her specialty is to expose the conduct of the very low class of Chinese, such as when she played the part of a half-nude Chinese maid in *Thief of Bagdad.*

Although she is deficient in artistic portrayal, she has done
more than enough to disgrace the Chinese race. Is there such a
thing as a half-nude maid in China?

The film was banned in China before it had the chance to debut
in America. The Chinese Nationalist government was likely extra sensitive to affronts, even of this superficial nature, because it had been
under siege for the last three months from Imperial Japan. The Land
of the Rising Sun had asserted a bold new vision for its nation at the
start of the twentieth century, one in which its government would
preside not only over Japanese citizens but also the entire continent of
Asia. Emboldened by its successful annexation of Korea in 1910 and a
backroom deal at the end of World War I to take over Germany's
concession territories in China, Japan marched forward with its plan
to gain control of Manchuria, a key territory in northern China sharing a land border with Korea.

In September 1931, Japan launched a false flag operation known
as the Mukden Incident to justify a full-blown invasion into Manchuria. By January 28, 1932, resentments between Chinese citizens and
Japanese expats in Shanghai's International Settlement boiled over.
Mob violence broke out, which rapidly devolved into full-on hostilities.
One week later, *Shanghai Express* premiered at the Paramount Theatre
in Downtown Los Angeles. Newspaper headlines described the film
as "the timeliest picture the Paramount ever played" and hinted that
it had been "rushed to theater screens" to capitalize on international
events then unfolding.

Whether the conflict between Japan and China intensified the
public's interest in *Shanghai Express* and sold more movie tickets is
impossible to know, but the sensational possibilities of a train being
waylaid by warring factions somewhere in the Far East were certainly
on the brain in 1932.

The critics were almost unanimous: as far as stories go, *Shanghai*

Express barely had two legs to stand on. But as a piece of cinematography, it was a stunning, unforgettable masterpiece.

In his review for the *Los Angeles Times*, Philip K. Scheuer called the film "an exquisite thing of lights and shades" but said that it "frequently grows so transfixed at the spectacle of its own beauty that its hand-maiden, Drama, is left stumbling by the wayside.

"Nothing, in the ordinary movie sense, happens," he continued. "A conjurer of glamour without equal in a very young art, [von Sternberg] will carry you, if you thrill at all to the mention of far places, into a world of snooty, stilted, and wholly irresistible enchantment."

People went crazy for Marlene Dietrich as they never had before. They loved every gorgeous frame of her. "Miss Dietrich gives an impressive performance. She is languorous but fearless as Lily," Mordaunt Hall wrote in the *New York Times*. "She glides through her scenes with heavy eyelids and puffing on her cigarettes. She measures every word and yet she is not too slow in her foreign-accented speech."

Prominent writer Ayn Rand told Jo personally that she'd never been so impressed by a film. The images he had created had been seared into her mind's eye. "The way the wind blows through the fur-piece around Marlene's shoulder when she sits on the back platform of the train!"

Moviegoers heartily agreed. The film's run at the Paramount was extended for a second week to keep up with demand. Within a month or so, *Shanghai Express* opened in London and Berlin, where moviegoers continued to swoon. Berlin's Mozartsaal theater sold out for many days in advance.

Industry accolades soon followed. *Shanghai Express* was nominated for three Academy Awards for the 1933 season in directing, outstanding production, and cinematography. Lee Garmes won for his work as cinematographer, but the genius behind it all, Josef von Sternberg, was coolly passed over by the Academy. The awards were a popularity contest, and he was decidedly unpopular.

Shanghai Express indisputably remains one of the best films any of the people involved in it ever made. Despite that, Anna May Wong was hardly mentioned in reviews. If her name came up at all, it was usually relegated to the last few lines: "Anna May Wong makes the most of the rôle of the brave Chinese girl." In a review in *Bioscope*, the British publication that had once fawned over her, there was no mention of Anna May at all.

A lone voice recognized the talent others overlooked. "Just a note of pleasant recollection on an excellent performance—Anna May Wong's in *Shanghai Express*," Edwin Schallert wrote a month after the film's debut. "That sliding gait of Miss Wong's when she is on dire deeds bent is something never to be forgotten. She gave amazing emphasis to those scenes in which the bandit leader was killed. Strange and haunting power of personality does this oriental star always seem to possess."

This piece of praise was buried at the end of Schallert's usual column. Not that it mattered. Paramount wasn't interested in finding out whether Anna May's performance had contributed to the film's success. A few days before *Shanghai Express* opened, an item appeared in the *Los Angeles Times* under the subhead "Off the List." The studio would not be renewing Miss Wong's contract. "Anna May Wong, another two-time discovery, has left Paramount." How quickly the fortunes turn on one.

A portrait of Anna May from her first session with Carl Van Vechten, newly initiated as a photographer, April 1932.

EATING BITTERNESS

I f 1931 was the year of Anna May Wong's exalted Hollywood homecoming—overflowing with bouquets, critical acclaim, and competing job offers—then 1932 was the year it all went to hell. Or at least back to the way things had always been. Her contract with Paramount quietly expired and she was once again a freelance actress auditioning for parts like any Dorothy or Barbara fresh off the bus from the Midwest.

By now Anna May had become an expert at stretching her salary to cover the lean weeks and months when film parts failed to materialize. She had made good money over the years—not nearly as much as her white or male counterparts, whose bank accounts seemed bottomless, but more than enough to afford a comfortable lifestyle, provide for her siblings' educations, and pay for her upscale apartment at the Park Wilshire. All this she was especially grateful for during a deepening global depression.

The studios were quick to make hay of China's conspicuous presence in the daily headlines. With a glut of China-themed films in the works, one would assume that Anna May stood to benefit. Ironically, her symbolic representation of China did not translate into better and more substantive roles. It didn't result in any roles, in fact. Not for her, at any rate.

A scourge of bad luck, which some might call by another name—racism—clung to her like a fly to flypaper.

It seemingly began when she gave up the lead female role in First

National Pictures' *The Honorable Mr. Wong* at the end of 1931 once she was engaged to appear in *Shanghai Express*. In her place, Loretta Young was cast to play the "almond-eyed" Sun Toya San opposite Edward G. Robinson as Wong Low Get. Both actors required hours in the makeup chair before they could assume their roles with any believability. In the eleventh hour the film was renamed *The Hatchet Man* and pitched to moviegoers with the logline: "He kills! She thrills!"

Around this time, a new Asian actress was being touted around Hollywood as a potential rival to Anna May Wong and "the second Chinese girl ever to get a break in American films." Her name was Toshia Mori, only she wasn't Chinese. She was from Kyoto, Japan.

They say imitation is the sincerest form of flattery. If this public attempt at launching another Asian actress to compete with Anna May irked her, she never mentioned it. She knew something Toshia didn't. As Asian actresses, they weren't competing just with each other for on-screen roles but with every leading lady in the industry who could, with the wave of a studio's magic wand, wake up the next day with her eyes taped up and her face powdered a shade or two darker.

Anna May was never one to wait around and see whether her name got called. So she commenced with plans to tour the country making personal appearances and doing vaudeville performances, then left for New York, no film contract in hand. She had only been away a couple weeks when RKO cast her in *Roar of the Dragon* with Richard Dix and Irene Dunne. By the time Anna May had rushed back to L.A., breaking her engagements to make it in time, Dunne had left to star in another film and was replaced with the latest Swedish import, Gwili Andre. Meanwhile, the script had been completely rewritten. The film was shaping up to be a carbon copy of *Shanghai Express*, which Anna May was not keen to repeat. She decided to leave the production and headed out on tour again, taking her vaudeville act north to San Francisco.

In April, she was back in New York City, headlining a stage act called *Spring in the Orient* at the Paramount Theater in Times Square. Box office receipts were suffering under the yoke of the Depression. Many theaters on Forty-Second Street went dark or became purveyors of crude strip shows. Desperate times called for desperate measures. Studios recruited a slew of mid-list Hollywood stars and sent them up and down Broadway to make personal appearances in hopes of bringing in moviegoers "during those months when the producers unload their so-so pictures."

To be clear, Anna May was not above adapting her talents for the vaudeville circuit. She may have even relished the way it brought her closer to her public. One journalist assigned to cover the show's run at the Mastbaum Theatre in Philly spent a good portion of his word count raving about Anna May. "The outstanding moments on the stage bill to the mind of this reviewer were those in which Anna May Wong appeared," he gushed. Dazzling the audience with her "delicately fashioned figure of old ivory," Anna May "sang in her enchanting and utterly individual voice an old Chinese folk song." She recited a Chinese poem and then its translation in English, mesmerizing listeners with her gentle incantations, and then closed her act with several American numbers. It was a demanding way to earn a living, but the buoyant energy of performing in front of a live audience was hard to beat.

On her days off, Anna May took in the pleasures of life in the big city. Carl Van Vechten and Fania Marinoff were a constant presence. The splendid drunken twenties might be over, but Carl was still a regular in the Harlem nightclub scene. Walter Winchell reported seeing Carl and Anna May at the Cotton Club one evening in early May. When the two got up to dance, Cab Calloway and his band played "a special Chinese tempo" in homage to the Chinese movie star in their midst.

It was no secret Carl Van Vechten's writing days were over. They'd ended with a whimper when his novel *Parties* came out and was universally panned. People were so sick of the twenties, it turned out, they couldn't even laugh about it. But Carlo, the man who was constantly reinventing himself, was already on to his next thing: portrait photography. He installed a darkroom in one of the kitchens in his and Fania's double apartment and began collecting props and eye-catching fabrics to hang as backdrops. Anna May Wong, with her striking Asian features, was the first to officially sit for Carl and his camera that spring.

The two friends spent hours improvising different looks and setups. For one series of pictures, Anna May donned a top hat, tuxedo jacket, and ascot while sipping slyly from a liquor-filled coupe. In another sequence she wore a silk dress and posed in profile in front of a chinoiserie-inspired tapestry, her long hair hanging down loosely for the camera.

Several weeks following their initial photo session, Anna May sent Carl a telegram with her thoughts on the resulting images while en route to Chicago, where she was due to perform at the Oriental Theatre and attend a groundbreaking ceremony for the Chicago World's Fair: "Wanted to tell you the later pictures were splendid am quite excited over them and writing as soon as I have a chance to collect my thoughts."

Of the images that she noted liking best in her next note to Carl, one stands out over and above the rest. In it, Anna May rests on a divan, surrounded by silk pillows patterned with peonies and other Eastern blooms. She is wearing a white feather wig that makes her look as though she's had an Eton crop and bleached her hair a startling peroxide blond. She stares into the camera from kohl-rimmed eyes, a serious, almost defiant, expression on her face. Timeless and irresistibly modern all at once. Carlo was onto something.

"To tell the truth," she told Carl, "I had much rather pose another time when I am either not feeling so happy or when I look more fit." Anna May apparently subscribed to the theory that one must suffer in order to create great art. There would be time enough for her to sit in front of Carl's camera, between seasons of grief and heartache, many more times in the coming years. But what, exactly, was she secretly feeling so happy about?

"Life is just a Pola Negri," Anna May quipped over a bottle of Chablis to reporter friend Cedric Belfrage, who was fresh off an Atlantic liner from England. They were having a laugh at Hollywood, sitting on the red plush chairs at "one of New York's smartest speakeasies" and riffing on "scores of variations on the 'Bowl of Cherries' number . . . the theme-song of America under the current depression." Cedric, a British reporter she'd met through the international set back in Los Angeles, was stopping through New York on his way to Hollywood, where he was to report on all the goings-on for his showbiz column in London's *Sunday Express*.

When the friends met again on another New York evening, Cedric brought a friend with him, a shy, wispy plank of a man named Eric Maschwitz, who was tagging along on holiday. Eric was an editor at the recently founded British Broadcasting Company with aspirations to one day write plays for the musical theater. His bashful smile belied his playboy tendencies. Anna May probably did not make much of Eric on this first meeting; he hardly spoke a word, so intimidated was he in the presence of her wit and loveliness. But perhaps she was flattered all the same by his obvious admiration.

The moment, however, lived on eternally in Eric's memory, as he later wrote of Anna May, "I can see her now, as she opened the door of her apartment to us, a slender exquisite person in a white blouse and long black skirt. I could not have known then what her friendship one day was going to mean to me, but I was entirely enchanted."

Did the smitten Eric Maschwitz ask to see Anna May again amidst the first daffodils that magical spring? Could that be the reason behind Anna May's good cheer? Were these budding lovers spied taking long walks through Central Park at dusk? And when they parted, did they exchange love letters and long, excited cables? Impossible to know, for each was careful not to leave a paper trail, but love was assuredly coming for them. Eric would have plenty of time to think it over on the SS *Île de France*, the gulls flying around it, during his return trip to England.

Anna May was waiting to hear when work on Columbia Pictures' *The Bitter Tea of General Yen* was to start. The controversial story was based on Grace Zaring Stone's best-selling book, a melodrama about a powerful Chinese warlord named General Yen who holds a white missionary woman, Megan Davis, captive; against Megan's better judgment, she falls in love with her captor but ultimately brings about his downfall. Seeing no way out, General Yen drinks a bitter poison tea to end his life.

Anna May's involvement in the project, along with Constance Cummings as the female lead and Herbert Brenon set to direct, had been announced one month earlier. Brenon's first request as director had been to hire her to play the role of Mah-Li. The studio, hastily plowing ahead, advertised the yet-to-be-filmed picture in a glossy two-page magazine spread that highlighted its two leading ladies. Nonetheless, Anna May's professional skepticism—"I never count too much on picture negotiations until the contract is signed"—turned out to be prescient. A scuffle ensued inside Columbia Pictures over who was going to direct *Bitter Tea*. Herbert Brenon, who had worked with Anna May on *Peter Pan* and *The Alaskan*, was out.

As the end of June neared, the studio announced that a young director named Frank Capra would take over the production. Not long after, studio brass replaced Cummings with Barbara Stanwyck. Anna May Wong's name was the last to drop from the production. Within a few days, a headline ran in the *Los Angeles Times* proclaiming, "Chinatown Girl Wins Role: Toshia Mori Newest Film Cinderella." Fickle Hollywood. Wasn't it only a decade ago that press mongers were spinning her, Anna May Wong, as the unlikely Chinese Cinderella? And yet, in all that time, they were still using the same overripe tropes.

The country was in the thick of the Depression. Studios were scrounging for ways to cut costs while keeping the A-list stars on their rosters happy. "To make these pictures safe for distribution," one Hollywood columnist explained, "producers are valiantly exchanging stars, writers, directors, and camera men if necessary." Maybe the execs at Columbia realized they could get an Anna May Wong lookalike for half the price, and eight years·younger to boot.

Having the role in *Bitter Tea* pulled out from under her was a disappointment, to say the least, but there was nothing for Anna May to do but hit the road once again.

In July, she joined Hollywood truants Jean Hersholt, Una Merkel, Lew Cody, Armida, Abe Lyman, and Jack Benny for a stage revue called *Hollywood on Parade*. Much like her other personal appearances, the show included song-and-dance numbers, comedy sketches, and other amusements. The troupe opened at the Capitol Theatre in New York and then bounced around the East Coast. One week Anna May was in Brooklyn, the next she was in Philly or Washington, D.C. With several performances a day, the work kept her busy: "You know what this 'Four a Day' life does to one," she wrote to Carlo.

Life on the road had its highlights. All that time together forged new bonds. Una Merkel was a woman after Anna May's own heart—"sympathetic, sincere, and as natural off the screen as on"—and the women struck up a friendship. In D.C. they shared a hotel suite. As Anna May remembers it, "My room was right at the back of the suite; the telephone was outside the bathroom. My friends kept ringing me up, and every time I had to dash across, through doors and across rooms." Una felt perfectly comfortable ribbing her new friend about the comic rigamarole she witnessed every time the phone rang: "Say, Anna, you oughta take yo' baggage and go live in the bathroom!"

The Olympic Games hosted in Los Angeles that summer came and went before Anna May made it out west again. It wasn't the Olympic hoopla but rather Wong Sam Sing's insistence that he would soon leave the United States to spend his retirement in the old country that compelled her to hurry homeward. Once she arrived in Los

Angeles and was safely ensconced in the Wong family fold again, her father changed his mind and decided he'd stay.

Still more China-themed scenarios were in development at various Hollywood studios. In September, MGM began auditioning actresses for *The Son-Daughter*, an adaptation of a David Belasco play, and asked Anna May to make a test at the studio. For once, the story was largely sympathetic to the Chinese cause. In it, two star-crossed lovers, both Chinese American youths, find themselves caught up in the San Francisco Chinatown community's secret efforts to fund rebels in China fighting to overthrow their oppressive Manchurian rulers.

Grace Kingsley was the first to champion Anna May being cast in the feature. "While nothing is settled in the matter, we are pleased to relate that there is every chance in the world that Anna May Wong will play the leading feminine role, the star part, in *The Son-Daughter*," Kingsley wrote in her column. "She could be ideal for the title part."

Several days following her audition, Anna May awoke to find her name making newspaper headlines across the country in connection with an international scandal: "Miss Wong Accused in an Auto Accident." The *New York Times*, apparently, believed the movie star capable of appearing in two places at once, for it reported that Austrian police had stopped "a motor car driven by the Chinese film actress, Anna May Wong," for striking and injuring a cyclist.

In this most egregious case of the "Wrong Asian" phenomenon, Austrian authorities, who apparently knew but one Chinese woman with the surname Wong, reported that they had detained Miss Wong and her companion, Rudolf Friml, an Austrian composer, and confiscated their passports while they investigated further. Of course, the real Anna May Wong was in Southern California at the time of the accident, more than 6,000 miles away. Despite speaking to Mr. Friml, the *New York Times* failed to verify whether the Miss Wong in question was indeed the same Miss Wong who had dazzled Viennese theatergoers two seasons prior.

Anna May was furious. Sure, she'd earned a few speeding tickets in her day, but that was back when she was a teenage flapper, high on the first flush of success and the purchase of a sleek new automobile. No one had even bothered to call her before they went to press with such a serious accusation.

"There is no excuse for such gross negligence on the part of the paper," Anna May wrote in response to the *New York Times* clippings Carl sent to her. "*The Herald-Tribune* took the trouble to phone and check with my agents before running the story. *The Times* carried a small paragraph in their September thirteenth issue that the police made a mistake in identifying the girl, which doesn't correct the damage done to me in their first story."

Anna May's bad luck was not about to subside anytime soon. An offer to do *On the Spot* in Honolulu fell through. Rumors that Samuel Shipman was writing an original play for Anna May to star in on Broadway, or that the actress might appear in Gordon Wong Wellesley's *Shanghai Interlude* at Universal, never materialized. Then came the final slap in the face.

"I made a test at Metro-Goldwyn-Mayer studios for the leading role in the *Son Daughter*, the Chinese play David Belasco produced years ago with Lenore Ulrich [sic]. I guess I look too Chinese to play a Chinese, because I hear Colleen Moore is going to do it," Anna May confided to Carlo privately, "although no definite decision has been made."

Colleen Moore with her dark bob and blunt-cut bangs was eventually passed over too. The ever handsome Ramon Novarro would play Tom Lee, while the part of Lien Wha ultimately went to Helen Hayes, thwarting any chance at reuniting Anna May and Ramon on-screen.

Anna May did her best to keep her chin up and play the role of supportive friend standing by in the wings. She accepted an invitation to visit the set for *The Son-Daughter* and watched Ramon and Helen Hayes shoot a scene, after which she was obliged to declare they looked "perfect" in their Oriental getups. But there was only so much public ostracism one woman could take. Anyone could see with their own two eyes what was being done to her. Hollywood had systematically shut her out of every single female Chinese role for the year 1932.

"Hollywood is experiencing an epidemic of oriental plays—with *Son-Daughter, The Bitter Tea of Gen. Yen,* and *Good Earth*—and everybody acts a part therein except the one actress qualified—Anna May Wong," Harry Carr lamented.

The situation she found herself in was absurd in the extreme. Only her fortitude, resourcefulness, and sardonic humor could see her through it. She was tired of trying so hard to be diplomatic, tired of smiling for the cameras despite her anger, tired of playing nice with the Hollywood honchos when it got her absolutely nowhere. So Anna May Wong made her true feelings known to Grace Kingsley, who printed it in her column: "Anna May Wong says a Chinese actor hasn't a Chinaman's chance in Hollywood."

———————

Of all the Chinese stories in development in Hollywood, there was one that stood to rise above the whole lot of 'em.

In the spring of 1931, a little-known author named Pearl Sydenstricker Buck published her second novel. *The Good Earth,* as she titled it, chronicles the lives of Chinese peasant farmer Wang Lung and his wife O-lan in rural China. Together, the couple persevere through famine, flood, plague, and war—trials of biblical proportions. Their fortunes rise and fall over the years according to the winds of fate, in an undulating style typical of Chinese literature. With a little luck and hard work, the House of Wang eventually rises to the status of wealthy landowner. Yet this long-sought-after prosperity threatens to alienate man from his family, husband from wife, and farmer from the true source of his wealth, the land.

How, one might ask, could an American woman named Pearl Buck hope to write about Chinese farmers with a modicum of authenticity?

Pearl Sydenstricker was American by birthright, born in Hills-
boro, West Virginia, in 1892. But as the daughter of Southern Presby-
terian missionaries who soon returned to their post in China along
with their new baby, her earliest memories were not of amber waves
of grain but rather of a landscape filled with paddy fields and pagodas.

Like Anna May, Pearl grew up hearing stories of a faraway homeland, except in her case it was a wondrous place called America. By
necessity, and as a consequence of her insatiable curiosity, the young
Pearl became an expert observer of Chinese life. She took to her supposedly alien environment like a fish takes to water. She learned to
speak Chinese first and more readily than English. She played with
Chinese friends her age in their family homes and listened to the local
gossip exchanged among villagers. Sometimes she even joined in, to
the shock and awe of onlookers.

"If America was for dreaming about, the world in which I lived
was Asia," Pearl later wrote. "I did not consider myself a white person
in those days."

As an adult in her late thirties, Pearl Buck found herself stuck in
a perfunctory marriage to agricultural missionary John Lossing Buck
and caring for two children, including one with special needs. Eventually, she wrote and published her debut novel to moderate success. Her
second book, *The Good Earth*, was published by the John Day Company a year later. Nothing could have prepared Pearl Buck or her
publisher for what happened next.

When Dorothy Canfield Fisher at the Book of the Month Club
picked this improbable novel "about agriculture in China" out of a pile
of proof copies, she changed Pearl Buck's fate forever. *The Good Earth*
was promptly crowned "Book of the Month" for March 1931. The
readers who soon found themselves picking up a copy of the must-read
book of the year were unexpectedly spellbound by *The Good Earth*'s
plain and honest tale of the working-class Chinese farmer.

"In its deeper implications it is less a comment upon life in China
than upon the meaning and tragedy of life as it is lived in any age in

any quarter of the globe," the *New York Times* wrote. Man and his struggle to live peacefully off the land, to feed and shelter his family, and to grow old and die in a warm bed is a story as old as time. Ordinary Americans, city dwellers and country folk alike, now caught in the grip of the Great Depression, could easily relate to Wang Lung and O-lan's precarious circumstances. They knew all too well what it felt like to be dealt a bad hand in lean times.

"Many stories and novels have been written about China," one reviewer observed, but no Western author had depicted the Chinese with such seeming accuracy, nor had any previous author imbued the characters with dignity and virtue. "One tends to forget, after the first few pages, that the persons of the story are Chinese and hence foreign," the *New York Times* added.

The novel was a runaway success, dominating bestseller lists well into 1932. Within its first eighteen months of publication, *The Good Earth* sold tens of thousands of copies and reached its twenty-second printing, netting more than $100,000 (about $2.3 million today) in royalties and related licensing deals. Pearl Buck was apparently "dusting in the attic" at home in Nanjing, China, when she received a cablegram informing her that her book had won the Pulitzer Prize.

Anna May Wong was an ardent supporter of the book. "I think *Good Earth* is one of the most wonderful books ever written on Chinese life," she told a reporter, "but I'm not sure it will make a good picture." Through the character of O-lan especially, one began to understand the taxing and thankless role wives and mothers played in the Chinese family unit. Maybe it gave Anna May occasion to reflect on the life her mother had lived, which was not so dissimilar from O-lan's.

Others in Hollywood were quick to recognize *The Good Earth*'s sudden and pervasive success. Irving Thalberg, cofounder and head of production at Metro-Goldwyn-Mayer, had his eye on snatching up film rights to the novel as early as September 1931.

Thalberg had a reputation for taking on difficult projects and turning them into hits. His induction into the filmmaking industry in 1920 as general manager of Universal at the ripe old age of twenty had earned him the moniker "Boy Wonder." A dramatization of *The Good Earth* for Broadway was already underway. Translating the book to the silver screen was a no-brainer in Thalberg's eyes. But Louis B. Mayer, the junk salesman turned motion picture impresario and Thalberg's partner at MGM, balked at the suggestion.

"Irving, the public won't buy pictures about American farmers," Mayer argued. "And you want to give them *Chinese* farmers?"

"*The Good Earth* isn't concerned with farming," Thalberg responded with conviction. "It's the story of how a man marries a woman he has never seen before and how they live a life of intense loyalty. The public will be interested in such devotion."

Thalberg prevailed and MGM inked the deal for screen rights to *The Good Earth* at the end of May 1932 for the whopping sum of $50,000 (more than a million dollars today), the most that had ever been paid for a book by a Hollywood studio. Pearl Buck, it was rumored, had stipulated that no changes be made to her original story and that the film be shot on location in China. Thalberg, apparently, was even willing to consider the author's suggestion that an all-Chinese cast be recruited, which would make for an intriguing first in Hollywood.

Despite her year of bad breaks, the gossip mill rushed to suggest Anna May Wong for the lead role of O-lan. Grace Kingsley stated the obvious: "We shouldn't be a bit surprised if Anna May Wong was borrowed to play it."

"The town is speculating over the star for MGM's *The Good Earth*," Chapin Hall surmised in the *New York Times*. "Rumor on the lot names Anna May Wong as the star."

Another columnist promptly parroted Hall's prediction: "As one Hollywood correspondent says, it would be the greatest role Miss Wong has had."

The greatest role she'd ever had.

Only time would tell. Anna May was up for the challenge. But was Hollywood?

———————

When Ruth Ferris, the resident palm reader at the Mary Louise Tea Room opposite Westlake Park, sat down to conduct a reading of Anna May Wong's hand, what she saw was startling. The "noted palmist" had studied 80,000 hands, including those of Hollywood screen stars Gloria Swanson, Joan Crawford, and Aileen Pringle. She was confident in her powers when she stated, "For overcoming obstacles in life, Anna May Wong's is one of the most significant palms I have ever seen."

Amidst the tea room's extravagant decor, where every chamber was furnished according to a different theme—Art Deco, French Baroque, mahjong—Miss Ferris deciphered what she saw written on Anna May's palm. It was clear, she said, that the Chinese American film star had developed her capabilities as an actress, writer, and conversationalist to a high degree. "All this," Ferris intoned, "was done in spite of great handicaps."

Well, Anna May didn't need a palm reader to tell her that. She knew she'd had it hard, more difficult than most actresses in the Hollywood pantheon. Still, such a declaration was at least validating to hear spoken aloud.

Nineteen thirty-three was a new year with new plans.

Anna May's year of touring the United States and trying out various vaudeville song-and-dance acts had proven to be a fruitful testing ground. Putting on as many as four shows a day, she had learned to gauge which numbers elicited the most enthusiasm from audiences and then tweak her performances accordingly. She had developed a greater confidence in her abilities to carry a live show and she was ready to take her act to farther-flung destinations. Her first idea was to fly down to South America, one of the continents she had yet to traverse, but that plan was soon scrapped for a visit to the United Kingdom, where she could try out her act in familiar waters.

The Wong family had seen a lot of comings and goings recently. Lulu had been away from home for nearly nine months. She'd finally broken into the family business—motion pictures, that is—and taken a role playing one of the wives in W. S. Van Dyke's film *Eskimo*, which was shot on location in the wilds of Alaska. Lulu returned at the end of March to the warm climes of Los Angeles wearing Arctic furs. Only a few weeks prior, James had taken his leave and sailed to China, where he would be teaching English to college students. Frank had been enlisted as Anna May's chauffeur in the meantime, though he held out hope big brother Jimmy might send for him shortly. And those still in L.A. had a new house to move into on North Figueroa Street, next to the old laundry, thanks to their actress sister and now benefactor.

Anna May, too, would be departing again in a matter of weeks for her next sojourn to Europe by way of New York. Harry and Tai Lachman, he a film director, she a singer and performer, had become good friends as of late. They would see to it that she got off on the right foot on her sojourn to Europe. She and Tai got along famously. They were each glamorous, well-traveled, cultured Chinese women. More importantly, they both loved a good party. The Lachmans hosted a farewell bash for Anna May that went so swimmingly that, by the end of the night, everyone went down to Venice Beach and rode scooters on the strand into the sunset. Life as a movie star was grand even when one wasn't making movies. Or at least that was the way it seemed from the outside looking in.

"Friends think I've been getting lazy: it's not at all that," Anna May told a reporter for the *New York Herald Tribune*. "But after going through so many experiences of doing roles that don't appeal to me, I have come to the point of finding it all pretty futile to keep repeating poor things."

Anna May slipped into New York by train and spent the week

seeing old friends and preparing for her voyage across the Atlantic. On her last day in town, movie columnist Marguerite Tazelaar caught up with her in her room at the Algonquin Hotel as she packed her belongings into trunks.

"I'm going to England, Scotland, and Ireland for a vacation until August when I expect to return unless I should have an offer to play on the stage over there," Anna May said with a frankness that surprised her interviewer.

"There is an integrity about this soft-voiced Chinese-American girl which is unique and somehow refreshing to find in a film star, in whom artifice is so often the chief characteristic," Tazelaar elaborated for her readers. "It is candor Oriental rather than Western, in its grave reserve and quiet freedom."

Anna May proceeded with her train of thought. "I have made only one picture since last summer in Hollywood, *A Study in Scarlet*. It's difficult when there aren't stories that producers think suitable, and especially because of the fact that I speak better English than many other Chinese players. They seem to feel that if they surround me with American players the effect would be too theatrical. I've made tests for all sorts of exotic parts, for I don't want to play only one type of role. . . . I feel by now I have earned the right to have a little choice in the parts I play."

It had been fourteen years since she started doing extra work in Alla Nazimova's *The Red Lantern*. In that time, she had acted opposite superstars like Douglas Fairbanks and Sessue Hayakawa, starred in silent era hits like *Song* and *Piccadilly*, and become an international movie star adored by millions. Yet here she was, beholden to the Hollywood machine that merely saw her as exotic fare used to occasionally refresh pictures from the steady stream of blondes, brunettes, and redheads who dominated the screen.

Was she interested in making films abroad? Marguerite Tazelaar wondered. Sure, there was always that possibility. That was why she was headed back to Europe. But why should a born-and-bred American have to look outside her country for gainful employment?

Anna May divulged that she would like to do another play on Broadway, particularly *Messer Marco Polo*, the story of Marco Polo's journeys written by Donn Byrne. There on a nearby table was the book in question, along with a pile of other tomes ready to be packed for the long trip: *The Moon and Sixpence* by W. Somerset Maugham (a friend), *The Canal Boat Fracas* by Louise Closser Hale, and *The Lives of a Bengal Lancer* by Francis Yeats-Brown.

"I supposed I am going through the state of the present generation," Anna May offered, "in not knowing exactly what I want to do at the moment. I have no resentment at all over the Hollywood situation as it has affected me. There are so many things up in the air out there at present, although everybody goes on making pictures. The salary cuts are most discussed at the moment. It's strange, but when there's a Depression on and you are working you scarcely notice it, while in good times if you are out of a job you suffer a great deal from your own depression."

What about marriage? Tazelaar prodded.

"No, I am not married. This is the way I feel about it. Either you settle down and make a home or you don't, in which case it is better not to marry, I think, for it is hardly fair to the man or yourself to live impermanently and always with another interest which must come first. I still want to rove a bit." That other interest, naturally, was her career, her freedom to remain duty-bound to no one.

In Tai and Harry Lachman, she saw an alternative to the life she was living. The couple had skirted American anti-miscegenation laws by getting married in Europe, and their successful entrance into Hollywood society showed that an interracial union like theirs could work despite public scrutiny. Harry Lachman's Chinese American wife did not affect his ability to work as a director like Mickey Neilan had feared when he scuttled his marriage proposal to Anna May ten years earlier.

Marriage to a man outside her race was no longer an impossibility for Anna May. The Cable Act of 1922, one of the more draconian laws that stripped American women of their citizenship if they married a foreigner ineligible for naturalization, had finally been amended. And Anna May was not without desirable suitors. Indeed, she was going to see about one in jolly old England presently, just as fast as the SS *Europa* could carry her across the Atlantic. After all, no one said you had to be married to have a little fun.

Anna May sports a top hat and tails for her cabaret tour
across Europe, circa 1933.

10
—

FORBIDDEN BLOSSOM

Anna May Wong's reintroduction into British society in the spring of 1933 started off on a high note. The Embassy Club, that exclusive Old Bond Street supper club where one might spot a famous movie star or accidentally trade glances with the Prince of Wales, was packed to the gills the evening of Anna May's debut performance. "Everyone in the world turned up at the Embassy," as one observer put it, "to see and hear Miss Anna May Wong, the exotic Chinese movie star."

Indeed, when she glided on stage to sing her opening number, a Chinese folk song called "Jasmine Flower," all eyes turned to her and were slowly transfixed as the strange, melancholy rhythm of unfamiliar words radiated from her delicate lips. The evening was not unlike the memorable scene in *Piccadilly* when Shosho dances for London nightclubbers, only Anna May had by now outgrown the slinky, midriff-baring getups of her youth, and instead of a Chinese zither and erhu for backup she had George Whelan accompany her on piano.

"The audience, of course, did not understand the words," a reviewer wrote, "but the alluring rhythm of the song, the simple and nicely balanced musical theme, and the rich colour of the singer's voice, had their effect, and Miss Wong knew that the audience had accepted her."

Among the audience that night were Mrs. Bryan Guinness, wife of the Guinness family brewing heir; former Labour MP Sir William and Lady Jowitt; the French Grand Slam–winning tennis player Suzanne Lenglen; Georgia's Princess Imeretinsky; as well as "a gentleman, startlingly like King Kong," who "sat at a table immediately behind [Anna May] and gazed at her ecstatically, with wide open mouth."

Anna May's presence alone was usually enough to enchant the casual onlooker, but tonight she did herself one better. She wore an exquisite gold satin gown—"The loveliest dress I have seen for some time," one style watcher exclaimed—with intricate Chinese embroidery in a deep lapis hue along the hem, pastel pink and green roses flecking the rest of the frock, and a plunging back line. On her nails she wore fine gold finger guards, custom-made by Asprey, the British jeweler and luxury brand, which gleamed under the spotlights. "The 'Wong' gave us rather short rations, but made up for it by the extreme length of her fingernails!" the pseudonymous Eve wrote in the *Tatler*.

This was Anna May Wong as Londoners had never seen her before, up close and personal in a cabaret of her own design. Throughout the evening, she entertained her audience with songs in French, English, and Chinese. One moment she was crooning "Parlez moi d'amour / Redites-moi des choses tendres . . ."; in the next she reappeared in a top hat and tails—the enduring symbol of gender-bending females— to sing about "the mannishness of the modern girl and the corresponding change in the other sex." Her mouth curled into a sly smile when she predicted that one day the courts would reverse the natural order of things and mandate that divorcees pay alimony to their ex-husbands.

A couple of her pieces involved original monologues set to musical arrangements, written for her by screenwriter Lynn Starling and Ealing Studios music director Ernest Irving. "Street Girl," inspired by her character Hui Fei in *Shanghai Express,* offers a rather cynical look at the prostitute's innermost thoughts and her desire to get revenge on the man who broke her heart: "I'll smile at him, flatter him, I'll play the loving wife, / And when he's lying in my arms, snuff out his life."

Her most affecting song and dance number, quite possibly, was the Noël Coward song "Half-Caste Woman." Anna May sang it as if it were her own, the lyrics so closely hinting at the liminal space she inhabited in show business and the world. "Half-caste woman, living a life apart / Where did your story begin?" The song glorifies the tragic beauty of a Eurasian woman who is prevented from leading a normal life because of her mixed racial background. Instead, she works as a prostitute in a port city, drinking with the sailors who pay her for sex. "Were you born of some queer magic / In your shimmering gown? / Is there something strange and tragic / Deep, deep down?" And yet it's her unusual appearance, an amalgam of Western and Eastern traces, and her forbidden status that make her so alluring.

Anna May Wong undeniably saw herself as a half-caste of sorts. Everywhere she went, society found a reason to exclude or censure her. She was Chinese and American but never enough of either to be fully accepted. When she sang, "Half-caste woman, what are your slanting eyes / Waiting and hoping to see? / Scanning the far horizon / Wondering what the end will be," perchance a few of her enthralled listeners stopped to muse whether the words were meant in jest or if they revealed the depths of an untold suffering.

Not all the Embassy's patrons that evening were beguiled by Anna May's charms, though. The columnist for the *Bystander* referred to her cabaret merely as "an interesting experiment" and confessed: "I think it would have been better had she sung in Chinese all the time. When she sang in English, it was not so original, and the words of one of her English songs would have been better in a language which everybody does not understand!"

Such comments failed to put a damper on the show's glowing success. Anna May wrote ecstatically to Fania of her triumph in London: "For the first time in my life, and in the history of the Embassy Club, I did Cabaret for them, and it was very agreeable to all concerned, as their business greatly improved as a result, and the experience was a novel one for me."

Her show ran for two weeks at the Embassy and then continued on to the Holborn Empire, one of London's storied music halls.

The spring of 1933 was a glorious one for Anna May Wong socially too. "I have been terribly busy since I arrived in London," she informed Fania, "and it goes, without saying, that I am very happy for all good things that come my way."

London had not forgotten her as Hollywood had, and she picked up right where she had left off three years ago. She mingled with members of the Bright Young Things like Cecil Beaton and Nancy Mitford at the Circus Ball held at Grosvenor House. On a trip to Paris, she marveled at Josephine Baker as she sang and danced in her zippy revue *La Joie de Paris* at the Casino de Paris. A bronze-cast bust sculpted of her was unveiled by Austrian sculptor Felix Weiss at the Warren Gallery alongside "the strong heads" of Emil Jannings and Conrad Veidt. Society columnists tracked her every appearance at events such as Derby Day at Epsom Downs, Patrick Balfour's soirée in Belgrave Square, and Mrs. Somerset Maugham's "tiara-party" on a sweltering July day (Prince George reportedly spent the party chiefly on the roof garden, trying to beat the heat). At the Punch Club gala dance, she was seen adjusting the cuff links of her dinner companion, Sir "Skipper" Ward. Occasionally, she hosted her own cocktail parties at Claridge's and served her guests pale green concoctions garnished with lychee fruits stacked on toothpicks.

Her professional life flourished. Following her engagement at Holborn Empire, she signed with Wyndham Productions to play the lead in a movie called *Tiger Bay* about a Chinese proprietress in a lawless South American port town. "When I left Hollywood, I vowed I would never act for the films again," she told a reporter with a bit of fire in her voice. "You see, I was so tired of the parts I had to play. . . . Why should we always scheme—rob—kill?" But Mr. Wyndham had convinced her to break her vow, she confessed. "And I am grateful. . . . For I think that 'Tiger Bay' is a good story."

While working on the film at Basil Dean's Ealing Studios, she had to learn how to throw a knife across a room for one of the final scenes in which her character Lui Chang kills Olaf, played by Henry Victor, the vicious gang leader who has kidnapped her adopted daughter. "All my spare moments were occupied in this deadly practice, which honestly used to give me cold shudders," Anna May relayed in an essay for *Film Pictorial*. "I doubt if they were half as gruesome as Henry Victor's feelings when the time came to make the 'shot' and he was acting as my victim."

She told Fania, whose friendship and artistic judgment meant a great deal to her, that Ealing Studios was the nicest she had ever worked in. "The Picture looks very promising so far, and I think it is going to be a success," she added. "I do hope you will see the Film eventually in New York—don't forget the name: *Tiger Bay*."

Production wrapped within two weeks' time, and while Anna May entertained a potential offer from theater producer Lawrence Langer to do *The Circle of Chalk* on Broadway, she made plans for a vacation to Juan-les-Pins on the French Riviera, Barcelona, and the island of Majorca off the coast of Spain.

Did she make time to reconnect with the bashful Eric Maschwitz? London could be a rather small place when you fraternized in artistic circles. Eric, in spite of his timid demeanor, was quite the gadabout. He was also married—to actress Hermione Gingold, who had in fact been wed to his boss when she and Eric first got into bed together. Following their transgression, Hermione swiftly divorced her first husband and married Eric. She thought they were in love until she discovered Eric was sleeping around. He advised her: "Get yourself a lover." Not wanting to end up in another marriage trap, the couple nixed divorce and decided to live separately in nearby flats. They remained married in name only as each pursued new romantic partners.

Hermione later recalled how they took turns one summer ushering their paramours to a friend's estate in the South of France. "Eric took his current girl friend to a villa in Juan les Pins to relax. When he left Juan les Pins, he gave me the keys to the villa and I went down there with a new boyfriend." Could Anna May have been the unnamed girlfriend? Certainly, one can speculate. The steamy details of her love life will likely never be ironed out, and that's just the way Anna May would have wanted it.

In Majorca, she was a guest of Ronnie and Deidre Balfour, and not knowing how to swim didn't stop her from playing in the crystal-blue waters surrounding the island. "Anna May Wong can't swim, but she *can* float. So Ronnie Balfour used to swim underneath her every time she got into the water, presumably to give her confidence," Mariegold reported in the *Sketch*. "However, it hadn't worked out like that, for every time she laughed so much that she nearly drowned!"

Anna May was back to work in London in September. Langer's offer to put on *The Circle of Chalk* in New York never came through in the end, but one thing after another kept coming her way, so she decided to stay on in England. Gaumont-British Picture Corporation signed her to play Zahrat in a remake of the popular "Ali Baba and the Forty Thieves" musical *Chu Chin Chow,* based on Oscar Asche's 1916 play. It was one of the rare films in which her character's initial treachery is redeemed and she lives to tell about it. Plus she would be the focal point in a spectacular musical number with dozens of backup dancers in the film's final scenes.

For most of fall 1933, Anna May reprised her cabaret show and toured throughout the British Isles. Her annual holiday greeting card was a special treat for those cherished friends and family who received it. She commissioned an artist to create a hand-colored lithograph illustrating her year abroad. Each card revealed a map of Great Britain with the stops on her vaudeville tour labeled, as well as insets for her trips to Spain and France. The sights and sounds of various destinations were brought to life in ink and paint: in Paris a miniature figurine version of Anna May stands next to the Eiffel Tower, newly purchased Parisian dresses dangling from her arms; in London she sings alongside a grand piano at the Embassy Club; in Barcelona she spectates ringside at a bullfight; she's shown clasping a pint of Guinness in Dublin and ordering fresh seafood from a stall in Aberdeen. When she'd said she still wanted to rove a bit, she meant it.

Newsman Harry Carr, who made the long journey from Los Angeles to London, caught up with his dear friend Anna May that autumn. Seeing how she had blossomed in the gray, wet climes of the Commonwealth, he felt perfectly correct in summing up her reputation to readers back home: "The most popular American actress in England is Anna May Wong. Her friends number the most charming people in London and she has as many titles in her telephone list as Douglas [Fairbanks], only she isn't so much impressed by the fact."

Good old Doug, the visionary who'd given a teenage Anna May her big break, was also in London to begin work on what would be his final film, *The Private Life of Don Juan*. "As a screen star in England, Douglas is deader than a last year's bird's nest," Carr declared. Even the King of Hollywood couldn't stay on top forever. But for Anna May Wong, the future was looking rosy.

———

For once, Irving Thalberg might have bitten off more than he could chew. Production on *The Good Earth*, or lack thereof, stalled from the very beginning. Six months after signing the deal with Pearl Buck, Thalberg suffered a heart attack at home. It wasn't his first either. The Boy Wonder's major shortcoming was the fact that he had been born with a congenital heart defect. Doctors said then that he would be lucky if he lived to see thirty.

Still twiggy and pale for an adult man, Thalberg was now thirty-three. He knew better than anyone that he was living on borrowed time. Why else would he push himself to the breaking point? Anyone could see he was working himself sick.

That he wasn't long for this world was becoming more and more obvious to his partner, Louis B. Mayer. Together, they had been in the trenches for more than a decade and transformed MGM into the best damn movie studio in town. They'd done pretty well for themselves too. But in the early days of their partnership, their roles had been clear: Mayer was the big boss who had the final say and controlled the studio purse strings; Thalberg was the creative mind with a nose for details, and he kept the trains running.

The two men were being compensated almost on equal terms, which suggested to Mayer that his dominance was slipping. He heard the talk around Hollywood. People thought that MGM's success was all due to the Boy Wonder and his genius for moviemaking, that Louis B. Mayer was an old hack whose empire would crumble the second Thalberg left him. Whether Mayer would have to build his own studio or Thalberg would have to face down the grim reaper, both were disastrous scenarios that loomed on the horizon.

When Mayer couldn't get access to Thalberg in the days following his latest heart attack—Norma Shearer, Thalberg's movie star wife, refused to admit anyone until the doctors cleared him—Mayer installed David O. Selznick at MGM and gave him his own independent unit. Selznick was only a few years younger than Thalberg and a prodigy in his own right who had produced commercial hits like *Of Human Bondage* and *King Kong*. It also helped that he was married to Louis B. Mayer's daughter; Mayer could happily envision turning the business over to his son-in-law one day.

Thalberg was livid when he learned what had been done in his absence. He refused to return to the studio, insisting he would take a much-needed vacation instead and travel by ship down the Panama Canal and then on to New York and Europe. Nearly nine months passed before Thalberg arrived back at MGM in August 1933, ready to get to work on *The Good Earth*.

Thalberg had it in his mind to hire the formerly married couple George Hill and Frances Marion, who remained friendly, to team up for his Chinese prestige picture. Marion, Hollywood's top screenwriter, would write the script and Hill would direct. A week and half before Christmas 1933, Hill and a company of eleven MGM studio personnel left port in San Francisco on the Matson-Oceanic liner *Monterey*, headed for China. They had no idea what lay in store for them in the so-called Land of Peach Blossoms.

To begin with, Thalberg's instructions were vague. No actors had been cast, nor the script finished. The idea was for Hill to do preliminary work in China by capturing the local scenery on film, scouting locations, auditioning local Chinese actors, and collecting authentic artifacts that could be shipped back to the United States and used to dress the eventual sets. The crew was not exactly welcomed when they landed on the other side of the Pacific. Navigating the web of Chinese authorities and figureheads and courting their approval was anything but straightforward.

MGM was willing to pay for cooperation. According to one account, a warlord agreed to aid the production with war scenes in exchange for a professional photograph of his army. The picture turned out exceptionally well and word about the American movie crew that was happy to provide professional photography services traveled quickly. In a short time, other armies began requesting portraits and "for a while it looked as though MGM had given over its crew to glorifying the Chinese war lord."

The warlords, it turned out, were the least of their worries. Filming the everyday Chinese, or laopaihsing, also proved vexing. Authorities stopped Hill and his men from photographing impoverished villagers in worn-out clothes. No, they wouldn't hear of it until "the coolies had been given new clothing." Women were asked to wear flowers in their hair. Streets were swept. Houses were scrubbed. At one point, the authorities even attempted to replace water buffalo—a beloved symbol of Wang Lung's connection to the land in the book—with a modern American-made tractor.

Pearl Buck recalled arriving in Shanghai and meeting with a harried George Hill. In a "state of despair," he complained that their efforts had been thwarted at every turn during their four-month stay. China was anything but peachy. Morale was terrible, and their makeshift studio had burned down, likely due to arson. Hill was at his wit's end.

There were *forces* that didn't want the picture made at all, he told Buck.

"Forces?" she inquired in disbelief.

Hill nodded but declined to elaborate further. Not long after, he and his crew were on a ship back to the United States.

"I discovered, as the months passed, that the 'forces' were familiar enough," Pearl wrote in her memoirs, "for they were simply the prickly inverted patriotism of some members in the new government who did not want an authentic film made of Chinese villages and peasants lest it might provide unflattering views of China to foreign audiences abroad."

Pearl Buck's famous novel was not so universally embraced by the Chinese it purported to lionize. The Chinese, after all, did not need to be reminded of their own humanity. Instead, in the story of Wang Lung and O-lan, they saw themselves portrayed as bumpkins, ignorant of the ways of the world. *The Good Earth* presented China as a poverty-stricken, broken-down place that many felt harkened back to a bygone era. Chinese elites especially did not appreciate the patriarchal tone taken by the book's American missionary author. Regardless of her fluency in the language, what could such a woman really know about the China that was now striving to become a recognized nation-state?

Pearl was ultimately sympathetic to Chinese objections and their desire to save face. The Chinese papers were full of editorials that read like this: "We fear that in spite of our government's every precaution, there will be some child in this film with an unwashed face or some farmer's wife with a dirty apron." Once she learned of the outcry against MGM's production, she distanced herself from the film completely.

The local news media in Los Angeles heralded the MGM crew's return enthusiastically in May 1934, claiming that the company was "bubbling with optimism." The crew arrived at the studio with "miles of film procured in the interior of China" as well as 250 cases filled with everything from "Chinese water-wheels to cooking utensils." The reports failed to mention that the reels and reels of footage made in

China, save for twelve minutes, were all destroyed during the return voyage—either by acid that leaked into the containers or due to a Chinese officer's insistence that the film reels be sent through an X-ray machine on the group's departure from the country.

Frances Marion, usually a whiz at adaptations, struggled to craft a viable script. Condensing the epic tale of *The Good Earth*, which follows the thirty-year saga of one family, into a two-hour screenplay was an unenviable task. The book itself had very little dialogue and when characters spoke to one another it was usually with the utmost economy. Rather, the narrative unfolds through Wang Lung's innermost thoughts. But telling the entire story through voice-over would be clunky and impractical. Marion generated multiple scripts from 1933 to 1934.

Then Hill was in a terrible car accident in June 1934, suffering a crushed chest and broken ribs. His recovery was painfully slow, and on the morning of August 10, 1934, his body was discovered in his Venice Beach home. The pistol George Hill used to blow his brains out was still clutched in his hand. Just the night before he had managed to attend a story conference at MGM for *The Good Earth*. However, the pain from his physical injuries had been too much to bear in the end.

All of Hollywood was shaken by George Hill's tragic end, including Irving Thalberg. Not only had *The Good Earth* lost its director, but its screenwriter, Frances Marion, was terribly devastated by Hill's death and dropped out of the production near the end of 1934.

Thalberg was back to square one. Two years had been devoted to preproduction, with little to show for it. The clock was ticking, so he turned presently to one of his tried-and-true methods: hiring a half dozen writers or so, telling them all to throw spaghetti at the wall as fast as they could, and seeing what stuck. Among the new blood brought in were Talbot Jennings, playwright Marc Connelly, Claudine West, Tess Slessinger, Jules Furthman (who had written the script for *Shanghai Express*), Marian Ainslee, and librettist DuBose Heyward.

It was important to Thalberg that the film appeal to women; otherwise he didn't think it could succeed at the box office. Hence, he told the writers to base their scripts on the Broadway adaptation and develop O-lan into a more likable, admirable matriarch. MGM was also under pressure from China's Nationalist government to present what associate producer Albert Lewin called "a completely sympathetic portrayal of Chinese life." Where the book revealed the futility and bitterness of rural life, the movie would produce a wholesome and uplifting narrative about man's elemental relationship with the "good earth." By recasting O-lan from a slavish, unlovable wife to a diligent, virtuous symbol of womanhood and, by extension, Mother Earth herself, the farmer's wife becomes the heroine of the story.

Among all the writers involved, Marc Connelly's script came out on top in August 1935. Irving Thalberg's opus was finally making headway. With a close-to-final script nailed down, he and Lewin could move on to the big question on everyone's mind: casting.

There were those who remained doubtful. One such skeptic wrote, "We're not convinced *The Good Earth* will ever see celluloid. If it does, we imagine Metro-Goldwyn-Mayer will be as surprised as anyone."

Another six months in London went by in the blink of an eye. During that time, Anna May played the lead in the Basil Dean/Associated Talking Pictures remake of *Java Head*—the first film in which she was allowed to kiss her costar on-screen.

Anna May had been absent from Hollywood for more than a year when Paramount got the itch to recall its Chinese American star. They had a part for her in a Chinatown number called *Limehouse Blues*, adapted from the English writer Thomas Burke's best-selling story collection *Limehouse Nights*. She was to play Tu Tuan, the jealous lover and dance partner of Harry Young, a mixed-race Chinese American import just arrived in London's Limehouse district. Harry, however, falls in love with an English street girl and pickpocket. George Raft would play Harry in yellowface and Jean Parker his taboo love interest. Lust, resentment, and suspicions swirl as this ménage à trois barrels toward its tragic conclusion. After Tu Tuan betrays Harry to the police, she pulls out a knife and dies by her own hand.

Tu Tuan wasn't the most enlightened role, but *Limehouse Blues* was a well-resourced picture with an established leading man. As a Limehouse native, Tu Tuan was supposed to speak British English. Paramount wanted Anna May specifically because of her studied British accent. It was about time those 100 guineas paid off. Anna May accepted the offer and set sail from London on the *Aquitania* at the beginning of July 1934. "I'm going to be awfully glad to get back to my family and Hollywood," she wrote to Grace Kingsley by postcard.

The Wong clan was there to welcome Anna May home from her world travels when the Chief pulled into the Pasadena train station. During her time away, she had grown out her famous bangs and begun sporting a bare forehead, widow's peak and all. At twenty-nine, Anna May looked older and more sophisticated, if a bit hardened, when she stepped off the train and into her family's arms. She wore a smart cream-colored traveling suit with a matching crescent hat, long gloves, and a patterned scarf tied at her collar. Her arms were filled with bouquets as she posed for the reporters and cameras present.

This joyous family reunion would be a relatively short one, for in a few weeks Anna May would be the one saying farewell to her father and siblings, Frank, Roger, Mary, Lulu, and Richard, as they embarked on a two-month trip to China. James, who had been working in China for a year, would meet them there. Wong Sam Sing had finally decided to retire and close the old Sam Kee Laundry for good. Four lonesome years had passed since Lee Gon Toy's tragic death. His kids were nearly all grown: Richard, the youngest, was twelve. Wong Sam Sing was in his seventies now and feeling more and more out of place—baffled, really—next to his modern-thinking American children. Though he himself had been born an American, he'd grown up

42 NOT YOUR CHINA DOLL

in a different time, when holding tight to the old ways, to culture and clan, was the only means for Chinese to survive in the Wild West.

"He does not understand our ways," Anna May explained in an interview with Louella Parsons. "He still worships after the manner of his fathers and he cannot understand young modern America." Wong Sam Sing, nearing the end of his life, decided it was time to return home to his first wife and eldest son and the grandchildren that awaited him there. The American Wong kids would accompany their father and make their first trip to "the land of their ancestors." Originally, Anna May had planned to join them, but taking on the role in *Limehouse Blues* made the timing impossible. She was expected back in Europe in November to tour her cabaret act through Italy, Sweden, Denmark, and Norway. China, unfortunately, would have to wait for a more opportune time.

Before they sailed, Anna May followed her family on board to say her farewells. There, on the deck of the SS *President Wilson*, with everyone dressed in their best traveling suits, Wong Sam Sing and his American brood gathered and smiled for a family picture. The ship soon pulled out of the port, leaving Anna May on her own.

Rumblings in the press about who would play the important role of O-lan in *The Good Earth* started up again shortly after her arrival home. No updates had been forthcoming from MGM since the grisly demise of its first director. But that didn't stop the rumor mill from churning.

"*The Good Earth* compass now points very strongly toward Anna May Wong. And wouldn't that be a sensation, if she were elected to this role!" gushed Edwin Schallert in the *Los Angeles Times*. "Long has Anna waited for a real chance in American pictures."

Edna B. Lawson, a reporter for the *Honolulu Advertiser*, conjectured that several Chinese players could be recruited for the cast. Irving Thalberg, it was rumored, was considering Shanghainese actress Butterfly Wu to play O-lan. In addition, Soo Yong, Keye Luke, and Anna May Wong were still in the running for the assumed all-Chinese cast. Lawson even suggested that cast members might speak their lines in Chinese, while the English dialogue could be furnished in subtitles. Walter Winchell offered a completely different take. Already assuming the worst, he remarked dourly, "Funny that nobody thought of Anna May Wong for *Good Earth*."

Louella Parsons, the queen bee of Hollywood gossip, didn't pussyfoot around. She went straight to the source and asked Anna May point-blank if she wanted the part in *The Good Earth*. Anna May deflected, suggesting that her sister, Lulu, would be a better fit for the role. "She has been a mother to all of us, although she isn't much older than we are," she said, referring to the Wong children.

Not satisfied, Louella tried again. But would she make a test for MGM if they asked her to? Anna May laughed. With an even-keeled coolness she said that she "refused to make any more tests for *Good Earth* or any other pictures just to prove she can look Chinese."

In fact, she added, "I know I look Chinese and so does everyone else."

Anna May was tired of playing the same old cat-and-mouse game with Hollywood. The industry's myopic worldview and the way the execs—not the artists—insisted on limiting roles for people of color like her had not changed much in the fifteen years she'd been working as a film actress. If anything, the strict implementation of the Hays Code that began in 1934 had only made things worse. On-screen interracial affairs, once a popular aspect of silent era hits like Sessue Hayakawa's *The Cheat*, were curbed by the code's miscegenation clause, which forbade any "sex relationship between the white and black races." She could never again play a romantic leading lady role opposite a white leading man as she had in *The Toll of the Sea*.

The ebb and flow of Anna May's career over the last several years—in Hollywood her fortunes seemed to dry up overnight, while in Europe the cup was always half full, brimming with opportunities—led her to turn inward in search of answers. She delved deeper into the teachings of Laozi, the great Taoist philosopher, and espoused many of his ideas when reflecting on her life. While she was home in L.A., she sat down with Harry Carr for a heartfelt tête-à-tête.

"With every passing year I feel myself more Chinese; it is as though I were taking up the heritage of my race. Yet I have never seen China," she told him. "My friends say that my appearance and manner have changed since my early Hollywood flapper days. I know that I feel differently in my consciousness. I don't believe that anything would ever worry me again. Those pig-tail pulling days of my terror and unhappiness could never come back.

"I found solace and philosophy in the traditions of my own people," she explained. "This is such a short life that nothing can matter very much either one way or another. I have learned not to struggle but to flow along with the tide. If I am to be rich and famous, that will be fine. If not, what do riches and fame count in the long run?"

This was not Anna May sitting back and throwing her life into the hands of fate. Passivity and inaction were not the way either. But, she had come to realize, there were some things that were more important than personal glory, on-screen or otherwise. Harmony would be restored only when all things in the universe were in balance with one another. The key was in trying not to try. Anna May could no more force a square peg into a round hole than she could convince Hollywood to see beyond its endemic racism. What she could do was continue to practice her art wherever it was welcomed, love and support her family, and give whatever joy and generosity came to her back into the world.

Anna May had already arrived at her own conclusion about *The Good Earth*. "I—that flustered, worried, defensive little Hollywood flapper—found happiness when I ceased to worry about time. No one can give me what belongs to someone else; and no one can take away that which is mine." Either MGM would offer her the part of O-lan or it wouldn't. The decision would not change the course of her life. Only she could do that.

By the time Irving Thalberg made up his mind over what to do about casting for *The Good Earth*, it was the fall of 1935. He'd settled on a new director, Victor Fleming, who coincidentally had just returned from his own travels in China. Fleming took one look at the piles of scripts stacked knee-high in associate producer Albert Lewin's office and said, "Throw 'em all out."

Thalberg had given some serious thought to Pearl Buck's recommendation that he employ an all-Chinese cast. He also knew that casting white actors to play the two lead roles would not go unnoticed, at least not without a bit of controversy. Yellowface was a clownish device used in lurid melodramas and lowbrow comedies. Even the practice of blackface had noticeably decreased with the emergence of Black actors like Stepin Fetchit and Hattie McDaniel. The NAACP was also to thank for its persistent activism on issues of representation. MGM was supposed to be making a realistic film about Chinese farmers, not a farcical Fu Manchu or Charlie Chan flick. Others at Thalberg's production unit warned him against resorting to yellowface, but Thalberg had been struck with a vision of who should play Wang Lung. And when he had a vision, nothing could deter him from pursuing it. "I'm in the business of creating illusions," he said, rebuffing his critics.

The man he wanted to play Wang Lung was Paul Muni, a Polish Jewish player on the Warner Bros. payroll known for his gifts as a character actor. Muni was born in Lemberg in the Austro-Hungarian empire (modern-day L'viv, Ukraine) and grew up in a Yiddish theater family. His parents immigrated to the United States and flung him into the family business at a young age; he'd been playing old men since he was twelve, as well as a wide assortment of personages and ethnicities, including French, Mexican, Polish, Cockney, Spanish, and African American in blackface. His recent roles as Louis Pasteur in a biopic about the French chemist and an Italian mobster in *Scarface* had been box office hits. Audiences marveled at his ability to transform himself. Thalberg believed Muni had it in him to make his biggest metamorphosis yet.

He invited Muni over to MGM studios that September and sprung the idea on him over lunch in his personal dining room.

"I'm about as Chinese as Herbert Hoover," Paul Muni protested. "I won't look Chinese, no matter how much makeup I use, and I won't sound it." He had a point, but Thalberg wouldn't hear it.

"You'll *be* it," Thalberg insisted, "which is what I want."

"I'm too old for the part," Muni objected. "Wang Lung starts out as a kid—twenty years old—on his wedding day. A couple of days ago, Mr. Thalberg, I was forty years old. How do you tell a camera— and an audience—that an old character actor is a kid? Hell, I never played a twenty-year-old when I was twenty years old!"

Thalberg kept working on Muni, eventually convincing him that his vision was the only one possible. In a matter of weeks, Paul Muni was signed to play Wang Lung and *The Good Earth* had its first star. MGM would negotiate with Warner Bros. and hammer out the terms of loaning Muni out to the studio. The role of O-lan remained unassigned.

There were other considerations to be made around casting. The Chinese Nationalist government was taking Hollywood's big China production quite seriously. In addition to the installation of Vice-Consul Yi-seng Kiang in Los Angeles, China sent a special envoy, Major General Ting-hsiu Tu, to observe and advise MGM's efforts to bring rural China to life.

Any number of actresses, Chinese, European, and American, had been under consideration at one time or another for O-lan. More than three hundred tests were made of actors in the United States and China. Anna May Wong was still vaguely in the running for the part, but Thalberg had never been fully convinced of her star power. In his eyes, she was a B-movie actress, not a leading lady. He doubted that any Chinese actor could carry a film of this stature and he had admitted as much to Pearl Buck. "I was told, however, that our American audiences demand American stars," Buck recalled. "So I yielded the point, as indeed I had to, for I had no control over the matter."

In the meantime, Anna May continued living her fabulous life. Nineteen thirty-five saw her voted "the best-dressed woman in the world" by the Mayfair Mannequin Academy, the modeling school responsible for launching New York Fashion Week. She often presided over dinners at friend Eddy See's newly opened Dragon's Den in Chinatown, where starstruck diners gaped at the movie star in their midst. Hollywood types like Peter Lorre and Walt Disney were also regulars, along with James Wong Howe and his longtime partner Sanora Babb. Due to anti-miscegenation laws, Dragon's Den was one of the few establishments that welcomed interracial couples and other marginalized groups. The basement restaurant's colorful murals, which were painted onto the exposed brick walls by artist friends Tyrus Wong and Benji Okubo, were a fitting backdrop for Anna May's sparkling repartee.

She returned to London for a seven-month stay, where Fania visited her and together they enjoyed fraternizing with mutual friend Paul Robeson and making new acquaintances with Chinese luminaries like Mei Lanfang, China's preeminent opera singer; S. I. Hsiung, author of the play *Lady Precious Stream*; and film star Butterfly Wu. Back in the United States in June, Anna May spent the summer and early fall months in New York City socializing and taking a month's rest at Briarcliff Lodge in Westchester County. When Major General Tu was asked his opinion of the Chinese American actress, he didn't pull any punches. He said plainly that her standing in China was "very bad."

"Whenever she appears in a film, the newspapers print her picture with the caption: 'Anna May Wong again loses face for China,'" he explained.

Chinese critics were constantly finding fault with her films. A few months earlier, one such reviewer was quoted in a British newspaper saying it was "unfortunate that Anna May Wong, in her capacity of employee of British companies, should appear in roles that reflect against her race."

Major General Tu, who was a Western-educated Chinese citizen, understood the impossible situation Anna May constantly found herself in. "I feel sorry for her because I realize that she has to play the parts assigned her," he admitted. "It is the *parts* China objects to. She is always a slave—*a very undressed slave*. China resents having its womanhood so represented."

In the meantime, MGM continued to audition prospective actresses. In September, one actress rose above the pack as the likely favorite. Her name was Luise Rainer, MGM's latest European import. Though born to a prosperous upper-middle-class Jewish family in Germany, her father disapproved of the theater and called acting "a low and vulgar profession." She was thrown out of the house around age sixteen when she decided to pursue a career as an actress. "I had to live on apples and eggs!" she later recalled. Her histrionic talents were quickly recognized. Rainer joined Max Reinhardt's troupe in Vienna and became one of his protégées.

In 1934 an MGM talent scout discovered Rainer in a stage production of *An American Tragedy* in Vienna. Within a short time MGM had signed her to a long-term option contract and put her on the next ship to the United States. She arrived in Hollywood in January 1935, just weeks after her twenty-fifth birthday. Her only companion was her beloved Scottish terrier, a special allowance she had negotiated with MGM as part of her contract.

Luise languished on the MGM payroll her first few months in Hollywood. No one had a project for her. Sure, it was nice getting paid to do nothing, but Luise was far away from home in a strange place. Then, when Myrna Loy walked off from a role opposite William Powell, Rainer got her chance. She would play the female lead in *Escapade*, her very first Hollywood film. The story was set in Vienna, and since MGM was eager to avoid arousing any anti-German sentiments, which had lately intensified in response to Hitler's meteoric rise, studio PR introduced Rainer to the public as Viennese, not German.

Critics and regular moviegoers were instantly taken with Luise's fragile, birdlike beauty, her penetrating eyes, and her dark hair worn in a "short raggedy bob." *Escapade*'s success demonstrated her latent star power. She "clicked" in a single picture, according to one observer. "She's a find! One can say that without question about Luise Rainer," Edwin Schallert gushed. "She is immensely clever, remarkably unself-conscious. Her acting has charm and freedom. She should go far."

In the public eye, Luise Rainer was a brilliant discovery. But privately there were whispers that Rainer was difficult. She had an air about her. "The greatest actress in Hollywood is Luise Rainer, if you believe Luise Rainer," went one snide comment in the celebrity pages.

"*Good Earth* forecasts are varied at the moment," Schallert reported in mid-September. "Fairly certain it is that if English-speaking players are used, Luise Rainer will have the leading feminine role." Two months later, Rainer was confirmed as the actress set to play O-lan. Anna May learned the news while she was still in New York. MGM, however, wanted her to test for another role in the film: that of Lotus, the bewitching teahouse girl whom Wang Lung becomes infatuated with after he grows rich and decides to take as his second wife.

So Anna May made the five-day train trip home to Los Angeles at the beginning of December 1935. She went to MGM studios, put on the costume and makeup for Lotus, and walked onto a provisional set to have her screen test made. German cinematographer Karl Freund was behind the camera and Bill Grady from the MGM casting office directed Anna May in her scene. All was quiet as a lone Hollywood reporter, Sidney Skolsky, watched silently from the wings. Then Luise Rainer walked in and sat down in the peanut gallery. Luise couldn't help herself: she was a fan. She marveled aloud to Skolsky at how beautiful and talented Anna May was; she was so excited to watch her work.

After a take or two, Bill Grady came over to where Luise was seated and in a hushed voice said, "Anna May Wong is very nervous. She's playing a difficult scene and I'm certain she wouldn't be so nervous if you weren't watching her."

"I'm sorry. I should have known better," Luise muttered, suddenly embarrassed. "I know how it is when I play certain scenes. I'll go and tell Anna May Wong that I'm sorry—I admire her very much."

Anna May made at least two screen tests at MGM that December. In his notes to Thalberg and others, Albert Lewin acknowledged that Anna May deserved "serious consideration" for the part of Lotus but he expressed concerns that she was "a little disappointing as to looks. Does not seem beautiful enough to make Wang's infatuation convincing."

Chinese or not, in their eyes she wasn't fit to play Wang Lung's wife or his mistress, and MGM ultimately decided against casting Anna May as Lotus. Instead, they condescendingly offered her the even lesser role of Cuckoo, the woman who brokers Lotus and Wang Lung's marriage and later serves as Lotus's lady-in-waiting.

The debacle of her screen test and the humiliation of having it recounted in the gossip columns for everyone to read about was insulting enough. Now she was nixed from playing Lotus entirely? Of all the low-down, dirty things she'd had to endure from Hollywood, this one took the cake. Whoever thought giving her the option to play Cuckoo was a suitable consolation prize must have been out of their mind. The part was minuscule, a supporting role to a supporting role. Did they think Anna May Wong was in the business of begging for crumbs?

Meanwhile, everyone was pumping her for news on the outcome of her audition. But Anna May had other plans in mind—and an idea about how to beat Hollywood at its own game. On December 16 she wrote to Fania in New York:

So far have not seen many people as I have been very busy getting settled and running back and forth to the M.G.M. studios.
Have made two tests for the "Lotus" part. From all appearances
Miss Rainer is definitely set for the part of Olan. No use bucking
up against a stone wall. Practically every one, including my
friends, seem to feel that I should take the Lotus part "if there is
lots of money in it."

I am still in the same frame of mind in regards to the thing
and feel a strong inclination to carry out my original plans of
going to China, however we shall see.

That same day she submitted a new Form 430 to the Los Angeles
immigration office so that she could leave the country on a trip to
China in January. Several days later, the half-truth that Anna May had
won the role of Lotus was leaked to the press. It would be easy to explain her rationale for walking away from the part without disclosing
that it was actually Cuckoo she'd been offered, not Lotus. Anna May
had played Lotus twice before in *Shame* and *The Toll of the Sea*, meeting her end in the latter by suicidal drowning. No, she was done being
Lotus, the forbidden blossom whose cloying scent always leads to
death and destruction. That's what she'd tell them.

MGM had made its decision; now it was time to make hers. If it
was China the American people wanted, then it was China she would
give them. Her response was flawless: for the first time in her life,
Anna May Wong was going to pay her respects to the land of her
ancestors, the *real* China—and she planned on bringing the cameras
with her.

ACT FOUR

Anna May stands inside the moon gate at Desmond Parsons's Peiping home
during her trip to China, 1936.

CHINA THROUGH THE LOOKING GLASS

From the moment she arrived in this world, it seemed, Anna May Wong had a remarkable capacity for defying expectations—and not always in a good way. Just as she had surprised her father by being born a girl, her public announcement that she had declined the role of Lotus sent Hollywood into an absolute tizzy. The only Chinese American actress of standing and name recognition had refused a principal part in *The Good Earth*? Irving Thalberg must have been thrown for a loop, his control over the narrative pulled right out from under him.

"It has long been my hope to see China and fill a gap in my life," Anna May said coyly. "I finally decided that, regardless of my work, I would sail for China." When she turned down the role of Cuckoo, she had made up her mind to give the American public something MGM couldn't . . . something better, a kind of counterprogramming: Anna May Wong in China.

She moved forward with plans to travel to the Far East. On Monday, January 20, 1936, Anna May hastened to the Port of Los Angeles in San Pedro and boarded the SS *President Hoover*, bound for Hong Kong. Some ten days later the ship reached its first port of call in Hawaii and docked for the day in Honolulu harbor. As Anna May breakfasted in the ship's dining room, she was accosted by a pack of local journalists who had been let loose on the ship after landing. Anna May was dressed to impress in an orange redingote made of light wool, a navy and white print dress, and a small pointed hat perfectly aslant on her head. Festooned with several fresh flower leis around her neck—a welcome gift bestowed upon her only moments before by the Chinese consul general, K. C. Mui—Anna May sipped her tea pleasantly and proceeded to address the questions lobbed her way.

The question on the tip of everyone's tongues: Was it true—could it be true—that she had said no to the Boy Wonder, the man who didn't take no for an answer, and walked out on MGM's biggest production in a decade?

"Anna May Wong, exotic celestial veteran of the silver screen and stage, offered up a Shanghai gesture to Hollywood yesterday," read the lede on the front page of the *Honolulu Advertiser* the next day. This was already going better than her wildest dreams. "She informed interviewers that she had refused the role of Lotus—a secondary role—in the film version of *The Good Earth*."

Speaking for herself, she reasoned, "I do not see why I, at this stage of my career, should take a step backward and accept a minor role in a Chinese play that will surround me entirely by a Caucasian cast."

In subsequent accounts, she made it clear that she had been upfront with MGM from the outset. "I'll be glad to take the test, but I won't play the part," Anna May had told the studio. "If you let me play O-lan, I'll be very glad. But you're asking me—with Chinese blood—to do the only unsympathetic role in a picture featuring an all-American cast portraying Chinese characters." What could they possibly say to that?

Back in Hollywood, once heads had stopped spinning, industry insiders tried to make sense of what had happened. "It was rather startling to hear that Anna May Wong, of her own volition, turned down the very fine role of Lotus in *The Good Earth*," Lloyd Pantages remarked in his column. "But then maybe it isn't so startling when you hear her story. The role of Lotus would be held in great disdain by the Chinese and she (being a Chinese lady) to play a secondary role to a Viennese, Luise Rainer (who is playing Olan), seemed just a little too ridiculous seeing as how Miss Wong wanted to play Olan from scratch—so there you be."

No one could fault Anna May for pushing back at the same studio bosses who had sidelined her for years despite the critical acclaim and adulation she'd won on Broadway and throughout Europe. Arriving at such a decision was all the more incredible since the film adaptation of *The Good Earth* was to be a historic first in American moviemaking by depicting the Chinese not only with compassion but also with a psychological realism that had been noticeably lacking until then. Charlie Chan, though a positive stereotype, as some would argue, was still a caricature, a kind of Oriental superhero, yet one who was effeminate and nonthreatening to white masculinity. Wang Lung and O-lan, on the other hand, were simple, salt-of-the-earth types and relatable to everyday Americans. But Anna May stuck to her guns and walked away from the chance to be a small part of this cinematic milestone.

By contrast, the Chinese American community up and down the West Coast had come to embrace MGM's production. The leads would be depicted by white actors in makeup, which, while not ideal, was a concession most Chinese Americans were willing to make in exchange for having their people's story told in a big way.

As the editorial notes in the *Chinese Digest* issue dedicated to *The Good Earth* would later express, "Do not think that because we made this issue . . . that we have succumbed to the fascination and glamour of Hollywood. Far from it. The chief reason was this: we recognize that the motion picture version of Pearl S. Buck's story of Man and the Soil will, like the novel, do an immeasurable amount of good in eliciting western understanding of and sympathy for China and the Chinese."

Anna May was pointed yet diplomatic in her comments to the reporters crowded around her on the SS *President Hoover*. Timing was also partly to blame. She had wanted to travel to China for years, she explained, and at last the ideal opportunity had presented itself.

All the groundwork had been carefully laid. First, she sent cards to her journalist friends announcing that she was leaving on her first visit to China. She also combed through her contacts abroad and wrote to friends and family in China, announcing her imminent arrival and tipping off the foreign press. Then she shrewdly arranged for respected photojournalist H. S. Wong, who captured world events for Hearst Metrotone News, to document her travels in China with his Eyemo camera and send the newsreel-worthy footage back to the United States, where the Hearst Corporation could potentially distribute it. Newsreel Wong, as he was more fittingly known, wasn't just any cameraman: he would later capture one of the most haunting images of war for *Life* magazine—a baby crying amidst the bombed-out debris of a train station in Shanghai during the Second Sino-Japanese War.

Anna May, who grew up speaking basic Cantonese at home and often cut her after-school Chinese classes, was turning over a new leaf and announced her plans to take Mandarin lessons and study Chinese theater technique during her extended stay in China. Maybe, some hypothesized, she would even make a picture there.

Finally, she negotiated a contract with the *New York Herald Tribune* to publish a series of five articles chronicling her impressions of China and demystifying its culture from the eyes of a fellow American. This was a small step toward the fruition of another dream Anna May had long held. She was an avid reader and aficionado of the written word. Stacks of books followed her wherever she traveled. A quick look at her datebook revealed a preference for keeping company with brilliant writers like Aldous Huxley, W. Somerset Maugham, Edward Knoblock, Carl Van Vechten, Eddy Sackville-West—not to mention her dear friends in the press pool.

Few knew it, but Anna May harbored a desire to write herself. Rob Wagner fondly remembered the days when little Anna and Lulu would arrive at his "writing shack" up the hill in the Arroyo Seco with a heavy bundle of laundry from Sam Kee's. The two girls would tarry awhile and visit Wagner as he worked at writing film scenarios. "Anna May wished to become a writer," Wagner recalled, "and so she would bring her little compositions to me for criticism. We became great friends."

It was this endeavor of chronicling her journey, instead of scribbling thank-you notes for the goodbye gifts she'd received, to which she directed her attention during the first few days of her ocean voyage. She'd been taking copious notes of all that she was seeing and experiencing. Now, sitting alone in her first-class stateroom on the SS *President Hoover* just weeks after her thirty-first birthday, "surrounded by the usual flowers, books, candy, and other going-away presents," Anna May reflected on what it felt like to be setting out on the trip of a lifetime.

"It is difficult to believe," she wrote, "that I am actually on my way to the East. Already the farewells of yesterday seem remote; a link with the past has been broken and I feel that I am suspended between two worlds."

Only a week or so ago, Tai Lachman had hosted a fabulous farewell party for Anna May and Erich Pommer and his wife, who would be departing in the opposite direction for London. More than two hundred people showed up at the cocktail hour, showering the guests of honor with warm wishes for their travels ahead. Several dozen stayed for dinner and noshed on "the grandest chop suey ever served." Having missed the epic goodbye party, Grace Wilcox flew up to San Francisco, the ship's second stop, several days later to give Anna May a potted lily and say her farewells in person before the SS *President Hoover* pulled out of port. The love her friends and family had shown her had done so much to lift her spirits and steady her for the voyage ahead, but as Anna May sailed forward into uncharted waters, the quotidian world as she had known it receded into the background.

All her life she had listened to her father and his friends tell wistful stories of their homeland. Their tales conjured up images of "tree-shaded villages set on the edge of old canals; of Buddhas seated on gold-leafed lotus flowers; of the kitchen-god who is burned with much ceremony every year after his mouth has been rubbed with sugar, so that when he ascends in smoke he will report only good things to the heavenly authorities."

She was in the somewhat perplexing position of being a Chinese who had never been to China. "Chinese in the United States suffer from a lifelong homesickness, and this somehow is communicated to their children, even though the children know nothing about their ancestral homeland," Anna May explained to the readers of the *New York Herald Tribune*. "I am very proud of being an American; for years, when people have asked me to describe 'my' native country, I've surprised them by saying that it is a democracy composed of forty-eight states.

"But," she continued, "I've always been aware of another country, in the background of my mind." Indeed, Anna May had settled into the rhythm of life on the SS *President Hoover* "punctuated by soft toned gongs," making new acquaintances with those also traversing the 6,000 miles between East and West. One afternoon, she ventured to the lower deck, where the "Oriental third class" was lodged. She moved with ease among her compatriots, Chinese who had made their livelihoods in America and were returning home after many years, sometimes decades, to see children and wives they had left behind (not unlike her own father) or to live out their final days so that their bones might be buried in ancestral tombs.

"One man proudly showed me a talented canary which he was taking home as a present for his brother," she told readers. "The Chinese are devoted to birds, and it is still customary for a gentleman of the older school to take a bird cage with him when he goes for a stroll in the park." The canary's cheerful song lingered in Anna May's ears as she made her way back to first class.

Before returning to her cabin, she stopped at the ship's bow. The unknown adventures that lay ahead galvanized her as the sun slowly dipped into the endless Pacific horizon. The massive ocean liner beneath her feet glided effortlessly through the swells, blowing salt mist into her hair. Flying fish leapt from the water against the fading sherbet sky. She understood that momentum was on her side, carrying her on a journey of self-discovery, to remember something that had always lived inside her.

"I am going to a strange country, and yet, in a way, I am going home," she wrote. "I have never seen China, but somehow I have always known it. . . . Just as I have never forgotten that my real name is Wong Liu Tsong."

———————

Back in Los Angeles, Irving Thalberg was anxious to get the rest of his supporting cast squared away for *The Good Earth*. A long and varied list of actresses with unusual backgrounds—Chinese, Polynesian, Hungarian, Russian—was trotted out to audition for Lotus: Steffi Duna, Princess Der Ling, Mamo Clark, Tamara Drasin, Isabel Jewell, Lotus Liu. Thalberg had articulated his intention to find Chinese players to fill principal roles, yet MGM's casting practices seemed to contradict that objective. In the *Los Angeles Times*, Edwin Schallert reported that Wang Lung's two wives would both be played by Caucasians, but weeks later the *Los Angeles Evening Post-Record* stated that "Producer Irving G. Thalberg desires all the characters, if possible, to be Chinese." So which was it?

MGM assumed it would be difficult to recruit Chinese fluent in English. "The cry has gone out for old Chinese who speak perfect English. It sounds like a gag but nevertheless it's a serious matter to the people making *The Good Earth*," one reporter explained. The last thing Thalberg wanted was a jarring split in accents between white and Chinese actors—though when it came to Luise Rainer, her German-accented English was apparently a nonissue.

"Paul Muni, who will play Wang, won't speak the horrible pidgin-English which most actors assume when they play a Chinese role." Motion pictures had taught moviegoers to associate Asian faces with

broken English. But in the context of *The Good Earth*, such stereotypical accents would elicit ill-timed laughter and remind viewers
that the story's subject was ultimately a foreign people. The easiest way
to make the characters relatable was to make them sound like Americans.

From the point of view of the MGM production staff, there just
weren't enough American-educated Chinese to fill all the Wang family
and household roles, especially parts like Wang Lung's father, uncle,
and aunt, which naturally called for older actors.

That autumn, studio scouts canvassed Chinese enclaves throughout California and the Northwest. Paul Muni and General Tu, along
with production associate Max Siegel, led the charge by making a
trip up to Oregon and Washington to look for suitable candidates.
Muni also hoped to embed himself among the Chinese American
communities they visited so that he could study how to emulate them
on-screen. He seemed happy enough to add casting duties to his acting
responsibilities as long as it meant he'd have more opportunities to
collect impressions of authentic Chinese atmosphere.

Hundreds of people excitedly volunteered to appear in the film. "I
suppose that every Chinese on the Pacific Coast except [Anna May
Wong] will be offered a part," Harry Carr wrote.

There were even rumors that the illustrious and world-renowned
Peking opera performer Mei Lanfang might play a part in *The Good
Earth* extravaganza, although exactly what role remained undecided.
However, by the time Muni and General Tu returned from their
scouting trip, just a dozen or so Chinese American players were approved and sent on to Hollywood. Bill Grady, who was in charge of
making screen tests, complained that most of the prospective actors
didn't actually look Chinese once they put their costumes on for the
camera. He'd gone through so many screen tests that Max Siegel wisecracked: "Bill Grady has shot more Chinese than the entire Japanese
army." All told, more than three hundred screen tests were made of

Chinese actors for nine principal roles and sixty-eight smaller speaking parts.

Out of this group of candidates, only a handful were signed onto the film. They included William Law, a San Francisco–based insurance broker and local politician; Chingwah Lee, a Chinatown tour guide and the editor in chief of the newly launched publication *Chinese Digest*; Laura Loew, a housewife and grandmother; Li Ta Ming, a cabaret performer; and Mary Wong, a clerk at the China Emporium in San Francisco who also happened to be Anna May's younger sister, though she was not initially identified as such. Veteran actors Keye Luke and Soo Yong were eventually added to the cast, along with newcomers Roland Lui, Caroline Chew, and Bessie Loo.

In the meantime, props and set design advanced full speed ahead. Since MGM's attempt at filming in China had failed miserably, the studio's only option was to bring China to Hollywood. Von Sternberg had nimbly carried off that magic trick in *Shanghai Express* with a mix of resourcefulness and inspired creativity. Thalberg had MGM's full resources at his fingertips. He didn't have to rely on clever camera angles or blocking the actors in restrictive ways to pull it off. He could build the Middle Kingdom from the ground up if he wanted to.

And so he did. Irving Thalberg would fabricate his very own Chinese countryside in the versatile topography of Southern California.

MGM leased five hundred acres in Chatsworth, a sleepy farm town northwest of Hollywood in the San Fernando Valley. It was said to be probably the largest swath of land any studio had ever appropriated for a production. Five acres of the property were set aside for Wang's house and fields. Another portion was designated for the nearby village where the great House of Hwang would be built. A whopping one hundred acres was to be planted with rice and wheat crops according to Chinese agricultural techniques, complete with a functional irrigation system.

Every day, crateloads of furniture, farming tools, and other props arrived from China. As early as George Hill's expedition in 1934, MGM scouts had descended upon unsuspecting villages in the Chinese hinterland and gone house-to-house with cash in hand, making offers to buy up whole lots. "How much—for everything?" they would ask. Anything they could pack into crates was bought and shipped back to California: pieces of old houses and disassembled junks, wooden plows, harrows, and flails, stone grain-grinding mills, waterwheels, windmills, gongs, ivory needles, colored joss paper, foo dogs, sundials, bronzes, earthenware pots, and teakwood furniture. In total, 18,000 items, from farm equipment and furnishings to ordinary objects were used to cobble together a convincing Chinese village and farmland.

To bring this farmland to life, MGM turned to the most obvious solution: they hired hundreds of Chinese Americans from nearby Chinatowns to work the land. Needless to say, the area was suddenly consumed by a frenzy of activity. Yee On, a knowledgeable gardener, led a group of Chinese farmers in cultivating crops. Under his supervision, they planted staples commonly used in Chinese cooking, such as water chestnuts and Chinese cabbage, and they tended to a growing stable of farm animals, which included water buffalo and donkeys. And when their work was done, these same laborers could blend seamlessly into the landscape they had helped build. Their very presence would imbue the vast acreage with the authentic Chinese atmosphere it lacked.

MGM painters were tasked with making hundreds of road signs in "Cantonese, Pekinese, and Mongolian ideographs" to direct the flow of Chinese workers from Los Angeles to their new job site. (Perhaps General Tu forgot to explain that the written Chinese language is the same regardless of one's spoken dialect.)

In truth, the job opportunities provided by MGM's *Good Earth* production were a significant boon to the local Chinese American community, and a much needed one at that. Just as a new Chinese village was being built in the San Fernando Valley, L.A.'s Old Chinatown quarter, many of its buildings dating back to the 1870s, was being prepped for demolition. Plans to erect a new train station and consolidate the three major train terminals in Los Angeles were announced in 1933. The site chosen for this public works project was adjacent to the original pueblo where the city in the desert had first sprung up centuries before with the arrival of the Spanish. It was there, south of the pueblo, that the Chinese had carved out a small district of their own for more than sixty years.

Though many planned to remain in the neighborhood up until the arrival of the wrecking ball, large sections of Chinatown had already been cleared to make way for L.A.'s Union Station. These were the same streets where Anna May Wong first glimpsed actors in greasepaint mugging for hand-cranked cameras. Unlike other Americans, she had never viewed the quarter's crooked alleys as a "mysterious place." To her, Chinatown was a place made up of familiar sights and sounds: "I accepted it as a matter of course—the narrow streets lined with grimy buildings, the shops where Chinese herbs and drugs were sold, the gambling places where white men and Chinese mingled, the over-crowded tenements where the Chinese lived, sometimes entire families in one room, the gaily painted chop-suey restaurants with their lanterns a soft, many colored blur in the dusk." By the time she returned from China, nearly all of it would be gone.

Local reporter Lee Shippey toured the transitioning area one day and wrote down his observations for the *Los Angeles Times*: "But a walk down Apablasa street gives one who knew old Chinatown something of a shock. It is cut off as abruptly as a movie set, and modern America is very busy on ground from which transplanted China has been rudely sliced." In the early days of the flickers, movie people had happily made use of Chinatown as if it were a ready-made set. Somehow that reputation seemed to stick, for most Angelenos saw it as a kind of amusement park, a place that could be easily dismantled and reassembled. But for the 3,500 Chinese Americans who called Los Angeles home, the loss of Old Chinatown was not so painless. "I doubt

that many of those Chinese know where they go from there," Shippey
remarked.

Six years into the Great Depression, many Chinatown residents,
chiefly those who were immigrants with limited English language
skills, lived paycheck to paycheck and could hardly afford to lose their
livelihoods. Thankfully, Hollywood's growing slate of China-related
films presented an alternative to help supplement family incomes and
could sometimes even lead to a steady wage for several months at a
time. Background work could be strenuous and the hours were unforgiving, but many of the Chinese Americans who were regularly employed as extras found the prolonged downtime in between setups and
shots a welcome change of pace from the rigors of blue-collar work.
And the pay wasn't too shabby: on average, Chinese extras in the mid-
1930s were paid anywhere from $5 to $15 a day and even as much as
$25 for speaking "atmosphere words." That sure beat making $1 to $3
a day as a cook in a Chinese restaurant or doing backbreaking farm-
work out in the fields.

In fact, recruiting Chinese Americans for the movies had become
a business unto itself. A feud within the Chinese American community erupted after the passing of James Wang, the former Baptist
minister who had helped Anna May get her start, when Tom
Gubbins—another longtime Chinatown recruiter sometimes referred
to as "the unofficial mayor of Chinatown"—tried to corner the market
on supplying Chinese extras for *The Good Earth*. Gubbins, a white
American who was born in China and spoke Chinese fluently, was
seen as an ideal go-between for studios in need of Asian extras, but his
tactics squeezed many vulnerable Chinese Americans. He reportedly
extracted a 10 percent commission off his recruits' wages, in addition
to charges for costumes he rented to them.

It wasn't long before a rival casting agency in Chinatown attempted to challenge Gubbins's primacy. MGM, refusing to get involved, stated plainly, "Anyone who can supply what we want will

certainly get a hearing." A faction of disaffected Chinese actors raised their grievances with Vice-Consul Kiang, who promptly filed a complaint with the California state labor commission. The dispute was quashed when the state labor commissioner brokered a deal with Hollywood's Central Casting Corporation to install Gubbins as a recruiter for the agency, thereby covering his commissions instead of passing them on to the background players themselves.

While work on the sets at MGM studios and the Chatsworth lot progressed, *The Good Earth*'s two principal actors, Luise Rainer and Paul Muni, threw themselves into preparations for their roles. Muni, though, had never fully bought into Thalberg's vision of him as Wang Lung. "Thalberg's the most tenacious person in the world," he told a journalist, confessing it was Thalberg's conviction, not his own, that made him say yes to the role. "What it came right down to, I suppose, was that I trusted his judgment more than I did my own. Or perhaps, that I hoped he was right and I was wrong. I'm still hoping."

The great character actor, whom the movie magazines declared was "the man who can't be typed," wasn't afraid of rolling up his sleeves and digging into the part, but he had his doubts. In a strange way, the challenge of becoming Chinese was galvanizing. Muni thrived on his desire to give the best performance possible. His process began with research. He read widely on Confucius and Chinese culture and enrolled himself in an extension course on Chinese music at UCLA. General Tu became a friend and frequent advisor; Paul spent many hours plumbing the depths of General Tu's knowledge.

During MGM's recruiting trip through San Francisco and other Chinese enclaves on the Pacific Coast, Muni devoted much of his time to studying every gesture, nuance, and rhythm of the Chinese he came into contact with. His goal was to find a family fully immersed in "the traditions of the Orient" and observe them in their element. "I thought I might live with a family of this kind for a week and perhaps steal something from them, something of their inner feelings; absorb some old country atmosphere," Muni explained. "But they're all American-ized. They are more American than Americans."

Luise Rainer was engaged in a somewhat different type of train-ing. Though she, too, made a similar trip to the Sacramento Valley to study her subjects where they lived, Rainer had spent a good portion of her first year in Hollywood learning English. She wasn't as preoc-cupied with portraying a Chinese peasant farmer in the same way that Muni was, but she was just as keen to take on the challenge of trans-forming herself. She was confident enough to rely on her acting abili-ties alone. For example, she refused to wear any of the exaggerated yellowface makeup used in earlier productions.

Muni also was wary of Hollywood's elaborate Oriental masks of yore. He and the studio agreed that an understated, natural look was what they were after. So Muni did what he could on his own: he slimmed down and shaved part of his head as well as the ends of his eyebrows. He enlisted a respected tailor from Chinatown to make the half dozen outfits his role required, ranging in style and taste from simple farmer's clothes to elaborate mandarin jackets made from silk brocades.

When it came to makeup, he and makeup man Jack Dawn spent many nights experimenting with various formulas. Their aim was for the makeup to be undetectable yet strong enough to hold his prosthetic eyelids in place. The method they arrived at involved using a semi-wax material that would harden and mold to the skin after being "applied in a small wedge shape next to the nose." In comparison to the well-worn practice of taping actors' eyes to make them appear slanted, this new and improved technique was hailed as "the most realistic makeup that has ever been used on the screen."

Despite these efforts, Muni's doubts remained.

"Will the public accept me as Chinese when I'm playing with real Chinese?" he wondered aloud. "I look at myself in the mirror and I don't look Chinese to me."

Somewhere in the Pacific Ocean, geographically and spiritually closer to China, Anna May Wong was about to get her first sighting of Asia as the SS *President Hoover* dropped anchor in Yokohama, Japan. From the ship's deck, she eagerly peered "through a veil of falling snow" at the city below and noted the people gathered on the dock: "women in thin kimonos, looking like half-frozen humming-birds; stevedores in straw raincoats that made them resemble shredded-wheat biscuits." This charming reverie was promptly interrupted when "a wildly trampling cavalcade came galloping up the gangplank" and surrounded Anna May, camera lenses and flashbulbs pointed in her direction. The pressmen had found her.

One by one, the Japanese reporters came forth, each presenting their card, held ceremoniously in both hands, and bowing low before the Chinese American movie star.

"Please, you got sweetheart?"

"Please, you think Oriental ladies should have permanent wave?"

"Please, you like Japan?"

As always, Anna May was a good sport. "I answered this machine-gun fire as best I could, explaining in answer to the first question that I was wedded to my art," she relayed to her readers in the *New York Herald Tribune*. "A few minutes later the reporters smiled in unison, made four or five deep bows and clattered down the gangplank as hurriedly as they had come."

When she returned to the SS *President Hoover* after a brief sightseeing trip in Yokohama, someone handed her a late edition of the day's paper. She was amused to learn that she was reportedly engaged to wed a wealthy Cantonese man named Art. "Such are the hazards of interviews in the East," she concluded wryly.

Anna May hadn't imagined how utterly electrifying her trip to the Far East would be. "I was so eager last night to set foot again in Asia that I found it almost impossible to sleep." Not since she and Lulu had blindly embarked for Berlin without speaking German or knowing what to expect had she felt this exhilarated. And she hadn't even made it to China yet.

A few days of trips to Tokyo, Kobe, Osaka, and Kyoto rounded out the ship's port of call in Japan, and after a one-day delay due to a storm the SS *President Hoover* was once again on the path toward China. Despite all the things Anna May had been told about the land of her forefathers, she found it hard to anticipate what it would actually be like when she got there. She pictured a country where life moved at a slow, tranquil pace. People were constantly saying the Chinese were a stoic, passive race. She doubted that many there would recognize her or know of her film fame, which would offer her some welcome anonymity.

The morning of their arrival in Shanghai, the butterflies in her stomach were all aflutter. Around 2:00 that afternoon, the SS *President Hoover* began winding its way up the Whangpoo River (known today as the Huangpu), traveling northward to China's biggest metropolis. Anna May cast her eyes upon these initial scenes like a veteran correspondent, committing every detail to memory so she could later describe them in her dispatch. She didn't want to miss a single moment.

"The first craft I saw there was a junk, with ribbed sails and large eyes painted on either side of the prow, so that the boat could see its way," she described in her dispatch to New York. "Flat fields, dotted here and there with peasant villages and curved roofed temples, stretched out to the horizon on either side of the stream. As we approached Shanghai great factories appeared on the river banks and the sky became smudged with smoke."

Once the river narrowed and the large luxury liner could go no farther, a smaller tender boat arrived to pick up Anna May and other departing ship guests and take them ashore to the customs jetty. But before she could even get off the ship, the Chinese press rushed aboard and demanded the movie star's cabin number from the information desk. A mad dash to cabin 414 ensued, but the room was empty. Reporters continued their frantic search until one spotted Anna May walking down a staircase. Seeing a band of newspapermen with their notepads and cameras trailing behind her, Anna May turned around and obligingly posed on deck before any of them could utter a word.

Soon she was reunited aboard the ship with her brother James, who was living in Shanghai and teaching at the Shanghai University Commercial College, and together they continued onto the tender. Their reunion was heartfelt but short, as the rabid mob of newspapermen waiting there, both Chinese and foreign, immediately closed in on Anna May. She had the strange experience of being more readily able to answer the British, German, and French reporters present than the Chinese, which required an interpreter since they spoke Mandarin and she only Cantonese.

In spite of the commotion and the barrage of questions in rapid-fire Mandarin that followed, she did not fail to catch sight of the gleaming city as they accelerated toward the port. The effect was dramatic and overwhelming: "My first glimpse of Shanghai, with its tall, modern buildings rising above the curving Bund, filled me with such a rush of emotion that I didn't know whether to laugh or weep." What had once seemed so distant and improbable suddenly appeared before her very eyes. She had finally made it to China.

"I have always wanted to come," Anna May told her interviewers. "You see I have always been so busy that I never felt that I could afford the time!"

Shanghai, if its newshawks were any indication, seemed to be equally as enthralled with Anna May Wong. She was alert and gracious and dazzled the crowd with very little effort as the press hung on her every word. The outfit she chose for her grand arrival was an elegant black dress topped with a mink coat and leather gloves. She gestured to her unusual hat, also black, which she explained had been specially designed for her and made in London; when worn, its rounded trapezoidal shape was meant to conjure up the image of a tiger's ears.

"When the Chinese go to America for the first time they are making a new beginning in life in one sense," she continued, "and now the process is just reversed with me. Here I am in China!"

A cluster of international cameramen edged their way to the front of the pack and Anna May obliged by posing for them against the Shanghai waterfront. German photographer Alfred Krause had photographed Anna May years before in his native Germany, so when he greeted her, she readily responded in German. This private conference ended, no doubt marked by pangs of jealousy from the rest of the throng, when Anna May pulled a tiny gadget off her own camera and handed it to Herr Krause as a token of her friendship.

As the tender pulled into the dock, six British guards marched aboard to escort Anna May through customs and on to her final destination, the Park Hotel. She was told they had been sent to protect her from the swarm of admirers waiting for her outside. She thought they were trying to put one over on her—that is, until she saw the gate for herself. "I realized that I was in danger of being overwhelmed. Old ladies teetering precariously on bound feet, scholarly looking gentlemen in long silk robes, schoolgirls in tight jackets and short skirts, and returned students in Western dress were pointing toward us and talking excitedly."

The crowd surrounding the taxi waiting to whisk her off to the Park Hotel was almost impenetrable. Somehow, after much difficulty, she reached the hotel. In the quiet of her suite overlooking the beautifully manicured Shanghai Racecourse, Anna May took a deep breath. The next day the English-language papers would tout her as the most exciting international personality to visit Shanghai in recent memory, and that was including U.S. vice president John Nance Garner.

If Anna May thought she would have a chance to rest and recover from her tumultuous arrival, she had better think again. A friend from her time in London, Madame Wellington Koo, wouldn't hear of it. She and her husband, Dr. Koo, the former Chinese ambassador to England, who was currently posted in Shanghai, had planned a spectacular welcome dinner for their American friend that same evening. The Koos would be leaving for Paris in less than a month so that Dr. Koo could assume the position of China's ambassador to France. What better way to spend their final weeks in Shanghai than with a round of receptions, luncheons, and dinner dances to say hello and goodbye to a good friend?

That night Anna May was toasted by Shanghai's well-to-do bankers, diplomats, and society matrons. Seated at her right was Dr. Koo and at her left was T. V. Soong, the reputed J. P. Morgan of China. She was rarely in her seat, for all the gentlemen present—except for Soong, who did not dance—delighted in twirling her around the dance floor. "I was kept busy tripping the entire evening," Anna May noted.

Mingling among the guests, she discovered that one of the ladies spoke Cantonese and enthusiastically launched into conversation in her native tongue. In a few minutes the woman was begging her pardon. "Miss Wong, do you mind going back to English? You speak Chinese charmingly, but you have such a marked American accent." Apparently, the British were not the only nationality to balk at Anna May's "terr-bul Amurrican" drawl. She took this criticism in stride, admitting to her readers back home, "I always said that only my family or people with ears of love could understand my Chinese, but I never really believed it until now."

The party carried on late into the evening, and when the group "adjourned" to the home of Dr. U. Y. Yen, an educator, it was merely to commence the next of the night's activities. Round after round of pai gow, a baccarat-like game played with Chinese dominoes, was pursued into the wee hours of the morning. "This went on until 5 am, not an unusual hour, I was told, for Shanghai parties to break up," Anna May clarified. "This is quite the gayest city I've ever been in, not excepting the more brilliant cities of Europe."

Boy, had she been wrong about China! Forget rice paddies and water buffalo: everything she'd seen that day showed her that China was emerging as an advanced and fashionable nation-state. Whoever came up with the notion that "the Chinese are always stolid and without emotion" was woefully mistaken.

Anna May was up again by noon to "take tiffin" (as they called lunching in Shanghai) with Madame Koo. The week's activities would only reinforce the fact that Shanghai, at least, was miles away from the quaint farm life depicted in Pearl Buck's books. While Luise Rainer was somewhere in Hollywood being fitted for O-lan's house slave rags, under Madame Koo's expert guidance Anna May was getting the royal treatment at the esteemed Laou Kai Fook silk emporium.

Among the major cities of Asia, Shanghai was celebrated for its cosmopolitanism. In the 1920s, fashionable Shanghainese women went through a phase of coveting all things Western. They shed their traditional jade for glittery diamonds set in platinum. However, the 1930s ushered in a return to Chinese classics but with a modern twist. As Madame Koo tells it, she single-handedly set the trend among her peers by wearing higher, more revealing slits in her cheongsams so that she could move without restriction. Similarly, her knack for fashion led her to don lacy stockings up to the knees to reveal "a few inches of creamy skin," to embellish her dresses with braided piping and fancy trimmings and to adorn her wrists and neck with jade trinkets— all trends that were soon picked up by the masses.

Although Anna May had arrived in China with some of her finest European dresses, just walking down Nanking Road in the International Settlement she could see that the modern cheongsams and flowing silhouettes worn by everyday Chinese women rivaled anything she could get back home.

The Chinese press was not nearly as kind to her as the foreign press and local English-language publications. They seized at once upon her European fashions and pronounced them dowdy representations of yesterday's trends. Leave it to her Chinese contemporaries to rip her a new one, "world's best-dressed woman" distinction notwith-standing. One Chinese reporter scorned her all-black arrival outfit, saying it made her look like "a girl from the convent." They also criti-cized her looks, suggesting that over her fifteen years in the movie business she had spent a little too much time under the klieg lights and looked older because of it—and that was the most tactful of the in-sults. One of the downright mean critics simply wrote, "Her youth is long gone. . . . I saw an old woman with a haggard face . . . and wrin-kles in the corners of her eyes."

Most of all, they attacked her track record in Hollywood of "losing face for China." "Is Anna May Wong Really Welcome?" journalist Hong Bingcheng titled his article on the star's arrival in Shanghai. "Whether Anna May Wong can be counted as Chinese is still a ques-tion," he argued. "For the sake of the country, we should order her to receive five or ten years of education here and then allow her to return to the U.S. to continue her career. . . . Otherwise, we should deport her and disavow her Chinese status."

Anna May didn't bother with their trifling reports. She was tak-ing a slightly different approach toward her Chinese education. Her first order of business was ordering several Chinese dresses made from the "shimmering bolts" of silk stacked in Laou Kai Fook.

Yet, in spite of these muckrakers, there were still more admirers eager to imitate the Hollywood-anointed star. Local artist Tsang Tsing-ying spent an entire morning with Anna May, sketching her figure in an array of ensembles she'd brought with her to China. The illustrations appeared across several days in the pages of the *China Press* for the benefit of Shanghai's style hounds.

Anna May's first week in Shanghai was a complete blur. The city's breakneck pace never let up. Each day's itinerary since she'd arrived felt as though it was scheduled down to the minute. Her day typically began with several interviews, followed by multicourse meals and ap-pearances at assorted parties and receptions. She couldn't get over the bountiful spreads placed before her at lunch and dinner. Her first tiffin at Sun Ya, a famous Cantonese-style restaurant, was no less than fifteen courses. "I'm thinking seriously of fasting for a week to let my digestion catch up," Anna May said in jest. "The worst of it is that at a Chinese party one must sample everything, for to refuse even a single course would be equivalent to insulting one's host. How the Chinese women keep their willowy figures remains a profound mystery."

Another day, another tiffin at Sun Ya. This time around, Anna May lunched with Victor Keen, an editor in the *New York Herald Tribune*'s Shanghai office, and was relieved to be able to pick at dishes without offending anyone "if I ignored the boiled water chestnuts or the Eight Precious Pudding." In the afternoon she went on a "delightful" shopping trip with Ada Lum, the sister of Australian Chinese tennis champion Gordon Lum. Saturday night was predictably overscheduled, with two parties on the docket. At the first party, hosted by the University of Southern California's Alumni Society at the Little Club, Anna May shared the spotlight with Mei Lanfang and the two were entertained by the sensational Chinese dancer H. M. Tan. When Anna May saw platters of food being brought out, she knew it was time to move on to the next event: a farewell party and costume ball at the Paramount Ballroom for Ambassador and Madame Wellington Koo. "I received a prize for wearing an American gown, foreign clothes counting as 'fancy dress' at a Chinese social affair."

The week came to a close with a dinner party at the Mayor and Madame Wu Tieh-cheng's home. By now Anna May was wise enough to stay out of the mahjong games being run at several tables. The woman who had on occasion staged "gambling hells" for her London friends was no match for these battle-hardened mahjong players. "Watching Chinese play is a remarkable experience, if one's eyes can travel enough to follow them," she remarked. "The players didn't even bother to look at their tiles, for they knew what each was merely by touch. Not being an expert, I soon was left miles behind."

In the few moments of calm she was able to steal away from the

constant whir of activity, Anna May reflected on her experiences of the
last week and the sensory overload that had come with it.

"It seems strange that Chinese dread the speed and noise of American cities, for surely there are more of both in Shanghai than I've ever
coped with anywhere else. For twenty-four hours a day one hears the
blare of automobile horns, the shouts of jinriksha coolies, the rattle of
buses and the high-pitched, blood-curdling squeak of the wheelbar-
rows that bring farm produce into the city. The tempo of the social life
is such a gallop that a person from quiet Hollywood can hardly keep
up with it. And my former mental picture was of people sitting in
walled courtyards and drinking tea all day long!"

"I really thought I was coming out here for a quiet trip," she told
a reporter at the *China Press*. "However, nothing surprises me anymore. So many of my preconceived ideas have been upset that I feel
like a Chinese Alice who has wandered through a very strange
looking-glass."

One aspect that impressed her quite a lot was seeing the freedom
and independence with which women went about their lives in the big
city. "The modern Chinese woman seems to be holding her own with
the outside world," she noted. "Japanese wives, trudging meekly after
their lords, seem far more repressed and dependent than the women
of China. Unlike the old-fashioned Chinese gentleman, a modern
Shanghai husband does not refer to his invisible wife as 'the mean one
of the inner compartments.'" She even ventured to add, "The women
in Shanghai actually have more freedom than many Europeans."

The ladies of Shanghai society whom Anna May had met during
her first week in China couldn't be further from the caricature of the
unappreciated, nevertheless loyal Chinese wife represented by O-lan
in *The Good Earth*. To think that she had wanted to play that role!
From where she stood now, MGM's undertaking seemed like a silly
game of make-believe. When a reporter asked her whether she thought
China had a right to bristle at Hollywood's treatment of its people, she
answered honestly: "I think that China has grounds for resentments

on the type of picture that has commonly been made in portrayal of Chinese characters. I believe that there is now a field for making a picture which would portray the finer type of Chinese woman as she really is."

Anna May conceded that she was tired of playing "sinister roles," which was in part why she had decided finally to travel to China. Her desire was "to learn something of the country" and to study Chinese women up close.

"She feels that she will be better able to play her parts in American films if she has firsthand knowledge of women in China," one journalist summarized.

Anna May was not above throwing a little shade in MGM's direction either. She brought up the fact that she had passed on taking a secondary role in *The Good Earth* and suggested that the project would ultimately have to be put on hold due to industry shortcomings—"Film technique has not yet reached the stage where it can portray an incident with all the fullness and meaning that two or three pages of a novel can do"—and a lack of authentic players to fill necessary parts.

The one thing she was grappling with was where she fit in the grand scheme of things. In the United States and Europe, most people saw her as irrevocably Chinese, her American twang notwithstanding. But in China she wasn't exactly Chinese. "It seems strange to meet people here who ask about the things that 'you in America do,'" Anna May said, attempting to parse her feelings into formal thoughts, "and I realize that in many ways I am considered American out here." Yet when a businessman took her to the bowling alley at the Columbia, an American country club, her presence caused a minor scandal. The club did not admit Chinese as members or guests and refused to let her bowl.

Her identity was never as straightforward as being one thing or another. When she dressed in Western-style clothing, people would ask, "Who is that Chinese girl in foreign dress?" So she slipped into her newly tailored cheongsams. "Once I changed to Oriental dress, I thought I might recede into the background and just enjoy being in China," Anna May later recalled. "But, no. Everyone who saw me now asked, 'Who is that foreign girl in Chinese dress?'"

In the first hour of her arrival, standing on the tender as it navigated the swells of the Whangpoo River, she herself had admitted to reporters that Anna May Wong still had much to learn about China.

Anna May chats with farmers in the Chinese countryside outside Peiping, 1936.

TRYING NOT TO TRY

When the man who would be Wang Lung surveyed the land he loved on the first day of principal photography for *The Good Earth*, what he saw before him was like a novelist's words brought to life.

The early morning sun crested the tops of the foothills in northern China and shone down on a small village in the valley below. A few peasants walked the dirt roads to town, some carrying produce to sell at market; their gait was unhurried, for time meant nothing here. In the distance, a half-crumbled stone wall marked the boundaries of this rural outpost of civilization. A deep moat that had to be crossed by a small bridge reinforced the town's medieval exterior. Branching outward from the city walls were rice fields flooded with water, shining in the sunlight. Men wearing grass-woven hats waded into the mud with their water buffalo and wooden plows to begin the day's work. The homes of modest farmers, huts made of earth and finished with thatched roofs, were interspersed across the landscape. Toward the long vanishing line of the horizon were row after row of neatly sown wheat, spry and green; their dewy stalks trembled as a cool breeze passed through their ranks.

None but the well-trained eye would have noticed that the chaparral-scrubbed hillsides captured in the camera frame were typical of Southern California, not China. To Paul Muni's mind, the transformation was complete.

"I don't believe it," he wrote in his notes from shooting. "I forget the camera and think I am really on a farm on the other side of the world."

It had taken four years to get to this moment. Four years of false starts, dozens of scripts, and hundreds of casting calls. There were disputes among the MGM producers and disputes with the Chinese Nationalist government. A new director was installed not once but twice: when Victor Fleming was forced to leave for medical reasons, Thalberg took the opportunity to replace him with Sidney Franklin. Even with production set to begin at the end of February 1936, MGM's fleet of writers continued to noodle and fuss over the script to the last second.

"I'd like to direct the picture," Franklin told Thalberg after he read the latest version, "but I can't do it as the script reads now."

"Why not?" asked Thalberg.

"Because it's too Occidental. I don't get the Oriental flavor at all. I'd have to work on it from beginning to end."

"Can you do it in a few weeks?" Thalberg pressed.

"No, it would take at least three months," Franklin pushed back.

"I can't wait. I'll give you six weeks."

The Boy Genius had spoken. Somehow the script underwent its umpteenth revision and was approved in time for filming to begin on schedule. Irving Thalberg was indeed the purveyor of illusions that he claimed he was. He and his crackerjack team of filmmakers had done the impossible: they had moved the mountain and brought it to Hollywood. The Chinese village that Pearl Buck had so faithfully transcribed in the pages of her book had sprung to life in the San Fernando Valley. There wasn't a soul in Los Angeles who could argue otherwise.

Whatever doubts lingered in Paul Muni's psyche seemed to melt away at the sight of Thalberg's masterful creation. He was buoyed by the rustic atmosphere he found himself immersed in and walked around the Chatsworth property as a single "Chinaman" among hundreds of Chinese extras. "I seem to hear the mournful call of doves and smell burning joss-sticks in the air. Buddha seems to brood. It's all old and oriental," Muni buzzed. "And just think, we are ten miles from the corner of Hollywood and Vine!"

Muni, of course, wasn't the only one satisfactorily fooled by the production design's Chatsworth farmland. Many of the Chinese American extras hired to play at working the land for the cameras felt as though they had been transported back in time. Like Anna May Wong, they were second- and third-generation Chinese Americans born in the United States who had never been to China. Instead, they grew up on stories from relatives about the distant land of their forefathers. It was a place, like something out of a dream, that existed in the heart and mind but not in the realm of lived experience.

Charles Leong, a recent college graduate, was one of the thousands of Chinese Americans who signed up to do extra work in *The Good Earth*. On his first day at the studio, a barber shaved off his black crop of hair and fastened a braided queue to his freshly bald head. Leong mourned the temporary loss of his thick, black locks. He wasn't too thrilled about wearing the "filthy-looking rags" with "cavernous holes and mud," either, despite assurances from the wardrobe lady that the costumes were sterilized nightly. But he was willing to make these small sacrifices for the guarantee of three months' work and a peek inside the dream factory.

The Chatsworth property and interior sets for *The Good Earth* inadvertently became a gathering place for Chinese young and old. A Chinatown away from Chinatown. Work in the movies wasn't always a piece of cake, but here there was a lighthearted spirit in the air. "It's a regular riot, like a colossal festive day in a Chinese village," Leong reminisced. The lavish Chinese lunches served to the cast of extras were the daily highlight. "Every noon hour was a holiday for everybody. . . . Three or four Cantonese dialects fluidly fill the air with banal, joyful, and happy Chinese talk and laughter. The cackling old men, smoking on willow pipes, would secretly glow at the generous spreads of good food, and openly grumble 'Huh, what food WE had when we were young men in the old country.'"

The peculiar implications of assuming the role of a Chinese farmer as a college-educated Chinese American man were not lost on Charles Leong. He wrote vividly of his scenes on location at the Chatsworth farm: "I was barefooted and hoeing a thin row of rice shoots. I felt the warmth of the soil. I was in China. And back of me, a camera followed my every move. Twenty other young brown bodies gleamed in the California sun, tilling the rice fields. Glistening, actually working and covered with more sweat than clothing." It was as though Leong and his fellow extras were being conveyed into a nostalgic past. "Here we were, twenty young American-born Chinese, trying to simulate, to reenact, for the movies a scene in which was part of the national fiber of our forefathers. My mind was far from the usual prosaic things. Was this a dream, a fantasy, realism? Was this China or Hollywood?"

Luise Rainer, too, was subsumed into the Chinese environment that materialized around her. Unlike Leong, who grimaced at the raggedy clothes he was given to wear, Rainer seemingly relished this intimation of realism. One columnist hailed her the "all-time champion of uncomplimentary makeup and costume." Her uniform as O-lan consisted of "tattered dirty clothes, with straggly hair, and with makeup deliberately applied to leave her as plain, vacuous, and uninteresting as possible." This was a far cry from her previous two roles, the first a Viennese socialite in *Escapade* and the second as Anna Held, the jilted showgirl in *The Great Ziegfeld*. There were no resplendent balls or glitzy stage numbers in *The Good Earth* and that suited Luise just fine.

A reporter from *Picture-Play* magazine interviewed her on set between takes for the scene in which O-lan, the former house slave, presents her baby son to the matriarch of the House of Hwang. "I enjoy this rôle better than Anna Held," Luise revealed. "This character is closer to the heart. I prefer to try to interpret everyday fundamental feelings."

Had she devoted months to preparation and research for the assignment just as Paul Muni had? "No," Luise answered. "I depend upon my own imagination. I read a script, then I think of that person all the time. Somehow instinctively I assume the right attitude. It disturbs me to be told how to portray emotions. To be convincing, I just do as I would do under the circumstances. That is, of course, if I were that particular woman."

Rainer, nonetheless, did allocate some of her prep time to visiting among the Chinese populations of San Francisco and Los Angeles. "I go many times to Chinatown and for hours I sit between the people there in their restaurants and theaters and I listen to them," she told another reporter. "But if I only imitate them that is nothing. I must look at them and listen to them, see how they behave and hear how they say things, then perhaps I know something about them—what they are and how they feel. It is only then I can hope to be the woman I play. I take her in and eat her."

The Viennese Teardrop, as many began calling her, truly had a gift for inhabiting the emotional realities of her characters. In one of the film's bleaker scenes, when the family has nearly starved to death in a time of terrible famine, Wang Lung realizes he must slaughter his beloved water buffalo in order to give his family sustenance. He cannot, however, bring himself to commit the final act, and so the stony, ever pragmatic O-lan is the one who must slit the animal's throat. Once takes were completed, Rainer was so overcome with emotion that she rushed off the set. Joan Crawford, who was also on the MGM roster and happened to be at the studio that day, ran into Luise sobbing in the street outside the soundstage. Afraid she would sound like a phony if she told Joan she was crying because of a scene she'd acted in, where no actual water buffalo was harmed, Luise fibbed and explained that she had just received terrible news from Europe about her family. Not long after this encounter, a bouquet of flowers arrived in her dressing room with a card from Miss Crawford.

Yet, as much as Hollywood acknowledged this newcomer's extraordinary talent, it was equally confounded by her. Luise Rainer was an enigma. She surprised many when she rose to star status in her very first MGM production, and critics were still abuzz about her stellar performance in *The Great Ziegfeld*. "Already word is whispered," one interviewer vouched, "Luise of the Laurels has walked off with still another million dollar film production, *The Good Earth*, as easily and lightly as she might with a bowl of rice." In spite of her success, Rainer professed no interest in fame, money, or Hollywood. She seemed happiest when toting her Scottie dog Johnny (which sounded more like "Jonnay" when she said it) around the Chatsworth set in a wheelbarrow.

"I am all wrong here in Hollywood," she told *Movie Mirror* in an interview published in October 1936, after her work on *The Good Earth* had wrapped. "I can't see myself as a film person. For me it is too impersonal. I intend to quit right now!"

Whether this is how Rainer truly felt or simply a reaction to the frustrations she experienced on set and behind closed doors with MGM execs is hard to say. The rumor was that she and Paul Muni didn't get along. Her uppity behavior, apparently, had rubbed him the wrong way. One day while watching rushes from her screen tests in the projection room, she asked a man sitting there to leave. Strangers made her nervous, she said. The unnamed man was Muni. Rainer later explained this blunder away by saying she had a bad memory for faces and hadn't recognized her costar.

During shooting, Luise complained to director Sidney Franklin that he wasn't giving her enough of an active role—that he was letting Muni steal scenes. "I told her that was his character," Franklin recalled. "Her character was the quiet one. The less she did, the more she did. The less she said, the more she conveyed. And when she spoke, be it one line or two, everybody would listen." *Screenland* reported that the two actors "couldn't see each other for a cloud of professional dust. Both have very decided temperaments, both are seriously concerned with their careers, both have illusions of greatness." Luckily, the Chatsworth location and its spacious five hundred acres served as a relief valve, alleviating the tension before it could explode. When one of them felt a tantrum coming on, they sprung for the hills and unleashed their pent-up emotions into the heedless wind. These self-imposed measures worked to keep the peace, and somehow, when Rainer and Muni came out the other side, each supposedly had nothing but "the greatest respect and admiration" for the other.

Incredibly, the Lotus character remained uncast until the end of summer 1936 as production was winding down. Lotus Liu, a Shanghai-born actress of Chinese and English ancestry who already had the name, was finally dropped as the top contender, even though she had previously been announced to play the role. The newly arrived Tilly Losch, a dancer from the opera ballet in Vienna, was selected instead, completing the Austrian trifecta of Muni, Rainer, and Losch. The rationale later cited in defense of MGM's decision to cast another white actress in one of the lead Chinese roles was that the Hays Office wouldn't stand for "mixing racials in romantic sequences." An Austrian man in Chinese clothes and makeup could no more kiss or consort with a Chinese woman on-screen than if he was wearing his native lederhosen.

Irving Thalberg knew it was absurd and he didn't care. He was more concerned with putting on a show. He was of the philosophy that every film should give moviegoers at least one great scene. For *The Good Earth*, his magnum opus, he intended to outdo himself. His goal was to pull off not one but four spectacles: the birth of Wang Lung and O-lan's first child; the death of another child in the depths of famine; the revolution in the big city and the looting of the palace; and the locust plague and the family's fight to save the land.

The chaotic looting scene—a pivotal moment in the film when O-lan discovers a pouch of jewels in a ransacked house—was scheduled to be shot at night on the MGM backlot. Central Casting called up as many Chinese Americans as they could find to fill the Chinese city streets with authentic-looking denizens. Mamie Louise Leung, the sole Chinese American journalist on staff at the *Los Angeles Times*, joined her peers at the recruiting office in Chinatown. A bus came by the Plaza in the late afternoon to pick up their motley crew, which Leung described as bringing together "youngsters, Hollywood-stylish in gaucho shirts and berets," along with "Chinatown grandfathers who had never become reconciled to American shoes" and "weary-eyed Chinese women in trousers and jackets."

At the studio, they were sent to wardrobe and makeup. The same shabby, loose-hanging Chinese clothes that had repelled Charles Leong were parceled out to the crowd with little attention to individual sizes. An auntie, one of the older Chinese ladies, asked if she could keep on the Chinese clothes she was already wearing. "No, Ma'am," the wardrobe girl responded. "Yuh gotta look dirty—plenty dirty, understand?" The girls who had arrived ready for their fifteen minutes of fame with waves in their hair and faces done up in lipstick and rouge were transformed into plain Janes. Their curls were brushed out and their "powdered faces were smudged generously with charcoal." There would be no China dolls at this revolution.

The last step in this barrage of realism was adding a final layer of dirt and grime. Before the extras could be let loose onto the set, a makeup man with a spray gun in hand showered the would-be looters with cold, slimy mud. A group of older women tried to run past the sludge station, but they were caught and dragged back: "They shut their eyes, trembled and yelled 'Ai yah, ai yah,' as they were splashed with mud."

The extras navigated the MGM backlot, and arrived at the set for the Chinese city. The tableau fabricated for the cameras included "groups of peasants strolling about the marketplace where dried ducks, salted fish and sausages were strung on bamboo poles. Men with queues wrapped about their clean-shaven heads carried baskets of choy and gwa—vegetables and melons—and brown crocks of soy bean sauce to the store in the center of the marketplace. Women rested on overturned straw baskets, their hands tucked into their sleeves for warmth. In the balconies of the rich men's houses, the light from dozens of colored lanterns glinted upon the rich robes and round hats of the mandarins who sat watching the scene below. The night air was filled with Chinese odors and the sound of Chinese voices."

The authenticity was astounding. Louise Leung noted that "the native Chinese looked at it all with a yearning nostalgia." It was enough to make one young lady, whose false eyelashes had escaped the makeup man's scrutiny, exclaim, "Gosh, this must be just like China."

Then a voice speaking Cantonese suddenly boomed over the PA system, ripping extras out of their personal reveries. It was old Tom Gubbins, barking orders in fluent and effective Cantonese: "This is supposed to be a revolution. Anything in the town is yours for the taking. Rush into the markets and loot. Grab things—fight over them. Be greedy—have fire in your eyes." As if he'd almost forgotten, he added, "And don't laugh."

Charles Leong later recalled Gubbins's "staccato Chinese commands" sardonically: "Imagine hiring a bunch of Chinese interpreters to relay the director's English instructions. And every son of old Mother China speaks English. That's Hollywood."

All along the artificial city streets, extras got to their feet and readied themselves for the mob scene they were about to enact. Then director Sidney Franklin shouted "Action!" and all mayhem broke loose. Chinese peasants swarmed the marketplace, overturning wares and grabbing at anything of value. Looters swiped poles hung with cured meat, piles of fresh-caught fish, even bewildered geese honking inside their cages. Someone got a fistful of Louise Leung's hair by mistake. It took a few beats before Franklin's calls of "Stop! Stop!" cut through the pandemonium and rioters returned to their ordinary selves. Leung thought for sure the trashed set would have to be abandoned, but production assistants emerged from the wings to clean up the mess. They steadily worked their magic "with brooms, brushes, and hammers" and put everything back in its place. "Even the man-handled fish, which were made of rubber, looked alive again after a good oil spray," Leung observed.

At Franklin's behest, the looting scene was staged another dozen times or more that evening. A makeshift hospital situated near the edge of the set received a series of patients throughout the night who had been battered and bruised by the frenzied crowd. One poor girl suffered a fractured ankle and was carried away on a stretcher. The older men and women among the extras had the good sense to keep themselves out of harm's way and "prudently stayed on the outskirts of the 'revolution.'" While the overzealous youths were receiving first aid, Chinese aunties and uncles sat on wooden crates, admiring their environs and shooting the breeze.

"In the village where I spent my childhood, there was a chicken store just like that one," a wizened old woman pointed out.

"But even in the poorest districts the sahm—clothes—weren't as bad as these," another chimed in before closing her eyes to snatch a few moments' rest.

Among them was Ah Bok, an old man squatting in front of a hut near a stone gate. "A far-away look came into his eyes," Leung recounted, as he took in the world around him. "To Ah Bok it was good. So long since he had been in Canton—thirty, no forty years. He shut his eyes in deep enjoyment."

"Places, everybody!" a voice rang out. "Let's get going!" And with that, the spell was broken.

————————

Across the Pacific, China was working its magic on Anna May Wong. She and Shanghai had gotten on famously. It was a surprise to both that each was presented with such a devastatingly charming and internationally minded partner. Why, Shanghai was just like her past lovers—Berlin, Paris, London, and New York—except even more swoon-worthy. But the "Paris of the East," as its nickname suggested, was not the real China, nor the reason she had sailed across the Pacific. (Others reserved a less flattering epithet for the country's sin city: they called her the "Whore of Asia.") In some ways, Shanghai was merely a distraction. Anna May's real desire was to see Canton, the land her grandparents had left behind for America.

On February 19, after a little more than a week in Shanghai, Anna May sailed south to Hong Kong on the SS *President Grant*. There in the British-ruled port city she was greeted by a flock of friends and fans waiting for her at the wharf. Actresses Lee Yi-Nin and Wong Sau-Nin and other well-known personalities, like Victor Hugo, manager of the Oriental Theatre, counted themselves among the welcome mob. Members of the Toisan Village Association, representing the region where her father was from, had also been sent to attend Anna May's reception. And of course there was the foreign and Chinese press ready to pummel her with questions.

Anna May's old friend Moon Kwan, who had returned to Hong Kong, cofounded the Grandview Film Company, and become a director in his own right, jostled through the crowd with a small entourage to receive Anna May. He was hopeful that he could convince her to star in one of his films while she was in China. Kwan could already picture it: a film starring Anna May Wong set against the backdrop of the Great Wall and the Forbidden City. American and European audiences eager for a glimpse of the East would eat it up. To grease the wheels ever so slightly, Kwan's Grandview colleagues, along with several Chinese film directors, had accompanied him with an offering of eight flower baskets tied up in pink satin ribbons bearing the message "Welcome Wong Liu Tsong, the Flower of Film."

What should have been a triumphant homecoming quickly soured into an ugly scuffle. Inside the ferryboat that had shuttled Anna May and her luggage from the ship to the port, a heated exchange transpired between her and another passenger. In the meantime, the people on the pier were restless for their idol to disembark and grew more and more agitated with each passing minute. Anna May finally emerged from the boat flustered, with a dour expression on her face. When Lee Yi-Nin and others reached out to shake her hand, Anna May ignored them. Representatives from the Toisan Village

Association felt similarly rejected. There was none of the expected glad-handing, waving to the cameras, or cheerful greeting of her fans. Apparently, she couldn't be bothered to address her fellow countrymen with the same courtesy?

Whatever the reason for her rudeness, Anna May's cold demeanor was interpreted as a grave insult. She had committed the cardinal sin of celebrity: ignoring those who held the reins of her popularity, the people and the press. An angry voice pierced through the din of the outraged mob, shouting: "Down with Wong Liu Tsong—the stooge that disgraces China. Don't let her go ashore."

If other Chinese citizens had yelled nasty comments at her in Shanghai, Anna May was none the wiser since she didn't speak Shanghainese or Mandarin. But the people here, of her homeland, spoke Cantonese just as she did and she understood the gist of their message. The verbal vitriol being hurled at her was so loud, as one reporter noted, it felt as though the sound shook the sky with fury. Distraught and paralyzed with fear when confronted with so many angry people, Anna May could only stand there and sob, where all could see the tears and snot streaming down her face. The throng eventually broke loose and smashed the flower baskets to pieces before finally dispersing. Anna May had to be rushed to Lulu's home in the upscale Happy Valley district of Hong Kong.

Meanwhile, Wong Sam Sing awaited her on the mainland in Toisan, where she had planned to travel in a few days' time. Since his return to China two years prior, her father had been living in Chang On, their ancestral village in the rural countryside, a trip several hours southwest of Canton. However, the snubbed Toisan delegation was prepared to launch a full-out campaign against Anna May, including enumerating her crimes against China. They sent an angry telegram to Wong Sam Sing in Chang On, threatening to chase his entire family out of Toisan if his daughter arrived in the village as planned. The same group lobbied local newspapers not to report on her visit. After receiving an urgent phone call from her father, who pleaded with her not to come to Chang On, Anna May acquiesced to meeting him and baby brother Richard in Canton instead.

Back in Hong Kong, she invited the Chinese press for an open-ended interview at the Hongkong Hotel so that she could explain herself and smooth over any ruffled feathers. She assured her critics that "she was not responsible for the interpretation of Chinese roles in American films" and, more importantly, to correct the notion that "she is in any way averse to being classed as a Chinese." How that rumor got started, she had no clue, but all the commotion had taken its toll. Soon after arriving in Hong Kong, Anna May excused herself from the public eye by claiming a case of the flu and made plans to escape to Manila in the Philippines for a breather. Hopefully the rancor in the air would die down by the time she returned.

The trip was not much of a vacation, for Anna May could not slip into Manila under the radar any more than she could in Shanghai or Hong Kong. But the tone shift did her waning spirit some good. Besides, she certainly wasn't one to say no to a dinner invitation from the president of the Philippines, Manuel Quezon, and his lovely wife, Aurora.

She quietly returned to Hong Kong after a week of sunshine in the Philippines. Her absence had successfully quelled the furor of her initial arrival. This was as good a chance as she would ever get to journey to Chang On. So Anna May absconded onto the mainland once more and made her way to her father's ancestral village. The gods must have been looking out for her this time around because somehow she managed to elude the press and her pesky detractors. The only cameras rolling were the ones she had brought along with her and Newsreel Wong to document what would become a life-changing experience.

The arduous journey into the rural countryside required Anna May to travel by train, bus, and on foot through tropical terrain abundant with palm trees, papayas, mangos, and bananas. She didn't know exactly what to expect when she made it there, but she dressed for the occasion nonetheless in a tasteful dark cheongsam and low heels. Walking up a dirt lane between rice fields and brick houses, she finally came upon her father, Wong Sam Sing. It had been about two years since she'd bid him goodbye in Los Angeles and watched him sail off to his retirement in China. His face lit up the moment he set eyes on his daughter. He was still the same man she remembered, kind and affable, wearing a simple gray suit jacket and slacks. Next to him, thirteen-year-old Richard was dressed in a dapper white linen suit, his school briefcase in hand. The family embraced each other and then waved Richard off to school for the day.

Wong Sam Sing proudly gave his daughter a tour of the village, showing her the community rice fields that were run on a cooperative basis by members of the Wong clan and introducing her to all their extended relations. She was honored with an unforgettable forty-three-course feast and to be polite, she "had to eat liberally of all of them."

Of course, many people from nearby rushed over to get their first look at an American movie star. It was a shock to some to discover that Anna May Wong was a flesh-and-blood person; rather, they had assumed she was a machine-generated illusion, like a hologram flickering before their eyes, not much different than a motion picture itself.

The highlight for Anna May was seeing her father so happy at having his American and Chinese families together at last. He was beaming. Walking arm in arm, she and her father strolled out into a shady grove of bamboo trees at that magic hour of the day when everything the light hits seems to sparkle. So this was the real China. It was almost too picturesque to believe.

When Anna May returned to Hong Kong, she wrote to Carlo of her recent travels: "Have been to Canton, which is to-date the most Chinese city I have visited. The surrounding country was simply heavenly." Life in the village of Chang On had made a powerful impression on her, and it would continue to deepen as her travels throughout China progressed over the coming months. She would journey to the mythical garden cities of Soochow and Hangchow; to the capital and seat of the Nationalist government in Nanking; to Chufu, the birthplace of Confucius; and to the Forbidden City in Peiping to the north.

Each and every place she visited taught her something, revealed a truth, or confirmed beliefs she had long held but never known the source of. Yet only one of these places could truly be called home, at least in the sense that it was the birthplace of generations and generations of Wongs who had come before her. Shanghai, glamorous though it was, could be any city in the world; it just so happened to be in China. Chang On—that was where the search for her origins definitively stopped. What did it all mean? Well, she was still working that out for herself.

Months later, a reporter asked Anna May about her possible plans to stage a Chinese drama for audiences in the West. She responded as if she were answering an entirely different question: "I am trying to sift through all the things that I see and hear in China. There is so very much—it is almost overwhelming. Perhaps you might say that I am trying to regain something that I have lost, trying to find out whether or not I am really Chinese."

Day by day, Anna May Wong was soaking up the sights and sounds of China. Before she left Hong Kong, she linked up with Warner Oland and his wife, who had arrived a month after she did on their first tour of Charlie Chan's homeland. Naturally, Oland received a warm welcome and none of the backhanded insults or confrontations about his film performances. Anna May treated her friend to a Chinese luncheon, at the end of which he "complained that he could not eat another thing for the rest of the day."

Back on the mainland, she made an official visit to the Mingxing Film Company in Shanghai. Zhang Shichuan, cofounder of the studio, and Butterfly Wu welcomed Anna May as Newsreel Wong's camera rolled.

Unlike their first meeting in London the summer before, there was a visible warmth between Butterfly and Anna May. The two actresses were dressed in tasteful cheongsams—Anna May in light blue silk and flower-embellished leather shoes, Butterfly in a somber dark gray, her hair curled for the occasion—and stood arm in arm, like sisters, chatting casually in Cantonese while posing for a photo op. Butterfly was one of the taller stars at Mingxing, but next to Anna May, who towered several inches above her, she looked quite small. "Butterfly Wu is shorter than Wong Liu Tsong!" one of the photographers called out. Butterfly laughed good-naturedly and declared, "Today I have shrunk."

Zhang Shichuan led Anna May inside on a tour of the studio facilities, introducing her to various staff members, and then on to a live set where scenes for a crime film titled *The Diamond Case* were in progress. Director Xu Xin-fu became noticeably ruffled when he saw Anna May Wong walk onto his set. In the footage captured by Newsreel's Eyemo camera, Anna May stands in the back corner of the interior set decorated with Chinese furnishings and respectfully watches as three actors playing gangsters count their stolen money. Later, the film's cinematographer chatted with Anna May on the side for a few minutes, plumbing her knowledge of lighting, makeup, and camera techniques. He left their conversation impressed: "Wong Liu Tsong has more than ten years of experience in the film industry, she seems to know it very well."

On her way north to Peiping by train, Anna May made several sightseeing trips. In the capital city of Nanking, the Nationalist government hosted a reception in her honor with the country's top brass in attendance. Anna May said a few words in English, complimenting her hosts and graciously explaining that she hoped "to promote the culture of our ancestral country" in the future. Still, her attempts to smooth things over did not exempt her from a litany of questions about her previous career choices.

"They made speeches that lasted for four hours," Anna May

recalled. "But instead of the usual stereotyped 'welcome to our city' speeches, they all took turns berating me for the roles I had played."

She arrived in Peiping in mid-May at just the right time to enjoy the ancient city's walled gardens fragrant with lilacs, tuberoses, and carnations. She immediately found the city to her liking. As in Toisan, she felt she was seeing the real China, the place she'd always imagined in her mind. Peiping, the ancient Chinese Empire's seat of power for centuries upon centuries, dynasty after dynasty, was filled with history. Shanghai had skyscrapers; Peiping had the Great Wall.

"Peiping has an extraordinary influence," Anna May said in a press interview. "For one thing, it's like a hidden treasure. Outside you may see only gray walls. You enter a gate and before you may be a most beautiful garden."

Soon after arriving, she gave up her hotel suite at the Grand Hôtel de Pékin, where she was continually mobbed by fans and autograph seekers. Originally, she had hoped to rent the charming courtyard home of British aristocrat Desmond Parsons, who was away in Europe, but his houseguest, travel writer Robert Byron, refused to let it to her. That, however, didn't stop her from having a portrait made of herself standing on the threshold of Parsons's octagonal moon gate.

Anna May rented a traditional Chinese-style house in the quiet hutongs of the old city. Inside the four-sided home was a small garden and courtyard "colored with pomegranate trees and perfumed with jasmine." The kindly lady landlord refused to let her pay more than one month's rent, stating it was a gesture of hospitality. The measured pace of life in this quiet abode was an agreeable change, and Anna May was happy to embrace "the beauty and charm of old customs" and the small delights of living in a Chinese neighborhood. The old man who sat outside the red gate to her house "dozing in the September sun or talking with his caged birds and cicadas" became a welcome fixture. Farther down the street were various vendors selling bowls of hot noodles and cool drinks, including one hawker who liked to pound out a ragtime rhythm on his porcelain cups in between customers. "A neighbor's child, nibbling at a bean cake" was just as likely to be seen giggling down the alleyway as he heeded his mother's call. "This is the world in which Anna May Wong has come to live," one journalist rhapsodized.

Anna May reconnected with Bernardine Szold Fritz, a Jewish American journalist and organizer of Shanghai's International Arts Theatre, whom she had first befriended years earlier in London. Bernardine was friends with all the celebrated artists and intellectuals of the era—Ernest Hemingway, F. Scott Fitzgerald, Harold Ross, members of the Algonquin Round Table, and of course, the Van Vechtens. She saw herself as a connector, and throughout her life curated salons from Paris to New York.

Through her correspondence with Bernardine, who now lived in Shanghai with her investment-broker husband, Chester Fritz, Anna May was sent cards of introduction to other expats and cosmopolitan Chinese living in Peiping. These included the esteemed intellectual Hu Shih, the man who had revolutionized and simplified the written Chinese language; Austrian novelist Vicki Baum, whose bestselling novel *Grand Hotel* became an Academy Award–winning film; and British writer Harold Acton, one of the Bright Young Things who had defected to China and was currently working on English translations of Chinese poetry and plays. Prominent Chinese of all backgrounds—actors, government officials, scholars, poets, and merchants—could be seen calling at Anna May's Peiping home. There over tea they would discuss various topics for hours at a time, almost like those days long ago when she held court in her bungalow behind the Sam Kee Laundry.

She also made friends with a West Point graduate named Frank Dorn, who was on assignment in Peiping as a U.S. military attaché and happened to live down the street from her in a picturesque residence with a garden that was replanted six times a year. Though he spent the majority of his time studying Chinese and writing up reports for his superiors, Dorn was an artist at heart. He had recently illustrated a historical map of Peiping that was reprinted en masse and sold to tourists on silk scarves. He was also the author of a novel based on the Indigenous people who lived in the Zambales Mountains in the Philippines. An astute observer of human relations, he and Anna May likely spent their afternoons together by his pool gabbing about the latest drama in the circle of foreign officials, eccentric expats, and Chinese elites they inhabited. Dorn's autobiography is filled with gossipy reports on which ambassadors' wives were the prettiest, who threw the best parties, and who could be counted on as a reliable bore.

Anna May herself makes an appearance in these annals. "Attractive and enveloped in the aura of Hollywood, men hovered around her wherever she went," Dorn noted. According to him, she received at least one marriage proposal from a British expat but demurred, stating she didn't think it right to bring "half-breed" children into the world—she who knew all too well what it felt like to be a kind of perpetual half-caste. "But that busted romance in no way stopped her from a sizzling fling with Robert Faure, a French Embassy attaché," Dorn continued in his zingy prose. Apparently, Anna May was as busy immersing herself in the culture of old Peiping as she was beguiling an array of suitors, for the "searing heat" from her intrigue with Faure "singed the beach tents at Peitaho resort, at Tientsin and way points. But by the end of summer, *l'affaire Faure* had petered out to cold ashes."

A few weeks into her stay, well-known Peiping hostess Tang Shunjun invited Anna May to attend a special springtime banquet at her home, where guests could enjoy the Taiping flowers blooming in her courtyard. Anna May came prepared with her trusty Leica camera and was so enchanted with the small white blossoms and their fragrant scent that she couldn't help herself from taking photo after photo. Seeing this, Miss Tang picked several flowers and arranged them in Anna May's hair. One day she would have to build a Chinese garden of her own.

Her education in all things Chinese continued in Peiping with visits to historical sites like the Forbidden City, the Summer Palace, the

Ming tombs, and the Great Wall at Badaling. One evening she walked alone to the Temple of Heaven and "sat in a flood of moonlight" admiring the age-old altar to the gods. "I did not really know what China meant to me until that night," she later recalled. "And if you asked me to tell you, I'm afraid I couldn't. It was an emotion born without words."

She enlisted Mr. Chou, Harold Acton's tutor, to teach her Mandarin and commenced with language lessons for two hours each day. Since Mr. Chou spoke neither English nor Cantonese, Anna May reasoned their mutual incomprehensibility would force her to learn Mandarin rather quickly. She devoted an additional two hours a day to studying Chinese drama as well as attending performances given by her friend Mei Lanfang. On one of her first days in Peiping, she toured a Chinese dramatic school where hundreds of pupils were trained in the art of Peking opera. Many of the pupils came from poor families and were brought to the school at a young age to begin the lifelong training required to become successful actors and musicians. She was amused to watch a male teacher, famous for impersonating women, teach a group of young girls how to move and gesture like proper ladies on the opera stage.

"I am simply crazy about the Children's Theater and have practically spent my first few days completely absorbing the Chinese Theater," she wrote in a letter to Bernardine. "Have been to the theater three times and expect to go every day as part of my education." By the end of her stay, Anna May had amassed a small collection of theatrical costumes—enough to fill several trunks—including an impressive and sizable warrior's headdress made of bright red pom-poms. "Have purchased three magnificent Chinese stage costumes and am thrilled with them," she wrote to Bernardine.

Anna May eventually convinced Bernardine, who had done so much to make her stay in China comfortable and whom she now considered a good friend, to come up to Peiping for a visit. One day the two women stole off into the countryside. Dressed modestly in a turtleneck, slacks, and long black double-breasted coat, Anna May explored the rural farmland with a walking stick in hand, stopping whenever they came upon one of the local farmers. The people out here were laopaihsing, ordinary folk who spent most days, from sunrise to sunset, toiling in the fields, harvesting crops, or in the kitchen preparing the next meal. They were the same hardworking people who had inspired characters like Wang Lung and O-lan. Anna May spoke to them animatedly in her fledgling Mandarin. Though their exchanges were relatively simple because of the language barrier, she felt that these experiences brought her closer to China. "The impressiveness of China is in its people," she later told a reporter. In them, she found "traces of the past."

As the torpid, humid days of summer began to lift and the scent of autumn arrived with the cool, breezy weather of September, Anna May Wong could feel her China sojourn gradually coming to a close. She had planned to spend three months in Peiping but ended up staying more than four. Her time in northern China yielded many meaningful experiences that she would savor for years to come. In mid-September, she returned to Shanghai by train. Once she was re-settled there with her belongings and newly acquired trunks packed with cheongsams and headdresses, she made plans to dash back to Hong Kong and Canton to say goodbye to her father and Richard in advance of her voyage back to the United States via Shanghai.

While she was in Canton, Anna May received a message from one of her managers in Paris notifying her of an offer from a London company to appear in a play there during the Christmas season. She accepted the offer, hastened her departure preparations, and booked a reservation to leave aboard the SS *President Adams* from Shanghai on October 20, which would sail to England via the Suez Canal.

Her last weeks in Shanghai were crammed with sparkling farewell parties. Butterfly Wu kicked off her goodbye tour with a dinner, after which Anna May had the honor of watching Butterfly shoot a scene for her upcoming movie *Always Keep Smiling*. More suppers and late-night gatherings followed. China's famous aviatrix Lee Ya-Ching threw a tiffin party on the day before Anna May's departure. Instead of departing the next morning, her Shanghai friends coaxed her into delaying her return for a few more days, if only to attend another round of soirées.

Journalists continued calling upon her for interviews up until the very last moments of her stay in China. A reporter from *Movietone* arrived at her hotel room one day and walked in upon the American movie star sitting comfortably on a couch, still in her yellow silk pajamas, her long hair draped over her shoulders. Even though it was already noon, she looked as though she had just woken up.

Had it been a successful trip coming home to the motherland? he asked. She puffed slowly on a cigarette and took a sip of her coffee before answering. "When I was in the U.S., I was interested in the affairs of the motherland, so I read books about China in the library. I searched a lot," she explained. The problem was that different books said different things. Which one was she to trust? "That's why I decided to come to China in person. Being told something is not the same thing as seeing it with your own eyes, which of course is a much more reliable and intimate experience."

Did she have plans in mind for the future of her career? She answered with a smile, "I can't predict what will happen in the future, let alone the next moment." At one point during her trip, Anna May pitched the idea of doing a movie "on the Chinese legend of the founding of Japan," where she would play the "sun goddess" leader of the new kingdom. Erich von Stroheim was tentatively interested in directing and Anna May had recruited Frank Dorn to write the story, but the project fell by the wayside. Ultimately, she didn't think prospects for developing Chinese films in Hollywood were great; bringing a traditional Chinese opera to the States likely wouldn't go over well with audiences there, nor could she see how elements of Chinese drama could be applied to American motion pictures. But as she had told previous interviewers, she did see another way that the two cultures might be bridged.

"There are infinite possibilities in China for movies," she argued. "It would be valuable for China if some large film corporation of America collaborated with a Chinese movie company in producing a movie depicting China. This would help to acquaint Hollywood with China and will also introduce to China some of the newest technical equipment." What she was suggesting was almost wholly antithetical to what MGM had done with *The Good Earth*. It would require Hollywood to put its ego in check and embrace a truly collaborative partnership, not one where it merely did enough to appease stakeholders. What's more, she proposed rendering a portrait of China that would include not only the humble farmer but also those who were educated city dwellers. "Such a picture," she added, "should be built around the lives of the people, the various classes of people."

Anna May was noncommittal about whether she would return to China to make films there herself. Still, an idea she had mentioned several months earlier lingered in her mind. In addition to the documentary footage she had collected, she thought she might play a Chinese travel guide of sorts "to show people about large Chinese cities with their clashing Eastern and Western elements." A fictionalized film narrative of this kind, she believed, could portray the contrasts of China "without asking the audience to stretch its imagination to the breaking point."

She summed up her tour of China as an enlightening trip, one that would help her to portray her heritage more authentically in any future endeavors. The reporter bid Anna May farewell and made his way down to the hotel lobby. Just as he was about to walk out, a waiter from the hotel restaurant came by with a tip: "Miss Wong has been busy being entertained all around town. She didn't get back to the hotel until 7 am this morning." Indeed, the sumptuous dinners and tiffin parties were never-ending.

"After missing three ships," she relayed to Fania and Carlo by letter, "I finally managed to turn a deaf ear to the persuasiveness of my good friends to remain in China, and leaped aboard the 'President

Pierce.'" She set sail from Shanghai on October 24. Due to her altered plans she would disembark in Los Angeles, then take a train to New York, and from there catch another ship to England so that she could arrive in time for her theatrical engagement.

"China has been wonderful," Anna May remarked in one of her final interviews with the Shanghai press. "It is very hard for me to leave—even harder than I had thought it would be. I have seen and felt so much that it is a little difficult for me to feel that it is a part of me as yet. I would like to go to California and think it over under one of our palm trees."

Many had doubted whether Irving Thalberg's Chinese farmer saga would ever see the light of day. Here, finally, was irrefutable confirmation: the picture was in the can. Principal photography on *The Good Earth* was completed by the end of summer 1936. Thalberg could breathe a little easier about one of the thorniest projects in his portfolio.

As postproduction work commenced to get the film ready for release, Thalberg and Albert Lewin continued to spend many hours together discussing how the film's editing and continuity were progressing. During one of these long conferences, which often took place on weekends at the Thalbergs' beachfront home in Santa Monica, a stray thought entered Lewin's mind. He and Thalberg were sitting poolside while Norma and the kids played in the water.

"Irving," Lewin appealed, interrupting his boss's train of thought.

"What?"

"If I were you, I'd be worried."

"About this dialogue?" Thalberg asked, slightly perplexed.

"No, no."

"About what, then?"

"I was looking at you and it occurred to me," Lewin explained. "You've just turned thirty-seven and you've got everything that a man could want. You've got millions. You're a captain of industry. You have a lovely, talented wife, and two beautiful, healthy children." Lewin paused as Thalberg smiled and nodded from his lounge chair in the shade. "The gods hate people like you. They're probably hiding behind that wall with a great big bat."

Thalberg laughed knowingly at his good fortune. "You're right," he said, "you're absolutely right."

With Thalberg, it always felt like he was running the clock down. In a recent meeting, one of his young protégés mentioned something about projects "ten years from now." Thalberg didn't skip a beat. "I'm not going to be here ten years from now," he said. "I might not be here ten days from now."

That very day he left with his family to spend the Labor Day holiday weekend at Del Monte Lodge near Pebble Beach on the Monterey Peninsula. When they returned to Los Angeles Monday evening, he had come down with a cold and a case of the chills. He spent the next few days in bed at home but in the evenings insisted on attending to business and social obligations: a dress rehearsal for a charity benefit, an afternoon tea hosted in honor of the Countess of Warwick, and the premiere of *Everyman* at the Hollywood Bowl.

By the end of the week, his ordinary cold had turned into something much worse: lobar pneumonia. Doctors and nurses were brought in. Norma Shearer ministered to her frail and wheezing husband throughout the weekend. Family, MGM colleagues, and friends like Douglas Fairbanks, who lived next door, shuttled in and out of Thalberg's sickroom, but his body was so wracked with fever and coughing fits that he could muster the energy for only a few words at a time. His condition steadily worsened. The following morning he beckoned to Norma and whispered, "The children, don't let them forget me." Irving Jr. and Katharine were hastily brought in to say goodbye to their father, but it was too late. Irving Thalberg had fallen into a coma and within a few hours, on September 14, 1936, he was pronounced deceased. The Boy Wonder was dead at thirty-seven.

Anna May takes English friend Val Gielgud on a tour of Paramount Pictures, 1938.

THESE FOOLISH THINGS

Back in the land of palm trees, the news of Irving Thalberg's death spread quickly on the MGM lot. Meetings were abruptly ended and all work stopped for the rest of the day. Staff were left to mill about aimlessly with tears in their eyes. Not everyone had the chance to work directly with Thalberg, but his reputation preceded him. His passion for the movies and his unerring drive to make pictures that meant something made even the most cynical of producers remember why they got into the movie business in the first place. Thalberg was the spiritual soul of MGM, and now he was gone.

The next day his death was announced on the front page of the *Los Angeles Times* and carried in papers across the nation. "Death of Irving Thalberg Shocks Film World," proclaimed the *Los Angeles Daily News*.

Remembrances from Hollywood's heavyweights came streaming in. "No recent news has been as shocking. . . . His leadership and accomplishments were a never-ceasing inspiration to all of us, and his place among us can never be filled," Mary Pickford affirmed. "One of the greatest friends a man could have; one of the greatest creative minds the world has ever produced," Lionel Barrymore said. The sitting president of the United States, Franklin D. Roosevelt, sent his condolences by wire: "The world of art is the poorer for the passing of Irving Thalberg."

By the end of October, editors at MGM had completed a rough cut out of the staggering and unruly amount of footage captured from six months of shooting *The Good Earth*. It was forty reels long, more than three times the length it would need to be in order to release it in theaters. Another twenty-eight reels would have to be painstakingly whittled away.

Meanwhile, Anna May was aboard the SS *President Pierce* on her way back across the Pacific, but all was not smooth sailing. Within six days of her departure, the Maritime Federation of the Pacific called a strike and brought all U.S.-operated ships in the Pacific to a standstill. When the *President Pierce* arrived in Honolulu Harbor, all passengers along with their baggage were summarily off-loaded. Anna May was one of six hundred hapless passengers who now found themselves stranded in the Hawaiian Islands. So she did what she did best and made lemons into lemonade.

"I am spending most of my time answering the telephone and letting people be kind to me," she told a reporter for the *Los Angeles Examiner*. "I am not going to fret, although I am anxious to return to my friends in Hollywood." She realized she was in a privileged position not to have to worry about the change of plans leaving her destitute. Whereas many less affluent passengers were anxious for the strike to end due to their dwindling travel funds, Anna May was able to broker a one-week personal appearance engagement at the local King Theatre.

"Here we are marooned on this heavenly island," she wrote to Fania and Carlo. "They couldn't have chosen a more delightful place; and except for the fact that it delays my return to the States and to seeing dear friends like yourselves, I would be enjoying this enforced vacation immensely, as I always wanted to see more of these islands." The impromptu layover was a much-needed vacation, as she told several reporters. In Hawaii, she recharged from three weeks of sleepless nights in Shanghai and meditated daily as she waited for the strike to resolve itself.

The stranded passengers were ultimately forced to circumvent the strike by boarding a pineapple barge one evening and ferrying to a Matson ocean liner anchored two miles offshore. After three weeks in Honolulu and another five days at sea, Anna May Wong stepped back onto American soil in San Francisco at the end of November 1936. The delay had forced her to cancel her engagement in London, for there was no way she could make it across the Atlantic in time. But it was no skin off her nose: she was just happy to be home. She had left the United States ten months before in her furs and European finery, and she returned a modern Chinese lady dressed in a polka-dotted cheongsam and cream-colored silk pantalettes. "I am proud to say I have a Chinese heart and the Western viewpoint," she told journalists as she disembarked.

Two days later, in Los Angeles, Anna May made her customary visit to the local U.S. Immigration and Naturalization Service offices. There, with a clerk and Chinese interpreter present, Inspector Boyd H. Reynolds subjected the world-renowned movie star to a rigorous interrogation. Even fame could not exempt her from the government-enforced surveillance conducted on all Chinese American residents.

"What is your name?" Inspector Reynolds began.

"Anna May Wong; my Chinese name is Wong Lew Tsong."

Next Reynolds produced a photograph and asked her to confirm whether it was her "photographic likeness" pictured.

"Yes, it is."

"Are you the same Anna May Wong who made a sworn statement before me December 16, 1935, in your application for a Form 430?"

"The same."

"When and where were you born?"

"At Los Angeles, California, January 3, 1905 at 351 South Flower Street."

"What is your occupation and residence at present?"

"Actress; I live at 2424 Wilshire Boulevard."

Reynolds proceeded to question Anna May about her family

members and their whereabouts, asking her to provide addresses and current occupations. One by one, he pulled out photographs and asked her to identify her siblings.

"Did you see your brother, Wong Wah Ying, and your father, Wong Sam Sing, while you were in China?" Reynolds asked.

"Yes, I saw my father in Hong Kong in the last of October, just before I sailed; and my brother Wong Wah Ying—he was at the 'President Pierce' to see me off."

"Was your father in good health when you saw him in Hong Kong in October, 1936?"

"Yes; I never saw him looking better."

Reynolds then produced a photograph of a Chinese man she had never seen before. Apparently, in an affidavit taken in the Chicago immigration office, the man had claimed he was her brother and testified that their father was deceased.

"In other words, he is an imposter?" Inspector Reynolds inquired.

"Yes; evidently assuming the identity," Anna May agreed. Upon further questioning, she stated for the record, "My father is not dead. . . . [T]his man is all mixed up. . . . [M]ost of this statement is 'screwy.'"

With that piece of chicanery cleared up, the interview concluded. Anna May Wong—a U.S. citizen, though treated as if she wasn't—was free to go.

Back in her apartment on Wilshire Boulevard, inhabiting the life she had previously known, Los Angeles felt smaller, provincial even. It wasn't L.A. that was different necessarily but something inside her that had changed. Anna May got to thinking: in almost two decades of working in the movies, she had bent and bowed to the demands of Hollywood, no matter how absurd or dismissive the requests. She had played conniving slaves, abandoned lovers, floozies, dancers, prostitutes, and half-castes. She'd done it because she desperately wanted to be an actress and those were the options available to her in the early days. Half the time, directors didn't even bother to tell her what the story was all about until she was in front of the camera. So it was either take what she could get or remain invisible. And while she knew that much of the vitriol directed at her by angry Chinese citizens was misplaced, she also saw that they had a point. Why should she continue to play in roles that cast a negative image of China and the Chinese? Her refusal to take a minor role in *The Good Earth* was not an aberration but the mark of a new chapter in her career.

Before long, Anna May's friends in the Hollywood press came to call on her. She regaled *Los Angeles Times* columnist Alma Whitaker with tales of the luminous personalities who had welcomed her to China and of her language travails: at one Peiping dinner she had comically flapped her arms like a bird to tell the waiters she preferred the duck over the fish. Rob Wagner was also happy to see his old friend back in town. Over lunch in Beverly Hills, Anna May told him, "I did not go to *see* China, but to *feel* it." She explained to Wagner how Chinese shopkeepers liked to bargain for sport, gave him a preview of the documentary travelogue she had made with Newsreel Wong's help, and laughingly informed him that her father was homesick for America. "Can you imagine Dad, who was supposed to be an old-fashioned Chinaman, impatient to teach the villagers American ways?"

Lloyd Pantages at the *Los Angeles Examiner* took notice when he saw Anna May looking sublime in one of her smartly tailored cheongsams. "I am disposing of all of my European clothes," she admitted to Bernardine Szold Fritz in a letter, "and just can't imagine wearing anything else but those lovely Chinese dresses." Just as she had transformed her outward appearance, Anna May's renewed Chinese identity also allowed her to be clear-eyed about where things stood in Hollywood. When journalist Henry Sutherland ran into her on a business call at Universal Studios, she was frank.

"I have just returned from China—my first visit—convinced I never could play in the Chinese theatre. I have no feeling for it," she said. "On the other hand, there seems little for me in Hollywood because, rather than real Chinese, producers here prefer Hungarians, Mexicans, or American Indians for Chinese roles."

Sutherland's article was syndicated in newspapers across the United States, under various headers. "These Fake Chinese Irk Anna M. Wong" went one headline. "Asserts Films Snub Chinese: Anna May Wong Still Looking for Job" ran another.

Sometimes the truth hurts. But Hollywood was skilled at deflecting it. "Her point that other races are used to represent Chinese is well taken, Metro's *Good Earth* being the outstanding current example," Sutherland wrote. "On the other hand, it's doubtful if discrimination against real Chinese was responsible. Casting *Good Earth* was one of the toughest jobs of the year, largely because few first rank Chinese actors were available."

If it was hard, it was only because MGM had made it so. But such complaints didn't register with the studio cavalcade.

Nothing was going to rain on *The Good Earth*'s parade. Irving Thalberg was barely cold in the ground, but the film was already being peddled as a living testament to his filmmaking genius. Whether it was good or not, Hollywood was ready to like it. Miraculously, MGM's editing team had brought the nearly 800,000 feet of footage down to a playing time of two hours and eighteen minutes. The final cut was submitted to the Chinese government for their review, which they readily approved with the contingency that they be allowed to censor portions of the film for distribution within China. The picture, verging on five years in production, was finally ready for the public. In sum, it had cost MGM $2,816,000 to make ($61.8 million in today's money).

One of Thalberg's lasting legacies was the fact that he refused to put his name on any of the films he produced. Credit, he claimed, didn't mean anything if you could give it to yourself. An exception was made in his absence, however. In the final cut of *The Good Earth*, Louis B. Mayer requested that a title card be inserted between the MGM lion's roar and the opening credits. It read: "To the Memory of

Irving Grant Thalberg We Dedicate this Picture, His Last Great Achievement."

The Good Earth made its world premiere at the Carthay Circle Theatre in Los Angeles on January 29, 1937. Floodlights streaked across the night sky and the theater's iconic Spanish-style bell tower could be seen from miles away, announcing the evening's historic spectacle. To build up the hype, MGM financed an extensive advertising campaign featuring the film's stars, Paul Muni and Luise Rainer. Angelenos could hardly open a local newspaper in the weeks leading up to the premiere without being hit over the head with half-page ads featuring the two lead actors posed in their peasant garb or circulars promoting Pearl Buck's book.

The convention of putting on extravagant prologues before screenings had largely fallen to the wayside due to Depression-era economies, but MGM still had a few tricks up its sleeves. All along the route to the theater, down Wilshire Boulevard and McCarthy Vista, and in the forecourt of the Carthay were props and set pieces from *The Good Earth* on display, refashioned into a behind-the-scenes exhibition. Behind the theater, an outdoor petting zoo was erected to house the water buffalo and other livestock used in the film.

For the first time in Hollywood history, the premiere would be broadcast live on radio networks nationwide, with the stars and bigwigs in attendance stopping along the red carpet to say a few words to listeners at home while an orchestra played in the background. Chao-Chin Huang, the Chinese consul general in San Francisco, and his wife made the trip down to Los Angeles to attend the world premiere. They, too, were given their due time at the radio microphone when they strolled through the Carthay courtyard in their evening attire. Other stars included Joan Crawford in a white gown, her famous seventy-carat star sapphire ring gleaming under the flashbulbs; Ginger Rogers on the arm of a young Jimmy Stewart; and Paul Muni looking anything but Chinese with a full beard and mustache. When Soo

Yong and Mary Wong ambled down the corridor toward the Carthay, fans in the grandstands gasped at their stunning Chinese dresses.

Conspicuously missing that evening was the actress whose performance everyone would soon be celebrating. Luise Rainer, along with the white ermine coat her husband had bought her for the occasion, was nowhere to be seen. Only weeks before, she and Clifford Odets, America's next great playwright, had wed in a private ceremony at Rainer's Brentwood home. The couple had met in Hollywood seven months earlier, and though the paparazzi often caught sweet moments between them while they dined at the Brown Derby, Odets was the jealous type. Rumor on the street was a lover's spat had kept her from attending the big night. Two days later, Rainer was on her way to New York, alone and without having seen the film she was currently starring in.

Private controversies aside, *The Good Earth*'s world premiere in Los Angeles was a triumph. The picture opened to similar fanfare four days later at New York City's Astor Theatre, where a second radio broadcast was picked up by stations in Shanghai and Nanking. In the meantime, Chinese newspapers waited eagerly to receive wires of the film's U.S. reviews. And when the reviews did come in, they were everything Thalberg could have hoped for.

"Once again Metro-Goldwyn-Mayer has enriched the screen with a superb translation of a literary classic," wrote Frank S. Nugent in the *New York Times*. "Its film of Pearl Buck's *The Good Earth* is one of the finest things Hollywood has done this season or any other." Once upon a time, another *New York Times*'s critic had said the same about Douglas Fairbanks's *The Thief of Bagdad*. Clarke Wales in the *Democrat and Chronicle* pronounced *The Good Earth* "the most flawless piece of screen production I have ever seen." The *National Board of Review Magazine* named the movie one of ten outstanding films for the year 1937. The *New Yorker* judged it "a vast and rich film."

While critics applauded Paul Muni's valiant efforts to evince the guise and mannerisms of a Chinese farmer, many observed that the illusion wore off as the film progressed. His costar's performance, by contrast, remained stunningly convincing throughout. "Luise Rainer's portrayal of O-Lan . . . establishes her beyond doubt as one of the truly great actresses of our day," Frank Nugent proclaimed. "Miss Rainer has given her majesty and haunting beauty." Sidney Franklin had been right about O-lan: less was more. "It's kind of a stunt role," the *New Yorker* admitted, "but that she hardly speaks throughout the performance, or makes a gesture, only serves to stress the fact that she actually dominates the film. She manages to seem more alive than whole mobs."

Pearl Buck, who had her misgivings about MGM's adaptation over the years, was greatly impressed when she snuck into a New York theater to watch the film. She called Luise Rainer's performance "incredibly perfect" and marveled "at the miracle of her understanding." Buck elaborated on her initial reaction years later in her memoir, writing that Rainer "not only looked like a Chinese woman but she moved like one and every detail of action, even to the washing of a rice bowl, was correct." When Buck had the chance to meet Rainer in person, she asked her how she had managed such an authentic characterization. "She told me that she had chosen from among the many Chinese employed on the set for the crowd scenes a young woman whom she thought most like O-lan. She had then followed this woman everywhere, watching her until she had identified with her."

Few critics had bones to pick with the white actors who assumed Chinese roles, which included Charlie Grapewin as Wang's old father, Walter Connolly as Uncle, Tilly Losch as Lotus, Jessie Ralph as Cuckoo, and Harold Huber as Wang's cousin. Only the *National Board of Review Magazine* felt the actors were too "obviously familiar and admired friends from Hollywood," arguing that "the miracle did not quite come off." The newcomer Chinese players were praised, though they were mentioned at the ends of reviews and without much individual distinction among them.

For their part, the Chinese American community came out in full support of *The Good Earth*. Many Chinese Americans had read Pearl Buck's novel and championed it as a sympathetic depiction of their heritage and community. The excitement around the film was palpable. Chingwah Lee, who played Wang's faithful friend Ching, used his publication the *Chinese Digest* to help promote the movie to Chinese Americans nationwide.

The magazine, in fact, deemed the release of *The Good Earth* significant enough to dedicate an entire issue to it. Gracing the cover of the March 1937 edition was a film still of O-lan on her deathbed surrounded by a coterie of women, including Mary Wong as the Little Bride. "The picturization of Pearl Buck's novel, *The Good Earth*, has been acclaimed from coast to coast by eminent critics as a great work of art and an outstanding achievement in the annals of the motion picture industry," the opening editorial announced with pride.

The pages were filled with articles highlighting Chinese American contributions to the film, whether as art department staff, technical advisors, or the actors who filled out the rest of the principal roles. Businesses and friends took out ads to celebrate those involved with the film's production. One advertisement placed by Moore's, a San Francisco clothing store, praised the performances of Roland Lui and Chingwah Lee. Another taken out by the China Emporium celebrated one of its employees: "Congratulations Mary Wong as 'Little Bride' in *Good Earth* and our Sales Director."

Madame Chiang Kai-shek, the American-educated, Christian wife of Generalissimo Chiang Kai-shek, viewed *The Good Earth* favorably and was deeply moved by Luise Rainer's performance. Soong Mei-ling, as she was alternately called, it being her maiden name, had become the softer, more approachable figurehead of modern China and was popular among Americans. Her public approval of the film was a huge publicity coup for MGM. As an expression of her appreciation, Soong Mei-ling sent Luise Rainer a gift of two hand-painted jars containing a special blend of Chinese tea, an elegant Chinese robe, and a bolt of the finest Chinese silk. Luise was delighted to be acknowledged in this way. In return, she sent six peach trees to Madame Chiang on the first direct China Clipper airmail service to Shanghai. The peach was not only a token of Rainer's gratitude and an auspicious symbol of longevity but also a subtle nod to the peach tree O-lan plants at the beginning of the film—a tree that eventually outlives her.

Along with this critical praise, the film continued to sell out engagements in Los Angeles and New York. Ticket sales at the Carthay Circle exceeded all previous records and the theater had to install additional telephones in the box office to deal with the volume of incoming requests. *The Good Earth* was a hit by every measure—except, that is, financially. Revenues carried on at a healthy clip, bringing in gross receipts of $3,557,000. Yet, with all the money poured into advertising, promotional activities, and distribution, MGM was left holding the bag for almost half a million dollars.

No one ever said prestige films came cheap. What they were principally good for was bestowing studios with the kind of glory and reputation that attracts top talent away from other studios. In that respect, MGM had maintained its eminence at the top of the heap. Pundits were already predicting that Luise Rainer would knock out the rest of the "Best Actress" competition come 1938's Academy Awards. The fact that she and Paul Muni both won Oscars at the 1937 Academy Awards for their respective roles in *The Great Ziegfeld* and *The Story of Louis Pasteur* augured well for their latest film.

Whether or not Anna May Wong wanted to follow the hoopla surrounding *The Good Earth*'s release, it would have been nearly impossible for her to ignore. Besides, there was also her sister Mary to think about and support in her role in the film. If Anna May was peeved by the admiration and accolades showered upon Luise Rainer, the woman who had effectively ended her bid for the role of O-lan, it was completely understandable. Only a German woman playing a Chinese peasant, the furthest thing from her reality, would receive the highest praise. But would the same commendations have been extended to a Chinese actress like Anna May had she been given the chance to play the part? Or would the critics and moviegoers have judged it a simple undertaking for a Chinese actress to impersonate one of her own?

In public at least, Anna May extended nothing but kindness and respect toward Luise. The two actresses met again in the fall of 1937 when Bernardine Szold Fritz, who had left Shanghai and resettled in Los Angeles, called Anna May up to join her at a charity reception hosted by Rainer and actress friend Gale Sondergaard in honor of dancer Angna Enters. Hollywood regulars like Claudette Colbert, Frank Capra, Peter Lorre, and Joan Crawford filed over to the party at the Sondergaard residence, decorated for the occasion with "many-colored blossoms and lighted tapers."

There, in a corner of the garden courtyard, the two hostesses and their guest of honor accosted the Chinese American actress. Luise, clasping Anna May's wrist, pulled her into their semicircle of women standing arm in arm. Anna May's splendid floor-length cheongsam with contrasting silk panels of light and dark cut a memorable figure against the staid dresses of the other three women. She towered over the petite Rainer, who looked up at her with a mixture of admiration and curiosity, almost as if she still doubted whether her onetime idol was real. Cordial words were exchanged. Perhaps Anna May told them stories of her travels in China and of her deepening concern for her family still in the country as warfare with the Japanese escalated. Bernardine recalled that Anna May was "rather in a state" because her sister Mary was to arrive back from war-torn China the very next day.

Several months later, the tenth annual Academy Awards banquet was held in a grand reception room at the Biltmore Hotel in Downtown Los Angeles. *The Good Earth* was nominated for five awards: Irving Thalberg and Albert Lewin for Outstanding Production, Sidney Franklin for Best Director, Luise Rainer for Best Actress, Karl Freund for Best Cinematography, and Basil Wrangell for Best Film Editing. Paul Muni was also nominated for Best Actor but for his role in *The Life of Emile Zola*, not as Wang Lung.

During the early years of Academy Awards, winners were announced at a press conference held before the awards banquet. For a second year in a row, Luise Rainer had to be compelled to attend and collect her Oscar for Best Actress. She and her husband, Clifford Odets, arrived late to the ceremony. Odets dismissed the Oscars as just another capitalistic institution, though perhaps a desire to trivialize his wife's moment in the limelight was also at work. But Louis B. Mayer had demanded she make an appearance at the Biltmore that evening, come hell or high water.

Looking at the photos in the papers the next day of Rainer and Louis B. Mayer holding up a golden Oscar statue and beaming, no one was any the wiser that the Viennese Teardrop was a difficult actress to wrangle, even when honors were being conferred upon her. The win made her the first actor in Academy history to win an Oscar two years in a row. Karl Freund took home the Oscar for Best Cinematography, and MGM walked away from the night's ceremony with five awards in hand, the most of any studio that year.

Many decades later, after Anna May Wong had passed away and the early Hollywood that she and so many of her friends had helped build became merely a legend of yesteryear, the so-called Golden Age, Luise Rainer was called to account for her yellowface impersonation in *The Good Earth*. A new generation of Asian Americans wanted to know why she had taken the role that many viewed as rightfully belonging to the first and only Chinese American actress of distinction. Why had she stolen Anna May Wong's one chance at Oscar glory? At ninety-three, she looked defiantly into the camera and said that portraying O-lan "doesn't have to do with a country. It has to do with the type of people—a peasant and a slave—that's what it has to do with. Not Chinese or European. No, no. That's all the same."

Anna May Wong put in her time underneath the palm trees, so to speak, contemplating all that she had experienced in her year in China and what it meant for her career moving forward. Her idea of doing a series of films as an "oriental detective" in the vein of Charlie Chan crystallized. She had seen with her own eyes how the Chinese welcomed Warner Oland with open arms on his trip to the Far East. Charlie Chan's crime-solving acuity and amusing aphorisms, Hollywood's silly salute to Confucius, endeared him to both the Chinese public and the Nationalist government. He was a good guy, a hero whom an entire nation could get behind.

Anna May saw no reason why she couldn't be a female version of this established trope. It was a win-win: she would get to represent a positive role model, and some enterprising studio would get a chance at developing its own Chinese sleuth to compete with Charlie Chan. Plus, unlike Oland, Anna May was a full-blooded Chinese who now spoke Mandarin and was knowledgeable of modern China.

She began shopping the concept around to different studios at the beginning of 1937. In truth, it wasn't the first time she had pitched the idea. Several years earlier she had offered the concept to Paramount but they quickly passed on it. This time around, Anna May decided to take a different tack. She asked the Paramount executive she was meeting with for some friendly advice. Which of two other studios did he think would be best to handle her detective series?

"Hey, what about us?" the executive demanded, suddenly sore that he was being cut out of a promising deal.

"But, I didn't think you would be interested in anything exotic, with Miss Dietrich on the lot," Anna May replied coolly.

Paramount signed Anna May to a one-picture contract in April 1937. "Movie to Star Her as Girl 'Chan,'" ran one headline, whose columnist averred that executives "recognize the popularity of Chan and fancy a lady Chan will be a riot." Several writers were assigned to begin work on a script for the starring feature, with production slated to begin in September. Until then, Anna May called on friends and commenced another personal appearance tour. Her public confrontation with MGM over *The Good Earth* was squarely in the past. She had stood up for herself by pointing out Hollywood's overt racism and she hadn't been blacklisted. Quite the contrary: she had a new studio contract in hand.

That spring, a freak incident garnered front-page coverage in the *Los Angeles Times* for several days. Anna May Wong and Mrs. David O. Selznick, wife of the well-known movie producer and daughter of Louis B. Mayer, each received an extortion letter threatening bodily harm to them and their loved ones unless they delivered $20,000 to one Dr. A. M. Foote, a retired chiropractor. But when Dr. Foote was brought in by the police, he knew nothing of the letters or the two women. He, too, had received a menacing letter ordering him to safeguard ransoms that would be delivered to him. Stranger still, in the letter sent to Anna May, the extortionist promised that the money was "a mere guarantee of co-operation to the fullest extent on your part." They clarified that their grand plan was to "induce Metro-Goldwyn-Mayer to have us in the same picture. When this is carried out, the money will be returned." The film, they said, would be about Jesus and include a role for evangelist Aimee Semple McPherson.

Initially, Anna May considered the letter a prank. "I have received many letters of a similar nature," she told a reporter, "but nothing has ever come of them and this one did not at first worry me." Kidnapping threats and ransom demands had been made on various stars over the years, including Mary Pickford and Marlene Dietrich. The detectives on the case believed the perpetrator was most likely "a crank or demented individual" but felt the threats were too serious to ignore. As a precaution, police were assigned to guard the Wong and Selznick residences. When a copycat letter arrived at Anna May's Wilshire apartment, she left town for an undisclosed location. The FBI opened its own investigation, but no suspects were ever prosecuted. After several weeks, news of the plot died down to a murmur and Hollywood went back to business as usual.

The arrival of Eric Maschwitz, Anna May's English beau, was just the thing to take her mind off such sordid affairs. She had last seen him two years earlier, during the second leg of her cabaret tour in Europe. Everything was coming up roses for Eric lately. He had been promoted to the BBC's director of vaudeville, and one morning in 1934, in need of a new song for an upcoming revue, he sat down in his pajamas and drafted the lyrics. It was called "These Foolish Things (Remind Me of You)" and catalogued a list of evocative images like "A cigarette that bears a lipstick's traces / An airline ticket to romantic places." The lines were reminiscent of a long-distance romance and almost indistinguishable from his ongoing flirtation with a certain movie star. Not a few eyebrows were raised. His wife certainly seemed to think it was written for Anna May. Needless to say, the song was enormously successful and became one of the most covered jazz standards of all time.

If that wasn't honor enough, at the end of 1936, Eric's musical *Balalaika* opened in London to critical acclaim and was on its way to a long, successful run at His Majesty's Theatre in the West End. MGM had made a generous offer for the film rights and invited Eric out to Hollywood to discuss the play. When he flew into Los Angeles, Anna May was there at the Burbank airport in her car to pick him up.

Talks at MGM proceeded and Eric was taken around to meet Louis B. Mayer and other bigwigs. By the end of his stay, MGM had not only staked a cool £25,000 (roughly $1.4 million in U.S. dollars today) to pick up the rights to *Balalaika*, but they were also offering Eric a six-month contract to leave his job at the BBC and come write for them. At ten times the weekly salary he currently made, the job was almost too good to be true. But leaving England and the London theater world behind for Hollywood, "perpetual sunshine among the orange-trees," was a big decision.

"I talked the problem over with Anna May," Eric recounted in his memoir. "In the state of mental confusion into which my various small and sudden successes had thrown me I was glad of her cool common-sense." He was wise to seek her counsel. "Calmly, kindly, shrewdly, Miss Wong analysed my situation for me, and as we said goodbye at the airport I knew that my time with the BBC was at an end." Eric accepted MGM's offer and returned to London to give notice and settle his affairs.

In tandem, Anna May made plans to travel to London for a few weeks' holiday in between professional appearances she was scheduled to make on the East Coast. She sailed from New York on the *Queen Mary* and on June 14, 1937, arrived in Southampton, where Eric was waiting to welcome her back to England. Though he was on his way out the door at the BBC, he had managed to finagle a last-minute contract for Anna May to appear on the BBC's Saturday night *Music Hall* program. One of the writers hastily put together a piece about an Englishman and a Chinese girl "aboard a steamer stranded in a lonely Chinese river."

Anna May got on splendidly in London as she always did and her presence was noted by the local papers as "adding a picturesque touch to several smart London parties." She wrote to her friends Fania and Carlos, who had sent her off from New York with a lovely present.

"Such fun to be in London again. Do you (Fania) remember it was two years ago that we left London, pouring with rain and boarded the Ile de France, and yet now that I am here, it seems only the day before yesterday," Anna May waxed nostalgic. "The theatre fare is not so exciting except for *Balalaika* which has been holding its own in a very successful way. It's written by Eric Maschwitz who you (Fania) have met—at Brighton."

For the last five years, Anna May and Eric had been like two ships passing in the night. They had had their fair share of overlapping ports of call and romantic rendezvous, but the realities of their careers had made it impossible to imagine being together in one place for any length of time. Under the terms of Eric's contract at MGM, he would be on Anna May's home turf for a solid six months, with the option to stay longer. The thought of a proper relationship with the shy but clever Eric Maschwitz became more and more real by the day.

Anna May continued on to Paris for a week, perhaps with Eric in tow, and then sailed back to New York the second week of July, knowing that she would soon see Eric on his return to the States. For now, she focused her energies on rehearsals for *Princess Turandot*, adapted from the eighteenth-century comedy by Carlo Gozzi. She would star as the princess alongside a promising young actor named Vincent Price at the Westchester Playhouse in August. The play was well-received, setting the record for the theater's highest-grossing show, and was revived for another week of shows. The play went on to the Westport Playhouse the next week. All of Broadway's leading ladies—Tallulah Bankhead, Alla Nazimova, Ethel Barrymore, Ina Claire—made the trip up to Westport, Connecticut, to see how Anna May would fare on the summer stock stage. Apparently, the tall, strapping Vincent Price was a little too convincing in his role as Prince Calaf, as he persuaded his scene partner to indulge in a brief liaison. Despite her affection for Eric, she was still an independent woman, after all.

While she was on the East Coast, armed conflict had broken out again between China and Japan following a minor clash on the Marco Polo Bridge outside of Peiping. Japan saw an opportunity to push deeper into China and seized it. The Nationalist government in Nanking scrambled to join forces with the growing Communist movement as part of a united front against Japan, but China was far outmatched in military power. The Japanese swiftly succeeded in occupying Peiping and Tientsin in the north. It was only a matter of time before Japanese troops reached Shanghai to the south.

The rumblings of war had the strange effect of intensifying studios' appetites for Asia-themed screenplays, just as they had with *Shanghai Express* in 1932 and the films that followed in the wake of Japan's earlier aggression. "That Sino-Japanese conflict has given a great upturn to the Wong fortunes in Hollywood," Edwin Schallert reported in the *Los Angeles Times*. In quick succession, a second film and then a third were tacked onto Anna May's contract with Paramount. Sure, war was good for business, but not so much for the conscience when you had family members living abroad in Asia. Her father, Richard, and Lulu remained in Hong Kong.

Anna May returned to Los Angeles at the beginning of September by way of the Super Chief to begin work on her first film for Paramount. As soon as she stepped off the train at the Pasadena station, she picked up the nearest newspaper and "with a furrowed brow" read the latest updates from the war. Mail service from China had become irregular as the country scrambled to defend itself. Anna May had not heard from any of her family there since the conflict erupted in July.

Luckily, she had her work to keep her mind from spiraling downward into worst-case scenarios. And then there was Eric, who had flown in from New York shortly after she arrived. Though he and his wife, Hermione Gingold, had lived apart for years, he'd brought her along on the New York leg of his trip because she had always longed to visit the United States. The two went their separate ways, however, when he left for Los Angeles.

Like clockwork, Anna May was there at the airport to rescue him from "a flock of minor reporters and cameramen" sent by MGM. Within a week he'd settled into a Mexican-style bungalow in Beverly Hills, replete with fruit trees, and hired a Packard sedan along with a Korean chauffeur recommended by Anna May to drive it. "I now had everything that a new young writer could aspire to, apart from a swimming pool and a British butler!" Eric recalled with verve. He neglected to mention the biggest bonanza of them all: Anna May Wong as his personal guide to Los Angeles.

While Eric settled into the routine at MGM (or lack thereof), Anna May went to work at Paramount. Two familiar faces would be joining her on the film, now titled *Daughter of Shanghai*. Robert Florey, Douglas Fairbanks's onetime foreign publicity director, had stuck around long enough to become a filmmaker and was set to direct. Then there was Philip Ahn, Anna May's childhood friend, who would costar opposite her as the leading male and love interest.

Despite his mother's denunciation of the movie industry, Philip Ahn had never quite given up on the idea of working in motion pictures. One day while finishing up his studies at USC, he caught the eye of director Lewis Milestone, who was then shooting a scene on campus. However, when Milestone heard Philip speak perfect English, he waved him off, explaining he wanted someone who spoke pidgin. Philip started to leave but, thinking better of it, turned back to the director and said, "Oh, so sollie, honorable sir. Me no talkie light lay, so go bye, chop, chop." This laughable performance apparently did the trick and Philip Ahn was on his way in the movies. Over the last three or four years, he'd worked his way up from bit parts in *The General Died at Dawn*, *The Good Earth*, and Shirley Temple's *Stowaway*. His most recent role in James Cagney's *Something to Sing About* promised to cement his position as "an exceedingly clever personality" on-screen.

Philip and Anna May had known each other since they were children, long before either one saw their name in lights. The fact that they, two Asian American kids who grew up in the heart of Los Angeles, were taking on the male and female leads in a major Hollywood production was quite frankly revolutionary. Philip and Anna May were the first Asian Americans to play a romantic couple on-screen in the sound era. And to get to do it as old friends was icing on the cake. It felt like they were getting away with something.

Daughter of Shanghai was based on a story supposedly ripped from the headlines about a human-trafficking ring smuggling undocumented immigrants into the country. When Lan Ying Lin, played by Anna May, and her father accidentally discover the culprits, her father is murdered and Lan Ying vows to avenge his death by exposing the crime syndicate behind the operation. Philip was cast as Kim Lee, the government agent who works in tandem with Lan Ying and at the same time falls in love with her.

The gossip slingers, however, only seemed to take note of how much time these actor friends were suddenly spending together, on set and around town. "In spite of the fact she says there's no romance," Read Kendall wrote in his *Los Angeles Times* column, "Anna May Wong is still constantly seen with Philip Ahn." On this occasion Anna

May didn't mind the speculation surrounding her love life because it gave her cover for what was really going on. But poor Philip wasn't used to this particular kind of media attention. "They said I was engaged to Philip Ahn, the Korean actor. He's terribly self-conscious about it," Anna May told a reporter while complaining about the untruths spread in gossip columns.

In actuality, Anna May was spending a good chunk of her off-screen time in the company of Eric Maschwitz. He had found MGM to be a soulless place where the likes of William Faulkner and other famous writers were paid to not write, which drove him rightly mad. At work, there was nothing to do but collect his weekly checks and idly hope for an assignment to come in. Outside the studio, life with Anna May was "pleasant in the extreme." She took him to all the places she held dear, the jewels of Southern California: "the beach at Santa Monica, the unreally beautiful racecourse of Santa Anita, the desert oasis of Palm Springs."

He was even brought into the Wong family fold as one by one her family returned from embattled China to the safety of Southern California—including her father and Richard at the end of the year and Lulu that following spring. The couple dined often with "the beloved Wong family" in Chinatown and other restaurants downtown. Under Anna May's steady instruction, Eric boasted of trying his hand at "chop-sticks and a few halting phrases of Chinese." And yet no one in the press was any the wiser. Save for a single line in the *New York Daily News*, buried at the end of a lengthy column: "Is Eric Maschwitz, lyricist of the London hit, *Balalaika*, in Hollywood to be near Anna May Wong?" Then, as if to insinuate another woman (and not his wife) was waiting for him back home in England, the columnist added, "A gal named Phyllis Gordon would like to know."

The highs and lows of the last several years of Anna May's life had been pronounced. But harmony and balance had arrived at last. She was not staging a comeback—at least, not in the style that Americans are wont to think of, she explained in an interview with *Modern Screen* around this time. Rather, she was beginning a career in the movies for a third time.

"You see, my movie life has really been divided into three distinct parts," she began. "The first period was taken up with my struggle to win recognition. After that was accomplished I got into sort of a rut, neither progressing nor being retarded. You know, there are so few roles that I can play and at the time they seemed to be always small ones.

"The result was that I had to stretch my salary over the lean weeks when I had no assignments. Well, just at this time, along came an offer to go to Europe and I accepted promptly. In Germany, they wrote stories for me and I became a star. This achievement, I consider my Second Beginning, for I went from there to London and was successful in films as well as on the stage.

"After finishing there, I returned to America where my picture progress once again seemed at a standstill, until recently when my Third Beginning got under way." With the wisdom of hindsight, Anna May credited her decision to bow out of *The Good Earth* and to travel to China as the linchpin guiding her third wind in Hollywood. "I had to be sure whether I was really playing a Chinese or merely giving an American interpretation of one. So—I saw China."

She had been back from her travels in China for a year now and could say with certainty that it had led her to one conclusion: "I feel that the real Chinese should be shown to the audiences of the world, if only to correct false impressions of the past. And so, with this thought in mind, I was happy to appear in *Daughter of Shanghai*." With a smile, she added, "Besides, this opportunity enables me to start my Third Beginning in the most unpredictable game in the world—the movies."

————

Eric Maschwitz, a self-professed romantic, was in love with Anna May Wong but decidedly not with Hollywood. He'd been hoodwinked like the best of them, Dorothy Parker and F. Scott Fitzgerald included, by the elusive, glistening mirage that is the dream factory. Fickle-hearted Hollywood had played as though she wanted him, pulled out all the stops when she was busy wooing her unsuspecting victim, but as soon as she had him right where she wanted him, wearing golden handcuffs in a hellacious paradise, she tightened her grasp.

"Go back to London!" theater impresario André Charlot, another victim of Hollywood's sweet nothings, told Eric. "Your roots are in Europe which is as far away from this circus as the planets! You'll never do any good in Hollywood; you care too much for what you are doing and too little for the money it can make you!"

Eric knew he was right. MGM had paid him $30,000 "for doing almost precisely nothing" and he'd never been more miserable. He idled away his free time with a hard-drinking crew of English expats whom Bernardine once had the displeasure of meeting and described somewhat disdainfully as "stinking drunks" with "drunken blonde sluts" hanging off their arms. As much as Eric cherished his time with Anna May, he knew this life in Hollywood was not for him. He charged forward with his work on the one screenplay worth the paper it was printed on—*Goodbye, Mr. Chips*—and counted down the days until his contract ended. At the little bar where he "had attempted to drown so many sorrows," he prayed that MGM would forgo their option to renew. Thankfully, his prayers were answered. His shackles unlocked, he was free to return to his former life.

On that April day of Eric's departure from Los Angeles, Anna May accompanied him to the train station where a swarm of friends were waiting to send him off. "The sky was burning blue," Eric remembered, "and as I stood there I felt a sudden pang, the sense of a chapter ended, another unknown chapter about to begin."

There was no mistaking his feelings for Anna May. Nor her love for him. "The Chinese are a remarkable people," he told his readers unequivocally. "Everyone should know and love at least one educated Chinese person in their lives."

The platform was crowded, but at times it felt as if they were standing there alone, just Anna May and Eric, prolonging the inevitable. "Most of all I hated leaving Anna May for, as the reader may have realized, she was somebody very precious to me, a friend, a counsellor, a piece of porcelain too delicate for my rough hands to handle with any safety."

And then "the bell sounded, the last farewells were said, and, all of a sudden, knee-deep in chocolates and novels by Pearl S. Buck, with tears in my eyes, I was on my way!"

The train pulled out of the station, smoke exhaling into the vast California blue, as a single lyric lingered in Eric Maschwitz's head: "The sigh of midnight trains in empty stations . . ."

The line was from the song he'd once told Anna May he'd written for her.

By the time he arrived several weeks later in London's Waterloo station—where he was heartily greeted by a reception committee of friends, including one Phyllis Gordon—Hollywood was a faint, orange-scented memory.

"Life seemed good," Eric wrote on the other side of the Atlantic. As usual, he professed, he was in love. But with whom, he didn't say.

Anna May Wong and her on-screen father Sidney Toler in a scene from *King of Chinatown*, 1939.

14

HEARTS THAT KNOW NO OTHER LAND

In her thirty-four years, Anna May Wong had seen and done more than most people accomplish in a lifetime. Ever since she first ventured across the Atlantic in 1928, she had restlessly crisscrossed the globe in service to her film and theater career. And she had more than her share of triumphs and failures. There were lean years, replenished by flush years, followed by lean years. She clinked glasses and broke bread with the international elite: artists, thinkers, businessmen, and heads of state. She fell in and out of love. She endured long separations from her family, which made their reunions all the more precious. She discovered what she was made of in tight situations when there was no one else to rely on but herself. Most of all, she learned to never allow others to define her. Instead, she claimed her own identity. She was neither a flapper nor a mythical Chinese maiden. She was simply an American who cherished both her Chinese heritage and her independence as a twentieth-century woman.

Anna May was still young but, having worked in Hollywood for twenty years and traveled the world, she was wise beyond her years. The heartache and disappointment she felt when her relationship with Eric Maschwitz ended was hard to encapsulate. He was, in many ways, the great love of her life. That he had given up on Hollywood so easily, and then given up on her, devastated Anna May.

She pursued everything she wanted in life with a steely determination and grit; she didn't force things, but she didn't quit either. Alas, other people were not like Anna May. They did not adapt as deftly to the obstacles strewn in their path. She, on the other hand, had learned from a young age to expect such setbacks, and in response she made herself pliable and resilient without diminishing her own agency. She was like a fast-moving river flowing effortlessly through the cracks, around rocks and fallen logs, and over cliffs until she arrived at her destination, a great lake, placid and calm to the casual observer but continually churning beneath the surface. Everywhere she went, she changed the landscape, her obdurate sense of purpose carving through rock like steadily dripping water, breaking down centuries of sediment slowly but surely.

"Anna May Wong possesses one of these strange powers—the ability to disappear and reappear at will. At least, so far as the screen is concerned. Not many people can do that," *Film Weekly* observed in 1939. By her own account, Anna May had reinvented herself several times in the span of her career. "It can't be called a 'come-back,'" *Film Weekly* clarified. "Anna has never faded away. She has simply decided, on several occasions, to have a change."

For the lone voice in the Chinese media that had urged her detractors to give her a chance—"She has an opportunity to understand the truth of China and fight for our country on the screen in the future"—Anna May was determined to make good on their faith in her. She vowed that she would no longer accept roles that "keep alive the 'cheap, preconceived notions' a great segment of the public entertains about the quaint, or inscrutable, Chinese." With this aim, Paramount developed several films that positioned her as unlikely but righteous heroines called on to right wrongs visited upon their families and communities. While she didn't exactly get the female Charlie Chan series she originally envisioned, she was fashioned into a brave amateur-sleuth type in several mystery thrillers. No one else in Hollywood was making films like these that revolved around Asian American characters played by Asian American actors.

Anna May Wong's new lease on life began with *Daughter of Shanghai*, released at the end of 1937, and progressed with *Dangerous to Know*, an adaptation of Edgar Wallace's *On the Spot*, and *When Were You Born?*, an astrology-inspired murder mystery, in 1938. She was loaned out to Warner Bros. for the latter to play an astrologist who solves a murder by deducing the zodiac signs of the suspects involved and ruling them out one horoscope at a time. Anna May was under no illusions that these movies constituted high art. They were one-hour B movies made on relatively modest budgets. As she wrote to Fania and Carlo, "I think [*Daughter of Shanghai*] will be a money maker although it's just plain hokum 'mellerdrammer.'" And yet, not insignificantly, Anna May took an active role in scripting these features and ensuring they promoted positive images of China and the Chinese. When she made *Island of Lost Men* the following year, she refused to wear a sarong, saying, "I'll stick to the Chinese styles. No Oriental girl would go wandering around in front of a camera in that get-up!" And nearly all the villain roles in this series of films were played by white actors. How's that for flipping the status quo on its head?

In the wake of Eric Maschwitz's departure in the spring of 1938, Anna May redoubled her focus on projects still in development at Paramount. Her next film was born from a friendship of mutual respect and was shaping up to be something quite unlike anything she'd done before. Over the years, she had come to know Dr. Margaret Chung, a prominent and beloved physician in San Francisco who counted many Hollywood names among her friends. (For instance, she once relieved Mary Pickford of her swollen tonsils.) Margaret and Anna May saw eye to eye on many things. Margaret, the daughter of a humble vegetable peddler in Santa Barbara, was the first Chinese American woman to become a doctor; Anna May was the first Chinese American woman to become a motion picture star. Both were familiar with the sound of doors slamming in their faces and didn't crumple easily in the face of rejection. Neither was married nor had plans to marry anytime soon. They were women wholly committed to their work, which they viewed as a duty and an honor.

Margaret Chung was also a selfless humanitarian. When war broke out in China again in 1937, Dr. Chung eagerly volunteered to serve as a frontline surgeon. However, both Chinese and American officials agreed that her skills would be far more valuable at home. Since childhood, it had been her dream to establish a modern hospital in China. She redirected her efforts toward funding medical aid to China, becoming one of its biggest boosters and recruiting hundreds of American pilots to fly supplies across the Pacific. Later, many of these same pilots would join the Flying Tigers aviation unit as part of a covert mission to beat back the Japanese invasion in China. Out of love and admiration for her friend's good deeds, Anna May would depict Dr. Margaret Chung on the screen in a fictionalized biopic.

The film was titled *King of Chinatown*, with a script focused on the story of Dr. Mary Ann Ling, a renowned surgeon, and her father, Dr. Chang Ling, who is a traditional Chinese herbalist with a shop in Chinatown. Nefarious schemes are afoot when associates of well-known racketeer Frank Baturin, also known as the "King of China-town," attempt to squeeze Chinese business owners by extorting money in exchange for so-called protection. However, when one of Baturin's own men turns on him and gives his rival the opportunity to shoot him down, the "King of Chinatown" is brought into the care of ace surgeon Dr. Mary Ling, who promises to save his life. As Dr. Ling nurses Baturin back to health, he begins to see the errors of his criminal ways, his redemption spurred on by a growing love for his faithful doctor. Before succumbing to another assault on his life, the King of Chinatown donates $5,000 to Dr. Ling so that she can fulfill her mission of shipping ambulances and medical supplies to the front lines in China.

To prepare for the role, Anna May spent two weeks in a Los Angeles hospital shadowing doctors and observing patients. She also arranged to sit through a major operation so that she could see for herself how a surgeon worked. The "hard-boiled" press agent who tagged along on this assignment had to excuse himself midway through the operation. She was even willing to file down her long, delicate fingernails. Paramount press shots captured Anna May enduring a painful manicure with the caption: "For Art's Sake—when told by Paramount studio that for her forthcoming role in *King of Chinatown* she would portray a Chinese surgeon Anna May Wong with many misgivings went to her manicurist to have her long fingernails trimmed for her surgeon role. Miss Wong is a stickler for accuracy."

Armenian actor Akim Tamiroff, who had previously costarred with Anna May in *Dangerous to Know*, was cast as Frank Baturin, the gangster with a heart of gold. Philip Ahn was enlisted once again to play Bob Li, the smart and good-looking Chinese American boy waiting to ask for Mary's hand in marriage one day. Despite Anna May's best intentions, her Paramount productions were not completely free of yellowface impersonations. Sidney Toler, who was about to become the new Charlie Chan, would play Mary's father, Dr. Chang Ling, with the aid of movie makeup. (That summer Warner Oland walked off the set for *Charlie Chan at the Ringside*, saying he wanted to return to his native Sweden one last time. Whether it was the drinking that finally caught up to him, the unforgiving pace of back-to-back film shoots, or the devastating reality of his wife serving divorce papers that drove him to the brink remains a mystery, but several weeks later Warner Oland was dead. He spent his final days in a Stockholm hospital with bronchial pneumonia.)

The opening scenes of *King of Chinatown* treat moviegoers with a lively montage of Chinese Lunar New Year festivities: children throwing bang snaps in the streets, confetti bombs exploding over parade processions, a dancing dragon winding through the crowds. Anna May, who was given time off from shooting to headline Moon Festival celebrations in Los Angeles Chinatown, suggested that the studio capture B-roll from the real-life festivities instead of re-creating the scene themselves. Paramount saved a bundle of money on extras and set construction, and Anna May got an authentic piece of Chinese America into her film. That's what Confucius called killing two birds with one stone.

What's more, the movie showed Chinese Americans living their lives both as modern Americans and as was members of immigrant communities who continue to honor their heritage. Mary brings her Caucasian colleagues at the hospital home for Chinese New Year at her father's shop. Together, she, her father, her colleagues, and Bob Li all enjoy a toast to the new year with a home-cooked Chinese meal and thimble-sized teacups of baijiu. Afterward they head to the charity boxing match arranged (and fixed) by Frank Baturin, where the Chinese American boxer Tommy Wu upsets the match with his unexpected win. When all is said and done at the end of the film, we see Bob and Mary sitting side by side, flying to China on a freight plane loaded with state-of-the-art ambulances, a diamond gleaming on her ring finger. Anna May finally got her happy ending.

Just as Anna May had acted as Hollywood's personal ambassador to Chinatown, feting friends like Ramon Novarro, Una Merkel, and Charles Rosher at Chinese restaurants and teaching them the time-honored traditions of her culture, she was now single-handedly exposing the American movie-watching public to a piece of her own little corner of Chinese America. She was a radical in sheep's clothing—or rather, silk cheongsams. The *New York Times* praised Anna May for her efforts "in molding the Paramount attitude, for she has long argued that her race should be portrayed as normal human beings."

All her squawking, as some might have called it, had eventually resulted in positive changes. "She also convinced the producers that not all Chinese can be relegated to two classifications, the dreamy poet and the sinister figure," the *Times* added. "Her reasoning, coupled with Chinese representation, has altered considerably Paramount's treatment of her race." On that account alone, *King of Chinatown* was a triumph and a motion picture that Anna May could be proud of forever after.

As the year 1938 came to a close, Anna May decided it was finally time that she set down roots. Tapping into the small pool of money she had saved throughout her career, plus the positive cash flow from her latest spate of films, she gave up her apartment at the Park Wilshire and bought a Spanish-style house on a one-acre plot at 326 San Vicente Boulevard in Santa Monica. Her middling star status put her in the top 20 percent of Hollywood salaries, but on average she earned just $4,000 to $6,000 per picture, a modest fee in comparison to the generous compensation packages doled out to actors like Marlene Dietrich and the late Warner Oland. Nevertheless, Anna May had learned how to live smartly without breaking the bank. She paid $18,000 in cash for the property and set to work renovating it into her dream home.

At the end of her trip to China, she had told a reporter, "When I have a home, it will be a Chinese home with a Chinese garden." Now she was making good on that promise to herself. Anna May envisioned constructing a house similar to ones she had seen in China but according to modern tastes. She commissioned Rudolf Schindler, a modernist architect and former associate of Frank Lloyd Wright, to design and manage the renovations. Santa Monica was at that time a small beach town just a stone's throw away from the rugged valleys of Pacific Palisades and Rustic Canyon. The city had a reputation for being a community of artists and bohemians, and its inhabitants—many of them Europeans in exile, like Bertolt Brecht, Thomas Mann, and Christopher Isherwood—were lured by the space, proximity to nature, and cool salt breeze that living fifteen miles west of Downtown Los Angeles afforded them.

Initially, Anna May planned for the entire Wong family to live with her on the property, but the idea was vetoed by her siblings, who preferred to live closer to Downtown L.A. Only her youngest brother, Richard, who had a few more years of high school, decided to move in with her, though other siblings bunked there from time to time. The house was converted into four separate apartments with a main suite designated for herself and a second apartment for Richard. The other two she would rent out to tenants.

Schindler built custom furniture for various rooms and an open fireplace in the living room. "The old ivy that smothered the walls" was pulled out and additional windows were installed to let in light. The exterior was painted white and a blue roof was put in—"like the blue roofs I saw in Peking." The final touch was a red octagonal door or moon gate opening onto the garden and main property from the street. Unusual by Western standards, the circular door was a nod to the many moon gates Anna May had passed through in gardens, temples, and palaces across China. Hence, she christened her home Moongate.

The move from her old apartment into the newly remodeled house initiated the upheaval of all that had come before. Anna May found herself not only sifting through the material possessions she had accumulated over the years but also reevaluating the emotional and intellectual underpinnings that had once guided her. She was in a contemplative, almost brooding mood when she spoke to journalist Alice Tildesley.

"We don't know how to live properly," said Anna May, looking plush in a red velvet housecoat. "Lately, as I've looked over my possessions, I've thought: 'Why do we cling to useless things?' For the matter of that, why do we cling to useless thoughts? And to useless people? That last is a hard thing to say, I know, but isn't it true?"

In this moment of personal reckoning, Anna May wondered whether she had wasted her time on all the wrong things: material gain; fame and prestige; people who were merely attracted by her celebrity; men who could never fully reciprocate or commit to her love. She pledged to rid her life of useless things and useless people, but most of all she expressed a desire to rid her mind of useless thoughts.

"We can't go back and live things over or correct mistakes already made, so let's forget the regrets," she concluded. Was Anna May think-ing specifically of her memories of Eric Maschwitz? She had remained publicly adamant, even while their affair continued behind closed doors, that she didn't see herself ever marrying. And that was alright by her.

There was the heartbreak of their relationship. And then there was the heartbreak of what was happening around the world. China, the peaceful sleeping giant, was locked in a war of resistance against Japan, whose conquest had swept down the coast, taking Peiping, Tientsin, Shanghai, Nanking, and Canton with it. For two years the Chinese had sustained massive casualties and experienced horrific war crimes at the hands of their hostile occupiers. Chiang Kai-shek and his Nationalist government were forced to flee to the west and set up a provisional capital in Chungking while Communist forces waged guerrilla warfare from their stronghold in the rural countryside out-side Japanese lines.

On the other side of the globe, the civil war in Spain was headed toward a bloody conclusion. Hitler's crusade against Jewish citizens escalated beyond anyone's worst fears and turned Germany into a po-lice state ruled by Brownshirts. Kristallnacht, the Night of Broken Glass, resulted in a violent pogrom of Jews and the destruction of their synagogues, businesses, and homes across Germany. The Nazi Party's consolidation of power foretold of terrors still to come. The iconoclas-tic, fast-living Berlin that Anna May had once inhabited was now but a reverie from her youth.

One day, in the midst of renovations for Moongate, a craftsman came to see her about some element of the decor. It turned out he was Jewish, and they got to talking. "We discussed the appalling state of the world and the persecution both our races are undergoing across the different oceans," Anna May recalled.

The man offered his perspective on matters. "I think it is wrong for us to let our minds dwell on the injustice and evils that are being done to our people. That is not a constructive thing to do," he explained. "No, the way to change these conditions is to change our own thoughts."

Anna May saw the wisdom of his words and adopted the attitude as her own. "The fault is in all of us, of course," she said to Alice Tildesley in her Moongate living room. "I haven't managed it yet, but I hope to get rid of useless thoughts of hate, also." It was purpose and meaning that she now craved, not the fleeting thrills of stardom nor the self-righteous anger of victimhood.

Moved by her family's harrowing tales of fleeing the war in China, and likely inspired by her friend Dr. Chung's fervor, Anna May devoted herself to the Chinese cause. She had been vocal about her support for Nationalist China and its struggle for self-determination since 1936, when she penned an essay on the topic for *Rob Wagner's Script* magazine.

Her earliest efforts were straightforward gestures: instead of buying her friends and family Christmas gifts, she donated her Christmas money to Dr. Margaret Chung's fund supporting medical supplies in China. "Please don't think that I neglected you at Christmas in not sending you some message," she wrote to Fania and Carlo, "but the need is so great out in China that I felt all my friends would understand when they know that my remembrance to them this year is in aid of a good cause." She auctioned off her movie costumes and other screen souvenirs. She attended charity galas in Hollywood and appealed to others in the film colony to contribute to the cause. She gave a talk at a charity event hosted by the Motion Picture Artists Committee and was rendered speechless when "several picture tycoons . . . rushed into the breach with $100 bills and checks for more hundreds." These deeds did not go unnoticed. Madame Chiang Kai-shek personally thanked Anna May for her contributions via cablegram in the summer of 1938.

The stakes increased with each day that saw the war continue. Then, as her contract with Paramount lapsed in 1939, Anna May saw an opportunity to redouble her efforts. That summer she booked a ten-week personal appearance tour of Australia to help raise funds for China. She returned to the United States at the beginning of September, on the heels of Hitler's invasion of Poland. In retaliation, France and England declared war on Germany. The world she had known was at its breaking point. After looming ominously for years like a black cloud on the far horizon, the Second World War had officially begun.

The lull in professional opportunities during this time privately worried Anna May. She confided in Carlo, "The Studios are extremely quiet and one wonders if one is going to work again. Hope it is just a passing phase." But her marching orders remained the same. Instead of bouncing to and from the typical parties in the Hollywood Hills, where industry names gathered to let loose and gossip about those not in the room, Anna May's social life increasingly revolved around China-related events. When Lin Yutang, a friend she had made in Shanghai and the author of the bestselling book *My Country and My People*, came to town to give a lecture titled "Can China Win?" at Los Angeles's Philharmonic Auditorium, Anna May took the opportunity to honor her friend with a tea party at Moongate. She had always been seen by the American public as a link between East and West, and here, in her beautiful home—American in construction, Chinese in sensibility—she could finally bring her two worlds together. Movie people like Myrna Loy, Hedda Hopper, Jimmy Gleason, and Rob Wagner mingled among the China contingent, helmed by Lin, Consul T. K. Chang, and Bernardine Szold Fritz.

For the foreseeable future, Anna May's calendar was stacked with charity benefits: luncheon at the Tropics in Beverly Hills; tea at Moongate hosting speakers knowledgeable about the war in China; an appearance at the *Cabin in the Sky* matinee at the philharmonic; charity auctions; screenings of her self-produced documentary of China; dinner at the Bowl of Rice gala ball; and even a stint at the Actors' Thrift Shop in New York City during the holiday shopping rush. Anna May, actually, was one of the committee members helping to organize the third annual Bowl of Rice drive in New York for 1940. The glitzy event was one of dozens of dinners and parties organized nationwide to raise funds for medical aid to China.

As if the world were not in a bad enough predicament, another tragedy was about to rock the Wong family. On July 25, 1940, during lunch with her father and sister Lulu, Mary Wong abruptly rose from the table and left the room. An hour later, a hired maid walked into the garage at 2845 Council Street and was confronted with a horrific sight: Mary's body, limp and lifeless, hanging from a clothesline suspended from the rafters above. She was only thirty-one.

Wong Sam Sing was still in shock when a police detective arrived on the scene. Lulu was in such a state of hysteria that the police couldn't question her until later. Wong could think of no reason why his youngest daughter would choose to die by suicide. There was no note left behind to explain the act. Was Mary depressed or lovesick? Following her role in *The Good Earth*, she worked for a time as Anna May's stand-in on films like *Dangerous to Know*, but that work had since dried up now that her sister was consumed with wartime charity activities. Had Mary been dejected about the lack of prospects for her acting career? Or mentally weighed down by the terrible state of the world?

Alas, Mary had escaped the ravages of war in China only to succumb to a hidden affliction of the heart and mind. Anna May was "prostrated" by the news when she was reached for comment at her home in Santa Monica. Overwhelmed with emotion, she could not think of a motive, either, and declined to comment further. For the Wongs, like many Chinese families, what happened in the family stayed in the family. If Mary had suffered from some form of mental illness, the topic was not to be broached, and especially not with outsiders. Without any evidence of wrongdoing, the police ruled the death a suicide. Anna May never spoke again of the incident in public. And in a letter to Fania and Carlo, she mentioned her sister's death only in the abstract:

"Dearest Fania and Carl: It was good of you to wire and we all deeply appreciated your helpful thoughts and kind sympathy at a time when we most needed the understanding of friends. It has all been so recent and tragic it is difficult to refer to it, so I will leave the subject alone."

It didn't help that being the sister of a famous actress meant that Mary's death was national news. Papers around the country carried the unhappy report. The *New York Times* callously printed the headline: "MARY WONG HANGS SELF: Sister of Anna May Wong Ends Life in California." The Wongs mourned the unspeakable loss of their youngest sister and buried her in the same plot as their mother at Angelus Rosedale Cemetery.

"The show must go on," that prevailing adage of lifelong entertainers everywhere, was burned into Anna May's brain. As at so many other points in her career, when disappointments and tragedies befell her—a contract was revoked, a nervous breakdown forced her to check into a sanatorium, her mother was killed by a reckless driver—she bore her suffering in private. Then she composed herself, put on her face, and strode back out into the world as the Anna May Wong her public expected. She delayed her summer stock appearance in a revival of *On the Spot* all of three weeks.

Anna May was back on fundraising duty in September to launch the Bowl of Rice drive at a New York press conference with Colonel Theodore Roosevelt Jr., Mayor Fiorello La Guardia, and Carol Bruce at the World's Fair City Hall. "China's need for medical aid is so great that it is hard for the imagination to grasp it," Colonel Roosevelt pronounced. "For three long years she has endured the same sort of war from the air that England is experiencing now; her cities have been laid waste and her people have been driven from one place to another in a pitiful search for safety where no safety can exist. These mass migrations and the hardships which the migrants have had to endure have resulted in untold suffering and sickness and widespread epidemics of dread diseases."

The same tone of seriousness was carried into the proceedings for the Bowl of Rice Ball on the evening of November 1, 1940. Over dinner in the opulent Basildon Room at the Waldorf-Astoria, guest of honor Dr. Hu Shih, who had ascended to the role of Chinese ambassador to the United States, spoke forcefully on why China could not give up its fight. "Peace is not possible," Hu Shih argued, "because we know that these aggressors cannot be appeased. They are insatiable."

Surrender would not only spell the end of China's national independence and freedom, which it had been struggling to defend for the last three years, but it would also signal "a great catastrophe in the larger world struggle of democracy against totalitarian aggression." Put in other words, China's plight against the Japanese, coupled with Germany's advances in the European theater of war, was nothing short of an existential crisis for global democracy. If China and England fell, the United States might very well be the last democratic government left standing.

Then came the day that would live on in infamy in American history. On December 7, 1941, the Japanese launched a surprise attack on Pearl Harbor, a U.S. naval base in Honolulu, Hawaii. This unprovoked act of aggression resulted in more than 2,400 American casualties, both military and civilian, and 1,178 more wounded. The next day President Franklin D. Roosevelt gave his famous speech imploring Congress to declare war on Japan. Within a few days, Germany and Italy, Japan's allies, declared war on the United States. America had officially entered World War II.

Fearing the Japanese population within our own borders, President Roosevelt issued Executive Order 9066, effectively granting the U.S. government the power to forcibly remove and relocate Americans of Japanese ancestry, regardless of their citizenship status. The facile assumption was that Japanese Americans disloyal to the United States might commit espionage or other acts of sabotage on American soil; yet the same suspicions were not applied to German or Italian Americans. Beginning in 1942, tens of thousands of Japanese Americans were forced to abandon their homes and businesses and report at meeting points throughout the West Coast. They could take only the possessions they were able to carry with them. The Santa Anita Racetrack, where Anna May and Eric Maschwitz once spent a romantic afternoon, was one of these meeting points. Stranded there until they were assigned to a camp, many Japanese Americans had to live temporarily in horse stables. Then the U.S. military transferred them to concentration camps in rural, often barren landscapes across the American West and incarcerated them for the remainder of the war.

Chinese and Japanese Americans were pitted against each other during this dark and tumultuous period. Whereas the Chinese were seen as democratic allies in need, the Japanese were vilified as cruel and unfeeling enemies. Most Americans could not tell the two ethnicities apart, so whether you were Chinese or Japanese, you were equally liable to experience the unwarranted wrath of your fellow American as you walked down the street. Presumably out of goodwill toward Chinese Americans, *Time* magazine ran a feature titled "How to Tell Japs from the Chinese." The page was printed with two photographs, one of a Chinese man, the other of a Japanese man. Superimposed on the images, and heavily influenced by the flawed theories of eugenics, were diagrams noting the features of each "race." The Chinese man was registered as having a "parchment yellow complexion," while the Japanese man was said to have an "earthy yellow complexion," and so on.

The verbal vitriol and physical violence unleashed upon Japanese Americans induced Chinese Americans, who similarly feared for their safety, to wear buttons and scraps of fabric pinned to their lapels with the words: "I am Chinese." Cinematographer James Wong Howe wore one of these signs during the war. Actor James Cagney, whom Howe photographed in *Yankee Doodle Dandy*, sported his own "I am Chinese" button in solidarity.

Once the United States entered World War II, wartime efforts became all-consuming. Patriotic Americans across the country reported for duty and committed to helping any way they could. Hollywood, too, was ready to play its part. Anna May Wong, still very much involved in her work to support China, signed on with Producers Releasing Corporation (PRC, representing "Poverty Row" B movie studios) to star in two wartime films. The first was *Bombs Over Burma* in which she played a teacher stationed in Burma who is secretly working for the Chinese army and attempts to track down a Japanese spy whose coded messages threaten the Burma Road supply route to Chungking. In *Lady from Chungking*, also a spy thriller, Anna May portrayed a Chinese aristocrat ordered to work in the rice fields in occupied China; in actuality, she is the guerrilla leader of a group of resistance fighters who uses her proximity to a Japanese general to smuggle information to the Flying Tigers, a volunteer group of American aviators fighting on behalf of the Chinese.

Critics panned both pictures. The movies were, after all, thinly veiled propaganda filmed with the singular purpose of shoring up support for the war in the Pacific. Anna May hadn't made them for prestige but for the cause, and in that spirit she donated the entirety of her paycheck, $4,000 total for both films, to United China Relief.

On the one-year anniversary of Japan's attack on Pearl Harbor, Anna May was sworn in as an air-raid warden at the Santa Monica City Hall. "Busy with bond sales, China relief and other war work," a local reporter noted, "the actress nevertheless felt, she said, that 'one can't do too much.'" Alma Whitaker, her old pal at the *Los Angeles Times*, applauded the actress's unwavering selflessness in her column. "Anna May Wong, the popular Chinese actress, is a special heroine. She is in such demand for Chinese War Relief, air-raid-wardening et al., that she hardly has time to earn a cent for herself."

Despite Anna May's relentless work on behalf of China, there were those who still viewed her as a scourge upon the nation's good name. At the end of 1942 through the spring of 1943, Madame Chiang Kai-shek made a highly publicized speaking tour across the U.S. to raise funds. Her final stop was Los Angeles, where she was greeted by thousands of Angelenos who lined the streets as her procession cruised through downtown. Although Anna May was among the guests at Consul T. K. Chang's reception at the Ambassador Hotel, an invitation to Madame Chiang's grand finale two days later at the Hollywood Bowl never arrived. Instead, in the spectacle produced by David O. Selznick, Mary Pickford handed Madame Chiang a bouquet of roses and many other Hollywood stars, including Norma Shearer, Ingrid Bergman, and Janet Gaynor, greeted the evening's illustrious guest. Anna May, it turned out, was intentionally omitted by special request from one of Madame Chiang's aides.

"There has been no more faithful worker for the cause of United China Relief than Anna May Wong," Rob Wagner, longtime friend and booster, wrote in his magazine *Script*. "Was she asked to greet Madame at the film reception? She was not." His wife, Florence Wagner, echoed his outrage on Anna May's behalf. "Where was Anna May Wong? Why was she not first in the parade of those glamorous picture girls who received the sainted visitor?"

Anna May, ever the diplomat, kept her head high. She insisted to Wagner, "The important thing is that Madame Chiang was heard by so many people and that the spectacle at the Bowl was such a big success."

Nothing could slow down or hinder Anna May's wartime efforts, not even the apparent public disapproval of China's first lady. By this time Richard, now twenty, was drafted into military service and shipped off to England to serve as a private first class in the U.S. military. While he was away, Anna May, too, was called on to serve her country. The Hollywood Victory Committee planned to send her to entertain troops for a month or more as part of a USO tour in the spring of 1944. She had hoped to be sent over to Europe, where she might check in on her brother and see old friends, but her assignment dispatched her to U.S. outposts in Edmonton, Alberta, and Alaska.

Days before she set out on tour, Anna May traveled first to New York City, where she partook in the celebrations for Paul Robeson's forty-sixth birthday extravaganza. She was just one of the notable names among the guest list of 8,000, which included the likes of Duke Ellington, Zero Mostel, Count Basie, and Mary Lou Williams. Still, she had her chance to broadcast her best wishes for Paul from the stage. Later she could be seen by Paul's side, peering at his five-tier birthday cake.

In the brisk north, still thawing out from winter, Anna May performed dramatic sketches and talked engagingly about life in China from makeshift stages. The muddy melting snow made for less-than-ideal conditions. "It was the first time in my life that I ever had to ask an audience to stop splashing so loud," Anna May laughed to a reporter. But she was encouraged by their bravery. "Many of the boys I met had fought the Japs in the Aleutians and in spite of the fact that they are terribly anxious to get home, they have an outspoken urge to take another shot at the enemy."

The tides of war were beginning to turn against the Axis powers in Europe as U.S. and British forces racked up victories in Italy and North Africa. A watershed moment for the Allies came on June 6, 1944. D-Day, as it is best remembered, marked the largest amphibious military assault in world history, with 160,000 American, British, and Canadian troops landing on the beaches of Normandy, France. Allied forces pushed back German defenses, and by the end of summer Paris was liberated. In less than seven months, Hitler and Mussolini were both dead and the Allies declared victory in Europe. Then in August 1945, the United States delivered the final crushing blow: President Truman gave the okay to drop two atom bombs on the civilian cities of Nagasaki and Hiroshima in Japan, instantly killing nearly 200,000 people. On September 2, 1945, General Douglas MacArthur accepted Japan's unconditional surrender. After six long years of war, around 60 million dead, countless lives disrupted and irrevocably altered, World War II was over.

Like everyone who lived through the earth-shattering decade of 1935 to 1945, Anna May Wong emerged from World War II somewhat the worse for wear. There was no going back to the time before. She could only look on those years through rose-colored glasses as a period of innocence and frivolity.

The life force that had once animated her, giving her the fortitude to keep pressing urgently forward and making her feel that she was fulfilling an important mission, vanished at war's end. Even so, the frenetic pace of the war years had not been good for her nerves, and she had begun drinking more than she should—not cocktails with friends as in the old days but alone, behind closed doors. She'd put her career on the back burner, and just when she was ready to return to the studio—any studio—there were slim to no pickings to be had.

She and Keye Luke were both passed over for the 1944 Pearl Buck book-to-film adaptation of *Dragon Seed*. Perhaps they were "much too authentically Chinese to play any important role next to the startlingly diverse group of European and American actors who essayed the leading roles." James Wong Howe had aspired to direct a screen version of Chinese novelist Lao She's best-selling book *Rickshaw Boy*. He had Anna May in mind for a part in it, but when civil war broke out in China again, the perfectionist in Howe couldn't see a way to film it anywhere else. Lester Cowan's announcement that he was going to make a biopic about Sun Yat-sen and cast Anna May Wong as Madame Sun Yat-sen merely got her hopes up.

Anna May, despite everything, had not lost her resourcefulness. To sustain herself, she took on technical consultant roles on China-centered films and pictures that sometimes featured white actors in Asian roles, like Dorothy Lamour in *Disputed Passage*. She also re-tooled herself as a kind of celebrity self-help guru and developed a women's lecture series on Chinese beauty customs. Lenthéric Perfumes sponsored her tour to twenty cities with a fragrance called

"Shanghai." "Spend a half hour or so a day watching the fish swim around the bowl," she would tell the ladies sitting in the audience, promising that it would help to "sharpen and beautify the eyes." This certainly wasn't the most glamorous thing she'd ever done to make a buck, but it kept her afloat.

The upkeep at Moongate was a constant burden, and at one point Anna May got pretty far along in a deal to sell the property to friend and Hollywood gossip columnist Hedda Hopper. But when she discovered she wasn't able to purchase property anywhere else due to racial covenants, Anna May sent Hopper an urgent telegram asking her to "make the generous gesture" and scuttle the deal, which she did.

Though she had originally intended to rent out the other units at Moongate, one or both remained vacant or partially leased for long stretches. But in these times of limited means, she made more of an effort to find tenants, while Richard took care of maintenance around the property. For a while she housed jazz guitarist Tal Farlow, who played in a trio with Red Norvo and Charles Mingus. Then one day in 1948 a young man named Conrad Doerr showed up on Anna May's doorstep. His only connection to show business was a distant relative, actress Cecil Cunningham, who had costarred with Anna May in *Daughter of Shanghai.*

"I was somewhat nervous as I rang the bell and my landlady-to-be for the next eight years opened the door," Conrad recalled. Anna May accepted him as a tenant and arranged for him to live in the apartment above the garage while he attended Santa Monica City College.

Her professional dry spell finally ended in 1948 when she was given a part as the key witness in *Impact,* a crime thriller about the lying heart of an unfaithful wife and her lover who together plot to murder her husband. Two months after filming wrapped, however, Anna May was rushed to the hospital. Just days before the Christmas holiday, Louella Parsons reported, "The many friends of Anna May

Wong will be sorry to hear she has been seriously ill, and may have to undergo an operation."

Her illness was not revealed to the public, but it was grave indeed. She was diagnosed with cirrhosis of the liver, an irreversible condition caused by scarring of the organ. Whenever the liver is damaged, either by disease or excessive alcohol consumption, it attempts to repair itself and scar tissue forms. Eventually, too much scar tissue impedes the liver from functioning properly and often results in death.

Quite possibly for the first time in her life, Anna May Wong was confronted with her own mortality. She was forty-three and fighting to stay alive. It was painful enough to think of her mother and sister Mary, who had been taken from her before their time. Soon she would have to confront another inevitability.

In the fall of 1949, Wong Sam Sing left his earthly body and rose to meet his maker. At age eighty-nine, he had lived long enough to see Los Angeles metamorphose into a first-rate city known around the world for its climate and its biggest export: the movies. His favorite daughter, the one he'd prayed to the gods would be a boy, had proven him wrong, and maybe even made him proud, by ascending to her place in the Hollywood firmament.

"I was always looking for my father in my films," Anna May once conceded. They had butted heads more than a few times over the years. Anna May always hated arguing with him in Chinese because he was sure to win while she stumbled inarticulately to find the right word. He was the reason, in part, why she could never see herself marrying a Chinese man: she wasn't about to let any husband dominate her. And yet, through it all, she loved him dearly and revered him more than she could say.

While working on *King of Chinatown*, Anna May had lobbied Paramount scriptwriters to remove all mentions of the phrase "Honorable Father." She'd been made to say that ridiculous phrase enough times in films like *Daughter of the Dragon*. Besides, it wasn't how

Chinese children, at least not American ones, addressed their elders. Her answer to this inauthenticity appears in the film itself, in a charming scene in which Mary Ling comes home on Chinese New Year to greet her father at his herbal shop.

> **MARY LING:** Hello Dad, Happy New Year!
>
> **CHANG LING:** My child, when you desired to become a modern up-to-date doctor I sent you to college.
>
> **MARY LING:** You've been a darling.
>
> **CHANG LING:** I even countenanced your working in a hospital. Perhaps if some of my herbs had proven unsuccessful, I might even have sent one of my patients to you. But please do not say, "Hello Dad."
>
> **MARY LING:** I'm sorry, Father. I'll try to remember. You know you're tickled to death I've got my degree.
>
> **CHANG LING:** You'll probably end up by operating on me.
>
> **MARY LING:** I like you just the way you are.

That was Anna May's tribute to her dear ol' dad. The honor was always implied.

Despite his long and abundant life, the loss of Wong Sam Sing proved to be the breaking point for Anna May. Following his death and burial, she suffered a nervous breakdown and was hospitalized again for several weeks. When she returned to Santa Monica, life became quieter than it had been in a long time as she cocooned herself inside the walls of Moongate.

A publicity headshot of Anna May Wong for her comeback performance
in *Portrait in Black*, 1960.

THE WOMAN WHO DIED
A THOUSAND DEATHS

Nineteen fifty was the dawn of a new era, a golden age in American life, when the land of the free returned to being a land of plenty—at least for some. The boys were home from overseas, getting an education thanks to the G.I. Bill and coming into jobs with good salaries and pensions. The ladies retreated from the factory line and the field hospital and retook their places in the home, running the household, making pennywise purchases from the Sears catalog, and rearing a bumper crop of young'uns, America's greatest hope for the future.

Anna May Wong celebrated her forty-fifth birthday that year. She was now old by Hollywood standards, and nobody wanted you when you were old. Why would they? With a steady flow of ingenues arriving in Los Angeles by the week with stars in their eyes, studios didn't have to try hard to reel in fresh meat. Norma Jean was dead, but Marilyn Monroe was undeniably on her way.

Work at the studios had dried up. But there was a new kid in town. Television, the budding entertainment medium that had studio executives shaking in their boots, was swiftly being adopted in homes across the country. In five years, the number of television sets in use rose dramatically, from 6,000 in 1946 to 12 million in 1951. There were only a handful of networks broadcasting during the day, and they were hungry for more material. Just as many established actors in the New York theater world had been reluctant to jump into the flickers for fear of tarnishing their reputations, Hollywood heavyweights saw no reason to lower themselves by appearing on television. Their faces and figures, larger-than-life on movie screens, would hardly take up any space at all on those tiny little boxes.

Anna May, though, was a pioneer through and through, just like her father. When she discovered a path leading forward, she always took it.

Fifteen years earlier she'd mentioned the idea of playing a Chinese travel guide who enlightens viewers on the dynamic differences between East and West through her excursions around the world. She refined this concept and combined it with elements of her track record as a crime-solving heroine to create a new series called *The Gallery of Madame Liu-Tsong* for the DuMont Television Network. In it, Madame Liu-Tsong, who shares Anna May's Chinese namesake, is the cosmopolitan proprietor of a string of international art galleries. Forgers, gangsters, and art thieves abound in this line of work, and the shrewd gallerist soon ends up solving mysteries and foiling global crime syndicates as part of her glamorous day job.

Conrad Doerr, who had established a friendly rapport with his celebrity landlady, attended a small dinner party Anna May held at Moongate on the eve of her departure for New York, where she would film *Madame Liu-Tsong* at the DuMont studios. "Early in the evening, she began to come apart," he remembered. Two years had elapsed since her last film. Conrad saw that she was "terrified not only over returning to work but over doing so in a new medium. But she went East, and came back stimulated and anxious to work."

The thirteen-episode series—the first program in television history to star an Asian American woman—aired at the end of August 1951 in a prime-time Monday evening slot. The first thirty-minute episode, "The Egyptian Idols," opened to Madame Liu-Tsong at her Paris gallery, where "a Madison Avenue gamin thrust a priceless Egyptian idol in her hand."

In spite of Anna May's best intentions, the program was under-realized thanks to bad writing and meager sets. DuMont, though a competitor with NBC and CBS, was a no-frills operation, and it showed. "Miss Wong, not to mention the viewing public, deserves much, much better than this," a disappointed critic concluded. The slim budgets and low production quality signaled the end for *Madame Liu-Tsong* before it had barely begun. DuMont canceled the show after one season, and the first Asian American–led television series came and went without a wink of recognition. Sadly, no copy of *Madame Liu-Tsong* is known to exist, for when DuMont went out of business several years later, the tapes were dumped into Upper New York Bay.

While Anna May in her professional life was still finding her footing again, she kept up a relatively active social diary. Conrad, who was young and interested in her Hollywood life, began accompanying Anna May on her visits with old industry friends as a chauffeur-escort.

She took Conrad along with her to see Anthony Quinn in a touring production of *A Streetcar Named Desire* in Santa Barbara, introduced him to Edith Head at a public talk in Pacific Palisades, and brought him to social appointments, where Conrad had occasion to meet other Hollywoodians like Philip Ahn, Wallace Reid Jr., and Aileen Pringle. Bernardine Szold Fritz, whom Anna May wrote letters to often, and Una Merkel remained good friends. On at least one evening, Conrad and Anna May enjoyed a few cocktails at the Mocambo nightclub, where she danced the rumba and bumped into gossip columnist Harrison Carroll.

Now and then, they had long conversations "about *The Good Earth*—her disappointment in the casting." Conrad felt that "playing O-lan would have made all the difference in the world to her career—and role in Hollywood." Still, everywhere Conrad went with Anna May, he couldn't help but notice that despite her absence from the screen she always seemed to cause a commotion. "She was tall for a

Chinese woman, had remained striking-looking, and her public wardrobe always had an Oriental flavor," he recalled. Even in her late for-
ties, Anna May never lost that movie star intrigue.

During these years, Anna May entertained at home, inviting close
friends like Eddy See, Sissee Leong, Tyrus Wong, James Wong Howe
and Sanora Babb, and Katherine DeMille, among others. Eddy and
Sissee, children of the well-known Chinatown merchant Fong
See, had grown up with Anna May in the streets of Old Chinatown. They were some of her few Chinese American friends from the
old days.

Stardom had its adverse effects, too: Anna May's celebrity often
made her inaccessible and seemingly remote in the eyes of her own
community, who approached her timidly or not at all. Yet inside the
confines of Moongate she felt secure among the select friends and family who had known her when she was just a girl with a dream working at her father's laundry. Eddy's son, Richard See, remembers going
over to Moongate as a teenager with his father and other relatives for
informal poker games. Anna May was always the consummate host,
refilling snack bowls and refreshing drinks in slacks and a black
sweater, cracking the occasional joke, "You know, fifty million Chinamen can't be Wong."

In public and in the presence of friends, Anna May tried her best
to keep up appearances, but she didn't always succeed. After a small
party at Moongate, Bernardine observed that Anna May "drank an
awful lot, and it did not make her gay, but rather, just downright
wretched." Richard Wong, who continued to live with his sister, was
there for her in those low moments behind closed doors. In the privacy
of her own home, she'd developed a self-destructive habit of binge
drinking. She wasn't the only one. Her generation had grown up on gin
fizzes and never fully weaned itself off them. Carl Van Vechten would
know: he wrote a whole novel about downing sidecars until the sun
came up. Hollywood was practically a community of high-functioning
alcoholics—high-functioning, that is, until somebody dropped dead.

Try as she might, Anna May had been unsuccessful in ridding her mind of useless thoughts as she had preached to a reporter a decade ago. "We fill our minds with thoughts of regret. We think: 'Why did I do this? Why didn't I do that? Now, I have made a dreadful mistake and it is too late to undo it. Oh, why can't I go back and do it differently?'" The past haunted her. "We let our thoughts wander over the past, living in past glories, smiling over the honors we once had, or in past happiness, reliving the sweetness of old days or dwelling on cruelties or injustices that have been visited on us or ours when such thoughts are of no use." Her lecture against this type of self-indulgence inadvertently revealed the thoughts that nagged at her heart and mind.

The worst of it was the way her looks had faded prematurely. The effects of cirrhosis aged her skin, causing her face to look puffy and jaundiced. It was sometimes difficult to look at herself in the mirror, to see the sagging skin and harsh lines where soft, easy beauty once prevailed. She was no longer the China doll, the temptress, or the siren. Those were the roles she had played for half her career, often unwillingly, and now no one would dare think of casting her in such parts. As her beauty deteriorated, her confidence shrank accordingly. She didn't feel fit to be seen in public. Under these conditions, her drinking habit worsened.

Anna May hit her bodily limit at the end of 1953. On December 9 she was hospitalized at Santa Monica Hospital under the care of Dr. Robert Skeels, who reported to the press that Anna May was "seriously ill but failed to comment concerning the nature of her illness." The Van Vechtens wrote immediately to Richard when they heard the news.

"At this moment I can report she is on the road to recovery but it will be a long period yet before she'll resume normal activities," Richard wrote to Fania and Carlo on December 15. "The trouble is her bad liver and physical rundown condition due to improper eating and self-isolation, emotional worries from the menopause and financial

worries from no work and all this led to a disregard of life and friends."
In spite of the seriousness of her condition, Anna May had not curbed
her habits to allay the onset of symptoms and the disease steadily advanced.

"So with these basic troubles, I guess the body gave in," Richard
explained, "and last Wednesday internal hemorrhage broke loose
in the esophagus-stomach region which didn't stop bleeding for
two days."

To Anna May and Richard's chagrin, word of her hospitalization
was picked up by major newspapers around the country. Walter
Winchell included a line about it in his regular column, stating "Anna
May Wong had a dozen transfusions. Still too ill . . ." The inclusion of
this sensational detail was sheer gossipmongering, but the report was
not far off from the truth. Dr. Skeels transfused his patient with no
less than eight pints of blood and ordered her to stay on bed rest. As
Anna May relayed to the Van Vechtens several weeks into her conva-
lescence, the doctor made clear that the transfusions were "just a temporary crutch to tide me over and he wasn't going to dig me out of the
grave again."

She headed to the Sierra Madre Lodge, a rehab and recovery center specializing "in the treatment of problem drinkers." From her temporary room situated in the idyllic foothills of the San Gabriel
Mountains, Anna May wrote to Fania and Carl with her characteristic
charm, as if trying to casually brush off the near-death experience she
had gone through:

"I am so dearly sorry to have given you my good friends so much
concern and worry with my recent siege at the Santa Monica Hospital.
Saul called on me there and no doubt has reported to you that I am on
the mend. . . . Just now your gorgeous chrysanthemums arrived. . . . I
now have them in my room where I can feast my eyes on them as I
write this letter to you. Many many thanks for your sweet thoughts."

At Richard's behest, Conrad made the trip east to Pasadena to visit
Anna May in recovery. Her brother thought a few social calls from

close and discreet friends would raise her spirits. She was to recuper-
ate at the lodge for two months but stayed only one before returning
home to Santa Monica. When Anna May wrote to Fania again, she
said the imposed period of rest had done her some good: "I decided all
the rush and wear and tear is of no avail. . . . I am enjoying a bit of long
lost peace, for which I'm so grateful."

Being faced with her own mortality this time around had the effect of jolting Anna May back into her old self: the upbeat and re-
sourceful actress who made her own luck. She read the self-help
bestseller *The Power of Positive Thinking* cover to cover several times.
"It is a great help . . . in ridding oneself of nervous tensions and having
the right attitude towards what appears to be colossal problems," she
told Fania. In the same breath, she detailed the meetings she lined up
as soon as she was discharged. A sudden burst of energy inspired her
to get back out there and pound the pavement over at the Hal Roach
Studio, Paramount, and Universal International. Plus, the hospital
bills and extended stay at the lodge had racked up a considerable tab.
She asked Fania to help her sell some of her jewelry to friends who
might be interested. "It isn't an easy thing for me to ask a good friend
like you to help me on such a matter, but it so happens I do need the
money, otherwise I wouldn't part with them."

Nothing definite came of her initial industry meetings, but reconnecting with familiar faces from the good old days like Cecil B. DeMille, Adolph Zukor, and Walter Wanger in the Paramount commissary
had the effect of lifting her spirits. She ran into Jesse Lasky on another
occasion and chatted with him briefly. "We made pictures during happier days," he told her, alluding to the sense that they were all part of
a dying breed of movie pioneers.

Around this time, Anna May and Richard reopened the idea of
selling Moongate. A steady drip of eager real estate developers made
it known that they had eyes on the lot; it was a prime location for a
new apartment complex. When Anna May had bought the land, she
acquired two parcels, one on the corner where Moongate currently

stood and another next to it with a copse of trees. In need of a quick cash infusion, Anna May sold the extra parcel to mitigate her financial woes and buy her and Richard time to mull over what to do about Moongate.

Although the next year passed without a peep from Hollywood, she did garner a small part in an episode of the television series *I Spy*. She began contemplating the idea of making a trip to London, Paris, and Munich to revisit some of her old haunts and see what was cooking in the film and theater industries abroad. The last time Anna May had been to England was 1937, before the war, before she and Eric called it quits. Nostalgia for the life she had once lived crept back in.

Even in her hometown, she sometimes had the feeling of being a relic left over from another era. Los Angeles had mushroomed into a city of nearly 2 million people. "When I went into Los Angeles to apply for my passport," she wrote to Fania in the summer of 1955, "the traffic and it's [*sic*] speed was rather bewildering, especially on the new Freeways. Even quiet little Santa Monica is such a busy place now, so to find peace one must retreat to the woods, which are getting more remote, as the suburbs grow."

Bennett Cerf, a friend and cofounder of Random House, suggested that Anna May write her autobiography for his publishing company. A trip to Europe would send her on a tour down memory lane and hopefully regenerate experiences from those pivotal years to collect in her memoirs. She flew to New York in September, where she saw Carl Van Vechten and Donald Angus. Her nerves about retreading the past, however, got the better of her and sent her on a drinking spree. She was so sloshed that before dinner had even begun Carl and Donald had to carry her out of the restaurant and take her back to her hotel.

Fania, who heard about the incident, later confronted Anna May about her drinking out of concern for her friend. "I thought she knew I cared for her enough to be honest with her," Fania relayed to Bernardine by letter. "So I begged her not to destroy herself—by drinking—a game nobody could beat." Anna May did not respond well to this intervention and broke her engagement to see Fania and Carl on her way back through New York.

"But because I understand the cause of her frustration," Fania continued, "I wrote to her shortly afterward as if nothing had happened. I am her friend and will remain so. I pity her lack of mental capacity, abstention, and experience, which prevents her from facing herself as she is, and not hoodwinking herself into believing she still remains what she represented many years ago."

Bernardine echoed Fania's sentiments in a letter of her own, writing, "It does seem though as she has been unable to accept the change that the years brings. . . . Old Lao Tze has said over and over in different words, that having success burdens man with the terror of losing it."

Written in confidence between two mutual friends, these words were harsh but presented an honest characterization of Anna May's unfortunate affliction. Fania added that Anna May had told her she felt as though she was letting her brother down. "Richard . . . doesn't understand why she isn't still the glamorous, sought after, personality she was then."

The final devastating blow was a line scrawled in the margins as an afterthought: "I say 'represented' for as you know she had no talent." Whether Fania was truly distraught over her good friend's alcoholism or simply stirring up petty rivalries of the past, she and Anna May never spoke of it again.

Anna May put her slipup in New York behind her and set off on her first commercial transatlantic flight aboard Pan-American Airways Flight 50 on the afternoon of September 18. After decades of traveling in first-class berths on top-of-the-line steamers and trains like the *Île de France* and the Super Chief, Anna May realized her present circumstances called for economy, so she booked her ticket in coach.

Contemporary London was baffling yet familiar. "Have been in a spin the moment I alighted on the ground and it has been very difficult to try and get my bearings and find my way around," she wrote to Fania and Carlo. "But it is really a joy to be back in London and after the first bewilderment at its 'new look'—the streets are still in the same places but the buildings have changed and the speed of traffic and people almost equals New York."

She stayed at the Westbury hotel in Mayfair, her former stomping grounds due east of Hyde Park, and reveled in the near-perfect weather. Her weeks were filled with the things she loved most: reuniting with old friends, chatting up industry people about upcoming projects, and taking in shows in the West End. She lunched with Somerset Maugham at the Dorchester on Park Lane, drank a gin and tonic or two with *Sketch* reporter Dick Richards, and sat for a portrait session with photographer Paul Tanqueray for old times' sake. "I was happy to find quite a few old friends and enjoyed our visits, although at moments I felt like an old cronie," she reported back to Fania.

F. Leslie Withers recounted his "sentimental reunion" with Anna May for the *Sunday Mercury*. Despite an eighteen-year absence, the British public had not forgotten her. "Wherever we went around London," Withers noted, "there were autograph-hunters eager to have the English and Chinese versions of her name on their often grubby pads."

"I am sure the British are more faithful to the favorites of yesterday than the Americans," Anna May admitted to Withers. "It really is wonderful to feel that so many still remember me." There was no doubt she was well loved in England. During the several hours she and Withers chatted at her hotel, a constant flow of friends arrived, including actors Ben Lyon and Bebe Daniels, to welcome her and deliver "huge bunches of flowers." At dinner that same evening, the headwaiter, "risking being tactless," came up to Anna May and "announced the fact that he was the waiter who used to serve her at the Kit Kat Club in 1928!"

Reliving the memories of those years long ago had not provoked the unpleasant emotions of past episodes as she had feared; rather, retracing her steps in London breathed new life into her. But the rush of activity during her three and a half weeks in the city—and the free-flowing cocktails—took a toll on her fragile health and her pocketbook. By early October she decided to forgo her original plans of visiting Paris and Munich and turned homeward. When she arrived back in Santa Monica, she admitted herself to the hospital at her doctor's urging.

Anna May had hardly walked over the threshold at Moongate before the real estate agents were knocking on her door again. Eventually someone made her an offer "too attractive to refuse." She and Richard had lived there for eighteen years, but with the property proving expensive and time-consuming to care for, coupled with Anna May's declining health, she realized it was time for a change. Richard had been single-handedly managing the maintenance and upkeep to save money, and Anna May was tired of the expectation that she cater to tenants or make idle small talk with them on a daily basis. Brother and sister decided to take the offer and sell the property.

They downsized into a smaller, more manageable house at 308 Twenty-First Place in Santa Monica in the summer of 1956, shortly after the sale closed. Conrad Doerr was the last to move out of Moongate. With him, he took a beloved desk given to Anna May by actress Judith Anderson and later bequeathed to him. The new owners swiftly razed the house to make way for a nondescript apartment building, and Moongate was no more.

———

Anna May settled into her new home with an enormous feeling of gratitude. She was thankful for her family. Lulu was a twenty-five-minute drive away and checked in on her often. Richard, more than anyone, had become her rock, and she relied on him greatly. He had always looked up to his famous older sister, but he was no longer a boy at thirty-three. For a while he had worked shifts at Douglas Aircraft and indulged in various creative endeavors, like the Chinese gift shop he opened in Brentwood and the home photography studio he'd

NOT YOUR CHINA DOLL

set up in the garage at Moongate. He photographed his sister and their pets, sending a few snapshots to the Van Vechtens now and then. One of his portraits of Anna May even made it into the *Sunday Mercury*. Whatever he was doing or working on, his sister remained the priority. Richard shouldered the majority of the work required to move them into the new house, including wallpapering the four rooms with Japanese grass cloth paper and transplanting many of the rare plants salvaged from Moongate.

Richard saw firsthand the price that fame and Hollywood's backhanded racism had exacted on Anna May. Drinking, perhaps, was one way to bury the grievances she refused to air in public. The taste of liquor on the tongue was also a reminder of days long since past. And yet, he understood how seriously Anna May took her career. Acting was her life and she was happiest when she was working. More than that, her refusal to let the Hollywood machine beat her into submission was an act of defiance.

Anna May had been moping long enough. It was time for her to buck up—especially if she still held to her belief that by being seen in the public eye, whether on screens or through her charity work, she was advancing a positive image of Chinese Americans and demonstrating their essential humanity. Clearly, the days of running home with Lulu to escape the racist taunts of their classmates had made an indelible mark on her.

The move to Twenty-First Place offered her a fresh start. Most important, Anna May was grateful to be alive. With her health improved, she was ready to make another go at television. She got her chance that fall in a live televised production of W. Somerset Maugham's play *The Letter* for the *Producers' Showcase* series. William Wyler, who had directed a film adaptation of the play in 1940 with Bette Davis in the lead role as Leslie Crosbie, wife to a plantation manager in Malaysia, and Gale Sondergaard playing the part of Mrs. Hammond, the Eurasian wife of Geoff Hammond, was set to direct the TV revival. Wyler, in fact, had originally wanted to cast Anna May

as Mrs. Hammond in the 1940 film, but the idea of presenting an actual Asian woman married to a white man once again was ruled out.
Sixteen years later, Anna May would finally get to take on the role of
Mrs. Hammond herself. She flew to New York for filming and while
she was there had a marvelous time with the Van Vechtens.

"I have so many wonderful remembrances from my recent visit to
New York," she wrote to Fania soon after she returned to Los Angeles.
"In a way, it was a kind of a turning point in my life, I hope I am now
on the right track."

Anna May Wong was beginning again once more. "She's gazing
into a TV future with a feeling of abandon that exceeds any period
during her long movie reign," Marie Torre reported in her TV
column.

"For the first time in my life," Anna May asserted, "I am free to
devote myself completely to the sheer joy of acting. I hope they will
like me in television."

Reflecting on the last several years, which had been difficult to say
the least, Anna May confessed, "Until recently, I was bogged down,
you might say. . . . And I had a personal problem too. I used to live
completely within myself. I was an extreme introvert. That's all right
if you're Garbo, or a sphinx, but it wasn't good for me. During these
last few years of rest, I had a good deal of time for soul-searching, and
now I have stopped floundering."

Anna May made good on this assessment. Over the next few years,
her TV career blossomed and she made numerous appearances in series like *Climax!*, *Adventures in Paradise*, *Mike Hammer*, *The Life and
Legend of Wyatt Earp*, and *The Barbara Stanwyck Show*. "After the war,
I did nothing for about five years. I had come to that transition when
I had to change from leading roles to character parts," she explained
to another journalist. "I think I have made it now. . . . And I find
character roles are more fun."

Her television revival led to another satisfying opportunity. At the
beginning of 1957, she was invited by ABC to present and narrate the

documentary she had made chronicling her 1936 trip to China on the program *Bold Journey*. Anna May's documentary, now titled *Native Land*, gave American viewers a glimpse of what life in China had been like two decades prior, before the Japanese invasion and the dramatic break between the Nationalists and the Communists, when the country seemed to be on the cusp of becoming a great democratic nation.

Around this time, though she had espoused the beliefs of Christian Science for most of her adult life, Anna May began attending classes at the Unity School of Christianity in Santa Monica. She found "a great deal of inspiration" in the teachings of Dr. Sue Sikking and looked forward to her classes every day—so much so, she often declined social invitations in order to attend them. When Bernardine met Dr. Sikking, she understood why: "This astonishing woman . . . who has been such a help to [Anna May] . . . impressed me very much." Anna May was happy to report to her friends that this new discipline had given her "a happy and joyful outlook on life."

––––––––––

Thanks to Anna May's renewed visibility, a role in the widely publicized melodrama *Portrait in Black* with Lana Turner and Anthony Quinn came her way at the end of 1959. Anna May was thrilled to return to the big screen. Press releases from Universal publicized it as her comeback moment, which they exaggeratedly claimed ended "a seventeen-year retirement from the motion picture screen."

In the original play for *Portrait in Black*, the script called for a Cockney house maid. Producer Ross Hunter changed the setting to San Francisco and the housekeeper to Chinese so that Anna May could take on the part. The role of Tawny, the Chinese housekeeper, one of several hired help in Sheila Cabot's upscale household, was a nominal one, in keeping with Anna May's new career as a character actor. Her scenes were few and far between and accompanied by a distinctly Oriental flourish in the soundtrack.

Nevertheless, she brought a dignity and strength to the character beyond what the script entailed. Some critics might have passed her performance off as typically "enigmatic" or "inscrutable," qualities many believed innate to the Asian psyche. But if one looks closer, there is so much brimming beneath the surface in Anna May's Tawny. She practically smirks as she delivers an incriminating letter to her mistress near the end of the film, as if to tell us she has known all along what we as moviegoers are only just now beginning to realize. Tawny, it seems, contains multitudes and is privy to a wisdom that only comes from a lifetime of hard knocks and deft recoveries.

Despite her small number of scenes, Anna May was accorded a royal welcome at the *Portrait in Black* premiere in Detroit in June 1960. No sooner had she touched down in Motor City than she received "the keys to the city, flowers from Chinese children in Windsor, and appeared on a radio program in whirlwind succession." She was back in picture-perfect form, wearing a scarlet Chinese dress and one of her unusual hats—"a copy of a Tibetan priest's hat, adorned with diamond pins set in platinum which spelled out her name in Chinese." Her fabulous getup inspired at least one newspaperwoman to compose the headline "Her Name's in Lights—and in Diamonds."

That same year Anna May was honored with her very own star on the brand-new Hollywood Walk of Fame. There, near the intersection of Vine and Hollywood Boulevard, her name was inscribed in a coral-colored star embedded into the terrazzo sidewalk and honored as one of the original Hollywood movers and shakers. Along with that distinction, she and Sessue Hayakawa shared the privilege of being the Walk of Fame's first Asian stars.

———

At the beginning of 1961, Conrad Doerr ran into his former landlady at a Santa Monica bank. They had lost touch in the intervening years, but he was glad to see Anna May looking so well. They chatted briefly and Conrad left with the impression that she was on a high.

Indeed, she had good reason to be cheerful about the future. Ross

Hunter told Anna May that he had just purchased the film rights to Rodgers and Hammerstein's hit musical *Flower Drum Song* and he wanted her to play an important role in it.

The musical, based on C. Y. Lee's novel of the same name, centers on a young Chinese man in San Francisco's Chinatown who is caught between the push and pull of traditional Chinese values and popular American culture. The dilemma—to adhere to one's heritage or to assimilate—was entirely familiar to Anna May. She had waited her whole life to see a story like this one come to the silver screen. Her part was that of Madame Liang, an advice-doling auntie and elder to the younger lead characters, played by Nancy Kwan, James Shigeta, Miyoshi Umeki, and Benson Fong. *Flower Drum Song* was set to be a groundbreaking achievement and the first film in Hollywood history with a majority Asian cast telling an Asian American story.

Filming was slated for mid-February 1961, at the beginning of Chinese New Year. In January, Anna May celebrated her fifty-sixth birthday. The Van Vechtens sent her and Richard their annual Christmas card a few weeks before, but she had yet to respond. On January 4, 1961, she wrote to Fania and Carlo: "I was sorry that I did not get my card off to you this year but was laid low just before Christmas with some kind of a virus which kept me busy travelling to the bathroom and to bed. However, I am happy to report that is a thing of the past and I am again feeling very fit."

Presciently, she added, "It is such a wonderful feeling to feel good again and you are one of the first people I want to write and at least I will be on time to greet you a happy Chinese New Years which is in February, the 15th to be exact. So Gung Hay Faht Choy to you both."

On Friday, February 3, 1961, less than two weeks before rehearsals were to start for *Flower Drum Song*, Anna May lay down for a nap in the afternoon and never woke up. She died in her sleep of a heart attack.

Only a year prior, she'd told a journalist, "When I die, my epitaph should be: I died a thousand deaths." She said this in jest, yet it was also true. "That was the story of my film career. Most of the time I played in mystery and intrigue stories. They didn't know what to do with me at the end," she reasoned, "so they killed me off."

Anna May Wong, the woman who had come to the most beastly and absurd endings on the big screen: strangled by irate lovers, buried alive, drowned in the ocean, suicide by poison—not once but twice— and the most fabulous finale of them all, falling on her own cabaret sword as the exotic dancing girl in *Song*. That death had been one of her most beautiful: expiring in the arms of her repentant lover, her lovely face enshrined in a halo of light.

For her final curtain call, she defied expectations yet again. The way to live, she had learned, was knowing what it is to die and to be reborn a thousand times over. When her time came, she did not struggle but passed peacefully, and in the most ordinary way possible, at home in her own bed with her boots still on.

A stunning portrait of Anna May Wong
by master of Hollywood glamour, photographer George Hurrell, 1938.

EPILOGUE

On the evening of March 15, 1961, the principal cast and crew for *Flower Drum Song* gathered on the newly erected set inside Stage 12 on the Universal City backlot. Thirty-seven-year-old producer Ross Hunter, Universal International's latest boy wonder, had grand plans for his first Rodgers and Hammerstein musical. "I want to welcome all of you to San Francisco Chinatown," Hunter said slyly as he launched into his prepared remarks. "You are now spilling your drinks on the largest and most costly sound stage set ever built at Universal studios, perhaps the largest ever built in Hollywood."

Indeed, director Henry Koster, actors James Shigeta and Miyoshi Umeki, and buzzworthy guests like Lana Turner, Mitzi Gaynor, and Roger Moore found themselves standing in an exact replica of St. Mary's Square, only a stone's throw away from a perfect duplicate of Grant Avenue, San Francisco Chinatown's main thoroughfare. No detail was spared. Fifty-four buildings, some as tall as three stories, were installed alongside sidewalks, steep sloping roads, and a trolley car on tracks, covering more than 50,000 square feet inside the cavernous soundstage. Gone were the days when flighty studios filmed in the Chinese quarter's back alleys. Now they built Chinatowns of their very own, and for a pretty penny too. The budget for the Grant Avenue set alone was $310,000—reportedly three times the cost of a standard "A" picture.

Though young and ambitious, Hunter held a special reverence for the old-world glamour of classic Hollywood. He also had a knack for reintroducing stars whose sparkle had faded over the years. In the span of a year, Hunter proved his mettle with two mega hits, *Pillow Talk* starring Doris Day and Rock Hudson and a remake of *Imitation of Life* with Lana Turner. Universal was assured that whatever Hunter wanted to take on next, lavish production budgets and all, it would undoubtedly be profitable.

In keeping with Hollywood traditions, Hunter thought it fitting to kick off his most ambitious movie production yet with a Chinese cocktail party for cast, crew, friends, and press. A spate of auspicious media coverage at the start of a project never hurt. "For your information," the *Film Daily* reporter wrote of the party, "the food was Chinese, but the drinks were strictly Scotch, bourbon, and Bristol Cream."

Two women were distinctly missing from the festivities that night. The first was Nancy Kwan, arguably the star and main attraction of *Flower Drum Song*, whom *McCall's* would later declare "the China doll that men like." She missed the opening cocktail party when her flight from France was delayed. Born in Hong Kong to a Chinese father and an English-Scottish mother, Kwan was the jet-setting "East-West Girl," as one Universal publicity man put it, a different type of exotic, one who was strangely familiar—she had freckles on her nose—still just as enigmatic. By happy accident, Kwan won her breakout role in 1960's *The World of Suzie Wong* playing a prostitute who falls in love with an American man in the seedy Wan Chai neighborhood of Hong Kong. One look at Kwan and Ross Hunter knew he'd found his Linda Low for *Flower Drum Song*.

The other woman missing in action was Anna May Wong. Scarcely six weeks had passed since her untimely death, but the memory of her seemed to have vanished along with her flesh and bones. Hunter did not mention the late actress in his remarks that evening, likely out of a desire to set an upbeat tone for the first day of production—though it's entirely possible, even probable, that her name was murmured among the guests. As much as Hunter had championed Anna May's return to the big screen and hand-selected her for the role of Madame Liang, now that she was gone, there was little he could do but keep the production moving. Twelve days after her passing, Universal publicists drafted a press release with the headline: "Juanita Hall Set for 'Flower Drum Song.'"

Actress Juanita Hall identified as Black, but because of her mixed ancestry, which included Scotch-Irish, Native American, and African lineage, she regularly took on unusual roles. Hall was a quick and necessary substitute. She originated the role of Madame Liang in the Broadway show and had performed the musical, including the popular number "Chop Suey," countless times. She had all the requisite skills, except that she was not Asian. From its inception, *Flower Drum Song* was touted as the first Hollywood film to feature an all-Asian cast. In the end, however, Universal's production fell short by one.

Sometime in the mid-1930s, the German psychotherapist and palmist Charlotte Wolff sat down with Anna May Wong while she was in London and read the lines on her hand, which she likened fancifully to Chinese calligraphy. Despite this rather clichéd observation, Wolff's assessment of Anna May was quite astute:

Imagination and instinct are the central forces in this personality. The low-lying Moon Mount is a sign of the suggestive influence which Anna May Wong has upon others, while the unusually well-shaped Finger of Mercury reveals special talent for acting.

The chief ethical motive in Anna May Wong's character is the idea of freedom and liberation, which she has followed from her youth onwards. (Note the large space between the fingers.) The Head-line, which forks below the Finger of Saturn, denotes a very early developed intellectual life which, combined with particular susceptibility to erotic influences, results in an overstrain of the nerves in youth.

The Luck-line is deeper and more uniform than the Line of
Destiny. Thus the course of Anna May Wong's life is determined
less by work and free will than by interplay of the constellations
which men call Chance.

No one could deny that Anna May held a "suggestive influence"
over others. She had "It," that undefinable, magical quality that made
people stop and stare and later think, *That girl is not like the rest of us.*
This much was clear from the time she stepped onto a crowded set
amidst hundreds of extras at the age of fourteen. She'd used that allure
to build a career and travel the world, dazzling artists and intellectuals, millionaire socialites and heads of state alike. And she had a ball
while she was at it too. Despite the hard knocks and racial barriers she
suffered, life as Anna May Wong was grand.

Indeed, there was a time when she could have had any man
wrapped around her delicately manicured fingers. But neither money
nor possession of a man was a motivating factor for her. No, she lived
for her art and devoted herself wholly to bringing the imaginary into
being. In order to practice her craft as that rare twentieth-century
species—the modern Chinese American woman—she had to claim
and protect her freedom, her independence.

"The only way to deal with an unfree world," Albert Camus
wrote in his novel *The Stranger*, "is to become so absolutely free that
your very existence is an act of rebellion." Anna May Wong, it seems,
embodied that ethos fully and wore it like a badge of honor. Her presence in Hollywood, no matter how many times they tried to push her
out or shut her down, was itself an act of resistance.

Some people say she never got her comeback, but they forget just
how many times the woman reinvented herself, moving from the silent flickers into talkies, from dancing girls in exotic melodramas to
earnest sleuths in crime thrillers, from live theater on Broadway to
broadcast television, all with apparent ease. She worked every decade
of her career, right up to the moment of her death. With more than

seventy credits to her name across film, television, and theater, what Anna May accomplished in any ten-year span of her career was more than many can boast of in a single lifetime.

Renowned photographers and artists like Man Ray, Edward Steichen, Madame d'Ora, Willy Pogany, and Cecil Beaton, just to name a few, immortalized her beauty in ink, paint, and silver gelatin. At one time or another, she was "the world's best-dressed woman" and "the world's most beautiful Chinese girl." Incredibly, she was the first internationally renowned Chinese American screen actress, the first born-and-bred Asian American movie star, the first Asian American to lead a television series, and the first woman of color to become a movie star within the Hollywood system.

In spite of these advances, Anna May was still a product of her time. Like many of her generation, she lived hard and died young. She dared to shine brilliantly and as physics teaches us, the flame that burns twice as bright burns half as long. In correspondence to Fania Marinoff from 1953, Anna May remarked on fellow actress Tallulah Bankhead's autobiography. "Her parting final lines I thought were very beautiful," she mused. The words were not actually Bankhead's but from poet Edna St. Vincent Millay, which Anna May included at the bottom of her letter:

> My candle burns at both ends;
> It will not last the night;
> But ah, my foes, and oh, my friends—
> It gives a lovely light.

I like to think this was Anna May's way of acknowledging the central truth of her own life. She flashed onto the scene in a blaze, then gradually sparked out. She was a Jazz Age baby, after all, when young Hollywood believed it their birthright to drink, smoke, and burn through cash as if tomorrow might never come. She was part of a pioneering class of picture stars who learned the fickle, fleeting nature of celebrity the hard way. Hollywood had a dark side—addiction, bankruptcy, rape, suicide—that nobody but the gossip rags liked to talk about.

In the decades following World War II, the peers Anna May had come of age with were either thoroughly forgotten or dead in the ground. Douglas Fairbanks, supposedly the picture of health, died of a heart attack at age fifty-six. Mary Pickford shrunk into retirement, cloistered away in her rooms at Pickfair. D. W. Griffith was all washed up, living in the shadow of his former glory at the Knickerbocker Hotel. Marshall Neilan's party days ended with a whimper, not a bang, and his alcoholism burned down every bridge back to Hollywood. Ramon Novarro was out of work and living off his savings in his Laurel Canyon home, where he occasionally entertained male prostitutes. Gilda Gray's shimmy days were long gone; so, too, was her fortune, gobbled up in the stock market crash of 1929. Jameson Thomas was dead at fifty of tuberculosis. Marlene Dietrich and Josef von Sternberg called it quits on their legendary collaboration, both on the screen and between the sheets. Warner Oland drank himself to death but Charlie Chan lived on. Luise Rainer swore off Hollywood and never went back, though she put her Oscar from *The Good Earth* to good use as a doorstop.

Anna May faced more challenges than most. Racism undoubtedly hindered her career, leading many to conclude that she was a woman before her time. But what if they're wrong? What if we have it backward? What if Anna May Wong was right where she was supposed to be all along?

Her popularity with the public was undeniable; many moviegoers wrote in to magazines to complain that their favorite actress had been baselessly sidelined for yet another white performer in yellowface. Five hundred fan letters a week don't lie. The critics felt much the same about Anna May and bemoaned the second-rate productions she was relegated to, as did many directors who recognized her talent but had little clout to change the mindset of studio executives. Truth be told,

EPILOGUE   381

Jesse Lasky, Irving Thalberg, or any one of those bigwig Hollywood
producers could have made Anna May an A-list sensation at the drop
of a hat. It was studio heads like them and their assumptions about
what America wanted that were out of touch, decades behind the mul-
ticulturalism sprouting up around the country.

Back then, Anna May Wong was the first and only. Today, thanks
to her struggle, she is the first of many. "She paved the way for those
who came after and continues to inspire," Gemma Chan, part of a
new generation of Asian American actors, has said. It has taken a
good hundred years, but things are beginning to shift. The success of
films like 2018's *Crazy Rich Asians*, 2019's *The Farewell*, 2020's *Minari*,
2021's *Shang-Chi and the Legend of the Ten Rings*, and 2022's *Everything
Everywhere All at Once*—all productions written, directed, and starring Asian American talent—has forced many in Hollywood to re-
think their production slates, in front of the camera and behind the
scenes. But we're not there yet.

Anna May's defeats, more than her triumphs, are lessons in what
must change in Hollywood if we want and expect filmmakers to represent the full spectrum of human experience. According to sociologist
Nancy Wang Yuen, as recently as 2015, more than half of all film,
television, or streaming stories in the United States failed to include at
least one Asian or Asian American actor in a speaking or named role.
What's more, the same biases that plagued Anna May—mainly, the
idea that Asian actors are not charismatic enough to carry a leading
role—are still at play in Hollywood in the twenty-first century. From
2007 to 2019, only 3.4 percent of top-grossing movies featured an Asian
American or Pacific Islander actor in a lead role. Of the forty-four
films led by Asian American Pacific Islander (AAPI) actors, a third
starred the same person: Dwayne "The Rock" Johnson. Similarly,
AAPI actors are cast as characters with some of the least complexity
and the lowest screen times on prime-time television.

The practice of yellowface has continued into the new millennium,
albeit in a more subtle form. White actors like Scarlett Johansson,

Emma Stone, and Tilda Swinton no longer have to powder their faces yellow or slant their eyes. Instead, characters that were originally scripted as Asian or Asian American are "whitewashed" so that white actors can impersonate them without repercussions. This practice denies actual Asian American actors the opportunity to take on roles specifically written for them.

Of course, Asian Americans are not the only ones to speak up about this type of whitewashing at the box office. In 2015, after the Academy gave all twenty acting nominations to white actors for a second year in a row, activists and industry insiders took to Twitter to voice their discontent with the hashtag #OscarsSoWhite. "It was a catalyst for a conversation about what had really been a decades-long absence of diversity and inclusion," director Ava DuVernay recalled. The hashtag has since become a common refrain during every award season, and the conversation about how Hollywood should change in order to accurately reflect the makeup of this country is still ongoing.

When Michelle Yeoh, a seasoned actress with many credits to her name, read the script for *Everything Everywhere All at Once*, she stopped and said to herself, *This is something*. Yeoh was in her late fifties; she had played everything from a sultry Bond girl opposite Pierce Brosnan to a kung fu warrior in *Crouching Tiger, Hidden Dragon*. After nearly four decades in the industry, she was finally setting eyes on a script that called on her to demonstrate her full range as an actress.

"This is something I've been waiting for, for a long time," she recounted tearfully, "that's going to give me the opportunity to show my fans, my family, my audience what I'm capable of. To be funny, to be real, to be sad. Finally, somebody understood that I can do all these things." Yeoh's words recall something Anna May Wong once said herself: "Some day some one will write a story *demanding* a real Chinese girl—then perhaps I'll have my chance." Of course, Anna May never got that chance, but Yeoh thankfully did. At the ninety-fifth Academy Awards in 2023, Yeoh became the first Asian woman to win an Oscar for best actress.

Anna May's final act was to hand on the torch to a new generation of Asian American hopefuls who would carry on the work she'd begun a half century earlier in Universal's groundbreaking production of *Flower Drum Song*. She passed to the other side before she could realize that dream, but her intention remains. "Anna May Wong lives on, in the minds of film scholars and fans," Margaret Cho has suggested. Her legacy and spirit live on, too, in actors like Cho, Michelle Yeoh, Lucy Liu, BD Wong, Sandra Oh, Awkwafina, Mindy Kaling, Steven Yeun, Kal Penn, Gemma Chan, John Cho, Constance Wu, Simu Liu, Ke Huy Quan, Ali Wong, Ming-Na Wen, Tzi Ma, James Hong, and so many more.

In 1923, an eighteen-year-old Anna May Wong was just at the beginning of her storied career, working long days on the Pickford-Fairbanks lot to prove her mettle and make a name for herself in Hollywood's biggest spectacle yet. A century later, her legacy looms larger than ever. As part of the U.S. Mint's American Women Quarters Program, in 2022 Anna May Wong became the first Asian American to have her image stamped on U.S. quarters. In fact, I can't think of another Hollywood star who has been enshrined on something as ubiquitous and consequential as American currency. The very same coins she once used to buy tickets at the movie theater now feature her indelible face, blunt-cut bangs and all.

Her story continues to resurface in popular culture in ways big and small. As of this writing, Anna May Wong has been the subject of numerous books, plays, and documentaries; her films have been revived in screenings at Paramount, the Academy Museum, UCLA, and the Museum of the Moving Image, and via streaming on the Criterion Channel and Turner Classic Movies; she has graced the Google home page in a Google Doodle and been featured as a clue on *Jeopardy!*; actresses Michelle Krusiec and Li Jun Li have brought her back to life on-screen in Netflix's *Hollywood* and Damien Chazelle's *Babylon*, respectively; and she has even inspired Mattel to create a Barbie doll in her image so that girls around the world will have a new role model to look up to.

As Mo Rocca, who devoted an entire episode of his podcast *Mobituaries* to her, has said: "Anna May Wong never won an Oscar, but someone may one day win an Oscar playing her. It's that kind of story." This prediction could very well come true in a few short years. Development has already begun on an Anna May Wong biopic with Gemma Chan signed on to play the lead, Nina Yang Bongiovi to produce, and Tony Award–winning playwright David Henry Hwang to write the screenplay for Working Title Films.

Anna May Wong has proven her staying power and then some. If she were alive today, I imagine she would smile, and perhaps shed a few tears of joy, at the realization that her hard-won achievements haven't been for naught. Truly, she has meant so much to so many. In death, her significance has risen decisively to the standing she sorely deserved. "We sometimes even surprise ourselves at what we can do," she once wrote in a letter to Carl Van Vechten. The phrase has been echoing in my mind ever since.

Anna May Wong, you bring honor to us all.

ACKNOWLEDGMENTS

They say that writing a book is a solitary pursuit. For much of my journey that maxim has held true. But it would be far from the truth to say I wrote this book all on my own when in fact so many people have helped shape it along the way.

I am forever grateful to my agent, Alia Hanna Habib, for understanding what this project was about from the very beginning and for pushing me to devote it to Anna May Wong and nobody else. I am equally indebted to Julia Cheiffetz, who taught me everything I know about what a book is and can be; thank you for championing my work every step of the way. Thanks also to Sophie Pugh-Sellers for cheering me on throughout this multiyear process: your enthusiasm always puts wind in my sails.

Thank you to Christina Kelly and John Parsley for believing in this book and giving it a home at Dutton. In addition, Amber Oliver and Grace Layer were excellent stewards. Jamie Knapp, Caroline Payne, Diamond Bridges, Allison Prince, LeeAnn Pemberton, Ryan Richardson, Susan Schwartz, Gaelyn Galbreath, David Chesanow, and Kristin del Rosario deftly managed the book's journey from production to publication. Hats off to Vi-An Nguyen for designing a cover more beautiful than my wildest dreams. And to Emi Ikkanda, who by a twist of fate, became my editor after having seen my proposal years before: what a joy it has been getting to work together. Thank you for your smart, thoughtful edits, for your passion for Anna May's story, and for steering me away from my long-winded tendencies!

To Anna Wong: Who would've thunk we'd just happen to meet at a photo exhibition in the same Chinatown streets our ancestors used to haunt?

Thank you for your generosity of spirit and for the stories you have shared with me about your aunt and the Wong clan. But most of all, I am thankful for your friendship. Here's to many more years of celebrating Anna May Wong's legacy together.

I am indebted to the biographers and scholars who came before me, especially Graham Russell Gao Hodges, Anthony B. Chan, Karen Leong, Shirley Jennifer Lim, Yiman Wang, Philip Leibfried, Chei Mi Lane, and Cynthia Walk. Thank you for laying the foundation for serious study of Anna May Wong's life. This book would not have been possible without your scholarship.

Thanks are also due to the many archives and institutions that aided me in researching Anna May Wong's life and career, including Yale Beinecke Library, the Fonoroff Collection at UC Berkeley, UCLA Film and Television Archive, the Rudolph Schindler Collection at UC Santa Barbara, the Cinematic Arts Library and East Asian Library at USC, Bobst Library at NYU, the New York Public Library, the Brooklyn Public Library, the British Library, the Museum of Chinese in America, the Chinese Historical Society of Southern California, the Hoover Institution Library & Archives at Stanford, and the Knole Estate. Special thanks to Rachelle Shumard, Michael Truong, and Gay Yuen at the Chinese American Museum of Los Angeles for your continued support. Thanks also to Louise Hilton, Benjamin Friday, Mona Huntzing, Andrea Livingston, Cole McCabe, Bijan S., Genevieve Maxwell, and the entire staff at Margaret Herrick Library for your consummate professionalism. You made me feel like one of the team during my four-week "residency" in special collections. And to Stephen Tollervey at the British Film Institute: thank you for teaching me how to spool 35mm reels like a pro and for our basement film chats. It was such a delight getting to watch Anna May's European films with a warm cup of tea and biscuits.

To Conrad Doerr, Jenna Rosher, Richard See, Maria Riva, and Nicholas von Sternberg, my deepest gratitude to you for sharing your memories with me and enriching my understanding of Anna May. To Lisa See and Paul Riva: thank you for facilitating these conversations with your parents.

Over the course of this journey, I ran into fellow travelers—writers and researchers who happily shared their own discoveries with me. Thank you to Susan Blumberg-Kason for introducing me to the storied world of Bernardine Szold Fritz and for connecting me with Bernardine's cousins, David Szanton and Nancy Lilienthal, who generously shared Bernardine's photos of Anna May. To William Gow for your meticulously researched dissertation on the Chinatown-Hollywood connection, which unearthed stories from the making of *The Good Earth* that I would have missed on my own. To Alexandra Chiriac for handing me the missing puzzle piece that solved the mystery of when and where Anna May took that infamous picture with Marlene Dietrich and Leni Riefenstahl. To Aimee Liu for enthralling me with tales of your father's and aunt's Hollywood careers.

My appreciation extends to Ventris Gibson, director of the U.S. Mint, who gamely sat for an interview about Anna May Wong's debut on the quarter: thank you for breathing new life into her legacy. Thanks also to Jennifer DeBroekert, Todd Martin, Brent Thacker, and the rest of the team at the U.S. Mint at Denver for making my visit there a dream come true.

To Mark Alesky: thank you for your artist's esprit de corps and for taking me to my first sound clash and making my stay in Brixton a truly memorable one. To Dr. Rossel: thank you for keeping me accountable during my monthly adjustments. Even when I wasn't reporting progress to my editor, I knew my chiropractor would set me straight. To all my English teachers throughout the years who taught me a reverence for the written word, but especially to Paul Childs: thank you for lighting a fire in me, "Oh Captain! My Captain!"

I am grateful to those who assisted me with some of the less glamorous aspects of archival research, including Mel Guo for clipping all those damn *Los Angeles Times* articles; my cousin Laura Sander for your brilliant help finding and translating German press articles; Xiaoxiao Du for transcribing and translating a copious number of Chinese movie magazines; Dr. Thuy-Van (Tina) Hang for your expert insights into Anna May's medical condition in her later years; Yan Chang for scouring Kamiyama Sôjin's memoir for any relevant tidbits. And to Teena Apeles for fact-checking this book to the moon. Because of your work, I can rest easy.

I am equally appreciative of the many Anna May Wong devotees who sent me tips or pooled their resources, including Victor B. D'Agostino, Eric

Rothe, Angela Wandesforde, Tom Shane, and the Goddess Anna May Wong Facebook page. A special thanks to Rebecca Grace Lee, who runs the Gallery of Anna May Wong on YouTube and the Anna May Wong Fans account on Instagram, for your constant sleuthing and for opening up your personal archive to me. Your work helps ensure that Anna May's films will be accessible to future audiences.

A small group of friends and family were kind enough to read early versions of this book. Their astute feedback most certainly made it better and gave me the confidence to keep going. Thank you to Shaw Yean Lim, Jane Salisbury, Chau Haber, Beverly Sameshima, Rebecca Grace Lee, Sandra Bark, Charlene Wang de Chen, and Kamala Nair.

Thank you to all the subscribers over at *Half-Caste Woman* for coming along on this journey with me and waiting patiently for the book to be finished. Thank you also to Ed Park, who listened to me wax poetic about Anna May Wong many years ago in our shared office at Amazon Publishing and never failed to respond to one of my newsletters with an interesting comment. And to my book club friends, who encouraged me through the ups and downs.

Of course, it almost goes without saying, I wouldn't be here if it weren't for the family and friends who have long supported me throughout this endeavor. Thank you to my parents, Lee and Emilie Salisbury, for housing and feeding me on my many research trips to Los Angeles—and for everything else too. To my brothers, Jack Salisbury and Scott Chase, for always cheering me on. And to my father-in-law, Steven Ciani, for your words of encouragement, penned with a writer's flair. To my friends, who are too numerous to name: thank you for everything. And guess what—my calendar is finally open so we can hang out again!

Last but never least, to Nicholas Ciani, my partner in all things, who was there for the late nights, unexpected roadblocks, and artistic meltdowns. Your love makes everything possible.

SELECTED BIBLIOGRAPHY

ARCHIVAL COLLECTIONS

Margaret Herrick Library, Academy of Motion Picture Arts and Sciences
Chinese Exclusion Act case files, National Archives and Records Administration, Riverside
Federal Bureau of Investigation
Los Angeles County Registrar-Recorder/County Clerk
Anna May Wong clippings file, New York Public Library
Anna May Wong collection of theatre programs, 1920s–1930s, New York Public Library
Carl Van Vechten papers, 1833–1965, Archives and Manuscripts, New York Public Library
Paul Kendel Fonoroff Collection for Chinese Film Studies, UC Berkeley
UCLA Film and Television Archive
Rudolph Schindler Collection, Art, Design & Architecture Museum, UC Santa Barbara
East Asian Library, University of Southern California
Cinematic Arts Library, University of Southern California
Museum of Chinese in America collections
Chinese American Museum of Los Angeles
Chinese Historical Society of Southern California
Carl Van Vechten Papers, Beinecke Library, Yale University
Bernardine Szold-Fritz correspondence, Beinecke Library, Yale University
Cedric Belfrage Papers, Bobst Library, New York University
Knole Estate records, UK National Trust
National Portrait Gallery, UK
British Film Institute
Frank Dorn Papers, Hoover Institution Library & Archives, Stanford University

PUBLICATIONS

Allmendinger, Blake. "Little House on the Rice Paddy." *American Literary History* 10, no. 2 (Summer 1998).
Baker, Josephine, and Jo Bouillon. *Josephine*. Translated by Mariana Fitzpatrick. New York: Marlowe & Company, 1988.

Bawden, James, and Ron Miller. *Conversations with Classic Film Stars: Interviews from Hollywood's Golden Era*. Lexington: University Press of Kentucky, 2016.

Baxter, John. "Berlin Year Zero: The Making of *The Blue Angel*." *Framework* 51, no. 1 (Spring 2010).

———. *Von Sternberg*. Lexington: University Press of Kentucky, 2010.

Beauchamp, Cari, ed. *My First Time in Hollywood*. Los Angeles: Asahina & Wallace, 2015.

Benjamin, Walter. "Gespräch mit Anne May Wong: Eine Chinoiserie aus dem Alten Westen." *Die Literariscme*, July 6, 1928.

Bennett, Arnold. *Piccadilly: Story of the Film*. Plainview, NY: Books for Libraries Press, 1975.

Bernstein, David E. "Lochner, Parity, and the Chinese Laundry Cases." *William & Mary Law Review* 41, no. 1 (December 1999).

Blumberg-Kason, Susan. *Bernardine's Shanghai Salon: The Story of the Doyenne of Old China*. Brentwood, TN: Post Hill Press, 2023.

Bogle, Donald. *Toms, Coons, Mulattoes, Mammies, and Bucks: An Interpretive History of Blacks in American Films*, New Third Edition. New York: Continuum, 1994.

Bowyer, Francesca Knittel. *Seen from the Wings: Luise Rainer, My Mother, the Journey*. Self-published, 2019.

Brownlow, Kevin. "Sidney Franklin and *The Good Earth*." *Historical Journal of Film, Radio, and Television* 9, no. 1 (1989).

Buck, Pearl S. *My Several Worlds: A Personal Record*. New York: John Day, 1957.

Carey, Gary. *Doug & Mary: A Biography of Douglas Fairbanks & Mary Pickford*. New York: Dutton, 1977.

Chan, Anthony B. *Perpetually Cool: The Many Lives of Anna May Wong (1905–1961)*. Lanham, MD: Scarecrow Press, 2007.

Chang, Gordon H. *Ghosts of Gold Mountain: The Epic Story of the Chinese Who Built the Transcontinental Railroad*. Boston: Houghton Mifflin Harcourt, 2019.

Chang, Iris. *The Chinese in America: A Narrative History*. New York: Penguin, 2003.

Chung, Hye Seung. *Hollywood Asian: Philip Ahn and the Politics of Cross-Ethnic Performance*. Philadelphia: Temple University Press, 2006.

Conn, Peter. *Pearl S. Buck: A Cultural Biography*. Cambridge, UK: Cambridge University Press, 1996.

Curtis, James. *William Cameron Menzies: The Shape of Films to Come*. New York: Pantheon, 2015.

de Silva, Annesley. *These Piquant People: Being a Collection of Conversations*. London: Cecil Palmer, 1932.

de Wolk, Roland. *American Disruptor: The Scandalous Life of Leland Stanford*. Oakland: University of California Press, 2019.

Dietrich, Marlene. *Marlene Dietrich: My Life*. Translated by Salvator Attanasio. London: Wieden & Nicolson, 1989.

Doherty, Thomas. *Hollywood's Censor: Joseph I. Breen and the Production Code Administration*. New York: Columbia University Press, 2007.

———. *Pre-Code Hollywood: Sex, Immorality, and Insurrection in American Cinema*. New York: Columbia University Press, 1999.

Dong, Arthur. *Hollywood Chinese: The Chinese in American Feature Films*. Los Angeles: Angel City Press, 2019.

Douglas Fairbanks Museum. *Douglas Fairbanks: In His Own Words*. Foreword by Keri Leigh. Lincoln, NE: iUniverse, 2006.

Du, Wenwei. "*The Chalk Circle* Comes Full Circle: From Yuan Drama through the Western Stage to Peking Opera." *Asian Theatre Journal* 12, no. 2 (Fall 1995).

Duberman, Martin Bauml. *Paul Robeson*. New York: Alfred A. Knopf, 1988.

Eisenstaedt, Alfred. *Eisenstaedt on Eisenstaedt: A Self-Portrait*. New York: Abbeville, 1985.

———. *People*. New York: Viking, 1973.

Fahlstedt, Kim Khavar. "Charlie Chan's Last Mystery, or the Transcultural Disappearance of Warner Oland." In *Nordic Film Cultures and Cinemas of Elsewhere*, edited by Anna Westerstahl Stenport and Arne Lunde. Edinburgh: Edinburgh University Press, 2022.

Fitzgerald, F. Scott. *This Side of Paradise*. New York: Scribner, 1920.

Gingold, Hermione. *How to Grow Old Disgracefully*. New York: St. Martin's, 1988.

Goessel, Tracey. *The First King of Hollywood: The Life of Douglas Fairbanks*. Chicago: Chicago Review Press, 2016.

Gow, William. "Performing Chinatown: Hollywood Cinema, Tourism, and the Making of a Los Angeles Community, 1882–1943." PhD dissertation, University of California, Berkeley, 2018.

Hanke, Ken. *Charlie Chan at the Movies: History, Filmography, and Criticism*. Jefferson, NC: McFarland, 1989.

Hardt, Ursula. *From Caligari to California: Erich Pommer's Life in the International Film Wars*. Providence, RI: Berghahn Books, 1996.

Hessel, Franz. *Walking in Berlin: A Flaneur in the Capital*. Cambridge, MA: MIT Press, 2017.

Higham, Charles. *Marlene: The Life of Marlene Dietrich*. New York: W. W. Norton, 1977.

———. *Merchant of Dreams: Louis B. Mayer, M.G.M., and the Secret Hollywood*. New York: Donald I. Fine, 1993.

Higson, Andrew, and Richard Maltby. "'Film Europe' and 'Film America': An Introduction." In *"Film Europe" and "Film America": Cinema, Commerce and Cultural Exchange, 1920–1939*, edited by Higson and Maltby. Exeter, UK: University of Exeter Press, 1999.

Hoban, James L., Jr. "Scripting *The Good Earth*: Versions of the Novel for the Screen." In *The Several Worlds of Pearl S. Buck*, edited by Elizbeth J. Lipscomb, Frances E. Webb, and Peter Conn. Westport, CT: Greenwood, 1994.

Hodges, Graham Russell Gao. *Anna May Wong: From Laundryman's Daughter to Hollywood Legend*. Hong Kong: Hong Kong University Press, 2012.

Hsu, Hua. *A Floating Chinaman: Fantasy and Failure Across the Pacific*. Cambridge, MA: Harvard University Press, 2016.

Huang, Yunte. *Charlie Chan: The Untold Story of the Honorable Detective and His Rendezvous with American History*. New York: W. W. Norton, 2010.

———. *Daughter of the Dragon: Anna May Wong's Rendezvous with American History*. New York: Liveright, 2023.

Jung, John. *Chinese Laundries: Tickets to Survival on Gold Mountain*. N.p.: Yin and Yang Press, 2010.

Kellner, Bruce. *Carl Van Vechten and the Irreverent Decades*. Norman: Oklahoma University Press, 1969.

Kinder, Larry Sean. *Una Merkel: The Actress with Sassy Wit and Southern Charm*. Albany, GA: BearManor Media, 2016.

Koo, Hui-Lan, as told to Mary Van Rensselaer. *Hui-Lan Koo (Madame Wellington Koo): An Autobiography*. New York: Dial Press, 1943.

Krist, Gary. *The Mirage Factory: Illusion, Imagination, and the Invention of Los Angeles*. New York: Broadway Books, 2018.

Kotsilibas-Davis, James, and Myrna Loy. *Myrna Loy: Being and Becoming*. New York: Alfred A. Knopf, 1987.

Lasky, Jesse L., with Don Weldon. *I Blow My Own Horn*. Garden City, NY: Doubleday, 1957.

Lawrence, Jerome. *Actor: The Life and Times of Paul Muni*. New York: G. P. Putnam's Sons, 1974.

Leibfried, Philip, and Chei Mi Lane. *Anna May Wong: A Complete Guide to Her Film, Stage, Radio and Television Work*. Jefferson, NC: McFarland & Company, 2008.

Leong, Charles L. "Mandarins in Hollywood." *Gum Saan Journal*, 2021, https://gumsaanjournal.com/special-edition-2021-the-eagle-and-the-dragon/mandarins-in-hollywood/.

Leong, Karen. *The China Mystique: Pearl S. Buck, Anna May Wong, Mayling Soong, and the Transformation of American Orientalism*. Berkeley: University of California Press, 2005.

Lim, Shirley Jennifer. *Anna May Wong: Performing the Modern*. Philadelphia: Temple University Press, 2019.

Lloyd, Stephen. *Constant Lambert: Beyond the Rio Grande*. Woodbridge, UK: Boydell Press, 2014.

Maschwitz, Eric. *No Chip on My Shoulder*. London: Herbert Jenkins, 1957.

Miyao, Daisuke. *Sessue Hayakawa: Silent Cinema and Transnational Stardom*. Durham, NC: Duke University Press, 2007.

Petro, Patrice. "Cosmopolitan Women: Marlene Dietrich, Anna May Wong, and Leni Riefenstahl." In *Silent Cinema and the Politics of Space*, edited by Jennifer M. Bean, Anupama Kapse, and Laura Horak. Bloomington: Indiana University Press, 2014.

Pickford, Mary. *Sunshine and Shadow*. Introduction by Cecil B. de Mille. New York: Doubleday, 1955.

Price, Victoria. *Vincent Price: A Daughter's Biography*. New York: St. Martin's, 1999.

Rainsberger, Todd. *James Wong Howe: Cinematographer*. New York: A. S. Barnes, 1981.

Richie, Alexandra. *Faust's Metropolis: A History of Berlin*. New York: Carroll & Graf, 1998.

Riva, Maria. *Marlene Dietrich: The Life*. New York: Pegasus Books, 1992.

See, Lisa. *On Gold Mountain: The One-Hundred-Year Odyssey of My Chinese-American Family*. New York: Vintage Books, 1996.

Silver, Alain. *James Wong Howe: The Camera Eye*. Santa Monica, CA: Pendragon Books, 2010.

Skal, David J., and Elias Savada. *Dark Carnival: The Secret World of Tod Browning, Hollywood's Master of the Macabre*. New York: Anchor Books, 1995.

Slide, Anthony. *A Special Relationship: Britain Comes to Hollywood and Hollywood Comes to Britain*. Jackson: University Press of Mississippi, 2015.

Spears, Jack. *Hollywood: The Golden Era*. New York: Castle Books, 1971.

Spoto, Donald. *Blue Angel: The Life of Marlene Dietrich*. New York: Doubleday, 1992.

Spurling, Hilary. *Pearl Buck in China: Journey to The Good Earth*. New York: Simon & Schuster, 2010.

St. Pierre, Paul Matthew. *E. A. Dupont and His Contribution to British Film: Varieté, Moulin Rouge, Piccadilly, Atlantic, Two Worlds, Cape Forlorn*. Madison, NJ: Fairleigh Dickinson University Press, 2010.

Swanson, Gloria. *Swanson on Swanson*. New York: Random House, 1980.

Sweet, Sam. *All Night Menu*. Vol. 4, July 2021 https://www.allnight-menu.com/home.

Tapert, Stephen. *Best Actress: The History of Oscar-Winning Women*. Newark, NJ: Rutgers University Press, 2020.

Thomas, Bob. *Thalberg: Life and Legend*. Garden City, NJ: Doubleday, 1969.

Van Vechten, Carl. *Parties: Scenes from Contemporary New York Life*. New York: Avon Books, 1977.

————. *The Splendid Drunken Twenties: Selections from the Daybooks, 1922–1930*. Edited by Bruce Kellner. Chicago: University of Illinois Press, 2003.

Vance, Jeffrey. *Douglas Fairbanks*. Berkeley: University of California Press, 2008.

Vieira, Mark A. *Irving Thalberg: Boy Wonder to Producer Prince*. Berkeley: University of California Press, 2010.

Von Sternberg, Josef. *Fun in a Chinese Laundry*. New York: Macmillan, 1965.

Wallace, Edgar. *On the Spot*. Garden City, NY: Doubleday, Doran, 1930.

Walk, Cynthia. "Anna May Wong and Weimar Cinema: Orientalism in Postcolonial Germany." In *Beyond Alterity: German Encounters with Modern East Asia*, edited by Qinna Shen and Martin Rosenstock. New York: Berghahn Books, 2014.

Walsh, Raoul. *Each Man in His Time: The Life Story of a Director*. New York: Farrar, Straus and Giroux, 1974.

Wang, Joan S. "Race, Gender, and Laundry Work: The Roles of Chinese Laundrymen and American Women in the United States, 1850–1950." *Journal of American Ethnic History* 24, no. 1 (Fall 2004).

Waugh, Evelyn. *The Diaries of Evelyn Waugh*, edited by Michael Davie. London: Wiedenfeld and Nicolson, 1976.

Wieland, Karin. *Dietrich & Riefenstahl: Hollywood, Berlin, and a Century in Two Lives*. Translated by Shelley Frisch. New York: Liveright, 2011.

Welsh, Tricia. *Gloria Swanson: Ready for Her Close-Up*. Jackson: University of Mississippi, 2013.

Wolff, Dr. Charlotte. *Studies in Hand-Reading*. London: Chatto & Windus, 1936.

Wollstein, Hans J. *Vixens, Floozies and Molls: 28 Actresses of Late 1920s and 1930s Hollywood*. Jefferson, NC: McFarland, 1999.

Young, Betty Lou. *Rustic Canyon and the Story of the Uplifters*. Santa Monica, CA: Casa Vieja Press, 1975.

Yuen, Nancy Wang. *Reel Inequality: Hollywood Actors and Racism*. New Brunswick, NJ: Rutgers University Press, 2017.

NOTES

LIST OF ABBREVIATIONS

LAT = *Los Angeles Times*
NYT = *New York Times*
NYHT = *New York Herald Tribune*
NYPL = *New York Public Library*
AMPAS = Margaret Herrick Library, Academy of Motion Picture Arts and Sciences
MPAA/PCA Records = Motion Picture Association, Production Code Administration
North-China Herald = *North-China Herald and Supreme Court & Consular Gazette*
SCMP = *South China Morning Post*
Movietone = 电声 (diansheng)
Screen Pictorial = 电影画报 (dianying huabao)
Film Age = 时代电影 (shidai dianying)
Young Companion = 良友 (liangyou)

PREFACE

xi **first Asian American movie star:** Some also bestow this distinction on Sessue Hayakawa, which I don't dispute. However, Hayakawa was born and died in Japan, and
it's unclear whether he ever considered himself Asian American. Anna May Wong
is the first American-born Asian film star and she identified as both Chinese and
American.

PROLOGUE

1 **sights they'd only read about:** Atchison, Topeka, and Santa Fe Railroad Company,
"Route of the California Limited," Rand McNally, 1903, in David Rumsey Historical
Map Collection, accessed Feb. 7, 2023, https://www.davidrumsey.com/luna/servlet
/detail/RUMSEY~8~1~24543~900046:Route-of-the-California-Limited-; Mrs. D. W.
Griffith (Linda Arvidson), in *My First Time in Hollywood*, ed. Cari Beauchamp (Los
Angeles: Asahina & Wallace, 2015), 6–8.

1 the klieg light: The Learning Network, "Oct. 21, 1879 | Thomas Edison Lights the Lamp," *NYT*, Oct. 21, 2011; "Klieg-Light Kliegl," The Talk of the Town, *New Yorker*, July 13, 1957, 20–21.

2 Edison concocted: "The Black Maria," *American Experience*, PBS, 2015, https://www.pbs.org/wgbh/americanexperience/features/edison-blackmaria/.

2 You could shoot scenes: Gary Krist, *The Mirage Factory: Illusion, Imagination, and the Invention of Los Angeles* (New York: Broadway Books, 2018), 58–61.

2 scribbled on postcards: Examples of vintage postcards advertising Southern California's orange groves, beaches, and temperate weather are plentiful online. Here is one example: "1921 Los Angeles CA USA Picture Postcard Cover to Auburn NY Orange Groves," accessed Nov. 7, 2022, https://www.hipstamp.com/listing/1921-los-angeles-ca-usa-picture-postcard-cover-to-auburn-ny-orange-groves/35196324.

2 "hardy pioneers": Mary Pickford, *Sunshine and Shadow* (New York: Doubleday, 1955), 77.

2 "It was like heaven": Cari Beauchamp, "Introduction," in *My First Time in Hollywood*, ii.

3 Harvey and Daeida Wilcox: Hadley Meares, "How One Ohio Native Became the 'Mother of Hollywood,'" *Curbed LA*, Feb. 20, 2014, https://la.curbed.com/2014/2/20/10142088/hollywood-history-daeida-wilcox-beveridge.

3 Whether Daeida borrowed the name: Lionel Barrymore, in *My First Time in Hollywood*, 58.

3 Notices advertising vacancies: Frances Marion, in *My First Time in Hollywood*, 20.

4 "Those locusts are swarming": Marion, in *My First Time in Hollywood*, 20.

5 "I would worm my way": Anna May Wong, "The Childhood of a Chinese Screen Star," *Pictures*, Sept. 1926.

5 the Curious Chinese Child: Betty Willis, "Famous Oriental Stars Return to the Screen," *Motion Picture Magazine*, Oct. 1931.

6 a set of tiny dolls: Anna May Wong, "I Am Growing More Chinese Each Passing Year," as told to Harry Carr, *LAT*, Sept. 9, 1934.

6 "I would register contempt": Anna May Wong, "I Am Lucky That I Am Chinese," as told to Alice B. Tildesley, *Honolulu Advertiser*, June 10, 1928.

6 "She must have been amazed": Wong, "I Am Lucky That I Am Chinese."

CHAPTER ONE

11 He'd attended a screening: Tracey Goessel, *The First King of Hollywood: The Life of Douglas Fairbanks* (Chicago: Chicago Review Press, 2016), 310–11.

11 Box office receipts: Goessel, *First King of Hollywood*, 300.

12 charmed the critics: Letters from R. H. Vail and Charles Albin, "Screen Points of View," *NYT*, Nov. 12, 1922.

12 that terrible d-word: Pickford, *Sunshine and Shadow*, 121–23.

12 she surprised him: Goessel, *First King of Hollywood*, 305.

13 "Last night I thought up": Goessel, *First King of Hollywood*, 305.

13 pirate paraphernalia: Goessel, *First King of Hollywood*, 305–6.

13   **a handsomely illustrated book:** *Motion Picture Magazine*, "Doug Hoists the Black Flag," June 1926; James Curtis, *William Cameron Menzies: The Shape of Films to Come* (New York: Pantheon, 2015), 35.

13   **he stayed up the whole night:** Jeffrey Vance, *Douglas Fairbanks* (Berkeley: University of California Press, 2008), 154.

13   **"Let's do an *Arabian Nights* story":** Goessel, *First King of Hollywood*, 305.

13   **"We looked at each other":** A scenario writer, "Evolution of a Picture," *NYT*, March 16, 1924.

14   **A sign that read BAGDAD:** Vance, *Douglas Fairbanks*, 166.

15   **his plans to make the pirate tale:** Goessel, *First King of Hollywood*, 310–11.

15   **a different kind of film:** "By Leaps and Bounds," *LAT*, Dec. 23, 1923.

16   **"I like roles that win sympathy":** Virginia Morris, "Nothing but the Truth," *Picture-Play*, Nov. 1927, 74.

17   **She had propelled her way:** Rob Wagner, "Better a Laundry and Sincerity," *Screenland*, Jan. 1928.

18   **the first Black character:** Donald Bogle, *Toms, Coons, Mulattoes, Mammies, and Bucks: An Interpretive History of Blacks in American Films*, new 3rd ed. (New York: Continuum, 1994), 3.

18   **Thirteen more years would pass:** Bogle, *Toms, Coons, Mulattoes, Mammies, and Bucks*, 6.

18   **relegated to the stereotypes:** Bogle, *Toms, Coons, Mulattoes, Mammies, and Bucks*, 4.

18   **white actors in blackface:** Bogle, *Toms, Coons, Mulattoes, Mammies, and Bucks*, 7.

18   **"a modest little person":** "Troubles of a Bagdad Thief," *NYT*, March 2, 1924.

19   **"the cleverest person in pictures":** Morris, "Nothing but the Truth."

19   **he sensibly hired his brothers:** Goessel, *First King of Hollywood*, 107–8, 193.

19   **"A day on his set":** Harry Carr, "Doug's Bagdad Is a Dazzler," *LAT*, July 15, 1923.

20   **painter Maxfield Parrish:** Vance, *Douglas Fairbanks*, 164.

20   **Menzies strode into the office:** Curtis, *William Cameron Menzies*, 34–35.

20   **"Look at these":** "Tale of Bagdad for Fairbanks," *LAT*, April 18, 1923.

20   **his vision was on its way:** Curtis, *William Cameron Menzies*, 36; Don Ryan, "Fantasy Arrives on the Screen," *Picture-Play*, May 1924.

20   **"A dream city":** Douglas Fairbanks, "Films for the Fifty Million," *Ladies' Home Journal*, April 1924.

21   **ARE YOUR FEET CLEAN?:** Carr, "Doug's Bagdad Is a Dazzler."

21   **re-enameled several times:** Vance, *Douglas Fairbanks*, 166–67.

21   **"If the plans of the artist":** "Tale of Bagdad for Fairbanks," *LAT*.

21   **Julanne Johnston in her dressing room:** Helen Carlisle, "A Chinese Puzzle," *Movie Weekly*, Aug. 30, 1924.

22   **The "worm turned":** Wong, "I Am Growing More Chinese."

22   **"This is the way we Americans walk":** Carr, "Doug's Bagdad Is a Dazzler."

22   **"The drab of historical accuracy":** Edwin Schallert, "Doug Rubs the Magic Lamp," *Picture-Play*, Sept. 1923, 45.

23   **"A dark-faced Mexican":** Raoul Walsh, *Each Man in His Time: The Life Story of a Director* (New York: Farrar, Straus and Giroux, 1974), 164–65.

23   **Costume designer Mitchell Leisen:** Vance, *Douglas Fairbanks*, 167.

23 **Bagdad's newest citizens:** Douglas Fairbanks papers, Margaret Herrick Library, AMPAS.

23 **wrangling his "cosmopolitan" cast:** "Troubles of a Bagdad Thief," *NYT*.

23 **as Anna May tells it:** Grace Kingsley, "I Shall Marry a Man of My Own Race," *Movie Weekly*, Nov. 17, 1923.

24 **Doug admitted with a wink:** "Troubles of a Bagdad Thief," *NYT*.

24 **some tawdry one-reeler:** Hanne Elizabeth Tidnam, "Watching Porn in Public: The Rise and Fall of the Adult Movie House," Medium, Aug. 12, 2016, https://timeline .com/rise-fall-porn-theater-172c45c7065f.

24 **"Sloe Gin":** Walsh, *Each Man in His Time*, 165.

25 **a man of the people:** Goessel, *First King of Hollywood*, 90, 152–53, 196–97, 227; Mathis Chazanov, "It Won't Be Pia-Fair," *LAT*, July 29, 1989; Mathis Chazanov, "Pickfair, Relic of Golden Age of Hollywood, Razed," *LAT*, April 20, 1990.

25 **Doug and Sam:** Goessel, *First King of Hollywood*, 318.

25 **"a huge darkey":** Marjorie Mayne, "A Dream Princess," *Picturegoer*, Dec. 1924, 58–59.

25 **when he traveled to China:** Goessel, *First King of Hollywood*, 403.

26 **entertain VIP guests:** Vance, *Douglas Fairbanks*, 174–75.

26 **"Working in a Fairbanks picture":** Goessel, *First King of Hollywood*, 259–60.

26 **Dinner was served:** Vance, *Douglas Fairbanks*, 65–67.

26 **a dedicated bedroom:** Goessel, *First King of Hollywood*, 258.

27 **around the dining room table:** Myrna Nye, "Society of Cinemaland," *LAT*, Sept. 16, 1928; Wanda Henderson, "Sawtelle's Blind Veterans Carol at Famous Pickfair," *LA Mirror*, Dec. 23, 1960; Chazanov, "It Won't Be Pia-Fair."

27 **"Just making a living":** Genova, "La petite Cendrillon chinoise," *Ciné-Miroir*, Nov. 27, 1931.

27 **her friend Philip Ahn:** Paul Henniger, "Wartime Villain: Philip Ahn—Really Not Such Bad Guy," *LAT*, Jan. 13, 1967; Hye Seung Chung, *Hollywood Asian: Philip Ahn and the Politics of Cross-Ethnic Performance* (Philadelphia: Temple University Press, 2006), 8–9; 71–72.

28 **"She lives in a movie fairyland":** Marjorie C. Driscoll, "Chinese Girl Becoming Star of Screen," *SF Chronicle*, Aug. 28, 1921.

28 **Back at the laundry:** Timothy G. Turner, "Maid of Orient Unspoiled by Success: Dips Her Hands in Suds," *LAT*, July 24, 1921; for accounts from children of Chinese laundrymen, see John Jung, *Chinese Laundries: Tickets to Survival on Gold Mountain* (n.p.: Yin and Yang Press, 2010).

28 **"a very hard worker":** *NYT*, "Troubles of a Bagdad Thief."

28 **"books to be kept":** Driscoll, "Chinese Girl Becoming Star of Screen."

CHAPTER TWO

31 **a snowstorm had blanketed parts:** "Deep Snow on Mountains," *LAT*, Jan. 2, 1905; "Brief Weather Report," *LAT*, Jan. 4, 1905; "Stiff Climb to the Snow," *LAT*, Jan. 4, 1905.

31 **thought he must be cursed:** Anna May Wong, "The True Life Story of a Chinese Girl," *Pictures*, Aug. 1926.

31 **the Chinese boy's cap:** Herb Howe, "Between Two Worlds," *New Movie*, July 1932.

32 **born in a mining town:** Wong Sam Sing, "True Life Story of a Chinese Girl"; Wong Sam Sing, file no. 14036-1459A, NARA–Riverside, 4–7.

32 **Anna had no interest:** Wong, "Childhood of a Screen Star."

33 **"Running a Chinese laundry":** Turner, "Maid of Orient Unspoiled by Success."

33 **caught her playing hooky:** Wong, "I Am Growing More Chinese."

34 **It wasn't long before:** Wong, "Childhood of a Chinese Screen Star"; Anna May Wong, "Bad Luck That Helped Me," *Picture Show*, Sept. 7, 1929.

34 **Like the invasive species:** Mrs. D. W. Griffith, in *My First Time in Hollywood*, 13; Nathan Masters, "A Brief History of Palm Trees in Southern California," KCET, Dec. 7, 2011, https://www.kcet.org/shows/lost-la/a-brief-history-of-palm-trees-in-southern-california.

34 **the first movie person:** Christine Lazzaretto and Heather Goers, "SurveyLA Citywide Historic Context Statement," City of Los Angeles, Sept. 2019, 10–11; Krist, *Mirage Factory*, 39–41.

34 **Selig's permanent studio:** Ren Kessler, "The Mystical, Magical Land of Hollywood, USA," The Movie Studios, accessed Feb. 10, 2021.

34 **Not long after, in fall 1909:** Krist, *Mirage Factory*, 50, 58.

34 **The population was just north:** "Historical General Population City & County of Los Angeles, 1850 to 2010," Los Angeles Almanac, http://www.laalmanac.com/population/po02.php.

35 **conventional jobs:** Myrtle Gebhart, "Jazz Notes on Old China," *Picture-Play*, May 1923; Wong, "Bad Luck That Helped Me."

35 **Her first extra part:** "Anna May Wong Earned $5 for Part in Her First Movie," *Edmonton (AB) Journal*, May 4, 1944.

35 **"It was grueling":** Wong, "Bad Luck That Helped Me."

35 **James Wang:** Genova, "La petite Cendrillon chinoise."

35 **the years before Will Hays:** Randee Dawn, "Entertainment Partners' Central Casting Unit Changes with the Times," *Variety*, Oct. 25, 2016, https://variety.com/2016/artisans/news/entertainment-partners-central-casting-unit-changes-with-the-times-1201898965/.

35 **the exceptional pay:** Wong, "I Am Lucky That I Am Chinese."

36 **"Consumed by my ambition":** Genova, "La petite Cendrillon chinoise."

36 **several hundred Chinese extras:** Wong, "I Am Growing More Chinese."

36 **Anna squealed with gratitude:** Genova, "La petite Cendrillon chinoise."

37 **"Why is it that the screen Chinese":** Anna May Wong, "I Protest," as told to Doris Mackie, *Film Weekly*, Aug. 18, 1933.

37 **"I felt the responsibility":** Wong, "I Am Growing More Chinese."

38 **she'd grown a thick skin:** Howe, "Between Two Worlds."

38 **tagging along with James Wang:** "Miss Yellow Willows Comes Home—a Star," *St. Louis Post-Dispatch*, July 25, 1931.

38 **fell ill with Sydenham's chorea:** Wong, "Childhood of a Chinese Screen Star."

39 **It was around this time:** Wong, "I Am Lucky That I Am Chinese"; Wong, "I Am Growing More Chinese."

39 **When Anna first announced her plans:** Wong, "I Am Growing More Chinese."

40 to "buy pretty dresses": Turner, "Maid of Orient Unspoiled by Success."

40 a boy in a car showed up: Wong, "I Am Lucky That I Am Chinese."

40 Lee Gon Toy had another reason: Wong, "Childhood of a Chinese Screen Star."

40 the Lumière brothers: Zack Sharf, "Lumière Brothers' 1895 Short 'Arrival of a Train' Goes Viral with Fan-Made 4K Restoration," *IndieWire*, Feb. 5, 2020, https://www .indiewire.com/2020/02/lumiere-brothers-arrival-of-a-train-4k-update-1202208955/.

41 "To us, of course, it was nothing": L. E. Winchell, "Honeymooning with Doug and Mary," *Atlanta Constitution*, Aug. 15, 1920.

42 Toisan was but a stone's throw: Gordon H. Chang, *Ghosts of Gold Mountain: The Epic Story of the Chinese Who Built the Transcontinental Railroad* (Boston: Houghton Mifflin Harcourt, 2019), 15–27.

42 substantiated the claims: James K. Polk, "December 5, 1848: Fourth Annual Message to Congress," Dec. 5, 1848, transcript, https://millercenter.org/the-presidency/presiden tial-speeches/december-5-1848-fourth-annual-message-congress.

42 100,000 men: William B. Lardner and Michael John Brock, *History of Placer and Nevada Counties California* (n.p.: Historic Record Company, 1924), 163.

42 "My father proved his originality": Wong, "True Life Story of a Chinese Girl."

43 owned two stores: Graham Russell Gao Hodges, *Anna May Wong: From Laundryman's Daughter to Hollywood Legend* (Hong Kong: Hong Kong University Press, 2012), 5–6.

43 Wong's own recollections: Wong Sam Sing, file no. 14036-1459A, NARA–Riverside, 4–5.

43 "He must have been very popular": Wong, "True Life Story of a Chinese Girl."

43 the "Big Four": Roland de Wolk, *American Disruptor: The Scandalous Life of Leland Stanford* (Oakland: University of California Press, 2019), 75–77.

43 Though Stanford had previously: Chang, *Ghosts of Gold Mountain*, 61–63, 85–86, 141–45.

44 The introduction of: De Wolk, *American Disruptor*, 116, 127.

44 the "Heathen Chinee": This pejorative term was made famous by Bret Harte's satirical poem "Plain Language from Truthful James," meant to critique anti-Chinese sentiment in the West. Ironically, the poem was retitled "The Heathen Chinee" and became a rallying cry behind the anti-Chinese movement, validating popular feelings that the Chinese were an inferior race. The poem launched Harte's writing career and was disseminated as an illustrated pamphlet in many different editions.

45 to find himself a bride: Hodges, *Anna May Wong*, 6–7.

45 Chinese Exclusion Act of 1882: Stephanie Hinnershitz, "The Chinese Exclusion Act," Bill of Rights Institute, accessed Feb. 24, 2021, https://billofrightsinstitute.org/essays /the-chinese-exclusion-act.

45 $12 for a dozen shirts: Iris Chang, *The Chinese in America: A Narrative History* (New York: Penguin, 2003), 48–49.

45 More than three fourths: Joan S. Wang, "Race, Gender, and Laundry Work: The Roles of Chinese Laundrymen and American Women in the United States, 1850–1950," *Journal of American Ethnic History* 24, no. 1 (Fall 2004): 61.

46 racism against the Chinese: Jung, *Chinese Laundries*, 92–93, 153, 186.

46 when Wong was arrested: David E. Bernstein, "Lochner, Parity, and the Chinese Laundry Cases," in *William & Mary Law Review* 41, no. 1 (Dec. 1999): 261–62.

47 Mary Pickford's father: Pickford, *Sunshine and Shadow*, 32.

47 **whose real name was Ullman:** Goessel, *First King of Hollywood*, 9.
47 **the bastard child:** Peter Ackroyd, *Charlie Chaplin: A Brief Life* (New York: Nan A. Talese, 2014).
47 **Anita Loos observed:** Anita Loos, *A Girl Like I* (New York: Viking, 1966), 121.
47 **Through the rose-hued lens:** "Biography of Douglas Fairbanks," Douglas Fairbanks Pictures Corporation, Jan. 1933, from *Douglas Fairbanks: In His Own Words*, 301.
47 **The Pickford patriarch:** Pickford, *Sunshine and Shadow*, 23–24.
48 **In a two-part memoir:** Wong, "True Life Story of a Chinese Girl."
49 **"Imagine that name in electric lights":** Howe, "Between Two Worlds."

CHAPTER THREE

51 **An expectant hush:** Carolyn Carter, "Doug Fairbanks Excels in *The Thief of Bagdad*," *Movie Weekly*, April 12, 1924; "Thief of Bagdad Film Took Long Time in Making," *LAT*, Oct. 26, 1924.
51 **"extensive and elaborate" preparations:** "Egyptian Theater Dark Three Days," *LAT*, July 7, 1924.
51 **a whopping $2 million:** Gary Carey, *Doug & Mary: A Biography of Douglas Fairbanks & Mary Pickford* (New York: Dutton, 1977), 145.
52 **"de luxe press-agent tactics":** McElliott, "Fantastic Fairbanks Film Packs Them in at Liberty," *NY Daily News*, March 19, 1924.
52 **5,000 fans:** Carey, *Doug & Mary*, 149.
52 **nearly bum-rushed:** "Colorful Throng Greets Colorful Doug in New Film," *NY Daily News*, March 19, 1924; "Police Clear Jam at Movie Premier," *NYT*, March 19, 1924.
52 **"the beating of drums":** "Police Clear Jam at Movie Premier," *NYT*.
52 **"A film which will exhaust fans' superlatives":** McElliott, "Fantastic Fairbanks."
52 **"The wealth of magic":** "Thief of Bagdad," *Variety*, March 26, 1924.
52 **"An entrancing picture":** "The Screen: Arabian Nights Satire," *NYT*, March 19, 1924.
52 **The film's rollout continued:** "'Thief of Bagdad' Next at Egyptian," *LAT*, June 19, 1924.
53 **Some 20,000 persons:** Picture and caption, in *Exhibitors Herald*, June 14, 1924, 27.
53 **an entire four-page spread:** "The Thief of Bagdad" section, *Hollywood Daily Citizen*, July 10, 1924, 9–12.
53 **a premiere extravaganza:** "Egyptian to Close 'Thief' This Month," *LAT*, Nov. 9, 1924.
53 **"beautiful gowns and handsome jewels":** L. B. Fowler, "Lensland's Elite View Doug's Best," *LA Daily News*, July 11, 1924.
53 **of Fleurs de Bagdad:** Schallert, "Film Banquet Is Dazzling"; Fowler, "Lensland's Elite View Doug's Best"; L. B. Fowler, "'Thief of Bagdad' Beggars Description: Triumph for Grauman and Fairbanks," *LA Daily News*, July 11, 1924.
54 **The lavish presentation:** "Egyptian to Close 'Thief' This Month," *LAT*; Joseph H. Steele, "Grauman Stages Master Prologue," *Hollywood Daily Citizen*, July 10, 1924; "Up Goes Presentation Cost: 'Thief of Bagdad' to Have Fine Frame," *LAT*, June 29, 1924; "Doug's New Film to Open Tonight," *Hollywood Daily Citizen*, July 10, 1924; "Special Perfume at Opening Here," *Hollywood Daily Citizen*, July 10, 1924.

54 **the movie prologue:** Kim K. Fahlstedt, "Prologue to Hollywood: Sid Grauman and the San Francisco Origins of Tinseltown Spectacle," *Bright Lights Film Journal*, July 25, 2020, https://brightlightsfilm.com/prologue-to-hollywood-sid-grauman-and-the-san-francisco-origins-of-tinseltown-spectacle/#.YQhiGFNuc_Y.

54 **"camels, flying rings":** "Up Goes Presentation Cost," *LAT*.

54 **"of bazaars and hanging rugs":** Schallert, "Film Banquet Is Dazzling."

54 **"a spectacle more brilliant":** "Up Goes Presentation Cost," *LAT*.

54 **Milton Sills took the stage:** "The Thief Another Great Adventure," *LA Evening Express*, July 11, 1924.

55 **most silent films were accompanied:** Scott Eyman, *The Speed of Sound: Hollywood and the Talkie Revolution, 1926–1930* (New York: Simon & Schuster Paperbacks, 1997), 38–40.

55 **classical composer Mortimer Wilson:** "Special Score for 'Thief of Bagdad,'" *LAT*, Jan. 20, 1924.

55 **a magical carpet ride:** Walsh, *Each Man in His Time*, 167–69.

56 **played to standing room only:** "Egyptian Hangs Out 'S.R.O.' at Thief of Bagdad," *LAT*, July 20, 1924.

56 **"the greatest cinema of its kind":** Fowler, "'Thief of Bagdad' Beggars Description."

56 **"a great artistic achievement":** Lola Kinel, "Keeping Abreast of the Screen," *Visual Education*, Oct. 1924.

56 **"No one but Douglas Fairbanks":** "'The Thief' Another Great Adventure," *LA Evening Express*, July 11, 1924.

56 **"I have no words":** Schallert, "Film Banquet Is Dazzling."

57 ***Photoplay* had predicted:** Portrait of Anna May Wong by Edwin Bower Hesser, in *Photoplay*, March 1924.

57 **"If Miss Johnston is to be considered":** Carter, "Doug Fairbanks Excels."

58 **"what do you think of Liu Tsong?":** Howe, "Between Two Worlds."

58 **"curious, exotic, and sinister types":** "With Doug in Bagdad," *Picture-Play*, Feb. 1924, 78–79.

58 **"Anna May Wong as the little slave girl":** Ibee, review of *The Thief of Bagdad*, *Variety*, March 26, 1924.

58 **could be seen modeling:** "Fashions," *LAT*, Dec. 16, 1923; "Blending the Oriental with the Artistic in Cars," *LAT*, Nov. 16, 1924.

58 **height of five foot six:** Government records are inconsistent with regards to Anna May's height. On her U.S.-issued certificate of identity and 1937 Form 430 application she is listed as five-five, while the ship manifesto from her trip to Canada in 1924 via Seattle, Washington, lists her as five-six and while her 1935 Form 430 application describes her as five-six and a half. Scholars generally agree she was tall compared to most women of her era, so I think it is reasonable to assume she was about five foot six.

58 **the two jarring personas:** Beverley N. Sparks, "Where East Meets West," *Photoplay*, June 1924.

58 **"Improbable as this sounds":** Carlisle, "A Chinese Puzzle."

59 **A special showing:** "Plays in Fantasy of Orient: Diminutive Star in Fairbanks Opus," *LAT*, Sept. 21, 1924.

59   a party going on somewhere: Merton, "Night Life of Hollywood," *Screen Secrets*, Dec. 1927, 45–47.

60   "Amory saw girls doing things": F. Scott Fitzgerald, *This Side of Paradise* (New York: Scribner, 1920), 58–59.

60   "I never seem to have any money": Carlisle, "A Chinese Puzzle."

60   "trying to beat a motor cop": Mary Winship, "The China Doll: Meet Anna May Wong of Hollywood," *Photoplay*, June 1923.

60   her traffic exploits: "Police Awaiting Picture Star on Speeding Charge," *LAT*, March 7, 1925.

60   "Who's your favorite movie star?": Carlisle, "A Chinese Puzzle."

60   made advances toward his underage actress: David J. Skal and Elias Savada, *Dark Carnival: The Secret World of Tod Browning, Hollywood's Master of the Macabre* (New York: Anchor Books, 1995), 74–75.

61   Gloria Swanson once described him as: Gloria Swanson, *Swanson on Swanson* (New York: Random House, 1980), 165.

61   Mickey was an Irish kid: Jack Spears, *Hollywood: The Golden Era* (New York: Castle Books, 1971), 279–313.

62   "I always said that": Elizabeth Peltret, "When 'Micky' Walked," *Motion Picture Classic*, April–May 1920.

62   He hated the egos: Spears, *Hollywood*, 300–301, 304.

62   for his film *Dinty*: Linton Wells, "Girl Refuses to Forsake Laundry for Film Fame," *Courier-Post* (New Jersey), Sept. 6, 1921.

62   there were only so many times: "The Life Story of Anna May Wong," *Picture Show*, Aug. 6, 1938.

62   as laid out by California law: *Michael M. v. Superior Court*, S.F. No. 23929. Supreme Court of California. November 5, 1979, accessed Nov. 12, 2022, https://law.justia.com/cases/california/supreme-court/3d/25/608.html.

62   the couple's affair was an open secret: Hodges, *Anna May Wong*, 31.

63   actress Blanche Sweet: "'Other Woman' in Neilan Case," *LAT*, March 17, 1921; "More Movie Weddings," *LA Evening Post-Record*, April 26, 1921.

63   Mickey was making moves: Swanson, *Swanson on Swanson*, 140.

63   he'd said the same thing: Tricia Welsh, *Gloria Swanson: Ready for Her Close-Up* (Jackson: University of Mississippi, 2013), 92.

63   over a weeklong tryst: Swanson, *Swanson on Swanson*, 178–81.

63   "an attractive little Chinawoman": Review of *Bits of Life*, *CAMERA!*, Nov. 26, 1921.

64   Ads for *Bits of Life*: Advertisement for *Bits of Life*, in *Ponca City (OK) News*, Dec. 26, 1921.

64   "Mickey Neilan is the prince of directors": Gebhart, "Jazz Notes on Old China."

64   she worked steadily: Hodges, *Anna May Wong*, 34.

64   At the end of May: "Brenon Company En Route to Alaska," *LAT*, May 31, 1924.

65   from her perch: "With Tom Meighan in the Canadian Rockies," *Photoplay*, Oct. 1924, 69.

65   "Cheerio, old top": Anna May Wong, "Anna May Wong Writes In," *LAT*, June 25, 1924.

65   "Anna May cannot swim": Grace Kingsley, "Brenon Doing Big Pictures," *LAT*, July 20, 1924.

65   **the law of the land:** "Chinese Exclusion Act (1882)," Milestone Documents, National Archives, accessed Nov. 12, 2022, https://www.archives.gov/milestone-documents/chinese-exclusion-act.

66   **the time her father was hauled off:** "Chinese Laundry to Be Tested in Court," *LA Evening Express*, Nov. 1, 1913; "Going Higher Up: Chinese Appeals Case," *LAT*, Nov. 2, 1913.

66   **James Wong Howe was no stranger:** Todd Rainsberger, *James Wong Howe: Cinematographer* (New York: A. S. Barnes, 1981), 11–18.

68   **For all the Wyckoffs:** Alain Silver, *James Wong Howe: The Camera Eye* (Santa Monica, CA: Pendragon Books, 2010), 19–28.

68   **Fearing a potential backlash:** Roger Cels, "Death Takes James Wong Howe at 76," James Wong Howe clippings file, Irvin Paik Collection, USC.

69   **"hyphenated American":** Sarah Churchwell, "America's Original Identity Politics," *New York Review*, Feb. 7, 2019, https://www.nybooks.com/daily/2019/02/07/americas-original-identity-politics/; Woodrow Wilson, "Address to the Daughters of the American Revolution," Oct. 11, 1915, The American Presidency Project, https://www.presidency.ucsb.edu/documents/address-the-daughters-the-american-revolution-0.

69   **as early as 1830:** "Timeline of Chinese Immigration to the United States," Bancroft Library, University of California Regents, accessed Nov. 12, 2022.

69   **the population grew to 150,000:** Chang, *Ghosts of Gold Mountain*, 44–45.

69   **the Chinese population had declined:** 1920 U.S. Census, Continental United States.

69   **the 1875 Page Law:** Sucheng Chan, "The Exclusion of Chinese Women, 1870–1943," in *Chinese Immigrants and American Law*, vol. 1, ed. Charles McClain (New York: Garland Publishing, 1994), 94, 105.

69   **4,582 Chinese women:** 1920 U.S. Census, California.

70   **Several months before:** T. Howard Kelly, "Why Was Thomas Meighan Stoned in Chinatown?" *Movie Weekly*, Jan. 19, 1924.

71   **Twenty-two-year-old journalist:** Gebhart, "Jazz Notes on Old China."

73   **Six months later:** Kingsley, "I Shall Marry a Man of My Own Race"; Jack Jungmeyer, "Anna May Wong Seeks to Recapture Her Racial Mannerisms and Modes," *Wilmington (DE) Evening Journal*, Dec. 4, 1923.

73   **"Anna May Wong as an Indian girl":** Fred, review of *The Alaskan*, *Variety*, Sept. 17, 1924.

73   **6 million moviegoers:** Paramount Pictures advertisement for *Peter Pan*, *Exhibitors Trade Review*, Jan. 17, 1925, 1.

74   **bought herself a new car:** Wong, "I Am Lucky That I Am Chinese."

74   **across the United States and Canada:** Wong Ying (Lulu Wong), file no. 14036-1266, NARA–Riverside, 50.

74   **At each stop:** "Film Folk Off on Long Tour," *LAT*, Feb. 15, 1925.

74   **a DIY affair:** "Train Home Cleaned by Film Stars," *LAT*, Jan. 31, 1925.

74   **went along on the tour:** Wong Ying, file no. 14036-1266, NARA–Riverside, 50.

74   **When the troupe turned up:** "Blank (Iowa) 'Angeling' Troupe of Hollywood Film Actors," *Variety*, March 11, 1925, 1, 8.

74   **A few bad checks later:** "Inside Stuff on Pictures," *Variety*, March 11, 1925, 34.

74   actor **Romney Brent:** Frederick Nolan, *Lorenz Hart: A Poet on Broadway* (New York: Oxford University Press, 1994), 61–62.

74   **a production company in her name:** "Chinese Girl Sues to Void Picture Pact," *SF Examiner,* July 18, 1924.

75   **movies based on classic Chinese tales:** Margaret Norris, "Flashes from the Eastern Stars," *Motion Picture Classic,* Dec. 1924, 54.

75   **the deal was rubbish:** "Chinese Girl Sues to Void Picture Pact," *SF Examiner.*

75   **she remained off the screen:** "Miss Yellow Willows Comes Home," *St. Louis Post Dispatch.*

76   **On a November day:** "Industrial Addition Is Important: McClintic-Marshall Plant Entertains Visitors for Start of Activity," *LAT,* Nov. 12, 1925.

CHAPTER FOUR

79   **on a "slumming" tour:** Jennifer 8. Lee, "When 'Slumming' Was the Thing to Do," *City Room* blog, *NYT,* July 6, 2009, https://archive.nytimes.com/cityroom.blogs .nytimes.com/2009/07/06/when-slumming-was-the-thing-to-do/.

79   **Chinatown filled with revelers:** "Chinese New Year," *LA Evening Citizen News,* Feb. 1, 1927; "Dragons, Fireclackee! It's Chinese New Year," *LA Evening Post-Record,* Feb. 2, 1927.

80   **in one of Chinatown's cafés:** Harry Carr, "The Lancer," *LAT,* Feb. 5, 1927.

80   **Chopsticks were passed around:** Details of the dinner are a composite of Chinese dinners AMW hosted over the years; see: "Anna May Wong's Party," *LAT,* Feb. 1, 1933, Anna May Wong clipping file, NYPL; Elza Schallert, "The Epicures of Hollywood," *Picture-Play,* Oct. 1927, 92.

80   **"Jimmy raises English bulldogs":** Carr, "The Lancer."

81   **Dressed to the nines:** Winship, "The China Doll."

81   **The strategy had worked so well:** Gebhart, "Jazz Notes on Old China."

82   **"Anna May Wong cannot make up her mind":** Cal York, "Studio News and Gossip— East and West," *Photoplay,* June 1925, 107.

82   **In a two-part commentary:** Wong, "True Life Story of a Chinese Girl."

83   **She recalled wryly:** Wong, "The Childhood of a Chinese Screen Star."

83   **Wong Tou Nan:** Wong Wah Ying (James Norman Wong), file no. 8402-080, NARA– Riverside, 9.

84   **a clipping of Anna May:** Anna May Wong clippings file, NYPL.

84   **put her foot down:** Wong, "True Life Story of a Chinese Girl."

84   **"Say, do you ever wonder":** Carlisle, "A Chinese Puzzle."

84   **"Do not think it is easy":** Wong, "True Life Story of a Chinese Girl."

85   **"I just tried to explain":** Wong, "Childhood of a Chinese Screen Star."

85   **she nearly lost herself:** Mamie Louise Leung, "Pretty Anna Is Ambitious," *LA Post-Record,* Aug. 7, 1926.

85   **"if you will come home":** Helen Carlisle, "Velly Muchee Lonely," *Motion Picture Magazine,* March 1928.

85   **"I had my fling":** Wagner, "Better a Laundry and Sincerity."

86 Life had changed: "Anna May Wong: The Charming Little Oriental of the Screen," *Picture Show*, Jan. 2, 1926.

86 James was studying business: Wagner, "Better a Laundry and Sincerity."

86 Mary and Frank: Mary Wong (Wong Lew Heung), file no. 9402-707, NARA–Riverside, 17–28.

86 her new lodgings: The details of her bungalow apartment are a composite of several descriptions: Carlisle, "Velly Muchee Lonely"; Wagner, "Better a Laundry and Sincerity"; Myrtle Gebhart, "A Lone Lotus," *Picture-Play*, Jan. 1932, 24; Kingsley, "I Shall Marry a Man of My Own Race."

86 "Many a celebrity": Carlisle, "Velly Muchee Lonely."

86 writer friend Grace Wilcox: Grace Wilcox, "Young China in Old Chinatown," *LAT*, May 22, 1927.

87 the Janningses threw a party: "Mr. and Mrs. Jannings Entertain," *LAT*, May 29, 1927.

87 every one of Mary's films: "Charles Rosher," IMDb, accessed Feb. 6, 2023, https://www.imdb.com/name/nm0003546/.

87 Mary had kindly: "Charles Rosher to Germany," *LAT*, Sept. 19, 1925; "Spectacular Effects in New Pickford Film," *Sioux City Journal*, July 17, 1927.

88 Now, one year later: "Rosher Returns to Photograph Murnau Feature," *American Cinematographer*, Oct. 1926.

88 a "camera operator": Author interview with Jenna Rosher, granddaughter of Charles Rosher, 2021.

88 a photographer of royals: Charles Rosher, "I Remember Way Back When," *American Cinematographer*, April 1936.

88 he rode with General Pancho Villa: "No Cameras Going to the Front," *The Moving Picture World*, Sept. 12, 1914; "Creators of Lasky Photography," *Motion Picture News*, Oct. 21, 1916.

88 to get caught in the crosshairs: H. M. Dean, "With Villa in Mexico," *Reel Life*, May 9, 1914.

88 "I had to film everything": Cynthia King, "From Villa to Earhart to Oscars," *Miami Herald*, Feb. 1, 1970.

88 the Battle of Ojinaga: King, "From Villa to Earhart to Oscars."

88 the Masonic pin on his lapel: Author interview with Jenna Rosher, 2021.

89 rendezvoused at his cottage: Betty Lou Young, *Rustic Canyon and the Story of the Uplifters* (Santa Monica, CA: Casa Vieja Press, 1975), 54–55, 59–62, 75.

89 a real-life Never Never Land: Ron Russell, "An Oasis of the Past," *LAT*, June 28, 1994; Young, *Rustic Canyon*, 84–85.

89 a local favorite at the club: Young, *Rustic Canyon*, 83.

89 built a shrine to her: Young, *Rustic Canyon*, 160.

89 Down a few steps: Details based on author interview with Jenna Rosher, 2021, and photographs taken by Victor B. D'Agostino.

90 "I don't suppose": Carlisle, "Velly Muchee Lonely."

90 too Americanized: Jungmeyer, "Anna May Wong Seeks to Recapture Her Racial Mannerisms and Modes."

91 "My philosophy": Leung, "Pretty Anna Is Ambitious."

91 how to use chopsticks: Cal York, "News and Gossip of All the Studios," *Photoplay*, March 1927, 48.

91 "WHY, oh WHY": M. H. Shryock, "She Didn't Know Her Chop Suey," *Photoplay*, Oct. 1927, 84.

92 Despite being billed third: "The Devil Dancer," *Picture Show*, Dec. 8, 1928; review of *The Devil Dancer*, AMPAS, Chamberlin Scrapbook, 23 of 46, 73.

92 In the latter film: Michael Orme, "At the Sign of the Cinema," *Sketch*, March 14, 1928, 24.

92 "The reviewers deplore": Norbert Lusk, "'The Dove' Is Above Usual," *LAT*, Jan. 8, 1928.

92 Even the director: Wagner, "Better a Laundry and Sincerity."

92 The two Asian actors: Kamiyama Sôjin, *Sugao no Hariuddo* (Tokyo: Yumani Shobo, 2006), 186.

93 *Old San Francisco's* premiere: Irene Thirer, "Greta Nissen Barrymore's Lead in 'Tempest'; 'Rose-Marie' in Color; News," *NY Daily News*, June 16, 1927.

93 "a cute, clever Chinese maiden": Irene Thirer, "Dolores Costello Leads Excellent Warner Cast in 'Old San Francisco'," *NY Daily News*, June 22, 1927.

93 her time in New York: Morris, "Nothing but the Truth."

94 She knew immediately: Grace Turner, "Shanghai Banquet," *Evening Star* (Washington, D.C.), Aug. 8, 1937.

94 But Harlem was more: Emily Bernard, *Carl Van Vechten and the Harlem Renaissance: A Portrait in Black and White* (New Haven, CT: Yale University Press, 2012), 25–30.

95 She had a press interview: Morris, "Nothing but the Truth."

95 at the Ambassador Hotel: "In Gotham," *LAT*, June 26, 1927.

96 She received fan mail: M. S., "To Anna," *Picturegoer*, Sept. 1925, 48.

96 "When a girl who": Wagner, "Better a Laundry and Sincerity."

96 "In picture after picture": Review of *Old San Francisco*, AMPAS, Chamberlin Scrapbook, 23 of 46.

96 "some day some one": Wagner, "Better a Laundry and Sincerity."

97 A couple weeks into filming: "To Yosemite for Second Start on 'Rose-Marie,'" *Variety*, Oct. 26, 1927.

97 "The directors seemed to believe": Genova, "La petite Cendrillon chinoise."

97 "a lovely slut": Lawrence Stallings and Ted Shane, continuity treatment for *Across to Singapore*, Nov. 3, 1927, AMPAS, Turner/MGM scripts—*Across to Singapore*, file A-106, 33.

98 Four years prior: James Kotsilibas-Davis and Myrna Loy, *Myrna Loy: Being and Becoming* (New York: Alfred A. Knopf, 1987), photo insert.

98 how to hold her chopsticks: Hodges, *Anna May Wong*, 61.

98 "They cast me as a Chinese": Kotsilibas-Davis and Loy, *Myrna Loy*, 52.

98 "There have been several attempts": Anna May Wong, "I Am Very Happy," *Mein Film*, no. 123, May 5, 1928, 6.

98 the German playwright: John Baxter, "Berlin Year Zero: The Making of *The Blue Angel*," *Framework* 51, no. 1 (Spring 2010): 172.

99 written with her in mind: Wong, "I Am Very Happy."

99 full of sorrow and misfortune: Walter Benjamin, "Gespräch mit Anne May Wong: Eine Chinoiserie aus dem Alten Westen," *Die Literariscme*, July 6, 1928.

99   The film was soon retitled: "Premiere in Berlin," *LAT*, Oct. 7, 1928.

99   "The role is perfect": Benjamin, "Gespräch mit Anne May Wong."

99   one of the continent's "starmakers": Cynthia Walk, "Anna May Wong and Weimar Cinema: Orientalism in Postcolonial Germany," in *Beyond Alterity: German Encounters with Modern East Asia,* eds. Qinna Shen and Martin Rosenstock (New York: Berghahn Books, 2014), 138.

99   as part of Film Europe: Andrew Higson and Richard Maltby, "'Film Europe' and 'Film America': An Introduction," in *"Film Europe" and "Film America": Cinema, Commerce and Cultural Exchange, 1920–1939* (Exeter, UK: University of Exeter Press, 1999), eds. Higson and Maltby, 2–3.

100 she was contracted to star: "Anna May Wong to Europe," *LAT*, March 17, 1928; Anthony Slide, *A Special Relationship: Britain Comes to Hollywood and Hollywood Comes to Britain* (Jackson: University Press of Mississippi, 2015), 170.

100 "I sought the advice": Ralph Parker, "Anna May Wong's Chinese Love Code," *Hollywood* 21, no. 2 (Feb. 1932).

CHAPTER FIVE

103 "It seems to us the greatest pity": "Anna May Wong to Europe," *LAT*, March 17, 1928.

103 a certificate of residency: "Chinese Exclusion Act (1882)," Milestone Documents, National Archives, accessed Nov. 12, 2022, https://www.archives.gov/milestone-documents/chinese-exclusion-act.

103 "As nothing was developed": Anna May Wong (Wong Liu Song or Wong Lew Song), file no. 14036-239, NARA–Riverside, 46.

104 Lulu didn't give it a second thought: Anne Howe, "In New York," *Screenland*, June 1928, 101.

104 Lulu Wong's Form 430: Wong Ying, file no. 14036-1266, NARA–Riverside, 20, 24.

104 the small group of well-wishers: Grace Wilcox, "Anna May Wong: A Story," *Oakland Tribune*, Nov. 4, 1934.

105 "in a class all by herself": Howe, "In New York."

105 wearing a fabulous fur-lined coat: Wong, "I Am Very Happy."

105 Berlin had risen from the ashes: Alexandra Richie, *Faust's Metropolis: A History of Berlin* (New York: Carroll & Graf, 1998), 284–86, 311–13, 321–24, 330–32.

106 "The first day on set": *St. Louis Post-Dispatch*, "Miss Yellow Willows Comes Home."

106 She hired a tutor: John Scott, "European Bouquets Get Notice," *LAT*, Aug. 23, 1931.

106 "Within a week": *St. Louis Post-Dispatch*, "Miss Yellow Willows Comes Home."

107 less than a thousand Chinese: Hodges, *Anna May Wong*, 66.

107 the press often referred to her: Walk, "Anna May Wong and Weimar Cinema," 149.

107 playing the role of spurned lover: "Berlin Praises Miss Wong," *NYT*, Aug. 22, 1928.

107 this special talent: Benjamin, "Gespräch mit Anne May Wong."

107 "I am very happy in Berlin": Wong, "I Am Very Happy."

108 two months into their stay: Benjamin, "Gespräch mit Anne May Wong."

110 cut her hair short only once: Wilcox, "Anna May Wong: A Story."

110 **her most valuable asset:** A. Rothstein, "Historical Hairstyles: From Victorian Times to Today," Minnesota School of Cosmetology, Oct. 25, 2018.

110 **As Anna May loosened her hair:** Benjamin, "Gespräch mit Anne May Wong."

110 **During her nearly three months:** Wong, "I Am Growing More Chinese."

111 **Their clothes were sophisticated:** Josephine Baker and Jo Bouillon, *Josephine*, trans. Mariana Fitzpatrick (New York: Marlowe, 1988), 48.

111 **Anna May went to see:** Program for "Ballets Russes de Serge de Diaghilev," Theatre Sarah-Bernhardt, June 21, 1928, Anna May Wong collection of theater programs, 1920s–1930s, Book 8414, NYPL.

112 **supping under the stars:** Gary Chapman, "The Chateau de Madrid," *Jazz Age Club*, Jan. 7, 2020, accessed Feb. 14, 2022, https://www.jazzageclub.com/the-chateau-de -madrid/5082/.

112 **a nightcap at Chez Joséphine:** Baker and Bouillon, *Josephine*, 68.

112 **After only a fortnight:** "Lots in a Name," *Weekly Dispatch* (London), Nov. 18, 1928.

112 **Anna May didn't care much:** Annesley de Silva, *These Piquant People: Being a Collection of Conversations* (London: Cecil Palmer, 1932), 49; "Lots in a Name," *Weekly Dispatch*.

112 **Pictures taken years before:** "Miss Anna May Wong," *Tatler*, July 11, 1928; "Ost Gegen West," *Kinematograph*, no. 196, Aug. 23 1929.

112 **Local artists and photographers:** "Long Shots," *Kinematograph Weekly*, Sept. 12, 1929; Nicholas Michailow, "Miss Anna May Wong, in National Dress," *Sketch*, Aug. 22, 1928; Swaine, "The Chinese Star of the 'Mandarin' Finger-nails by Daylight," *Sketch*, Dec. 26, 1928.

113 **seeing the sights of London:** G. S. J., "Oriental Film Artist's Triumph: The Rise to Fame of Anna May Wong," *Staffordshire Sentinel*, Jan. 9, 1929.

113 **Paparazzi captured Anna May:** "The Chinese Screen Star Visits London's China-town," *Sketch*, Aug. 8, 1928.

113 **Noël Coward's hit musical:** AMW collection, Book 8405, NYPL.

113 **potboilers that had been circulating:** "Welcome, Arnold Bennett," *NYT*, Oct. 14, 1911.

114 **"This youthful creature":** Arnold Bennett, *Piccadilly: Story of the Film* (Plainview, NY: Books for Libraries Press, 1975), 24–25.

115 **"just what her admirers want":** Review of *The Devil Dancer*, *Illustrated Daily News*, from *The Devil Dancer* press book, United Artists Collection, Wisconsin Center for Film and Theater Research.

115 **a role that entailed more:** Gilda Gray, "Me," *Picturegoer*, Nov. 1928, 13.

116 **"The story of this production":** "The Screen," review of *The Devil Dancer*, *NYT*, Dec. 19, 1927.

116 **"girl of swaying hips":** Review of *The Devil Dancer*, *Motion Picture News*, Dec. 2, 1927.

116 **and was paid $250,000:** "Flashes from Filmland," *Screen Secrets*, Jan. 1928, 10.

116 **in Gilda's case:** "The Devil Dancer," *Picture Show*.

117 **Filming for *Piccadilly* began in earnest:** "British Studios To-day," *Bioscope*, Aug. 15, 1928.

117 **a striking blue-and-silver kimono:** Louise E. Johnston, "What the Fans Think: British Studio Gossip," *Picture-Play*, Jan. 1929, 11.

117   The costume was provided by Nathan's: "Costumes and Courts," *Bioscope*, Dec. 12, 1928.

118   she recruited Noranna Rose: "Noranna Rose to the Occasion," *People*, Feb. 17, 1929.

118   in excess of £8,000: Edith Nepean, "A Week in My Life," *Picture Show Annual*, 1930, 107; "Piccadilly Night Club in Studio," *Bioscope*, Aug. 15, 1928.

119   far away from the censure: Paul Matthew St. Pierre, *E. A. Dupont and His Contribution to British Film: Variete, Moulin Rouge, Piccadilly, Atlantic, Two Worlds, Cape Forlorn* (Madison, NJ: Fairleigh Dickinson University Press, 2010), 12–13.

119   three hundred extras: "Piccadilly Night Club in Studio," *Bioscope*.

119   "calm and cold as a statue": Bennett, *Piccadilly*, 113–14.

120   "The strangest dancing": Bennett, *Piccadilly*, 25.

120   the premiere for *Song*: "Berlin Praises Miss Wong," *NYT*; "Song," *Der Kinematograph*, Aug. 23, 1928.

121   a live orchestra: Walk, "Anna May Wong and Weimar Cinema," 140.

121   "Maia Wong": Scott, "European Bouquets Get Notice."

121   scenes from the script: Walk, "Anna May Wong and Weimar Cinema," 143, 161–62.

121   In the version screened that evening: "Alternative Endings to 'Show Life,'" *Bioscope*, Sept. 19, 1928.

121   a full twenty minutes: "Premiere in Berlin," *LAT*, Oct. 7, 1928.

121   "I seemed suddenly to be standing": Wong, "I Am Growing More Chinese."

122   "He discovers Anna May Wong": "Song," *Der Kinematograph*.

122   "With Anna May Wong in the leading rôle": Auberon, "Do Foreign Stars Eclipse British?," *Bystander*, Nov. 28, 1928.

122   Her reply made its way: Grace Kingsley, "Baclanova's New Lasky Contract Leads Toward Stardom; Josephine Dunn Has Feature Role with Fox; Anna May Wong Returning Home Soon," *LAT*, Nov. 3, 1928.

123   On the set that day: Edmond Gréville, "Anna May Wong vedette chinoise de 'Piccadilly,'" *Pour Vous*, Feb. 14, 1929.

124   a West End theater was booked: "'Piccadilly' Film," *Daily Mirror* (London), Jan. 29, 1929.

124   "Acting honours": "Film News," review of *Piccadilly*, *Stage*, Feb. 7, 1929.

124   "It was England": "Anna May Wong," *Picture Show Annual*, 1931.

124   Gilda presciently sailed back: "Piccadilly Stars: News of Gilda and Anna," *Kinematograph Weekly*, Jan. 10, 1929.

124   Her swift fame: "Citing Exception When the Twain Did Meet," *Brooklyn Times-Union*, March 22, 1931; Hodges, *Anna May Wong*, 72.

124   Her style, too: Audrey Rivers, "Anna May Wong Sorry She Cannot Be Kissed," *Movie Classic*, Nov. 1931, 39.

125   "the originator of the 'Shimmy'": Auberon, "'Piccadilly'—But Little Pleasure," *Bystander*, Feb. 13, 1929.

125   "Just a whisper": Douglas Fox "Film Makers Take Cue from Wagner, Daddy of the Theme Song," *Exhibitors Herald World*, April 27, 1929, 39.

125   "Whoever permitted Gilda Gray": Freddie Schader, "Piccadilly: A Fair Melodrama of London Life," *Motion Picture News*, July 20, 1929.

128   not in the original story: Walk, "Anna May Wong and Weimar Cinema," 155–56.

128   **As a German émigré:** St. Pierre, *E. A. Dupont and His Contribution to British Film*, 84–85, 104–7.

128   **"Shosho and Valentine may not see":** Review of *Piccadilly*, *National Board of Review Magazine* 4, no. 4 (April 1929): 8–9.

128   **strangely, said nothing:** "The Screen," review of *Piccadilly*, *NYT*, July 15, 1929.

128   **The British media:** "Our Greatest Effort Yet: Why 'Piccadilly' Must Rank as Film of the Highest Grade," *Sunday Mirror* (London), Feb. 3, 1929; London correspondent, "A Memorable British Success," *Dundee Evening Telegraph*, Feb. 8, 1929.

128   **Anna May renewed her contract:** "News in Headlines," *Bioscope*, Oct. 24, 1928, contents page.

129   **Against Dupont's directorial wishes:** St. Pierre, *E. A. Dupont and His Contribution to British Film*, 107–8.

129   **Australia cut scenes showing:** MPAA/PCA records, AMPAS.

CHAPTER SIX

131   **another thinly veiled variation:** Walk, "Anna May Wong and Weimar Cinema," 140.

131   **filmed on location:** "Eichberg's Next: 'Pavement Butterfly,'" *Kinematograph Weekly*, March 14, 1929.

131   **The boisterous parade:** "The Passing Pageant of the Present Day," *Sphere*, Feb. 9, 1929; Geraldine Phillips Oppenheim, "Geraldine Phillips Oppenheim on Beaulieu: New Ideas in the Nice Carnival," *Bystander*, Feb. 13, 1929.

132   **the air of an Erté design:** Walk, "Anna May Wong and Weimar Cinema," 146.

132   **The mountains of fan mail:** Alma Whitaker, "Sugar and Spice," *LAT*, March 17, 1929.

132   **On a previous trip:** Morris, "Nothing but the Truth"; "Gilbert Miller Sails," *NYT*, June 16, 1927.

132   **In Germany:** Anna May Wong, "My Story," *Leven Advertiser and Wemyss Gazette*, Sept. 15, 1928.

133   **the first English production:** Wenwei Du, "*The Chalk Circle* Comes Full Circle: From Yuan Drama Through the Western Stage to Peking Opera," *Asian Theatre Journal* 12, no. 2 (Fall 1995).

133   **a series of long-distance telephone calls:** G. S. J., "Oriental Film Artist's Triumph"

134   **she was on her merry way:** "Film Star for the Footlights," *Era*, Jan. 16, 1929; "Aubrey Hammond," *Era*, Feb. 20, 1929; "Studios et plein air," *Pour Vous*, March 7, 1929, 14.

134   **retyping them wholesale:** Author interview with Richard See, 2020.

134   **like a florist shop:** Mayme Ober Peak, "Life of Anna May Wong Is Like a Chinese Fairy Tale," *Hartford (CT) Courant*, July 19, 1931.

134   **Princess Beatrice:** Wilcox, "Anna May Wong: A Story."

134   **"ever so much too long":** Herbert Farjeon, "The London Stage," *Graphic*, March 23, 1929.

135   **"as rich and bright":** J. T. Grein, "Criticisms in Cameo," *Sketch*, March 27, 1929.

135   **"There is a lack of austerity":** Farjeon, "The London Stage."

135   **"a dainty personality":** Grein, "Criticisms in Cameo."

135 **"exquisitely graceful"**: Charles Morgan, "Anna May Wong in a London Play," *NYT*, March 31, 1929.

135 **"To watch her"**: Trinculo, "The Passing Shows," *Tatler*, no. 1450, April 10, 1929.

135 **"It comes as a shock"**: Vernon Woodhouse, "At the Theatre: Old Days and Old China," *Bystander*, March 27, 1929.

135 **"Speaking with an American accent"**: Farjeon, "The London Stage."

135 **"Her speech is tinged"**: Grein, "Criticisms in Cameo."

136 **"talking so American"**: "A Guide for London Playgoers," *Graphic*, March 30, 1929.

136 **people who assumed**: Wong, "True Life Story of a Chinese Girl."

136 **only five weeks**: "London Amusements," *Daily Mirror* (London), April 20, 1929.

137 **"quite gently and charmingly"**: "If Gossip We Must," *Bystander*, May 22, 1929.

137 **invested a hundred guineas**: Wilcox, "Anna May Wong: A Story."

137 **acquire an English accent**: Scott, "European Bouquets Get Notice."

137 **"Now I will speak"**: Louella O. Parsons, "After 15 Months in London She Returns to Hollywood for Film Role," *LA Examiner*, Aug. 12, 1934.

137 **"the only leading lady"**: "A Canna-Balliol Yarn," *Bystander*, May 22, 1929.

137 **"Londoners liked the Chinese plot"**: "Broadway Chinese Scored," *LAT*, July 2, 1929.

138 **Any of her films**: Whit, "What to See at the Cinemas," *Liverpool Echo*, Jan. 15, 1929; "A Chinese Madame Butterfly: 'Crimson City' at Regent," *Leader,* March 22, 1929; "Pavilion Theatre," *Bucks Herald*, April 5, 1929; Scott, "European Bouquets Get Notice."

138 **"I like the English people"**: De Silva, *These Piquant People*, 53.

138 **"the only country"**: The Editor, "Looking 'Round," *Era*, Feb. 27, 1929.

139 **lunched at the Ivy**: Madame X, "A Woman's Letter," *Graphic*, March 23, 1929.

139 **old friend Edward Knoblock**: Grace Wilcox, "Whose Shoulders Do the Stars Cry on When They Are Blue?" *Oakland Tribune*, June 23, 1935.

139 **Her visit to the Law Courts**: W. H. M., "British Studios To-day," *Bioscope*, June 5, 1929, 43; "Home News in Brief," *Daily Mirror* (London), June 5, 1929.

139 **"I did not buy myself"**: Rivers, "Anna May Wong Sorry She Cannot Be Kissed."

139 **plays and musical revues**: AMW collection, Book 8407, NYPL.

139 **Constant Lambert accompanied her**: Mariegold, "Mariegold in Society," *Sketch*, June 5, 1929; "Expert's Eye," *Sunday Mirror* (London), June 2, 1929; "Chinese," *Daily News* (London), May 31, 1929.

139 **not so secretly obsessed**: Stephen Lloyd, *Constant Lambert: Beyond the Rio Grande* (Woodbridge, UK: Boydell Press, 2014), 80–81.

139 **It was whispered**: "If Gossip We Must," *Bystander*, Jan. 22, 1930.

140 **"When I was in Europe"**: Howe, "Between Two Worlds."

140 **She modeled Chinese shawls**: "In the Boudoir," *Graphic*, March 23, 1929.

140 **riding a horse through Hyde Park**: Fred Byron, "Comment le cinéma britannique combat la concurrence américaine," *Pour Vous*, Feb. 21, 1929.

140 **The photographers loved her**: G. S. J., "Oriental Film Artist's Triumph."

140 **"What I like about English country life"**: "'Mail' Mustard and Cress," *Hull Daily Mail*, June 12, 1929.

140 **all too happy to accept:** "People Who Play Active Parts," *Tatler*, May 22, 1929.

140 **She returned the favor:** Eleanor Smith, "From My Window in Vanity Fair," *Weekly Dispatch* (London), May 26, 1929.

141 **the "flapper election":** "London Notes," *Yorkshire Post*, May 31, 1929; "Echoes from Town," *Nottingham Evening Post*, May 31, 1929.

141 **Anna May had met them:** Bruce Kellner's transcripts of Carl Van Vechten's daybooks, Box 208, Carl Van Vechten papers, 1833–1965, Archives and Manuscripts, NYPL.

141 **on a holiday tour:** Carl Van Vechten, *The Splendid Drunken Twenties: Selections from the Daybooks, 1922–1930* ed. Bruce Kellner (Chicago: University of Illinois Press, 2003), 232.

141 **His reputation as patron saint:** Bernard, *Carl Van Vechten*, 1–2, 34–35, 40–41, 61–69.

142 **another well-known figure:** Martin Bauml Duberman, *Paul Robeson* (New York: Alfred A. Knopf, 1988), 4–10, 113–15.

143 **"To the white world":** Duberman, *Paul Robeson*, xi.

143 **One day while walking home:** Duberman, *Paul Robeson*, 6.

143 **beaten within an inch of his life:** Duberman, *Paul Robeson*, 19–23.

144 **at one college dance:** Duberman, *Paul Robeson*, 24–25.

144 **his acting and singing career:** Duberman, *Paul Robeson*, 32, 43–44.

144 **Robeson was hired by the law firm:** Duberman, *Paul Robeson*, 54–55.

144 **His first notable role:** Duberman, *Paul Robeson*, 55–59.

144 *All God's Chillun* **opened:** Duberman, *Paul Robeson*, 63–67

145 **sit down for a meal:** Duberman, *Paul Robeson*, 87.

145 **By the summer of 1925:** Duberman, *Paul Robeson*, 77–78, 86.

145 **Paul found English society:** Duberman, *Paul Robeson*, 118.

146 **"Everyone who is anyone":** "The Business Genius Who Entertains London on Election Night," *Sketch*, May 29, 1929.

146 **closed off an entire floor:** "The Passing Hour," *Bystander*, June 5, 1929.

146 **"On to the . . . election party":** Van Vechten, *The Splendid Drunken Twenties*, 247–48.

146 **ordinary Londoners:** G. Eden, "Election Platform," *Daily News* (London), May 30, 1929.

146 **Grace Wilcox traveled to England:** Alma Whitaker, "Sugar and Spice," *LAT*, May 5, 1929.

147 **husband's sudden death:** "Stricken Man Dies Trying to Summon Help," *LAT*, May 15, 1929.

147 **It was decided that Lulu:** "Dietz Rites Delayed," *LAT*, May 18, 1929; "Lulu Wong, Actress, Homesick; Returning," *LA Examiner*, May 30, 1929.

147 **She had her fun:** "Rum Runners' Retreat," *Era*, June 12, 1929.

147 **Anna May much preferred:** Grace Wilcox, "Hollywood Buries Its Nose in a Book as Stars Go Literary," *Oakland Tribune*, Feb. 3, 1935.

147 **Godden Green sanatorium:** UK National Trust records; Conrad Doerr, "Anna May Wong," *Films in Review*, Dec. 1968, 661; author interview with Conrad Doerr, 2022.

147 **the first stop:** "Henley and Hymen," *Tatler*, July 10, 1929.

147 **A reporter from the French movie magazine:** Louis Delaprée, "Une matinée au Louvre avec Anna May Wong," *Pour Vous*, July 18, 1929.

150 **If they wanted to keep up:** Ursula Hardt, *From Caligari to California: Erich Pommer's Life in the International Film Wars* (Providence, RI: Berghahn Books, 1996), 126–29.

150 **a few plays here and there:** AMW collection, NYPL.

150 ***Dear Carl Van Vechten*:** AMW to CVV, Sept. 26, 1929, Carl Van Vechten Papers, Yale Beinecke Library.

151 **a deal to make four "supers":** "News in Headlines," *Bioscope*, Oct. 24, 1928.

152 **Robeson had announced:** Duberman, *Paul Robeson*, 122–23.

152 **a letter Paul had written:** "The Colour Bar: Mr. Paul Robeson's Hotel Experience; A London Incident," *Scotsman*, Oct. 23, 1929.

152 **the first Black actor:** Samantha Ellis, "Paul Robeson in Othello, Savoy Theatre, 1930," *Guardian*, Sept. 3, 2003, accessed Feb. 16, 2022, https://www.theguardian.com/stage/2003/sep/03/theatre.

152 **the production was troubled:** Duberman, *Paul Robeson*, 133–36.

153 **sat prominently in the audience:** Duberman, *Paul Robeson*, 136; Mariegold, "Mariegold in Society," *Sketch*, May 28, 1930.

153 **"A.M.W. like a brontosaurus":** Evelyn Waugh, *The Diaries of Evelyn Waugh*, ed. Michael Davie (London: Wiedenfeld and Nicolson, 1976), 309.

153 **"Hopeless production":** Waugh, *Diaries of Evelyn Waugh*, 311.

153 **the ill-advised headline:** "When It's Wong to Kiss: Censor's Ban on New Film," *Weekly Dispatch* (London), Nov. 10, 1929.

154 **"It's all absolute rot!":** "John Longden Is Very Emphatic," *Derby (England) Daily Telegraph*, Nov. 23, 1929.

154 **"We are to have many love scenes":** "And Ne'er the Lips Shall Meet," *Daily News* (London), Nov. 11, 1929; "Mr. Longden and Miss Wong," *Daily News* (London), Nov. 12, 1929.

154 **"Once again, I have to die":** "Ne'er the Lips Shall Meet," *Daily News* (London).

154 **Black Tuesday came and went:** "Global Impact 1929–1939," Encyclopedia.com, accessed Feb. 8, 2023, https://www.encyclopedia.com/education/news-and-education-magazines/global-impact-1929-1939.

154 **Clubs like Clärchens Ballhaus:** Michael Waters, "People in 1920s Berlin Nightclubs Flirted via Pneumatic Tubes," *Atlas Obscura*, June 21, 2017, https://www.atlasobscura.com/articles/pneumatic-tube-table-phone-flirting-berlin.

154 **"Visitors who like to dance":** Franz Hessel, *Walking in Berlin: A Flaneur in the Capital* (Cambridge, MA: MIT Press, 2017), 43.

154 **mad for costume balls:** "Berlin Dance Craze Grows," *NYT*, Dec. 2, 1926; Lincoln Eyre, "Berlin Will Dance Through Holidays," *NYT*, Dec. 25, 1927; "Pleasure Palace Is Being Built in Berlin with Seven Large Halls for 10,000 Guests," *NYT*, Nov. 19, 1927.

155 **Reimann School of Art and Design's Gauklerfest:** "Snapshots from the Reimann Ball 1930," *Farbe und Form*, Feb./March 1930, 55; C. Arthur Croyle, *Hertwig: The Zelig of Design* (Ames, IA: Culicidae Architectural Press, 2011), 148.

155 **Two little-known German actresses:** Alfred Eisenstaedt, *People* (New York: Viking Press, 1973), 22–23.

156   **"a friendly touch of colour"**: Marlene Dietrich, *Marlene Dietrich: My Life*, trans. Salvator Attanasio (London: Wieden and Nicolson, 1989), 43–44.

156   **the symbolic flower of "the girls"**: Maria Riva, *Marlene Dietrich: The Life* (New York: Pegasus Books, 1992), 58.

156   **The revue was a smash hit:** Karin Wieland, *Dietrich & Riefenstahl: Hollywood, Berlin, and a Century in Two Lives*, trans. Shelley Frisch (New York: Liveright, 2011), 71–74.

156   **A young photographer:** Eisenstaedt, *People*, 5; Alfred Eisenstaedt, *Eisenstaedt on Eisenstaedt: A Self-Portrait* (New York: Abbeville, 1985), 8, 28.

156   **Only one of them:** Patrice Petro, "Cosmopolitan Women: Marlene Dietrich, Anna May Wong, and Leni Riefenstahl," in *Silent Cinema and the Politics of Space*, eds. Jennifer M. Bean, Anupama Kapse, and Laura Horak (Bloomington: Indiana University Press, 2014), 297–301.

157   **Austrian by birth:** "Josef von Sternberg, Film Director, Is Dead," *NYT*, Dec. 23, 1969.

157   **he'd added the "von":** Charles Higham, *Marlene: The Life of Marlene Dietrich* (New York: W. W. Norton, 1977), 81; Riva, *Marlene Dietrich*, 60–61.

158   **negotiated a deal:** Higham, *Marlene*, 82; Baxter, "Berlin Year Zero," 166–67.

158   **An exhaustive search was held:** Baxter, "Berlin Year Zero," 170–71.

158   **Marlene was spending long days:** Riva, *Marlene Dietrich*, 127.

158   **Marlene dominated "the little man":** Baxter, "Berlin Year Zero," 176, 183.

158   **"It's amazing the skill":** "Direktor Goldschmid über Elstree," *Der Kinematograph*, Nov. 26, 1929.

158   **a premiere of her own:** Weiland, *Dietrich & Riefenstahl*, 172; Riva, *Marlene Dietrich*, 78.

159   **urged Paramount to sign her:** Riva, *Marlene Dietrich*, 75–77; Dietrich, *Marlene Dietrich*, 57–58.

159   **Silence fell upon the entire theater:** Baxter, "Berlin Year Zero," 187.

159   **thirty-six pieces of luggage:** Higham, *Marlene*, 94.

159   **as if he could kill her:** Photo of Marlene Dietrich and Emil Jannings: https://www.pinterest.com/pin/366832332142596817/.

159   **"I don't leave Berlin lightly":** Baxter, "Berlin Year Zero," 187.

160   **She bounced around Europe:** "Anna May Wong in Budapest," *Bioscope*, April 2, 1930; "More Horses for Your Note Book," *Bystander*, April 23, 1930; Captain C. E. Ward, "Flying Notes: Advantages of the Moth," *Bystander*, May 14, 1930; "On the Set!" *Tatler*, April 9, 1930.

160   **While there, she:** AMW collection, NYPL; Waugh, *Diaries of Evelyn Waugh*, 311.

160   **She hired a strict tutor:** H. J., "Anna May Wong learnt Französlilch: Und wird im Herbst in Wien am Theater spielen," *Mein Film*, June 1930, 7.

160   **the police were called:** "Citing Exception When the Twain Did Meet," *Brooklyn Times-Union*.

160   **"the most popular stage star":** "Productions, Projections, Reflections," *Pasadena Post*, Sept. 24, 1930.

160   **After twenty-five performances:** Hodges, *Anna May Wong*, 94–96.

160 **preoccupied with a dream:** E. Le Berthon, "Anna May Wong Was a Laundryman's Daughter," *Picturegoer*, Oct. 17, 1931.

161 **embarked on the RMS *Aquitania*:** "Seven Liners Leave Today, Four Arrive: Stage Notables on the *Aquitania*—Other Ships Due from Europe and South," *NYT*, Oct. 17, 1930.

161 **with only one trunk:** Scott, "European Bouquets Get Notice."

161 **she had every intention:** Mordaunt Hall, "The Screen: Anna May Wong, Homesick, Returns," *NYT*, Oct. 18, 1930.

161 **theater producer Lee Ephraim:** "All for Mr. Wallace: A Chinese Actress Reaches Broadway, and If She Is Not Wong, Sue Her," *NYT*, Nov. 16, 1930.

161 **"bogus wop gang leader":** J. Brooks Atkinson, "The Play," *NYT*, Oct. 30, 1930.

161 **She arrived in New York:** Scott, "European Bouquets Get Notice."

161 **The play opened on Broadway:** Rowland Field, "The New Play," *Brooklyn Times-Union*, Oct. 30, 1930.

162 **come to regret:** Peak, "Life of Anna May Wong Is Like a Chinese Fairy Tale."

162 **Her mother had been struck:** "Mother of Anna Wong Car Victim," *LAT*, Nov. 11, 1930.

162 **Two days later:** "Anna Wong's Mother Dies," *NYT*, Nov. 12, 1930.

162 **"I've just been admitting it":** Carl Van Vechten, *Parties: Scenes from Contemporary New York Life* (New York: Avon Books, 1977), 79.

CHAPTER SEVEN

165 **two-week-long heat wave:** "Los Angeles Weather in 1930," Extreme Weather Watch, accessed March 19, 2023, https://www.extremeweatherwatch.com/cities/los-angeles/year-1930#november.

165 **she'd been a child herself:** Anna May Wong, file no. 14036-239, NARA–Riverside, 92–93.

165 **observing her mother:** Wong, "True Life Story of a Chinese Girl."

165 **Lee Gon Toy struggled to make sense:** Harry Carr, "The Lancer," *LAT*, Nov. 15, 1930.

166 **the dimly lit street:** "Driver Freed in Death of Anna Wong's Mother," *LA Evening Citizen News*, Nov. 13, 1930.

166 **a car suddenly appeared:** "Anna May Wong's Mother Hit Down," *LA Daily News*, Nov. 11, 1930.

166 **with devastating force:** "Mother of Anna Wong Car Victim," *LAT*, Nov. 11, 1930.

166 **was not held by police:** "Driver Freed in Death of Anna Wong's Mother," *LA Evening Citizen News*.

167 **Her father told her:** Howe, "Between Two Worlds."

167 **"Then the terrible news":** Grace Kingsley, "Paramount Casts Unknowns," *LAT*, Nov. 18, 1930.

167 **"It was unthinkable":** Howe, "Between Two Worlds."

167 **Jeanne Winters was announced:** "Theatre Notes," *NY Daily News*, Nov. 11, 1930.

168 **the beliefs of Christian Science:** Howe, "Between Two Worlds."

168 **the prolific author:** Michael Mallory, "Edgar Wallace: The Man Who Wrote Too Much?," *Mystery Scene Magazine,* Summer Issue #130, accessed Nov. 18, 2022, https://www.mysteryscenemag.com/article/3241-edgar-wallace-the-man-who-wrote-too-much; "Edgar Wallace Dead," *Dundee Courier,* Feb. 11, 1932; "Edgar Wallace, Noted Writer, Dies," *NYT,* Feb. 11, 1932; "Word of Death Shocks London," *NYT,* Feb. 11, 1932.

168 **"the gangster's grotesque jargon":** J. Brooks Atkinson, "The Play," review of *On the Spot, NYT,* Oct. 30, 1930.

168 **"tremendously entertaining":** Trinculo, "The Passing Shows: 'On the Spot,' at Wyndham's Theatre," *Tatler,* May 7, 1930.

169 **The subject hit a little too close:** "Cermak to Ban Plays on Chicago Gang Life," *NYT,* April 29, 1931.

169 **stripped all mentions of Chicago:** "Play 'Eased' for Chicago," *NYT,* April 30, 1931.

169 **"refreshingly amusing":** Atkinson, "The Play."

169 **earning her praise:** David Carb, "Seen on the Stage," *Vogue,* Dec. 22, 1930, 78.

169 **"the best suicide":** Percy Hammond, "Coming Over the Hill," *Harper's Bazaar,* March 1931, 96, 113.

169 **a literal knife to the heart:** Edgar Wallace, *On the Spot* (Garden City, NY: Doubleday, Doran, 1930), 310–13.

169 **One night a stagehand:** Anna May Wong, "My Film Thrills," *Film Pictorial,* Nov. 11, 1933, 6.

169 **167 performances:** Amnon Kabatchnik, *Blood on the Stage, 1925–1950: Milestone Plays of Crime, Mystery, and Detection: An Annotated Repertoire* (Plymouth, UK: Scarecrow Press, 2010), 288.

169 **a five-city road tour:** "Drama of Gangland Is Lone Opening Booked for Monday," *Courier-Post* (New Jersey), March 16, 1931; W. W. S., review of *On the Spot,* by Edgar Wallace, *Brooklyn Standard Union,* March 24, 1931; review of *On the Spot, Boston Globe,* April 6, 1931; "Play 'Eased' for Chicago," *NYT;* "Actresses Prominent in Coming Stage Plays," *Pittsburgh Press,* April 24, 1913; "One Play Opens This Week," *Philadelphia Inquirer,* May 17, 1931.

170 **"to glow and dazzle":** Carr, "The Lancer," *LAT,* Nov. 15, 1930.

170 **"Because Miss Wong":** Rosa Reilly, "Is the Stage the Port of Missing Screen Stars?" *Screenland,* Feb. 1931.

170 **"slip through their fingers":** Grace Kingsley, "Paramount Casts Unknowns."

170 **Various offers:** "Remember Her?" *Screenland,* Oct. 1931, 83.

170 **a contract with Paramount:** "Anna May Wong Signs Long Term Contract with Movie Company," *Brooklyn Standard Union,* March 31, 1931.

170 **Paramount announced the deal:** "Finds Preference for Clean Films," *NYT,* April 17, 1931.

170 **"Back in the old days":** "Productions, Projections, Reflections," *Pasadena Post,* April 14, 1931.

171 **rented herself an apartment:** Grace Kingsley, "Former Screen Stars Return," *LAT,* June 9, 1931.

171 **"the finest address in Hollywood":** Image of Castle-Argyle Arms, Calisphere, University of California, accessed Nov. 18, 2022, https://calisphere.org/item/d125c c1bccd1e092e386e73cd05eab16/.

171 **rehearsals regrettably kept her:** Kingsley, "Former Screen Stars Return."

172 **talked of buying a house:** "Remember Her?," *Screenland.*

172 **$50,000 in damages:** "Family Sues for Mother's Death," *LAT*, Feb. 3, 1931.

172 **At long last:** Howe, "Between Two Worlds."

172 **Fu Manchu was the summation:** Sax Rohmer, *The Insidious Dr. Fu-Manchu* (New York: A. L. Burt, 1913), 25–26.

174 **"absurdly fantastic and unreal":** "Daughter of the Dragon," *Bioscope*, Nov. 4, 1931, 23, 25.

174 **especially with the kids:** Mordaunt Hall, "Fu Manchu's Daughter," review of *Daughter of the Dragon*, *NYT*, Aug. 22, 1931.

174 **"with dragons on the walls":** Hall, "Fu Manchu's Daughter."

174 **The final budget:** Paramount Pictures production records, AMPAS.

174 **"a preposterous and draggy story":** Review of *Daughter of the Dragon*, *Film Daily*, Aug. 23, 1931, press clippings, Core Collection, production files, AMPAS.

174 **"Too much effort":** Review of *Daughter of the Dragon, Variety*, Aug. 25, 1931, press clippings, Core Collection, production files, AMPAS.

175 **an interview of the two actors:** Willis, "Famous Oriental Stars Return to the Screen."

175 **"Unimportant as a picture":** Muriel Babcock, "'Daughter of Dragon' Shown," *LAT*, Aug. 29, 1931.

175 **Hayakawa had left Hollywood:** Daisuke Miyao, *Sessue Hayakawa: Silent Cinema and Transnational Stardom* (Durham, NC: Duke University Press, 2007), 214, 223–24.

175 **which culminated in:** "The Immigration Act of 1924 (The Johnson-Reed Act)," Milestones: 1921–1936, Office of the Historian, U.S. State Department, accessed Nov. 20, 2022, https://history.state.gov/milestones/1921-1936/immigration-act.

175 **sensed the growing agitation:** Miyao, *Sessue Hayakawa*, 231.

175 **he traveled to greener pastures:** Willis, "Famous Oriental Stars Return to the Screen."

175 **a $10,000 flat fee:** Paramount Pictures production records, AMPAS.

175 **"I am very happy to be filming":** Genova, "La petite Cendrillon chinoise."

176 **crazed lady fans:** Epigraph by Miyatake Toyo, in Miyao, *Sessue Hayakawa*, 1.

176 **"He does moderately well":** Hall, "Fu Manchu's Daughter."

176 **"He does not manage":** Babcock, "'Daughter of Dragon' Shown."

176 **Hollywood's first heartthrob:** Miyao, *Sessue Hayakawa*, 3–4, 227.

176 **"As a general thing":** Harry Carr, "The Lancer," *LAT*, Sept. 3, 1931.

177 **Hollywood's favorite villain:** S. R. Mook, "The Villains Are Coming!," *Screenland*, Nov. 1931.

177 **paid him handsomely:** Paramount Pictures production records, AMPAS.

177 **Oland had just returned:** Yunte Huang, *Charlie Chan: The Untold Story of the Honorable Detective and His Rendezvous with American History* (New York: W. W. Norton, 2010), 143.

177   **Chan was a gentleman:** E. G. Cousins, "A Chinaman Who Isn't," *Picturegoer Weekly*, July 4, 1936.

177   **Earl Derr Biggers from Pasadena:** Ken Hanke, *Charlie Chan at the Movies: History, Filmography, and Criticism* (Jefferson, NC: McFarland, 1989), xi–xii.

178   **Born Johan Verner Ölund:** Frank Perrett, "Chan Alias Oland," *Democrat & Chronicle*, March 14, 1937.

178   **"the Swede who became a Chinese":** J. C. M., "The Swede Who Became a Chinese," *Kansas City Star*, Aug. 4, 1929.

178   **required almost no makeup:** H. H. Niemeyer, "Warner Oland Is the Screen's Best Oriental," *St. Louis Post-Dispatch*, Jan. 11, 1935.

179   **"You have no idea":** J. C. M., "The Swede Who Became a Chinese."

179   **"So far as the picture proves":** Review of *Daughter of the Dragon, Variety*, press clippings, AMPAS.

179   **"a flaming and brilliant personality":** Harry Carr, "The Lancer," *LAT*, April 4, 1931.

179   **"It may yet come to pass":** Grace Kingsley, "Powell Weds Actress Soon: Miss Wong's Next Film," *LAT*, June 12, 1931.

180   **"It is my hope":** J. C. M., "The Swede Who Became a Chinese."

180   **Fox purchased the rights:** Hanke, *Charlie Chan at the Movies*, xiii.

180   **more than twenty actors:** Perrett, "Chan Alias Oland."

180   **"This Charlie Chan":** Niemeyer, "Warner Oland Is the Screen's Best Oriental."

180   **"Much as I love the part":** Grace Kingsley, "Warner Oland Even Gets His Fan Mail in Name of Famous Charlie Chan," *LAT*, June 30, 1935.

181   **He began speaking to his wife:** "Warner Oland Feels Chinese: Wife Heartily Confirms Statement," *China Press*, March 15, 1936.

181   **"He imbibed between shots":** Hanke, *Charlie Chan at the Movies*, 81.

181   **a very rich man:** Huang, *Charlie Chan*, 259–60, 262.

181   **acquired four homes:** Kingsley, "Warner Oland Even Gets His Fan Mail in Name of Famous Charlie Chan"; Niemeyer, "Swede Who Made Fortune as Chinaman."

181   **"Husband and wife?":** Hodges, *Anna May Wong*, 101.

182   **Negotiations with Edward Belasco:** Muriel Babcock, "Coast Lures Colorful Trio: Anna May Wong May Do 'On the Spot' Here," *LAT*, June 2, 1931.

182   **Contracts were inked:** Muriel Babcock, "'On the Spot' Stars Signed," *LAT*, July 16, 1931; "Star Trio Will Play in Drama," *LAT*, Aug. 5, 1931; "Current Drama," *LAT*, Aug. 23, 1931.

182   **her "sensational rise":** Babcock, "Coast Lures Colorful Trio."

182   **One journalist saw the outpouring:** "Even Bootleggers Take Gangster Play Seriously," *LAT*, Sept. 6, 1931.

182   **"hoydenish and slightly crude":** Grace Kingsley, "Cinema Nomads Achieve Fame," *LAT*, June 20, 1931.

182   **"to now be back in Hollywood":** Genova, "La petite Cendrillon chinoise."

182   **"I always say":** Willis, "Famous Oriental Stars Return to the Screen."

183   **"Wasn't it Byron who said":** Harold W. Cohen, "Film Facts," *Pittsburgh Post-Gazette*, May 1, 1931.

184   **"It is my dream":** Berthon, "Anna May Wong Was a Laundryman's Daughter."

CHAPTER EIGHT

188   **"[Jo] kept raving":** Jesse L. Lasky, with Don Weldon, *I Blow My Own Horn* (Garden City, NY: Doubleday, 1957), 221.

188   **she lopped off:** The Oracle, "Information, Please," *Picture-Play*, September 1932.

188   **Jo had long harbored:** Author correspondence with Maria and Peter Riva, 2022.

188   **When Marlene arrived:** Riva, *Marlene Dietrich*, 83–85; Wieland, *Dietrich & Riefenstahl*, 182.

190   **Production on *Shanghai Express*:** Paramount Pictures production records, AMPAS.

191   **a new mandate:** Thomas Doherty, *Hollywood's Censor: Joseph I. Breen and the Production Code Administration* (New York: Columbia University Press, 2007), 41–46, 352.

191   **"a single page":** Josef von Sternberg, *Fun in a Chinese Laundry* (New York: Macmillan, 1965), 263; John Baxter, *Von Sternberg* (Lexington: University Press of Kentucky, 2010), 142.

191   **He'd already proven:** Higham, *Marlene*, 108.

191   **"He smiled when I told him":** Von Sternberg, *Fun in a Chinese Laundry*, 242.

192   **"A sea of banners":** Riva, *Marlene Dietrich*, 125.

192   **B-roll footage:** Rainsberger, *James Wong Howe*, 18.

192   **Another fiction peculiar:** Anthony B. Chan, *Perpetually Cool: The Many Lives of Anna May Wong (1905–1961)* (Lanham, MD: Scarecrow Press, 2007), 227–28.

194   **They were cultured women:** Riva, *Marlene Dietrich*, 123.

194   **records by Richard Tauber:** Hans J. Wollstein, *Vixens, Floozies and Molls: 28 Actresses of Late 1920s and 1930s Hollywood* (Jefferson, NC: McFarland, 1999), 253.

194   **They sipped coffee:** Riva, *Marlene Dietrich*, 127.

195   **left nothing to chance:** Riva, *Marlene Dietrich*, 115–20.

195   **More than $1,600:** Paramount Pictures production records, AMPAS.

195   **On the first day of filming:** Donald Spoto, *Blue Angel: The Life of Marlene Dietrich* (New York: Doubleday, 1992), 86; Riva, *Marlene Dietrich*, 114–15.

195   **"If *you* believe I am skilled enough":** Riva, *Marlene Dietrich*, 119.

195   **Marlene's look had all eyes on her:** Riva, *Marlene Dietrich*, 116–19, 125–26.

196   **"An actor is turned on":** Von Sternberg, *Fun in a Chinese Laundry*, 165–66.

196   **preposterous demands:** Baxter, *Von Sternberg*, 145–46.

196   **he barked commands:** Lasky, *I Blow My Own Horn*, 222.

197   **"First, he was Clive Brook":** Higham, *Marlene*, 115.

197   **A swig here or there:** Hanke, *Charlie Chan at the Movies*, 81.

197   **"It took me hours":** Von Sternberg, *Fun in a Chinese Laundry*, 106.

197   **Grace was extended solely:** Riva, *Marlene Dietrich*, 99, 126–27.

198   **"She wasn't sure of herself":** Higham, *Marlene*, 105–6.

198   **found Jo's direction invigorating:** Marguerite Tazelaar, "The Occidental Anna May Wong Is Found in Oriental New York," *NYHT*, April 3, 1932.

198   **she pulled an all-nighter:** A. H. T., "Miss Wong Won Way by Hard Work," *China Press*, Feb. 15, 1936.

198   **The MPAA also submitted changes:** MPAA/PCA records, AMPAS.

199 **lacked the teeth:** Doherty, *Hollywood's Censor,* 52–56.

202 **"I was glad for once":** Kathryn Applegate, "Famous Movie Actress Enjoys Visit Here After Strenuous Days in East," *Muncie (IN) Star Press,* June 1, 1932.

202 **an assistant designer:** Peter Ballbusch, Josef von Sternberg papers, AMPAS.

202 **the great Dietrich's affairs:** Author interview with Maria Riva, 2022.

203 **Marlene invited actor friend:** Higham, *Marlene,* 114–15.

203 **"Paramount Utilizes Anna May Wong":** MPAA/PCA records, AMPAS.

204 **it had been under siege:** Erin Blakemore, "How Japan Took Control of Korea," History.com, July 28, 2020, accessed Nov. 25, 2022, https://www.history.com/news/japan -colonization-korea.

204 **One week later:** "'Shanghai Express' Due Today," *LAT,* Feb. 4, 1932.

204 **Newspaper headlines:** "'Shanghai Express' Is Booked," *LA Record,* Feb. 1, 1932; Edwin Schallert, "Timely Movie Released Soon," *LAT,* Jan. 29, 1932.

205 **In his review:** Philip K. Scheuer, "'Shanghai Express' Here," *LAT,* Feb. 6, 1932.

205 **"an impressive performance":** Mordaunt Hall, "The Screen: Marlene Dietrich in a Brilliantly Directed Melodrama Set Aboard a Train Running from Peiping to Shanghai," *NYT,* Feb. 18, 1932.

205 **writer Ayn Rand:** Von Sternberg, *Fun in a Chinese Laundry,* 263.

205 **in London and Berlin:** Albert A. Sander, "German Producers Facing Crisis," *Era,* April 27, 1932.

205 **Lee Garmes won:** "The 5th Academy Awards, 1933," Oscars.org, accessed Nov. 25, 2022, https://www.oscars.org/oscars/ceremonies/1933.

205 **a popularity contest:** Baxter, *Von Sternberg,* 150.

206 **"the brave Chinese girl":** Hall, "The Screen: Marlene Dietrich in a Brilliantly Directed Melodrama."

206 **there was no mention:** "Shanghai Express," *Bioscope,* March 23, 1932, 19.

206 **"That sliding gait":** Edwin Schallert, "New Players' Stock Rises: The Rhythmic Anna May," *LAT,* March 1, 1932.

206 **A few days before:** John Scott, "Filmdom Tough on Cinderellas," *LAT,* Jan. 31, 1932.

CHAPTER NINE

209 **stretching her salary:** Robert McIlwaine, "Third Beginning," *Modern Screen,* Dec. 1937.

210 ***The Honorable Mr. Wong:*** Grace Kingsley, "Unsympathetic Roles Scorned," *LAT,* Nov. 2, 1931.

210 **a new Asian actress:** Dan Thomas, "Hollywood Gossip," *Journal* (Connecticut), Aug. 26, 1932.

210 **Her name was Toshia Mori:** Grace Kingsley, "New Oriental Star Appears," *LAT,* Sept. 25, 1931.

210 **RKO cast her:** Irene Thirer, "Orient in Newsreel Spotlight," *NY Daily News,* Feb. 8, 1932.

210 **breaking her engagements:** Hubbard Keavy, "Screen Life in Hollywood," *Burlington Free Press* (Vermont), March 2, 1932.

210 **completely rewritten:** Louella O. Parsons, "Barbara Stanwick to Star in Play by Sam Behrman," *Fresno Bee*, March 1, 1932.

210 **headlining a stage act:** Mordaunt Hall, "Screen," *NYT*, April 4, 1932.

211 **Box office receipts:** Cedric Belfrage, "Broadway's Talkies, Shows and Speakeasies," *Sunday Express* (London), April 17, 1932.

211 **"unload their so-so pictures":** Karen Hollis, "They Say in New York—," *Picture-Play*, Oct. 1932, 25.

211 **One journalist:** "Anna May Wong in Person, Mastbaum," *Philadelphia Inquirer*, June 25, 1932.

211 **at the Cotton Club:** Walter Winchell, "On Broadway," *Wisconsin State Journal*, May 3, 1932.

212 **the first to officially sit:** Bruce Kellner, *Carl Van Vechten and the Irreverent Decades* (Norman: Oklahoma University Press, 1969), 258–60.

212 **"Wanted to tell you":** AMW to CVV, May 5, 1932.

212 **Of the images:** Carl Van Vechten Papers, Yale Beinecke Library.

212 **"To tell the truth":** AMW to CVV, July 21, 1932.

213 **"Life is just a Pola Negri":** Cedric Belfrage, "Talkies—and Show People—in an Atlantic Liner," *Sunday Express* (London), April 10, 1932; Belfrage, "Broadway's Talkies, Shows and Speakeasies."

213 **a British reporter:** Cedric Belfrage, "Off to Hollywood," *Sunday Express* (London), April 3, 1932.

213 **a shy, wispy plank of a man:** Eric Maschwitz, *No Chip on My Shoulder* (London: Herbert Jenkins, 1957), 59–60.

214 **time to think it over:** Maschwitz, *No Chip on My Shoulder*, 62; lyrics to "These Foolish Things (Remind Me of You)."

214 **waiting to hear:** Applegate, "Famous Movie Actress Enjoys Visit Here."

214 **involvement in the project:** Relman Morin, "Russian Star Returns to Pictures," *LA Evening Post-Record*, May 2, 1932; "Pictures and Players," *NYT*, May 8, 1932.

214 **Brenon's first request:** "Brenon Gets Story of Chinese Intrigue," *Detroit Free Press*, June 5, 1932.

214 **two-page magazine spread:** *The Bitter Tea of General Yen* magazine ad, 1932, source unknown.

214 **"I never count too much":** Applegate, "Famous Movie Actress Enjoys Visit Here."

214 **a young director:** "Screen Notes," *Brooklyn Times-Union*, June 21, 1932.

214 **studio brass replaced Cummings:** Louella O. Parsons, "Hollywood Highlights," *Modesto Bee*, June 22, 1932.

214 **a headline ran:** "Chinatown Girl Wins Role: Toshia Mori Newest Film Cinderella," *LAT*, June 27, 1932.

215 **"To make these pictures":** Mollie Merrick, "Studios Back Up Their Big Stars on Salaries Despite Economy," *Spokane Spokesman-Review*, July 3, 1932.

215 **Hollywood on Parade:** Brooklyn Paramount ad, *Brooklyn Daily Eagle*, April 11, 1932, 13; Mastbaum Theater ad, *Courier Post* (New Jersey), June 25, 1932, page 5; E. de

S. Melcher, "An Essay Goes Forward to Movies of the Future," *Evening Star* (Washington, D.C.), July 24, 1932.

215   **"'Four a Day' life":** AMW to CVV, July 31, 1932.

215   **Una Merkel was a woman:** "Anna May Wong Has Never Been to China," *Film Pictorial*, May 27, 1933, found in Larry Sean Kinder, *Una Merkel: The Actress with Sassy Wit and Southern Charm* (Albany, GA: BearManor Media, 2016), 81.

215   **shared a hotel suite:** Philippa, "Almost in Confidence," *Hong Kong Sunday Herald*, March 22, 1936, found in Larry Sean Kinder, *Una Merkel*, 81–82.

215   **he would soon leave:** AMW to CVV, Sept. 21, 1932.

216   **"She could be ideal":** Grace Kingsley, "Studio Looks for Hercules," *LAT*, Sept. 8, 1932.

216   **awoke to find her name:** "Miss Wong Accused in an Auto Accident," *NYT*, Sept. 12, 1932.

216   **Anna May was furious:** AMW to CVV, Sept. 21, 1932.

217   **Rumors that Samuel Shipman:** Wood Soanes, "Curtain Calls," *Oakland Tribune*, June 14, 1932.

217   *Shanghai Interlude*: Grace Kingsley, "Universal Buys War Story," *LAT*, March 14, 1932.

217   **"I made a test":** AMW to CVV, Sept. 21, 1932.

217   **role of supportive friend:** "Screen Scraps," *Philadelphia Inquirer*, Dec. 25, 1932.

218   **"Hollywood is experiencing":** Harry Carr, "The Lancer," *LAT*, Nov. 21, 1932.

218   **"Anna May Wong says":** Grace Kinsgley, "Hobnobbing in Hollywood," *LAT*, Nov. 15, 1932.

218   **fortunes rise and fall:** Hilary Spurling, *Pearl Buck in China: Journey to* The Good Earth (New York: Simon & Schuster, 2010), 133–34.

219   **American by birthright:** Spurling, *Pearl Buck in China*, 1–2, 6–7, 10–11.

219   **"If America was for dreaming":** Spurling, *Pearl Buck in China*, 2.

219   **stuck in a perfunctory marriage:** Spurling, *Pearl Buck in China*, 137–39.

219   **When Dorothy Canfield Fisher:** Peter Conn, *Pearl S. Buck: A Cultural Biography* (Cambridge, UK: Cambridge University Press, 1996), 122–23.

219   **"its deeper implications":** "'The Good Earth' and Other Recent Works of Fiction," *NYT*, March 15, 1931.

220   **"Many stories and novels":** "'The Good Earth' Story of Chinese by Pearl S. Buck," *Brooklyn Times-Union*, March 15, 1931.

220   **"One tends to forget":** "'The Good Earth' and Other Recent Works of Fiction," *NYT*.

220   **dominating bestseller lists:** "Fast, Fun Facts About *The Good Earth*," Oprah.com, Sept. 15, 2004, https://www.oprah.com/oprahsbookclub/fast-facts-about-the-good-earth/all.

220   **reached its twenty-second printing:** "Guild Will Present 'The Good Earth,'" *NYT*, April 22, 1932.

220   **netting more than $100,000:** Spurling, *Pearl Buck in China*, 203.

220   **she received a cablegram:** Alexander Woollcott, "Shouts and Murmurs: The Vanishing Lady," *New Yorker*, Aug. 13, 1932.

220   **"I think *Good Earth*":** Applegate, "Famous Movie Actress Enjoys Visit Here."

220   **Thalberg had a reputation:** Mark A. Vieira, *Irving Thalberg: Boy Wonder to Producer Prince* (Berkeley: University of California Press, 2010), 8.

221   **A dramatization:** "Guild Will Present 'The Good Earth,'" *NYT*.

221 **Translating the book:** Bob Thomas, *Thalberg: The Life and Legend* (Garden City, NY: Doubleday, 1969), 303–4.

221 **the deal for screen rights:** Spurling, *Pearl Buck in China*, 202.

221 **it was rumored:** Grace Kingsley, "Long Location Trips Planned," *LAT*, April 11, 1932; Florabel Muir, "'The Good Earth' Must Be Earthy, Says Film Pact," *NY Daily News*, April 12, 1932.

221 **an all-Chinese cast:** James L. Hoban, Jr., "Scripting *The Good Earth*: Versions of the Novel for the Screen," in *The Several Worlds of Pearl S. Buck*, eds. Elizabeth J. Lipscomb, Frances E. Webb, and Peter Conn (Westport, CT: Greenwood Press, 1994), 130; Wood Soanes, "Curtain Calls," *Oakland Tribune*, Sept. 20, 1933.

221 **"We shouldn't be a bit surprised":** Grace Kingsley, "Oriental Film Plays Planned," *LAT*, Sept. 19, 1931.

221 **"The town is speculating":** Chapin Hall, "Hollywood in Review: The Studios Are 'Borrowing' Actors and Directors—Other Recent Events," *NYT*, July 10, 1932.

221 **"one Hollywood correspondent says":** Robert G. Tucker, "Film Barons Consider New Program Ideas," *Indianapolis Star*, July 17, 1932.

222 **the resident palm reader:** Mary Louise Tea Room advertisement, *LAT*, Feb. 12, 1930.

222 **sat down to conduct a reading:** Ruth Ferris, as told to Mary Alice Parent, "What I Learned from 80,000 Hands," *LAT Sunday Magazine*, Feb. 19, 1933.

222 **the tea room's extravagant decor:** The Mystic Tea Room, "California Tea Rooms," accessed June 3, 2022, http://mystictearoom.com/wiki/California_Tea_Rooms.

222 **"in spite of great handicaps":** Ferris, "What I Learned from 80,000 Hands."

222 **four shows a day:** AMW to CVV, July 31, 1932.

222 **fly down to South America:** Grace Kingsley, "Hobnobbing in Hollywood," *LAT*, March 20, 1933.

223 **Lulu had been away:** "Here's Hollywood," *Screenland*, Aug. 1932, 78–79.

223 **returned at the end of March:** Grace Kingsley, "Hobnobbing in Hollywood," *LAT*, March 22, 1933.

223 **a few weeks prior:** Alma Whitaker, "Sugar and Spice," *LAT*, April 9, 1933.

223 **a new house:** Reine Davies, "Hollywood Parade," *LA Examiner*, Sept. 2, 1933.

223 **Harry and Tai Lachman:** Grace Kingsley, "Hobnobbing in Hollywood," *LAT*, Dec. 4, 1932.

223 **a farewell bash:** Grace Kingsley, "Hobnobbing in Hollywood," *LAT*, April 26, 1933.

223 **"Friends think I've been":** Marguerite Tazelaar, "Film Folk in Person: A Chat with Miss Wong," *NYHT*, April 30, 1933.

226 **as fast as the SS *Europa*:** "Anna Wong Sojourn in England Nearing," *LA Evening Citizen News*, April 15, 1933.

CHAPTER TEN

229 **"Everyone in the world":** Eve, "The Letters of Eve," *Tatler*, May 24, 1933.

229 **a Chinese folk song:** Program for Cabareten, Sweden, March 8–10, 1935, AMW collection, Book 8402, NYPL; Shirley Jennifer Lim, *Anna May Wong: Performing the Modern* (Philadelphia: Temple University Press, 2019), 108.

229 **"The audience, of course":** "Chinese Actress at Tivoli," *Aberdeen Press and Journal,* Oct. 10, 1933.

229 **Among the audience:** "The Passing Hour," *Bystander,* May 24, 1933; Eve, "The Letters of Eve," *Tatler,* May 24, 1933.

230 **"The loveliest dress":** Jane Gordon, "Jane Gordon Talks on Style," *Daily News* (London), May 23, 1933.

230 **fine gold finger guards:** W. J. Bishop, "First Vaudeville Appearance in England of Anna May Wong," *Era,* June 7, 1933.

230 **"The 'Wong' gave us":** Eve, "The Letters of Eve," *Tatler,* May 24, 1933.

230 **Throughout the evening:** "Anna May Wong," *Western Morning News,* Nov. 22, 1933.

230 **Her mouth curled:** "Chinese Actress at Tivoli," *Aberdeen Press and Journal.*

230 **original monologues:** Program for National Scala, Copenhagen, Denmark, Feb. 1–14, 1935, AMW collection, Book 8402, NYPL.

230 **the lyrics so closely hinting:** Noel Coward, "Half-Caste Woman," 1931.

231 **"an interesting experiment":** "The Passing Hour," *Bystander,* May 24, 1933.

231 **"I did Cabaret for them":** Letter from Anna May Wong to Fania Marinoff, July 5, 1933, Carl Van Vechten Papers, Beinecke Library, Yale University.

232 **the Circus Ball:** "Whoopee-là! All the Fun of the Circus Ball," *Sketch,* May 17, 1933.

232 **marveled at Josephine Baker:** Program for *La Joie de Paris* at the Casino de Paris, 1932–1933, NYPL; Lim, *Anna May Wong,* 92–96.

232 **A bronze-cast bust:** Mariegold, "Mariegold Broadcasts," *Sketch,* May 24, 1933.

232 **Derby Day:** Eve, "The Letters of Eve," *Tatler,* June 7, 1933.

232 **Patrick Balfour's soirée:** Mariegold, "Mariegold Broadcasts," *Sketch,* June 21, 1933.

232 **Mrs. Somerset Maugham's "tiara-party":** Mariegold, "Mariegold Broadcasts," *Sketch,* July 12, 1933.

232 **Punch Club gala:** "When London Dances," *Tatler,* June 28, 1933.

232 **her own cocktail parties:** "The Little Season in London," *Harper's Bazaar,* Jan. 1935.

232 **"When I left Hollywood":** Wong, "I Protest."

232 **how to throw a knife:** Wong, "My Film Thrills."

233 **She told Fania:** AMW to FM, July 5, 1933.

233 **Barcelona, and the island of Majorca:** "Miss Anna May Wong Visits Nottingham Council House," *Nottingham Journal,* Aug. 18, 1933.

233 **He was also married:** Hermione Gingold, *How to Grow Old Disgracefully* (New York: St. Martin's, 1988), 35–44, 50–51.

234 **a guest of Ronnie and Deidre Balfour:** Mariegold, "Mariegold Broadcasts," *Sketch,* Sept. 6, 1933.

234 **back to work in London:** "News and Gossip of Broadway," *NYT,* July 23, 1933.

234 **Gaumont-British Picture Corporation:** Edwin Schallert, "'Chu-Chin-Chow' Will Star Anna May Wong, Thalberg Programs Story of Criminal," *LAT,* Nov. 1, 1933.

234 **Her annual holiday greeting card:** "Lithograph Souvenir of Anna May Wong's 1933/34 European Tour," 1934, National Portrait Gallery, UK, https://www.npg.org.uk/collections/search/portrait/mw243779/Lithograph-souvenir-of-Anna-May-Wongs-19334-European-tour.

235 **Newsman Harry Carr:** Harry Carr, "Young Doug Bests Father," *LAT,* Dec. 11, 1933.

235   **suffered a heart attack:** Vieira, *Irving Thalberg*, 220.

235   **a congenital heart defect:** Vieira, *Irving Thalberg*, 3.

236   **Mayer couldn't get access:** Vieira, *Irving Thalberg*, 220.

236   **Selznick was only a few years:** Thomas, *Thalberg*, 236–41, 247–48.

236   **Hill and a company:** "Monterey Late Leaving Port," *San Pedro (CA) News-Pilot*, Dec. 14, 1933.

237   **preliminary work in China:** "'Good Earth' Company Returns from China," *Whittier (CA) News*, May 21, 1934; Pearl S. Buck, *My Several Worlds: A Personal Record* (New York: John Day, 1957), found in the Irvin Paik Papers at USC, 393.

237   **According to one account:** George Lewis, "Cine . . . . . . matters," *LA Evening Post-Record*, Sept. 17, 1935.

237   **flowers in their hair:** Buck, *My Several Worlds*, 393–94.

238   **not so universally embraced:** Hua Hsu, *A Floating Chinaman: Fantasy and Failure Across the Pacific* (Cambridge, MA: Harvard University Press, 2016), 36–39.

238   **sympathetic to Chinese objections:** Buck, *My Several Worlds*, 393–94.

238   **The local news media:** "'Good Earth' Company Returns from China," *Whittier (CA) News*; Edwin Schallert, "'Good Earth' Troupe Through in China," *LAT*, April 30, 1934.

238   **The reports failed to mention:** Buck, *My Several Worlds*, 394; Conn, *Pearl S. Buck*, 159.

239   **struggled to craft a viable script:** Hoban, "Scripting *The Good Earth*," 131–36.

239   **a terrible car accident:** "George Hill Kills Self," *LAT*, Aug. 11, 1934.

239   **George Hill's tragic end:** "Film Director Suicide Victim," *Whittier (CA) News*, Aug. 10, 1934; Vieira, *Irving Thalberg*, 323.

239   **back to square one:** Hoban, "Scripting *The Good Earth*," 131.

240   **It was important to Thalberg:** Vieira, *Irving Thalberg*, 323.

240   **under pressure:** Hoban, "Scripting *The Good Earth*," 139; Kevin Brownlow, "Sidney Franklin and *The Good Earth*," in *Historical Journal of Film, Radio, and Television* 9, no. 1 (1989): 80–82.

240   **Marc Connelly's script:** Philip K. Scheuer, "Charles Boyer Will Delineate Leonardo da Vinci in Wanger Production," *LAT*, Aug. 24, 1935.

240   **"We're not convinced":** Lewis, "Cine . . . . . . matters."

240   **Another six months:** "Ocean Travelers," *NYT*, June 25, 1935.

240   **Paramount got the itch:** "Chinese Screen Actress Home," *LAT*, July 24, 1934.

241   **"I'm going to be awfully glad":** Grace Kingsley, "Hobnobbing in Hollywood," *LAT*, July 7, 1934.

241   **The Wong clan:** "Chinese Screen Actress Home," *LAT*.

241   **the one saying farewell:** "Actress' Family Sails for China," *St. Louis Post-Dispatch*, Aug. 13, 1934.

241   **finally decided to retire:** Louella O. Parsons, "Anna May Wong—Amazing Person," *SF Examiner*, Aug. 12, 1934.

242   **The American Wong kids:** "Wong Family Takes Vacation in Orient," *Hartford (CT) Courant*, Aug. 19, 1934.

242   **expected back in Europe:** Parsons, "Anna May Wong—Amazing Person"; "The Life Story of Anna May Wong," *Picture Show*.

242 **Before they sailed:** "Actress' Family Sails for China," *St. Louis Post Dispatch.*

242 **"*The Good Earth* compass":** Edwin Schallert, "Will Anna May Wong Play in 'Good Earth'?" *LAT*, July 30, 1934.

242 **considering Shanghainese actress:** Edna B. Lawson, "Little Theatre Gossip," *Honolulu Advertiser*, Aug. 12, 1934.

243 **"Funny that nobody thought":** Walter Winchell, "On Broadway," *Decatur (AL) Daily*, Sept. 17, 1934.

243 **straight to the source:** Parsons, "Anna May Wong—Amazing Person."

243 **the strict implementation:** Doherty, *Hollywood's Censor*, 60–63; Thomas Doherty, *Pre-Code Hollywood: Sex, Immorality, and Insurrection in American Cinema* (New York: Columbia University Press, 1999), 363.

244 **sat down with Harry Carr:** Wong, "I Am Growing More Chinese Each Passing Year."

245 **made up his mind:** Thomas, *Thalberg*, 304.

245 **the practice of blackface:** Bogle, *Toms, Coons, Mulattoes, Mammies, and Bucks*, 25–26.

245 **"the business of creating illusions":** Vieira, *Irving Thalberg*, 323.

245 **The man he wanted:** "Paul Muni," Britannica, last updated Sept. 18, 2022, https://www.britannica.com/biography/Paul-Muni.

245 **the family business:** Frederick L. Collins, "Paul Muni Becomes a Heathen Chinese," *Liberty*, Aug. 22, 1936, from Irving Paik Papers, USC.

246 **Thalberg believed Muni had it:** Vieira, *Irving Thalberg*, 324.

246 **Paul Muni was signed:** Edwin Schallert, "Activity Starts on 'Good Earth'," *LAT*, Nov. 12, 1935.

246 **a special envoy:** Rob Wagner, "Horrible Hollywood," *Rob Wagner's Script*, July 13, 1935, 21.

246 **More than three hundred:** Brownlow, "Sidney Franklin and *The Good Earth*," 82.

246 **had never been fully convinced:** Vieira, *Irving Thalberg*, 323.

247 **"I was told, however":** Buck, *My Several Worlds*, 393.

247 **Nineteen thirty-five saw her voted:** "Best Dressed Woman," *Big Springs News* (Nebraska), Jan. 3, 1935.

247 **Dragon's Den in Chinatown:** Lisa See, *On Gold Mountain: The One-Hundred-Year Odyssey of My Chinese-American Family* (New York: Vintage Books, 1996), 193–98, 214–15.

247 **seven-month stay in London:** "Paul Robeson with others, England," photograph, Photographs of Prominent African Americans, James Weldon Johnson Collection, Yale Beinecke Library; "London Notes and Comment: Orientals at Tea," *Yorkshire Post*, June 12, 1935; "Film Industry in China: Miss Butterfly Wu's Visit to London," *Observer* (London), June 2, 1935.

247 **taking a month's rest:** "Anna May Wong . . . ," *Yonkers Herald Statesman*, Sept. 21, 1935.

247 **"Whenever she appears in film":** Wagner, "Horrible Hollywood."

247 **one such reviewer:** Era Staff, "Talking Shop," *Era*, May 22, 1935.

248 **"I feel sorry for her":** Wagner, "Horrible Hollywood."

248 **one actress rose above:** Edwin Schallert, "Luise Rainer Rated Most Likely Choice for 'Good Earth' Feminine Lead," *LAT*, Sept. 17, 1935.

248 **Her name was Luise Rainer:** Claudia Luther, "Luise Rainer Dies at 104; 1930s Star Had Meteoric Rise and Fall in Hollywood," *LAT*, Dec. 30, 2014.

248 **Her histrionic talents:** Stephen Tapert, *Best Actress: The History of Oscar-Winning Women* (Newark, NJ: Rutgers University Press, 2020), 79–70; James Bawden and Ron Miller, *Conversations with Classic Film Stars: Interviews from Hollywood's Golden Era* (Lexington: University Press of Kentucky, 2016), 241.

248 **on the MGM payroll:** Tapert, *Best Actress*, 70–71; Edwin Schallert, "Luise Rainer Acclaimed Bergner of Light Comedy," *LAT*, July 5, 1935; Robbin Coons, "In Screenland," *Monrovia (CA) News-Post*, Aug. 9, 1935.

249 **instantly taken:** Mayme Ober Peak, "Reel Life in Hollywood," *Boston Globe*, May 21, 1935.

249 **She "clicked":** George Shaffer, "Star, 8, Loses Teeth in Midst of Film Making," *Chicago Tribune*, Sept. 10, 1935.

249 **"She is immensely clever":** Schallert, "Luise Rainer Acclaimed Bergner of Light Comedy."

249 **"The greatest actress":** "King George and Queen Mary Have 'Tiff' During Parade," *Des Moines Register Sunday Magazine*, July 14, 1935, 3.

249 **"*Good Earth* forecasts":** Schallert, "Luise Rainer Rated Most Likely Choice for 'Good Earth' Feminine Lead."

249 **Rainer was confirmed:** Edwin Schallert, "Metro Will Transform Five Hundred Acres into Northern Chinese Community," *LAT*, Nov. 20, 1935.

249 **wanted her to test:** Lloyd Pantages, "Democratic Party to Use Films in Presidential Campaign with Appropriation of $500,000 Made," *SF Examiner*, Dec. 4, 1935.

249 **She went to MGM studios:** Sidney Skolsky, "Hollywood," *NY Daily News*, Dec. 17, 1935.

250 **at least two screen tests:** Arthur Dong, *Hollywood Chinese: The Chinese in American Feature Films* (Los Angeles: Angel City Press, 2019), 78–79.

250 **they condescendingly offered her:** Lloyd Pantages, "I Cover Hollywood," *LA Examiner*, Feb. 3, 1936.

251 **"So far have not seen many people":** AMW to FM, Dec. 16, 1935.

251 **That same day:** Anna May Wong, file no. 14036-120, NARA–Riverside, 20–24.

251 **the half-truth:** "What's Planning and Doing at the Studios," *St. Louis Globe Democrat*, Dec. 22, 1935.

CHAPTER ELEVEN

255 **"It has long been my hope":** "Anna May Wong Sailing Monday to Visit China," *Great Falls (MT) Tribune*, Jan. 19, 1936.

255 **its first port of call:** Margaret Kamm, "Anna May Wong Gives Views on Theater of East, West," *Honolulu Advertiser*, Jan. 30, 1936.

255 **several fresh flower leis:** Anna May Wong, "Anna May Wong Relates Arrival in Japan, Her First Sight of the Orient," *NYHT*, May 24, 1936.

256 **"offered up a Shanghai gesture":** Ray Coll, Jr., "Anna Scorns Minor Role," *Honolulu Advertiser*, Jan. 30, 1936.

256 **"I'll be glad to take the test":** McIlwaine, "Third Beginning."

256 **"It was rather startling":** Lloyd Pantages, "Mae West's Contract Is Renewed by Paramount with New Clause Banning Show of Temperament," *SF Examiner*, Jan. 23, 1936.

257 **"Do not think that":** "Editorial Notes," *Chinese Digest*, March 1937, 23.

258 **she sent cards:** O. O. McIntyre, "New York Day by Day," *Waterloo (IA) Courier*, Feb. 10, 1936.

258 **She also combed through:** Hodges, *Anna May Wong*, 138–41.

258 **announced her plans:** Kamm, "Anna May Wong Gives Views on Theater of East, West"; Louella O. Parsons, "All-Male Cast Will Trek to Africa to Make Film Drama About Boer War," *Waterloo (IA) Courier*, Jan. 22, 1936.

258 **fruition of another dream:** Wagner, "Better a Laundry and Sincerity."

259 **It was this endeavor:** Anna May Wong, "Anna May Wong Tells of Voyage on 1st Trip to China," *NYHT*, May 17, 1936.

259 **a fabulous farewell party:** Parsons, "All-Male Cast Will Trek to Africa to Make Film Drama About Boer War."

259 **flew up to San Francisco:** Grace Wilcox, "The Hollywood Reporter," *Brooklyn Times-Union*, Feb. 23, 1936.

259 **Anna May sailed forward:** Wong, "Tells of Voyage on 1st Trip to China."

261 **actresses with unusual backgrounds:** Edwin Schallert, "The Pageant of the Film World," *LAT*, Dec. 5, 1935; Edwin Schallert, "Princess Der ling Noted Authoress Tested for 'Good Earth'," *LAT*, Dec. 6, 1935; Edwin Schallert, "The Pageant of the Film World," *LAT*, Dec. 27, 1935; Louella O. Parsons, "Absolute Quiet Is Chosen As Jean Harlow Picture," *Modesto Bee*, Dec. 13, 1935; Edwin Schallert, "Tilly Losch May Make . . . ," *LAT*, Jan. 6, 1936; Louella O. Parsons, "Isabel Jewell Takes Best Test for Lotus Role in 'Good Earth'," *Philadelphia Inquirer*, Jan. 22, 1936; Relman Morin, "Stardom in Movies Predicted for Lotus Liu, Young Eurasian Girl," *San Bernardino County Sun*, April 29, 1936.

261 **"the horrible pidgin-English":** Mollie Merrick, "Silly English to Be Barred in 'Good Earth,'" *South Bend (IN) Tribune*, Dec. 2, 1935.

262 **studio scouts canvassed:** "MGM Conducts a Search for Chinese Players," *LA Evening Post-Record*, Dec. 2, 1935; Jerome Lawrence, *Actor: The Life and Times of Paul Muni* (New York: G. P. Putnam, 1974), 223.

262 **hoped to embed himself:** Edwin Schallert, "No Pigeon English for These Chinese," *LAT*, Nov. 25, 1935.

262 **Hundreds of people excitedly volunteered:** "Filming of 'Good Earth' to Start Soon," *Chinese Digest*, Dec. 13, 1935, 5.

262 **"I suppose that every Chinese":** Harry Carr, "The Lancer," *LAT*, Dec. 7, 1935.

262 **Peking opera performer:** Edwin Schallert, "Mei Lan-Fang May Play in 'Good Earth,'" *LAT*, Oct. 31, 1935.

262 **returned from their scouting trip:** "Filming of 'Good Earth' to Start Soon," *Chinese Digest*, Dec.13, 1935, 5.

262 **"Bill Grady has shot":** Sidney Skolsky, "Hollywood," *Tampa Tribune*, Dec. 11, 1935.

262 **three hundred screen tests:** Dong, *Hollywood Chinese*, 80.

263 **a handful were signed:** "Four Chinese Signed for 'Good Earth'," *LA Evening Post-Record*, Dec. 9, 1935; "San Francisco Supplies Actors," *LAT*, Dec. 5, 1935.

263 **Chingwah Lee:** Sometimes styled as Ching Wah Lee.

263 Veteran actors: "Who's Who Among the Chinese in 'The Good Earth,'" *Chinese Digest*, March 1937, 9.

263 MGM leased five hundred acres: Schallert, "Metro Will Transform Five Hundred Acres."

263 crateloads of furniture: Lloyd Pantages, "Democratic Party to Use Films in Presidential Campaign'; Blake Allmendinger, "Little House on the Rice Paddy," *American Literary History* 10, no. 2 (Summer 1998): 371–72.

264 18,000 items: Brownlow, "Sidney Franklin and *The Good Earth*," 82.

264 a knowledgeable gardener: Allmendinger, "Little House on the Rice Paddy," 371–72.

265 being prepped for demolition: Suellen Cheng and Munson Kwok, "History of New Chinatown," from *The Los Angeles Chinatown 50th Year Guidebook* (June 1988), Chinese Historical Society of Southern California, accessed June 21, 2022.

265 a new train station: Union Station Los Angeles, "History," accessed June 21, 2022, https://www.unionstationla.com/history.

265 The site chosen: Krist, *The Mirage Factory*, 7.

265 for more than sixty years: "Old Chinatown in Los Angeles to Be Razed," *Chinese Digest*, March 1937, 23.

265 the same streets: Wong, "Childhood of a Chinese Screen Star."

265 toured the transitioning area: Lee Shippey, "The Lee Side o' L.A.," *LAT*, Aug. 24, 1936, found in William Gow, "Performing Chinatown: Hollywood Cinema, Tourism, and the Making of a Los Angeles Community, 1882–1943" (PhD diss., University of California, Berkeley, 2018), 75.

265 3,500 Chinese Americans: "Historical Census: Racial/Ethnic Numbers in Los Angeles County, 1850 to 1980," *Los Angeles Almanac*, accessed Nov. 29, 2022, https://www.laalmanac.com/population/po20.php.

266 many Chinatown residents: Gow, "Performing Chinatown," 86–88.

266 passing of James Wang: Grace Wilcox, "The Hollywood Reporter," *Brooklyn Times-Union*, May 12, 1935.

266 another longtime Chinatown recruiter: "L.A. Chinatown 'Mayor' Probed on Film Extras," *Variety*, Dec. 18, 1935, found in Gow, "Performing Chinatown," 92.

266 "Anyone who can supply": John Scott, "'Good Earth' Casting Stirs Feud Among Chinese Actors," *LAT*, Dec. 1, 1935.

267 A faction of disaffected Chinese actors: Gow, "Perfoming Chinatown," 92.

267 threw themselves into preparations: Ida Zeitlin, "The Man Who Can't Be Typed," *Motion Picture*, Aug. 1936, 89.

267 The great character actor: Lawrence, *Actor*, 223.

267 devoted much of his time: Franc Dillon, "Paul Muni Worries Along," *Picture-Play*, Nov. 1935, 55.

268 made a similar trip: Schallert, "Metro Will Transform Five Hundred Acres"; Pauline Gale, "An Interview with Paul Muni and Luise Rainer," *Motion Picture Studio Insider*, Jan. 1937, 60.

268 she refused to wear: John Schwarzkopf, "On Location with *The Good Earth*," *Motion Picture*, Oct. 1936, 63.

268 did what he could: Lawrence, *Actor*, 223.

268 enlisted a respected tailor: "Lands Tailor but His Woes Are Not Over," *Great Falls (MT) Tribune*, Jan. 19, 1936.

268 makeup man Jack Dawn: Schwarzkopf, "On Location with *The Good Earth*," 63.

268 "Will the public accept me": Dillon, "Paul Muni Worries Along," 55, 91.

269 Somewhere in the Pacific Ocean: Wong, "Relates Arrival in Japan."

269 Anna May Wong: "Recalls Shanghai's Enthusiastic Reception," *NYHT*, May 31, 1936.

270 Chinese press rushed aboard: "Anna May Wong's Homecoming Special," *Screen Pictorial*, March 1936.

271 who was living in Shanghai: Anna May Wong, file no. 14036-120, NARA–Riverside, 15.

271 had the strange experience: Wong, "Recalls Shanghai's Enthusiastic Reception"; "A Paltry Welcome," *Movietone*, Feb. 21, 1936.

271 "My first glimpse": Wong, "Recalls Shanghai's Enthusiastic Reception."

271 "I have always wanted to come": "Many Friends Greet Anna May Wong," *China Press*, Feb. 12, 1936.

271 equally as enthralled: "Mob Meets Chinese Film Star," *North-China Herald*, Feb. 19, 1936; "Many Friends Greet Anna May Wong," *China Press*.

272 "When the Chinese go to America": "Many Friends Greet Anna May Wong," *China Press*.

272 cameramen edged their way: "Newsmen, Photographers Rush on Hoover to See Noted Film Star," *China Press*, Feb. 12, 1936.

272 German photographer Alfred Krause: "Krause Clicks Clever Camera," *China Press*, Feb. 16, 1936; "Many Friends Greet Anna May Wong," *China Press*.

272 pulled into the dock: Wong, "Recalls Shanghai's Enthusiastic Reception."

272 the English-language papers: "Newsmen, Photographers Rush on Hoover," *China Press;* "Highlights of the Week," *China Press*, Feb. 17, 1936.

272 have a chance to rest: Wong, "Recalls Shanghai's Enthusiastic Reception."

274 Whoever came up: "Newsmen, Photographers Rush on Hoover," *China Press*.

274 celebrated for its cosmopolitanism: Hui-Lan Koo, as told to Mary Van Rensselaer, *Hui-Lan Koo (Madame Wellington Koo): An Autobiography* (New York: Dial Press, 1943), 294–96.

274 "a few inches of creamy skin": Wong, "Recalls Shanghai's Enthusiastic Reception."

274 not nearly as kind: "Miss Anna May Wong Is Buying Chinese Clothes," *China Press*, Feb. 14, 1936; "A Paltry Welcome," *Movietone*.

275 They also criticized her looks: "Anna May Wong's Homecoming Special," *Screen Pictorial*.

275 "Her youth is long gone": Chen Jiazhen, "An Impression of Anna May Wong," *Movietone*, Feb. 21, 1936.

275 they attacked her track record: Hong Bingcheng, "Is Anna May Wong Really Welcome?," *Film Age*, Feb. 1936.

275 ordering several Chinese dresses: Wong, "Recalls Shanghai's Enthusiastic Reception."

275 admirers eager to imitate: "Styles of Actress Are Noted Here," *China Press*, Feb. 26, 1936; "Latest from Fashion World," *China Press*, March 6, 1936; "Among Anna May Wong's Dresses," *China Press*, March 8, 1936.

275   **Her day typically began:** Anna May Wong, "Anna May Wong 'Amazed' at Chinese Appetite," *NYHT*, June 7, 1936.

276   **lunched with Victor Keen:** Anna May Wong, "Anna May Wong Finds Shanghai Life Glamorous," *NYHT*, June 14, 1936.

276   **Saturday night:** "Little Club Party to Have 2 Honor Guests," *China Press*, Feb. 12, 1936.

276   **she knew it was time:** "Vice-President Tan Is Host at Dinner," *China Press*, Feb. 12, 1936.

276   **"I received a prize":** Wong, "Finds Shanghai Life Glamorous."

276   **"Watching Chinese play":** Wong, "Recalls Shanghai's Enthusiastic Reception."

277   **"It seems strange that":** Wong, "Finds Shanghai Life Glamorous."

277   **"I really thought":** "Shanghai Fast Enough: Actress Says Shanghai Night Life Eclipses Paris and N.Y.," *China Press*, Feb. 16, 1936.

277   **"nothing surprises me":** Wong, "'Amazed' at Chinese Appetite."

277   **"The modern Chinese woman":** "Anna May Wong Feted in South: Wears Chinese Dress While In Manila," *China Press*, March 17, 1936.

277   **"Japanese wives":** Wong, "Finds Shanghai Life Glamorous."

277   **"China has grounds for":** "Many Friends Greet Anna May Wong," *China Press*.

278   **"Film technique has not":** "Mob Meets Chinese Film Star," *North-China Herald*.

278   **she wasn't exactly Chinese:** "Shanghai Fast Enough," *China Press*.

278   **"Who is that Chinese girl":** McIlwaine, "Third Beginning."

CHAPTER TWELVE

281   **the first day of principal photography:** Schwarzkopf, "On Location with *The Good Earth*," 40.

281   **"I don't believe it":** Lawrence, *Actor*, 225.

282   **A new director:** Leighton Early, "Some Odds and Ends in Production News," *LA Evening Post-Record*, Jan. 22, 1936.

282   **with production set to begin:** Thomas, *Thalberg*, 304–6.

282   **"I seem to hear":** Lawrence, *Actor*, 225.

283   **a recent college graduate:** Charles L. Leong, "Mandarins in Hollywood," *Gum Saan Journal*, 2021, accessed June 29, 2022, https://gumsaanjournal.com/special-edition -2021-the-eagle-and-the-dragon/mandarins-in-hollywood/.

284   **One columnist hailed her:** Paul Harrison, "Stars Cover Up Beauty for Sake of Photoplays," *News and Observer* (Raleigh, NC), Dec. 20, 1936.

284   **A reporter from *Picture-Play*:** Ben Maddox, "Old-Fashioned As Eve," *Picture-Play*, Oct. 1936.

285   **"I go many times to Chinatown":** Charles Darnton, "Will Luise Rainer Really Leave the Screen?," *Movie Mirror*, Oct. 1936.

285   **Rainer was so overcome:** Weston East, "Here's Hollywood!," *Screenland*, Sept. 1936; "On and off the Set," *Picture-Play*, Sept. 1936; Tapert, *Best Actress*, 72–73.

285   **equally confounded by her:** Gordon Crowley, "There's No Explaining Luise Rainer!," *Motion Picture*, Sept. 1936.

286   **"Already word is whispered":** Darnton, "Will Luise Rainer Really Leave the Screen?"

286 **professed no interest in fame:** "Petting Permitted," *Screenland*, Aug. 1936.

286 **"I am all wrong here":** Darnton, "Will Luise Rainer Really Leave the Screen?"

286 **while watching rushes:** Read Kendall, "Around and About in Hollywood," *LAT*, Dec. 18, 1935.

286 **"I told her that was his character":** Vieira, *Irving Thalberg*, 325–26.

286 **the Chatsworth location:** Elizabeth Wilson, "What Happens on Movie Locations?," *Screenland*, Oct. 1936, 84.

287 **the Lotus character:** Jerry Asher, "The Hollywood Reporter," *Nashville Banner*, Aug. 2, 1936.

287 **Lotus Liu, a Shanghai-born:** Barbara Miller, "Austrians Favored in 'Good Earth,'" *LAT*, Aug. 16, 1936; Relman Morin, "Stardom in Movies Predicted for Lotus Liu, Young Eurasian Girl Given Leading Role in First Film Showing," *San Bernadino County Sun*, April 29, 1936.

287 **newly arrived Tilly Losch:** Miller, "Austrians Favored in 'Good Earth.'"

287 **"mixing racials":** "'Good Earth' a Bad Casting Headache," *Variety*, Dec. 18, 1936.

287 **every film should give moviegoers:** Vieira, *Irving Thalberg*, 326.

287 **the sole Chinese American journalist:** Louise Leung, "Night Call—in Chinatown," *LAT Sunday Magazine*, July 26, 1936.

289 **Gubbins's "staccato Chinese commands":** Leong, "Mandarins in Hollywood."

289 **along the artificial city streets:** Leung, "Night Call—in Chinatown."

291 **sailed south to Hong Kong:** "Anna May Wong: Famous Chinese Film Star in Colony," *SCMP*, Feb. 22, 1936: "A Welcome Turns into Expulsion; Toisan Association Rejected; "Anna May Wong Quietly Leaves Hong Kong for the Philippines," *Movietone*, March 27, 1936.

291 **an ugly scuffle:** "Anna May Wong: Severely Criticised by the Chinese Press," *SCMP*, Feb. 28, 1936; "A Welcome Turns into Expulsion," *Movietone*; AMW to FM and CVV, Feb. 22, 1936.

292 **"Down with Wong Liu Tsong":** Hodges, *Anna May Wong*, 166–67.

292 **awaited her on the mainland:** Hodges, *Anna May Wong*, 6–7, 160.

292 **the snubbed Toisan delegation:** "Miss Anna May Wong Back: Chinese Actress Meets Her Father in Canton," *North-China Herald*, April 1, 1936; "A Welcome Turns into Expulsion," *Movietone*.

293 **She assured her critics:** "Anna May Wong: Severely Criticised by the Chinese Press," *SCMP*.

293 **excused herself from the public eye:** "Miss Anna May Wong Back," *North-China Herald*; "Anna May Wong Feted in South: Wears Chinese Dress While in Manila," *China Press*, March 17, 1936.

293 **quietly returned to Hong Kong:** "Miss Anna May Wong Back," *North-China Herald*.

293 **absconded onto the mainland:** Anna May Wong's travelogue documentary, *Bold Journey: Native Land*, ABC, aired Feb. 14, 1957, UCLA Film and Television Archive.

294 **forty-three-course feast:** Louise Leung, "East Meets West," *Hollywood*, Jan. 1937.

294 **"Have been to Canton":** AMW to CVV, March 14, 1936.

295 **asked Anna May about her possible plans:** "Actress Plans Production of Historical Play," *China Press*, May 9, 1936.

295 **she linked up with Warner Oland:** "Mr. Warner Oland in Shanghai," *North-China Herald*, March 25, 1936.

295 **Oland received a warm welcome:** "Miss Anna May Wong Back," *North-China Herald*.

295 **she made an official visit:** "Butterfly Wu Graciously Hosts Anna May Wong's Visit to Mingxing Motion Picture Company," *Movietone*, May 8, 1936; "Anna May Wong Visits Shanghai, China," May 1, 1936, UCLA Film and Television Archive, https://youtu.be/9mDJDt2vD7w.

296 **On her way north:** "The Capital's Various Sectors Hosted a Tea Party for Anna May Wong," *Movietone*, May 22, 1936.

296 **"They made speeches":** Leung, "East Meets West."

297 **She arrived in Peiping:** "Anna May Wong Sees Infinite Possibilities for China Movies," *China Press*, Sept. 17, 1936.

297 **gave up her hotel suite:** Letter from Anna May Wong to Bernardine Szold-Fritz, May 19, 1936, Bernardine Szold-Fritz correspondence, Beinecke Library, Yale University.

297 **she had hoped to rent:** Paul French, *Destination Peking* (Hong Kong: Blacksmith Books, 2021), 40.

297 **Inside the four-sided home:** Jack Foster, "Anna May Wong Discovers China," *Oklahoma News* (Oklahoma City), Oct. 11, 1936.

297 **The kindly lady landlord:** Rob Wagner, "A Chinese Girl Comes Home!," *Rob Wagner's Script*, Dec. 12, 1936.

297 **"the beauty and charm of old customs":** McIlwaine, "Third Beginning."

297 **The old man who sat outside:** Foster, "Anna May Wong Discovers China."

298 **Bernardine Szold Fritz:** Susan Blumberg-Kason, *Bernardine's Shanghai Salon: The Story of the Doyenne of Old China* (Brentwood, TN: Post Hill Press, 2023).

298 **correspondence with Bernardine:** AMW to BSF, May 19, 1936; June 9, 1936; Aug. 8, 1936.

298 **could be seen calling:** Foster, "Anna May Wong Discovers China."

298 **down the street from her:** Huang, *Daughter of the Dragon*, 236.

299 **historical map of Peiping:** Frank Dorn, *After the Flag Is Lowered*, unpublished autobiography, part 3, page 379, Frank Dorn Papers, box 5, folder 3-5, Hoover Institution Library & Archives.

299 **author of a novel:** Dorn, *After the Flag Is Lowered*, 376.

299 **"Attractive and enveloped":** Dorn, *After the Flag Is Lowered*, 386.

299 **Peiping hostess Tang Shunjun:** "Peking Socialite Entertains Anna May Wong?," *Movietone*, June 19, 1936.

299 **Her education in all things:** "Anna May Wong Visits the Great Wall," *Movietone*, June 5, 1936; Wong, "Bold Journey: Native Land."

300 **Temple of Heaven:** Foster, "Anna May Wong Discovers China."

300 **commenced with language lessons:** AMW to BSF, May 19, 1936; "Anna May Wong Begins Studying Mandarin," *Movietone*, Feb. 21, 1936.

300 **spoke neither English:** Harold Acton, *More Memoirs of an Aesthete* (London: Methuen & Co, 1970), 2.

300 she toured a Chinese dramatic school: Wang Fan, "Peking Opera School Being Brought to Life on TV," *China Daily*, Nov. 30, 2015, http://www.ecns.cn/2015/11 -30/190601.shtml.

300 She was amused to watch: Wong, "Bold Journey: Native Land."

300 "I am simply crazy": AMW to BSF, May 19, 1936.

300 amassed a small collection: "Anna May Wong Sees Infinite Possibilities for China Movies," *China Press*; untitled, *SCMP*, Sept. 17, 1936, 15.

300 "Have purchased three": AMW to BSF, Aug. 8, 1936.

300 to come up to Peiping: AMW to BSF, June 9, 1936; Blumberg-Kason, *Bernardine's Shanghai Salon*.

300 Dressed modestly: Photos taken by Bernardine Szold Fritz, 1936, courtesy of David Szanton.

301 "The impressiveness of China": "Anna May Wong Sees Infinite Possibilities for China Movies," *China Press*.

301 "traces of the past": "Actress Plans Production of Historical Play," *China Press*.

301 While she was in Canton: "Anna May Wong Returning from Canton by Plane," *China Press*, Oct. 4, 1936.

301 She accepted the offer: "Anna May Wong to Reflect on China Under U.S. Palm," *China Press*, Oct. 9, 1936.

301 Butterfly Wu kicked off: "Butterfly Wu Invites Anna May Wong to Dinner, Anna May Wong Watches Butterfly Wu Shoot a Movie," *Movietone*, Oct. 23, 1936.

301 China's famous aviatrix: "Rainbow Restaurant Is Scene of Tiffin Parties," *China Press*, Oct. 20, 1936.

302 A reporter from *Movietone*: "Anna May Wong's Farewell Chat," *Movietone*, Oct. 23, 1936.

302 a movie "on the Chinese legend": Dorn, *After the Flag Is Lowered*, 386.

302 prospects for developing Chinese films: "Actress Plans Production of Historical Play," *China Press*; "Anna May Wong Will Study Mandarin Here," *China Press*, March 28, 1936.

303 "There are infinite possibilities": "Anna May Wong Sees Infinite Possibilities for China Movies," *China Press*.

303 an idea she had mentioned: "Actress Plans Production of Historical Play," *China Press*.

303 "Miss Wong has been busy": "Anna May Wong's Farewell Chat," *Movietone*.

303 sumptuous dinners and tiffin parties: "Miss Wong Entertains at Luncheon Party," *China Press*, Oct. 22, 1936.

303 "After missing three ships": AMW to FM and CVV, Nov. 8, 1936.

304 "China has been wonderful": "Anna May Wong to Reflect on China Under U.S. Palm," *China Press*.

304 breathe a little easier: Vieira, *Irving Thalberg*, 355–56.

305 In a recent meeting: Vieira, *Irving Thalberg*, 362.

305 he left with his family: Vieira, *Irving Thalberg*, 363–68; "Thalberg, Noted Film Maker, Dies," *LAT*, Sept. 15, 1936.

CHAPTER THIRTEEN

307 **news of Irving Thalberg's death:** Vieira, *Irving Thalberg*, 369–70.

307 **on the front page:** "Thalberg, Noted Film Maker, Dies," *LAT.*

307 **"Death of Irving Thalberg":** Eleanor Barnes, "Death of Irving Thalberg Shocks Film World: Pneumonia Closes Meteoric Career of 'Boy Producer,'" *LA Daily News*, Sept. 15, 1936.

307 **"No recent news":** "Screen Genius' Death Stuns Industry's Heads," *LAT*, Sept. 17, 1936.

307 **"The world of art":** Morton Thompson, "Film Great Pay Tribute to Thalberg," *LA Evening Citizen News*, Sept. 16, 1936.

307 **editors at MGM:** Coons, "'Good Earth' Is Last Picture of Irving Thalberg."

308 **Within six days of her departure:** "600 Stranded in Honolulu," *LA Examiner*, Nov. 8, 1936; "F. E. Likely to Get Trade from Hawaii," *China Press*, Dec. 3, 1936.

308 **"I am spending most of my time":** "600 Stranded in Honolulu," *LA Examiner.*

308 **a one-week personal appearance:** China Clipper, "Shanghai Man Breaks Hawaii Tie-Up"; John B. Peck, "Seen & Heard at the Theaters," *Honolulu Star-Bulletin*, Nov. 17, 1936.

308 **"Here we are marooned":** AMW to FM and CVV, Nov. 8, 1936.

308 **The impromptu layover:** "Strike Delays Actress' Trip," *Pasadena Post*, Nov. 29, 1936; "Stranded Travelers in Hawaii Have Troubles," *Long Beach Sun*, Nov. 21, 1936.

308 **The stranded passengers:** "447 Board Monterey at Honolulu for U.S.," *San Pedro (CA) News-Pilot*, Nov. 24, 1936.

309 **three weeks in Honolulu:** "Island Strike Victims Home," *LA Examiner*, Nov. 29, 1936; "Strike Victim," *San Pedro (CA) News-Pilot*, Nov. 30, 1936.

309 **ten months before:** "Young Stock Raiser Dreams of Prize—Strike Detained Travelers Return," *LAT*, Nov. 30, 1936.

309 **"I am proud to say":** "Strike Delays Actress' Trip," *Pasadena Post.*

309 **her customary visit:** Anna May Wong, file no. 14036-120, NARA–Riverside, 15–16.

310 **what the story was all about:** Anna May Wong, "My Story," *Young Companion*, Feb. 1936.

311 **the Hollywood press came to call:** Alma Whitaker, "Sugar and Spice," *LAT*, Dec. 11, 1936.

311 **Over lunch in Beverly Hills:** Wagner, "A Chinese Girl Comes Home!"

311 **her smartly tailored cheongsams:** Lloyd Pantages, "I Cover Hollywood," *LA Examiner*, Dec. 17, 1936.

311 **"I am disposing of all":** AMW to BSF, Jan. 15, 1937.

311 **"I have just returned from China":** "These Fake Chinese Irk Anna M. Wong," *Courier Post* (New Jersey), Dec. 17, 1936.

312 **"Asserts Films Snub Chinese":** Henry Sutherland, "Asserts Films Snub Chinese: Anna May Wong Still Looking for Job," *Des Moines Register*, Dec. 17, 1936.

312 **nearly 800,000 feet:** Frank S. Nugent, "The Screen," *NYT*, Feb. 3, 1937.

312 **The final cut was submitted:** "Chinatownia—'Good Earth' O. K'd by China," *Chinese Digest*, Feb. 1937, 9; "Nanking Glad at Release of 'Good Earth,'" *China Press*, April 25, 1937.

312 **five years in production:** Thomas, *Thalberg*, 306.

312 **refused to put his name:** Samuel Marx, "Thalberg Made Movies, Not Deals," *LAT*, Sept. 14, 1986.

312 **requested that a title card:** Vieira, *Irving Thalberg*, 377.

313 **made its world premiere:** "Sweethearts in Carthay," *LA Daily News*, Jan. 27, 1937; "Tonight World Premier at 8:30," *LA Daily News*, Jan. 29, 1937.

313 **a behind-the-scenes exhibition:** "'The Good Earth' Sets a New High Mark in Entertainment," *LA Daily News*, Feb. 9, 1937; "Muni Awaits Initial View of Own Film," *LA Evening Citizen News*, Jan. 26, 1937; "Popularity of 'Good Earth' Continues," *LAT*, Feb. 6, 1937.

313 **an outdoor petting zoo:** *The Good Earth*, Metro-Goldwyn-Mayer production and biography photographs, AMPAS.

313 **broadcast live on radio:** "Carthay Starts Seat Sale This Morning," *LA Daily News*, Jan. 25, 1937; "M-G-M's 'The Good Earth' Has Gala World Premiere," *Springfield News-Sun*, Feb. 15, 1937.

313 **the Chinese consul general:** "Chinatownia," *Chinese Digest*, March 1937, 17.

313 **Other stars included:** Tip Poff, "That Certain Party," *LAT*, Feb. 7, 1937.

314 **Mary Wong ambled:** R. R., "Roaming 'Round with R. R.," *Chinese Digest*, March 1937, 8.

314 **Conspicuously missing that evening:** Tip Poff, "That Certain Party."

314 **she and Clifford Odets:** "Luise Rainer and Odets Wed in Quiet Home Ceremony," *LAT*, Jan. 9, 1937.

314 **The couple had met:** "Luise Rainer and Clifford Odets, the Playwright, Dine Out Together," *LAT*, Aug. 9, 1936; Read Kendall, "Around and About in Hollywood," *LAT*, Dec. 30, 1936; Francesca Knittel Bowyer, *Seen from the Wings: Luise Rainer, My Mother, the Journey* (self-published, 2019), 23–34.

314 **a lover's spat:** Read Kendall, "Around and About Hollywood: Everything Okeh with Newlyweds," *LAT*, Feb. 3, 1937.

314 **without having seen the film:** "Luise Rainer Hasn't Seen 'Good Earth,'" *LAT*, Feb. 24, 1937.

314 ***The Good Earth*'s world premiere:** "M-G-M's 'The Good Earth' Has Gala World Premiere," *Springfield News-Sun*.

314 **"Once again Metro-Goldwyn-Mayer":** Frank S. Nugent, "The Screen," *NYT*, Feb. 3, 1937.

314 **"the most flawless piece":** Clarke Wales, "Reviews of the New Films," *Rochester (NY) Democrat and Chronicle*, Feb. 21, 1937.

314 **one of ten outstanding films:** "The Outstanding Films of 1937," *National Board of Review Magazine*, Jan. 1938, 3.

314 **"a vast and rich film":** John Mosher, "The Current Cinema," *New Yorker*, Feb. 6, 1937, 59–60.

315 **illusion wore off:** Nugent, "Screen Time"; Eleanor Barnes, "Good Earth," *LA Daily News*, Jan. 30, 1937.

315 **"Luise Rainer's portrayal of O-Lan":** Frank S. Nugent, "Off with the Gun: The 1937 Cinema Achieves a Flying Start, with 'The Good Earth' Leading," *NYT*, Feb. 7, 1937.

315 **"It's kind of a stunt role":** Mosher, "The Current Cinema."

315 **who had her misgivings:** Buck, *My Several Worlds*, 394–95.

315 **felt the actors were:** J. S. H., "The Good Earth," *National Board of Review Magazine*, March 1937, 8–9.

316 **to dedicate an entire issue:** "Editorial," *Chinese Digest*, March 1937, 2.

316 **friends took out ads:** Moore's ad, *Chinese Digest*, March 1937, 3.

316 **the China Emporium celebrated:** China Emporium ad, *Chinese Digest*, March 1937, 14.

316 **an expression of her appreciation:** Edith Lindeman, "Amusements: Norma Shearer Plans Return to Pictures," *Richmond Times-Dispatch*, June 17, 1937.

317 **she sent six peach trees:** "First Clipper Reaches China," *Hawaii Tribune-Herald*, May 2, 1937; "Sports," *Chinese Digest*, June 1937, 17.

317 **the film continued to sell out:** "Popularity of 'Good Earth' Continues," *LAT*, Feb. 6, 1937; "Matinee Trade at Carthay Heavy," *LA Daily News*, Feb. 2, 1937.

317 **gross receipts of $3,557,000:** Thomas, *Thalberg*, 306.

317 **with all the money:** Vieira, *Irving Thalberg*, 377.

317 **Pundits were already predicting:** Gus McCarthy, "Miracle in Academy Awards; Most of Hollywood Agrees," *Motion Picture Herald*, March 13, 1937.

318 **called Anna May up:** BSF to FM, Nov. 17, 1937.

318 **Hollywood regulars like:** May Hobart, "Actresses Hostesses at Party for Dancer," *LA Evening Citizen News*, Nov. 17, 1937.

318 **in a corner of the garden:** Photographs from this event of Wong with Rainer, Sondergaard, and Enters can be found in various photo collections online.

318 **was "rather in a state":** BSF to FM, Nov. 17, 1937.

318 **the tenth annual Academy Awards:** James Francis Crow, "Banquet Marks Rebirth of Film Academy," *LA Evening Citizen News*, March 11, 1938.

319 **During the early years:** Charles Higham, *Merchant of Dreams: Louis B. Mayer, M.G.M., and the Secret Hollywood* (New York: Donald I. Fine, 1993), 258–59, 280.

319 **Looking at the photos:** Marion Nevin, "M.G.M. Leads Field in Academy Awards," *Venice (CA) Evening Vanguard*, March 11, 1938.

319 **Luise Rainer was called to account:** Dong, *Hollywood Chinese*, 76.

320 **in the vein of Charlie Chan:** Edwin Schallert, "Anna May Wong to Play Sleuth," *LAT*, Jan. 28, 1937, 8; Regina Crewe, " 'Frosted Willow': Never Having Seen Homeland Before, Actress Has Many Varied Experiences," *New York American*, May 16, 1937, in AMW clippings, NYPL.

320 **she had offered the concept:** McIlwaine, "Third Beginning."

320 **a one-picture contract:** Edwin Schallert, "Anna May Wong Signs at Paramount," *LAT*, April 5, 1937, 40.

320 **"fancy a lady Chan":** Bland Johaneson, "Movie to Star Her as Girl 'Chan,'" unknown publication, undated, in AMW clippings, NYPL.

321 **a freak incident:** "Miss Wong Plotter Stirs Wide Inquiry," *LAT*, March 25, 1937.

321 **considered the letter a prank:** "Ink Snares Woman in Aimee Threat," *LAT*, March 26, 1937.

321   **"a crank or demented individual"**: "Extortion Case Inquiry Pushed," *LAT*, March 29, 1937, 22.

321   **police were assigned**: "Threat Note Guard Posted," *LAT*, March 27, 1937.

321   **a copycat letter**: "Anna May Wong Again Target of Threat Letter," *LAT*, April 3, 1937.

321   **no suspects were ever prosecuted**: FBI file for Anna May Wong, file no. 9-HQ-2639.

321   **had last seen him**: AMW to FM and CVV, June 19, 1937.

322   **coming up roses**: Maschwitz, *No Chip on My Shoulder*, 64–66, 78–79.

322   **"These Foolish Things"**: Eric Maschwitz wrote the lyrics under the name Holt Marvell, and his writing partner, Jack Strachey, composed the song to accompany them.

322   **His wife certainly seemed to think**: Gingold, *How to Grow Old Disgracefully*, 54.

322   **a long, successful run**: Maschwitz, *No Chip on My Shoulder*, 96–102.

322   **made a generous offer**: Maschwitz, *No Chip on My Shoulder*, 87–88, 102, 113.

323   **made plans to travel to London**: AMW to FM, April 19, 1937.

323   **where Eric was waiting**: "Long Shots," *Kinematograph Weekly*, June 17, 1937.

323   **contract for Anna May**: Tuner, "A New Pair in the Music Hall," *Nottingham Journal*, June 19, 1937.

323   **"adding a picturesque touch"**: Star-Gazer, "On Stage and Screen," *Merthyr (UK) Express*, July 10, 1937.

323   **"Such fun to be in London"**: AMW to FM and CVV, June 19, 1937.

323   **continued on to Paris**: "Ocean Travelers," *NYT*, July 12, 1937.

324   **rehearsals for *Princess Turandot***: "Anna May Wong on Summer Stage," *NYT*, Aug. 3, 1937.

324   **The play was well-received**: "News of the Stage," *NYT*, Aug. 9, 1937; "Goings on About Town," *New Yorker*, Aug. 7, 1937.

324   **Broadway's leading ladies**: Victoria Price, *Vincent Price: A Daughter's Biography* (New York: St. Martin's, 1999), 77.

324   **persuaded his scene partner**: Price, *Vincent Price*, 77.

324   **armed conflict had broken out**: "Second Sino-Japanese War (1937–1945)," Britannica, last updated Aug. 29, 2022, https://www.britannica.com/event/Second-Sino-Japanese -War.

324   **intensifying studios' appetites**: Edwin Schallert, "Anna May Wong in Two Pictures," *LAT*, Sept. 15, 1937; Edwin Schallert, "Another Wong Subject Preparing," *LAT*, Oct. 8, 1937.

325   **returned to Los Angeles**: "Anna May Wong Back for Work on Picture," *LA Evening Citizen News*, Sept. 9, 1937.

325   **picked up the nearest newspaper**: United Press, "The Hollywood Roundup," *Columbus (NE) Telegram*, Sept. 10, 1937.

325   **then there was Eric**: Maschwitz, *No Chip on My Shoulder*, 102–3.

325   **Two familiar faces**: "News of the Screen," *NYT*, Sept. 9, 1937.

325   **Anna May's childhood friend**: Edwin Schallert, "Korean Actor Cast Opposite Anna May Wong," *LAT*, Sept. 18, 1937.

326   **he caught the eye**: Henniger, "Wartime Villian: Philip Ahn—Really Not Such a Bad Guy."

326 **"an exceedingly clever personality":** Edwin Schallert, "Korean Actor Cast Opposite Anna May Wong."

326 **the first Asian Americans:** Chung, *Hollywood Asian*, 85.

326 **ripped from the headlines:** "Alien Smuggle Racket Told in New Picture," *LA Examiner*, Jan. 3, 1938.

326 **"there's no romance":** Read Kendall, "Around and About in Hollywood," *LAT*, Dec. 2, 1937.

327 **Anna May didn't mind:** Paul Harrison, "Anna May Wong Outlines Ideas About Movie Column," *Missoulian*, Nov. 13, 1938.

327 **her off-screen time:** Maschwitz, *No Chip on My Shoulder*, 104–5.

327 **her family returned:** Wong Kim Ying (Richard Wong), file no. 14036-3617A, NARA–Riverside, 2-3; Lulu Wong, file no. 14036-1055A, NARA–Riverside, 1–2.

327 **Eric boasted of:** Maschwitz, *No Chip on My Shoulder*, 112.

327 **a single line:** Dan Walker, "Broadway," *NY Daily News*, Dec. 21, 1937.

327 **The highs and lows:** McIlwaine, "Third Beginning."

328 **He'd been hoodwinked:** Maschwitz, *No Chip on My Shoulder*, 113–16

329 **a hard-drinking crew:** BSF to FM, Nov. 10, 1937.

329 **Hollywood was not for him:** Maschwitz, *No Chip on My Shoulder*, 115–17.

329 **"The Chinese are a remarkable people":** Maschwitz, *No Chip on My Shoulder*, 88.

330 **The platform was crowded:** Maschwitz, *No Chip on My Shoulder*, 117–19.

CHAPTER FOURTEEN

334 **"Anna May Wong possesses":** John K. Newnham, "Chinese Puzzle," *Film Weekly*, June 17, 1939, 19.

334 **the lone voice:** "The Life Story of Anna May Wong and How She Became Famous," *Movietone*, Feb. 14, 1936.

334 **She vowed that:** Frank Eng, "Frank Eng," *LA Daily News*, Oct. 25, 1948.

335 **"plain hokum 'mellerdrammer'":** AMW to FM and CVV, Jan. 3, 1938.

335 **took an active role:** Douglas W. Churchill, "Respectfully Yours, Hollywood," *NYT*, Oct. 23, 1938.

335 **refused to wear a sarong:** F. Leslie Withers, "Eight Stars Go to School," *Birmingham (UK) Sunday Mercury*, July 9, 1939.

335 **a prominent and beloved physician:** Sherman Montrose, "San Francisco's Chinatown Proud of Its Three Women Physicians," *Decatur (IL) Daily Review*, Sept. 16, 1934; Cecilia Rasmussen, "Chinese American Was 'Mom' to 1,000 Servicemen," *LAT*, June 24, 2001.

336 **To prepare for the role:** "U.S. Screen Briefs," *Paterson (NJ) News*, March 16, 1939.

336 **The "hard-boiled" press agent:** Paul Harrison, "Anna May Wong Outlines Ideas About Movie Column," *Missoulian*, Nov. 13, 1938.

337 **"For Art's Sake":** Paramount Pictures publicity stills, accessed Dec. 3, 2022, https://www.instagram.com/p/ClZehVMPppt/.

337 **That summer Warner Oland:** Hanke, *Charlie Chan at the Movies*, 4; Louella O. Parsons, "George Bernard Shaw Plays Will Appear in Pictures," *SF Examiner*, Aug. 8,

1938; Kim Khavar Fahlstedt, "Charlie Chan's Last Mystery, or the Transcultural Disappearance of Warner Oland," in *Nordic Film Cultures and Cinemas of Elsewhere*, eds. Anna Westerstahl Stenport and Arne Lunde (Edinburgh: Edinburgh University Press, 2022), 47–48.

337 **suggested that the studio:** "Festival of the Moon in Chinatown," *LA Examiner*, Aug. 8, 1938; "Anna May Saves Her Studio Money," *Portland (ME) Evening Express*, Sept. 28, 1938.

338 **praised Anna May for her efforts:** Churchill, "Respectfully Yours, Hollywood."

339 **Her middling star status:** Hodges, *Anna May Wong*, 175.

339 **She paid $18,000:** Los Angeles County, California, Deed Book 16095: 20–21.

339 **"When I have a home":** "Anna May Wong Sees Infinite Possibilities for China Movies," *China Press*.

339 **She commissioned Rudolf Schindler:** "Rudolf (aka Rudolph) Michael Schindler (1887–1953)," US Modernist, accessed July 26, 2022, https://usmodernist.org/schindler.htm.

339 **a community of artists and bohemians:** Hodges, *Anna May Wong*, 175; Scott Timberg, "A Bohemian and His Kind," *LAT*, July 11, 2004.

339 **Only her youngest brother:** Ella Wickersham, "Hollywood Parade," *LA Examiner*, Nov. 23, 1939; author correspondence with Conrad Doerr, 2022.

340 **Schindler built custom furniture:** R. M. Schindler papers, Architecture and Design Collection, Art, Design & Architecture Museum, University of California, Santa Barbara.

340 **"The old ivy":** Alice L. Tildesley, "Why Waste Your Time?," *Oakland Tribune*, April 9, 1939.

340 **the circular door:** Wickersham, "Hollywood Parade."

340 **"We can't go back":** Tildesley, "Why Waste Your Time?"

341 **didn't see herself ever marrying:** Ruth Reynolds, "And Never the Twain Shall Mate?: Anna May Wong and Mai-Mai Sze Discuss East-West Romances," *NY Daily News*, July 18, 1937.

341 **locked in a war:** "Second Sino-Japanese War, 1937–1945," Britannica, last edited Nov. 10, 2020, accessed July 27, 2022, https://www.britannica.com/event/Second-Sino-Japanese-War.

341 **Hitler's crusade against Jewish citizens:** Michael Berenbaum, "Kristallnacht: German history," Britannica, last edited Nov. 1, 2021, accessed July 27, 2022, https://www.britannica.com/event/Kristallnacht.

341 **a craftsman came to see her:** Tildesley, "Why Waste Your Time?"

342 **She had been vocal:** Anna May Wong, "Manchuria," *Rob Wagner's Script* 6, no. 153 (Jan. 16, 1932).

342 **donated her Christmas money:** AMW to FM and CVV, Jan. 3, 1938.

342 **auctioned off her movie costumes:** Read Kendall, "Around and About in Hollywood: Screen Souvenirs Will Be Sold," *LAT*, March 12, 1938; "Actress to Aid China War Fund," *NYT*, June 22, 1938.

342 **attended charity galas:** "Hollywood Throws a Party," *Tatler*, April 6, 1938; Chester

Paul, "Filmdom to Frolic for War Victims," *LAT*, Oct. 2, 1938; "Benefit to Aid Victims of War," *LAT*, Dec. 11, 1938.

342 **gave a talk at a charity event:** Grace Wilcox, "Hollywood Reporter," *Detroit Free Press*, March 27, 1938.

342 **personally thanked Anna May:** "Wong Gets China Cable," *Chicago Defender*, July 16, 1938.

343 **a ten-week personal appearance tour:** "Anna May Wong Off to Australia," *LA Examiner*, May 5, 1939.

343 **She returned to the United States:** "Anna May Wong Returns from Tour," *LAT*, Sept. 5, 1939, 27.

343 **"The Studios are extremely quiet":** AMW to CVV, Feb. 20, 1940.

343 **tea party at Moongate:** Wickersham, "Hollywood Parade"; "Anna May Wong Honors Chinese Author at Tea," *LAT*, Nov. 26, 1939.

343 **stacked with charity benefits:** "Chinese Benefit Plans Formed," *LAT*, April 26, 1941; "Chinese Film Star to Appear at Light Opera Matinee," *LAT*, June 19, 1941; "Anna May Wong at Thrift Shop," *NYT*, Dec. 2, 1941. "Anna May Wong Backs Benefit," *LAT*, May 26, 1940; "Celebrities Entertained," *LAT*, June 9, 1940; "LaGuardia Leads U.S. Mayors in Bowl of Rice Party Drive," *Wilmington (CA) Daily Press Journal*, Oct. 8, 1940.

344 **another tragedy was about to:** "Chinese Woman Commits Suicide," *LAT*, July 26, 1940; "Motive for Suicide of Star's Kin Secret," *Oakland Tribune*, July 26, 1940; "Movie Star's Sister Is Suicide," *Pittsburgh Courier*, Aug. 3, 1940.

345 **"Dearest Fania and Carl":** AMW to FM and CVV, Aug. 12, 1940.

345 **callously printed the headline:** "Mary Wong Hangs Self: Sister of Anna May Wong Ends Life in California," *NYT*, July 26, 1940.

345 **delayed her summer stock:** AMW to FM and CVV, July 16, 1940; Aug. 12, 1940.

345 **the Bowl of Rice drive:** "Aid for China," *NYHT*, Sept. 22, 1940; "LaGuardia Leads U.S. Mayors in Bowl of Rice Party Drive," *Wilmington (CA) Daily Press Journal*; "Bowl of Rice Drive Launched by Mayor," *NYT*, Sept. 17, 1940.

346 **guest of honor Dr. Hu Shih:** "Chinese to Gain by Friday's Ball," *NYT*, Oct. 27, 1940; "China to Fight On, Dr. Hu Shih Says," *NYT*, Nov. 2, 1940.

346 **Then came the day:** "Pearl Harbor," History, Oct. 29, 2009, last edited Dec. 2, 2021, accessed July 31, 2022, https://www.history.com/topics/world-war-ii/pearl-harbor.

346 **forcibly remove and relocate:** "Executive Order 9066: Resulting in Japanese-American Incarceration (1942)," National Archives, accessed July 31, 2022, https://www.archives.gov/milestone-documents/executive-order-9066.

347 **ran a feature titled:** "How to Tell Japs from the Chinese," *Time*, Dec. 22, 1941, 81, accessed July 31, 2022, http://digitalexhibits.wsulibs.wsu.edu/items/show/4416.

347 **wear buttons and scraps:** Rainsberger, *James Wong Howe*, 22.

348 **signed on with Producers Releasing:** Hodges, *Anna May Wong*, 183–86.

348 **she played a teacher:** "What the Press Agents Say: Arcadia," *Portsmouth (NH) Herald*, June 18, 1942.

348 **also a spy thriller:** "'Chungking' Film Drama on at Vogue," *LA Evening Citizen News*, Dec. 23, 1942.

348   **Critics panned both pictures:** "The Screen," *NYT*, Aug. 10, 1942; S. L. S., "'Lady from Chungking' Offered on Capitol Screen," *Philadelphia Inquirer*, Dec. 17, 1942.

348   **the entirety of her paycheck:** Karen Leong, *The China Mystique: Pearl S. Buck, Anna May Wong, Mayling Soong, and the Transformation of American Orientalism* (Berkeley: University of California Press, 2005), chap. 3, 147n.

348   **"Busy with bond sales":** "Anna May Wong Adds Work of Air-Raid Warden to Duties," *LAT*, Dec. 8, 1942.

348   **"a special heroine":** Alma Whitaker, "Sugar and Spice," *LAT*, Dec. 10, 1942.

348   **viewed her as a scourge:** "Consul Host at Reception," *LAT*, April 1, 1943; "Thousands Line Procession Route," *LAT*, April 1, 1943, A; "Mme. Chiang 'Captures' City," *LAT*, April 1, 1943, 1; "Mme. Chiang Bowl Fete Set," *LAT*, April 4, 1943; Leong, *The China Mystique*, 104, 142–45.

349   **"The important thing is that":** Leong, *The China Mystique*, 104.

349   **Richard, now twenty, was drafted:** Elliot Norton, "Anna May Wong Has Two Prides," *Boston Post*, Aug. 5, 1943, in AMW clippings folder, NYPL; "Anna May Wong Leaves on U.S.O. Tour," *LAT*, March 30, 1944.

350   **Paul Robeson's forty-sixth:** Ruth Miller, "Mapping Brooklyn," *Chicago Defender*, April 29, 1944.

350   **she had her chance:** Anna May Wong gives a speech at Paul Robeson's birthday, April 16, 1944, https://www.youtube.com/watch?v=-K6gOH0czeg; photo of Paul Robeson and Anna May Wong, WorthPoint, accessed March 14, 2023, https://www.worthpoint.com/worthopedia/vint-1944-actor-paul-robeson-anna-92244846.

350   **performed dramatic sketches:** "Noted Movie Star Is Visiting City," *Edmonton (AB) Bulletin*, April 28, 1944.

350   **"Many of the boys":** "Anna May Wong Tells of Alaska Camps Tour," *LAT*, July 25, 1944; today the term "Jap" is considered a racial slur and not a word one should ever use, but in Anna May's time it was used somewhat indiscriminately, whether hostility was intended or not. While Anna May at times felt anger and despair over Japan's onslaught into China and other parts of Asia during the 1930s and '40s, she also tried her best to "think good thoughts" and promote peaceful relations with all.

350   **the final crushing blow:** "Atomic Bombings of Hiroshima and Nagasaki," Britannica, Dec. 3, 2022, https://www.britannica.com/event/atomic-bombings-of-Hiroshima-and-Nagasaki.

350   **After six long years:** World War II Foundation, "Timeline of World War II," accessed Aug. 3, 2022, https://wwiifoundation.org/timeline-of-wwii/; "D-Day," History, Oct. 27, 2009, last edited June 5, 2019, accessed Aug. 3, 2022, https://www.history.com/topics/world-war-ii/d-day; "D-Day: The Beaches," fact sheet, accessed Aug. 3, 2022, https://dod.defense.gov/Portals/1/features/2016/0516_dday/docs/d-day-fact-sheet-the-beaches.pdf; "How many people died during World War II?," Britannica, accessed Aug. 3, 2022, https://www.britannica.com/question/How-many-people-died-during-World-War-II.

351   **were both passed over:** Eng, "Frank Eng."

351   **aspired to direct:** Rainsberger, *James Wong Howe*, 23.

351   **Lester Cowan's announcement:** Hugh Dixon, "Hollywood: Movie Memos," *Pittsburgh Post-Gazette*, Feb. 3, 1948.

351   **Dorothy Lamour in *Disputed Passage*:** Author correspondence with Conrad Doerr, 2022.

351   **She also retooled herself:** "Anna May Wong at Famous-Barr on Thursday," *St. Louis Globe Democrat*, Oct. 13, 1947; "Miss Wong Returns to Films After 4 Years," *Valley Times* (North Hollywood), Oct. 29, 1948.

352   **"Spend a half hour":** Patricia Clary, "Eyeful of Goldfish Beautifies Peepers," *Long Beach Press-Telegram*, Dec. 4, 1948.

352   **a deal to sell the property:** AMW to Hedda Hopper, April 3, 1946, Hedda Hopper papers, file 3266, AMPAS.

352   **a young man named Conrad:** Doerr, "Anna May Wong," 660.

352   **Two months after filming:** Louella O. Parsons, "Kay Thompson Gets Bid to Play Musical Comedy Lead in London," *LA Examiner*, Dec. 23, 1948.

353   **cirrhosis of the liver:** Mayo Clinic, "Cirrhosis," accessed Aug. 6, 2022, https://www.mayoclinic.org/diseases-conditions/cirrhosis/symptoms-causes/syc-20351487.

353   **left his earthly body:** "Father of Film Actress Anna May Wong Dies," *LAT*, Oct. 13, 1949.

353   **"I was always looking":** Hodges, *Anna May Wong*, caption in photo insert.

353   **while she stumbled:** Peak, "Life of Anna May Wong Is Like a Chinese Fairy Tale."

353   **lobbied Paramount scriptwriters:** Churchill, "Respectfully Yours, Hollywood."

354   **she suffered a nervous breakdown:** Erksine Johnson, "In Hollywood," *Pomona Progress Bulletin*, Nov. 15, 1949.

CHAPTER FIFTEEN

357   **the number of television sets:** Mitchell Stephens, "History of Television," Grolier Encyclopedia, accessed Aug. 3, 2022, https://stephens.hosting.nyu.edu/History%20of%20Television%20page.html#:~:text=The%20number%20of%20television%20sets,all%20U.S.%20homes%20had%20one.

358   **established a friendly rapport:** Doerr, "Anna May Wong," 661.

358   **The thirteen-episode series:** Leibfried and Lane, *Anna May Wong: A Complete Guide to Her Film, Stage, Radio and Television Work*, 162–63.

358   **the first program in television:** Nicole Chung, "The Search for *Madame Liu-Tsong*," *New York Magazine*, Sept. 2017, https://www.vulture.com/2017/09/the-search-for-the-gallery-of-madame-liu-tsong.html.

358   **The first thirty-minute episode:** "Television Review," *NYT*, Aug. 28, 1951.

359   **"deserves much, much better":** Chung, "The Search for *Madame Liu-Tsong*."

359   **The slim budgets:** Marie Torre, "Out of the Air," *East Liverpool (OH) Evening Review*, Oct. 9, 1956.

359   **the tapes were dumped:** Chung, "The Search for *Madame Liu-Tsong*."

359   **"her disappointment in the casting":** Doerr, "Anna May Wong."

359   **"playing O-lan":** Author correspondence with Conrad Doerr, 2022.

360   **During these years:** See, *On Gold Mountain*, 284.

360 **Eddy's son, Richard See:** Author interview with Richard See, 2021.

360 **"fifty million Chinamen":** See, *On Gold Mountain*, 284.

360 **"drank an awful lot":** BSF to FM, Nov. 19, 1952.

361 **"We fill our minds":** Tildesley, "Why Waste Your Time?"

361 **hit her bodily limit:** "Anna May Wong Ill in Hospital," *LAT*, Dec. 12, 1953.

361 **"At this moment":** Richard Wong to FM and CVV, Dec. 15, 1953.

362 **"had a dozen transfusions":** Walter Winchell, "Gossip of the Nation," *Philadelphia Inquirer*, Jan. 13, 1954.

362 **"just a temporary crutch":** AMW to FM and CVV, Dec. 28, 1953.

362 **the Sierra Madre Lodge:** "1954 Business Directory," *South Pasadena Review*, Jan. 19, 1954.

362 **"I am so dearly sorry":** AMW to FM and CVV, Dec. 28, 1953.

363 **the self-help bestseller:** AMW to FM, March 6, 1954.

363 **she detailed the meetings:** AMW to FM, Jan. 31, 1954.

363 **sell some of her jewelry:** AMW to FM, March 6, 1954.

363 **reconnecting with familiar faces:** AMW to FM, Jan. 31, 1954.

363 **"We made pictures":** AMW to FM, Feb. 28, 1955.

363 **the idea of selling Moongate:** AMW to FM, March 6, 1954.

364 **sold the extra parcel:** AMW to FM and CVV, Oct. 29, 1954.

364 **garner a small part:** Walter Winchell, "On Broadway," *Terre Haute (IN) Tribune*, Sept. 26, 1955.

364 **nearly 2 million people:** "Historical General Population: City & County of Los Angeles, 1850 to 2020," Los Angeles Almanac, accessed Aug. 6, http://www.laalmanac.com /population/po02.php.

364 **"When I went into":** AMW to FM, Aug. 26, 1955.

364 **suggested that Anna May write:** Hodges, *Anna May Wong*, 196; Doerr, "Anna May Wong," 661.

364 **tour down memory lane:** "Anna May Wong in London," *Tatler and Bystander*, Oct. 26, 1955.

364 **She flew to New York:** FM to BSF, Feb. 4, no year, though likely from 1956.

365 **"It does seem though":** BSF to FM, Dec. 5, 1955.

365 **Fania added that:** FM to BSF, Feb. 4.

365 **put her slipup:** AMW to CVV, Sept. 8, 1955.

365 **"Have been in a spin":** AMW to FM and CVV, Oct. 6, 1955.

366 **stayed at the Westbury:** AMW to FM and CVV, Oct. 6, 1955; Dick Richards, "The Bright Lights," *Sketch*, Oct. 5, 1955; "Anna May Wong in London," *Tatler and Bystander.*

366 **"I was happy to find":** AMW to FM, Oct. 27, 1955.

366 **"sentimental reunion":** F. Leslie Withers, "Yellow Willow (That's Anna May)," *Birmingham (UK) Sunday Mercury*, Oct. 9, 1955.

367 **she admitted herself:** "Anna May Wong to Leave Hospital," *LA Examiner*, Oct. 20, 1955; AMW to FM, Oct. 27, 1955.

367 **"too attractive to refuse":** AMW to FM, Oct. 27, 1955.

367 **They downsized:** AMW to FM, July 15, 1956.

367 **the last to move out:** Author correspondence with Conrad Doerr, 2022.

367 **had become her rock:** AMW to FM, June 16, 1952; Oct. 3, 1952; undated card, 1958; Aug. 11, 1958.

368 **One of his portraits:** Withers, "Yellow Willow (That's Anna May)."

368 **Richard shouldered the majority:** AMW to FM, July 15, 1956.

368 **a live televised production:** Marjory Adams, "Anna May Wong Lovely in Comeback Role," *Boston Globe*, June 14, 1960.

369 **"I have so many wonderful":** AMW to FM, Nov. 5, 1956.

369 **"gazing into a TV future":** Marie Torre, "Out of the Air," *East Liverpool (OH) Evening Review*, Oct. 9, 1956.

369 **"After the war":** Bob Thomas, "Died Thousand Deaths, States Anna May Wong," *Anniston (AL) Star*, Dec. 15, 1959.

369 **invited by ABC:** "Television: Program Preview, Feb. 18, 1957," *Time*, Feb. 18, 1957, https://content.time.com/time/subscriber/article/0,33009,809126,00.html.

370 **classes at the Unity School:** AMW to FM, Oct. 26, 1959; April 4, 1960.

370 **"This astonishing woman":** BSF to FM, Sept. 7, 1960.

370 **this new discipline:** AMW to FM, April 4, 1960.

370 **"seventeen-year retirement":** Press release dated Dec. 16, 1959, Bob Werden and Don Morgan papers, File 18, AMPAS; Barbara Holliday, "Her Name's in Lights—and in Diamonds," *Detroit Free Press*, June 28, 1960.

370 **In the original play:** Paine Knickerbocker, "'Portrait in Black' Takes on Glamor," *SF Chronicle*, Jan. 20, 1960, in Bob Werden and Don Morgan papers, AMPAS; Eng, "Frank Eng."

371 **Some critics might have:** Elspeth Grant, "Cinema," *Tatler and Bystander*, Nov. 1960; A. H. Weiler, "Lana Turner in Film at 2 Theatres," *NYT*, July 28, 1960.

371 **"the keys to the city":** Holliday, "Her Name's in Lights—and in Diamonds."

371 **Anna May was honored:** "'Walk of Fame' Gets Under Way," *LA Evening Citizen News*, Feb. 8, 1960; Anna May Wong, Hollywood Walk of Fame, accessed Dec. 4, 2022, https://walkoffame.com/anna-may-wong/.

371 **ran into his former landlady:** Doerr, "Anna May Wong," 662.

372 **wanted her to play:** AMW to FM and CVV, July 17, 1960.

372 **"I was sorry that I":** AMW to FM and CVV, Jan. 4, 1961.

372 **"When I die, my epitaph":** Thomas, "Died Thousand Deaths."

EPILOGUE

375 **On the evening of March 15:** Bob Werden and Don Morgan Papers, File 14, AMPAS.

375 **an exact replica:** Army Archerd, "Just for Variety," *Variety*, March 17, 1961; Phil M. Daly, "Phil M. Daly in Hollywood," *Film Daily*, March 22, 1961.

375 **the Grant Avenue set:** Larry Glenn, "'Flower Drum Song' Reprised Close to Home," *NYT*, April 30, 1961.

376 **"For your information":** Daly, "Phil M. Daly in Hollywood."

376 **"the China doll that men like":** *McCall's*, February 1962.

376 **She missed the opening:** Archerd, "Just for Variety."

376 **Kwan was the jet-setting:** Hedda Hopper, "Gift to Science: Nancy Kwan Plays an Ichthyologist," *Cincinnati Enquirer*, March 22, 1964.

377 **drafted a press release:** Bob Werden and Don Morgan Papers, File 14, AMPAS.

377 **German psychotherapist and palmist:** Dr. Charlotte Wolff, *Studies in Hand-Reading* (London: Chatto & Windus, 1936), 131–33.

379 **At one time or another:** "The World's Most Beautiful Chinese Girl," *Look*, March 1938.

379 **"My candle burns at both ends":** AMW to FM, July 28, 1953; Edna St. Vincent Millay, "First Fig," 1920, https://poets.org/poem/first-fig.

380 **she put her Oscar:** Bowyer, *Seen from the Wings*, 410.

381 **"She paved the way":** Gemma Chan, Instagram, Sept. 13, 2021, https://www.instagram.com/p/CTx7eGNofYH/?hl=en.

381 **According to sociologist:** Nancy Wang Yuen, *Reel Inequality: Hollywood Actors and Racism* (New Brunswick, NJ: Rutgers University Press, 2017), 26.

381 **From 2007 to 2019:** Kimmy Yam, "A Third of Lead Asian American, Pacific Islander Roles in Top Films Played by 'The Rock,' Study Shows," *NBC News*, May 21, 2021, https://www.nbcnews.com/news/asian-america/third-lead-asian-american-pacific-islander-roles-top-films-played-n1268086.

381 **AAPI actors are cast:** Yuen, *Reel Inequality*, 27.

381 **White actors like:** Keith Chow, "Why Won't Hollywood Cast Asian Actors?," *NYT*, April 22, 2016.

382 **"It was a catalyst":** Reggie Ugwu, "The Hashtag That Changed the Oscars: An Oral History," *NYT*, Feb. 6, 2020.

382 ***This is something:*** Michelle Yeoh, "Michelle Yeoh Breaks Down Her Most Iconic Characters," *GQ* on YouTube.com, April 6, 2022, https://youtu.be/DHOSiFzcHJ8.

382 **"Some day some one":** Wagner, "Better a Laundry and Sincerity."

383 **"Anna May Wong lives on":** Margaret Cho, "Imagine," MargaretCho.com, Dec. 14, 2004, https://margaretcho.com/2004/12/14/imagine/.

384 **"never won an Oscar":** Mo Rocca, "Anna May Wong," *Mobituaries with Mo Rocca*, Feb. 2020, accessed Jan. 17, 2023, https://www.mobituaries.com/news/my-favorite-mobits-anna-may-wong/.

384 **Development has already begun:** Rebecca Sun, "Gemma Chan, Nina Yang Bongiovi Developing Anna May Wong Biopic with Working Title Films (Exclusive)," *Hollywood Reporter*, March 24, 2022, https://www.hollywoodreporter.com/movies/movie-news/anna-may-wong-biopic-gemma-chan-1235118243/.

384 **"We sometimes even surprise ourselves":** AMW to CVV, Sept. 26, 1929.

ILLUSTRATION CREDITS

The frontispiece photograph is by Otto Dyar. The preface photograph is courtesy of the Chinese American Museum, Los Angeles. The prologue photograph
is courtesy of Marc Wanamaker, Bison Archives. Chapter 1, from the collections
of the Margaret Herrick Library, Academy of Motion Picture Arts and Sciences. Chapter 2, courtesy of Anna Wong. Chapter 4, Bettmann / Getty Images.
Chapter 5, courtesy of the BFI National Archive. Chapter 6, photograph by
Alfred Eisenstaedt, courtesy of the LIFE Picture Collection / Getty Images,
reprinted by permission of Harvard Art Museums / Busch-Reisinger Museum,
Gift of Lufthansa German Airlines. Chapter 7, CPA Media Pte Ltd / Alamy
Stock Photo. Chapter 8, courtesy of Universal Studios Licensing, LLC, from
John Kobal Foundation / Getty Images. Chapter 9, photograph by Carl Van
Vechten, © Van Vechten Trust, from Carl Van Vechten Papers, Beinecke Li-
brary, Yale University. Chapter 10, photograph by George F. Cannons, courtesy
of Condé Nast / Shutterstock. Chapter 11, courtesy of Goddess Anna May
Wong. Chapter 12, photograph by Bernardine Szold Fritz, courtesy of David
Szanton. Chapter 13, courtesy of the Gielgud family. Chapter 14, courtesy of
Universal Studios Licensing, LLC, from the collections of the Margaret Herrick Library, Academy of Motion Picture Arts and Sciences. Chapter 15, Ever-
ett Collection. Epilogue photograph by George Hurrell, courtesy of Mark A.
Vieira, the Starlight Studio. Page 460, photograph by Frank Dorn, courtesy of
the Frank Dorn Papers, Hoover Institution Library & Archives.

INDEX

Note: Italicized page numbers indicate material in photographs or illustrations.

ABOUT THE AUTHOR

Katie Gee Salisbury is a writer and photographer. Her work has appeared in the *New York Times*, *Vanity Fair*, the *Ringer*, and the Asian American Writers' Workshop. She also writes the newsletter "Half-Caste Woman." She was a finalist for the Jerome Hill Artist Fellowship in 2021 and gave the TED Talk "As American as Chop Suey." She has spoken about her work at the Museum of Chinese in America, Barnard College, New York University, and elsewhere. A fifth-generation Chinese American who hails from Southern California, she now lives in Brooklyn, New York. *Not Your China Doll* is her first book.

A somber yet stately Anna May Wong stands beneath a willow tree, her namesake, in Frank Dorn's Peiping garden, July 1936.